MOON

HANDBOOKS

W9-BNU-368

HUDSON
RIVER VALLEY

NIKKI GOTH ITOI

DISCOVER THE HUDSON RIVER VALLEY

Nostalgic for the simplicity of rural life, today's travelers and weekend warriors crave the small-town experience with a modern flair. They are finding it, increasingly, in the Hudson River Valley.

From Blue Hill at Stone Barns to the Dia:Beacon museum, America's first vacation destination is making headlines once again. Home décor retailers are shooting catalogs in the antique mecca of Hudson, business owners are reporting celebrity sightings, triathletes are swimming in the river, and the Food Network is promoting chefs from Westchester County to Saratoga Springs.

The towns of Beacon, Catskill, Hudson, and Kingston have reinvented themselves. Antiques hot spots are emerging around Saugerties and Millerton, and the valley's farms are going organic. It's enough to make you pack your bags and head for the hills.

homes along the Kingston shoreline

But it's not the first time the region has come en vogue. For nearly four centuries, travelers have ventured up the Hudson River in search of opportunity, inspiration, and a breath of fresh air. It is here that Washington Irving wrote "The Legend of Sleepy Hollow" and Thomas Cole created the landscape paintings that marked the dawn of the Romantic Era.

Old-world roots, dramatic scenery, and an ever-changing economy give the Hudson River Valley the depth and complexity of an aged red wine. Dutch names alternate with Algonquin Indian words to produce tongue twisters like Kinderhook and Rhinebeck, Taghkanic and Minnewaska. Timeless legends of haunted houses and enchanted woods entertain children and adults alike.

Measured by numbers, the Hudson River is unexceptional – only 315 miles long, 3.5 miles across at its widest point, and 216 feet at its

Catskill mountain laurel in early summer

deepest. Carved by a glacier 75 million years ago, the river originates from Lake Tear of the Clouds in the rugged Adirondack Mountains and becomes navigable at Troy, above Albany. From the Federal Dam at Troy all the way to New York Harbor, the Hudson is a 150-mile-long estuary that ebbs and floods with ocean tides, mixing saltwater with fresh as far up as Kingston in Ulster County. The Algonquins called it "Muhheahkantuck," meaning the river that flows both ways, or great waters constantly in motion. In winter, chunks of ice near the shore might flow south, while those in the middle flow north.

The constant mixing supports the largest single wildlife resource in New York State, according to environmentalist Robert Boyle, author of *The Hudson River: A Natural and Unnatural History*. Deciduous trees, rocky bluffs, and gentle foothills line both shores. Mallard ducks paddle across narrow inlets, while fishing boats troll for striped bass. Beyond the river's edge, narrow country lanes lead to historic parks, working fruit and dairy farms, and mountains that stretch 4,000 feet into the sky.

In any season, the Hudson Valley's natural beauty triumphs

the Great Jack O'Lantern Blaze at Van Cortlandt Manor

over ever-growing suburban sprawl. Weeping willow trees bend over brooks and streams. Stately oaks and sugar maples form a canopy over quiet country lanes. Yellow forsythia announces the arrival of spring. Ranks of split firewood, signs for tractor crossings, one-lane bridges, and the honk of Canada geese overhead are all part of the valley's bucolic charm. From wine trails to snowboard terrain parks, the valley continues to adapt to changing traveler interests.

Unlike California's Napa Valley or the Loire Valley in France, few travelers select the Hudson River Valley as their vacation destination; more often, it chooses them. Maybe you've been invited to a riverside wedding or family reunion, or you are planning to tour Vassar, Bard, and other schools with a college-bound teen. Business might land you in Westchester or Albany, within striking distance of the Great Estates and Catskill Mountains. Or perhaps you need a weekend getaway from Manhattan. Whatever prompts your first visit, take some time to explore, and it's very likely you'll to want to return – again and again.

Your next visit might be a spa weekend, a yoga retreat, or the

kayaks for rent in Cold Spring

triple-summit hike over the High Peaks of the Catskills. Soon you'll be a regular at the local farm stands and scheming how to avoid the crowds during leaf-peeping season. And then you'll be scanning real estate ads for your own country escape. It's a slippery slope.

Today's Hudson Valley continues to evoke a sense of wonder. You can't ride the train along the Hudson's eastern shore without contemplating the Revolutionary War, the viability of community-supported agriculture, or the fate of the American shad. All the while, you feel the unmistakable presence of those who came before: Alexander Hamilton, Ulysses S. Grant, Henry James, and Mark Twain, to name a few.

At its heart, the Hudson River Valley today is a place of contrasts – where dairy farmers mingle with concrete factory workers, where hunters share the forest with conservationists, and where the cosmopolitan meets small-town America. Along this historic river, the familiar still has the power to surprise.

the best ice cream in Columbia County

Contents

MAP CONTENTS

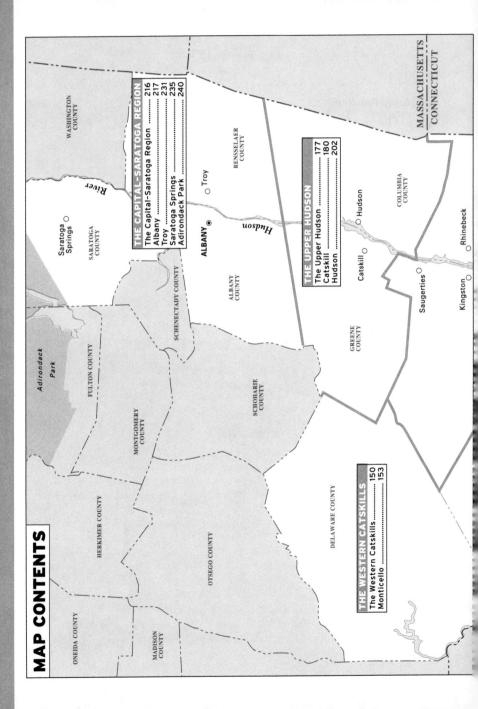

ONEIDA COUNTY

MADISON COUNTY

HERKIMER COUNTY

FULTON COUNTY

Adirondack Park

MONTGOMERY COUNTY

SCHENECTADY COUNTY

OTSEGO COUNTY

SCHOHARIE COUNTY

DELAWARE COUNTY

WASHINGTON COUNTY

Saratoga Springs

SARATOGA COUNTY

Hudson River

ALBANY COUNTY

ALBANY

Troy

RENSSELAER COUNTY

GREENE COUNTY

Catskill

Saugerties

Hudson

COLUMBIA COUNTY

Rhinebeck

Kingston

MASSACHUSETTS

CONNECTICUT

The Lay of the Land

THE LOWER HUDSON

The Hudson River Valley begins at the borders with New York City and New Jersey and includes many densely populated bedroom communities of Westchester and Rockland counties. Several attractive mansions and gardens line this stretch of the river, including Kykuit, the magnificent Rockefeller residence in the Pocantico Hills. And along with the historic estates come several wilderness areas all the more impressive for their proximity to Manhattan. For example, any Rockland County itinerary should include a visit to Harriman State Park. The quaint villages of Tarrytown and Piermont, on opposite sides of the river, are an easy day trip from Grand Central Station. Outstanding international cuisine and lively nightlife are additional highlights of the area.

THE HUDSON HIGHLANDS

Above the Lower Hudson, the Hudson Highlands encompass Orange and Putnam counties along the most distinctive stretch of the river. A solid granite mountain range called the Appalachian Plateau crosses the Hudson here, and the river has carved a narrow and deep path through the range. The resulting fjords and vistas resemble the banks of the Rhine. To complete the picture, a dreamy mist often clings to the peaks of Storm King and Breakneck Mountains on opposite shores. In addition to admiring the scenery, you can browse the shops along Main Street in Cold Spring, visit the historic West Point campus, or drive through the Black Dirt Region. For outdoor recreation in winter and summer, head to Greenwood Lake on the New York–New Jersey state line.

THE MID-HUDSON

The "Gunks" of Ulster County and the riverside mansions of Dutchess County define the Mid-Hudson River Valley region. Here, the valley expands into rolling hills and farm fields interspersed with lakes, streams, and forests. Plan your trip around a visit to a gourmet restaurant or local arts festival. Wine trails on either side of the river guide visitors along rural back roads. Scenic drives through both counties cover miles of idyllic countryside. The towns of New Paltz, Saugerties, or Woodstock make a convenient home base for exploration. This part of the valley features several cultural highlights as well: Dia:Beacon is a nationally recognized museum for artwork from the 1960s to the present, and the Culinary Institute of America trains first-rate chefs, many of whom stick around to influence local menus.

THE WESTERN CATSKILLS

Health spas and yoga retreats have replaced yesterday's summer boarding houses in the Western Catskill region. Communities here are a mix of longtime farming families and newer second-home owners. Several historic covered bridges span the Willowemoc and Beaverkill Rivers, while hundreds of lakes and streams entertain anglers and bird-watchers alike. Spend an hour inside the Catskill Fly Fishing Museum, even if you're not the fishing type. Most travelers will want at least a full weekend to explore the back roads of these two counties; serious fishing and hiking enthusiasts could easily find a week's worth of entertainment.

THE UPPER HUDSON

The Catskill and Berkshire Mountains frame the upper section of the Hudson River Valley. In between, small lakes and dense hardwood forests alternate with rolling hills and cultivated fields. Rural communities dot the landscape, welcoming visitors with historic sites, antique shops, and the promise of outdoor adventures. The dramatic topography of the Catskills inspired the first generation of Hudson River School painters, who depicted natural wonders like Kaaterskill Falls in colorful Romantic landscapes. Across the river, agricultural Columbia County borders the Berkshire Mountains of New England. Several historic mansions are worth a half-day visit, including the Livingston family home at Clermont and the Persian-style Olana, which belonged to painter Frederick Church.

THE CAPITAL-SARATOGA REGION

The Capital-Saratoga region of Albany, Rensselaer, and Saratoga Counties marks the end of the navigable Hudson River and the gateway to the rugged Adirondack wilderness. There is much more to New York's state capital than first meets the eye—highlights include modern art, a rich colonial history, active state government offices, exceptional dining, and easy access to outdoor fun. Add a lively entertainment scene that revolves around the youthful college culture, and you have a surprisingly dynamic urban community. By contrast, quiet Rensselaer County consists of industrial Troy, a top-notch engineering school, and many small rural towns; while Saratoga Springs is a well-developed resort town steeped in the cultures of horse racing, apple picking, and natural spa treatments.

Planning Your Trip

The Hudson River Valley includes 12 New York State counties, which are commonly divided into six regions: the Lower Hudson River Valley, Hudson Highlands, Mid-Hudson River Valley, Upper Hudson River Valley, Western Catskills, and Capital-Saratoga region. You can drive or take a train the length of the valley, approximately 180 miles from New York City to Albany, in well under three hours; however, the area offers ample entertainment for a weekend- or week-long adventure in any season.

Whether you explore the valley by car, bike, train, motorcycle, foot, or private plane, you will find boundless opportunities for outdoor recreation and entertainment on either side of the Hudson River. Out-of-state visitors often combine a Lower Hudson Valley excursion with a trip to New York City, or a tour of the Upper Hudson with a New England itinerary. Local residents may want to plan a series of weekend getaways to explore each county in the region. Wherever you choose to begin, be sure to venture away from the river's edge to the hills and mountains that lie beyond.

Generally speaking, the Hudson River Valley gets prettier the farther north you travel, so if you're looking for a real contrast to New York City, it's best to keep going at least until you reach the highlands near Cold Spring. That said, public transportation, international cuisine, and first-rate museums are more prevalent the closer you get to the Big Apple, and the Lower Hudson River Valley does have its share of beautiful outdoor spaces.

Most itineraries will cover more than one county in the region, especially if you stay near the river. You can visit one or two sights and enjoy a good meal in any of these counties in a one-day trip. For the weekend traveler, a couple of museums or historic sights would leave time for an outdoor adventure as well. If you want to take in most of the available sights and attrac-tions, Dutchess, Ulster, and Greene Counties will require the longest stay for exploration—allow two to three days for each of these counties. Also, remember that destinations are more spread out in rural counties like Sullivan and Delaware, so you'll need extra time to get from place to place. For those who plan to explore the region from top to bottom—whether by car, train, or bike—a full week would allow plenty of time for a cross-section of activities.

Some of the most spectacular river views are only accessible by train, but for travelers who want to explore the area's hidden gems, a car affords more flexibility and spontaneity. Motorists have many options in this area, from winding country roads to open interstates. Route 9 and its many permutations (9D, 9G, 9H, 9J) hug the eastern shoreline, except for Route 9W, which runs parallel on the Hudson's west side. A faster choice is the scenic Taconic State Parkway, which runs north to south through Westchester, Putnam, Dutchess, and Columbia counties. Farther east, Route 22 runs along the New York State border with Connecticut and Massachusetts. The speediest way to get from the wilderness to the sea is the New York State Thruway (I-87), a mul-tilane toll road that connects New York City to Albany.

Today's leisure travelers tend to choose rustic country inns and upscale bed-and-breakfasts for overnight stops. The region also has the usual assortment of standard motels and mod-erately priced chains, including TraveLodge, Best Western, and Days Inn. Camping is per-mitted in many state and county parks, as well as at private campgrounds, with more choices the farther north you travel.

WHEN TO GO
The best times to visit the Lower Hudson Val-ley are late spring to early summer, and early

to mid-fall. July and August tend to be hot and muggy, especially close to New York City. For cooler temperatures in summer, or winter activities, head to the Upper Hudson, the Catskills, or the Capital-Saratoga Region.

The fall foliage season begins in mid-September and can last until late October, depending on the weather. A heavy rain or snow will end the season early. Most years, the colors are best around Columbus Day weekend in mid-October. The prime leaf-peeping window varies by as much as a week or two from the lower to upper parts of the valley (and from lower to higher elevations), so if you can't catch the peak in one county, you can often travel north or south to see an earlier or later show.

November can be cold, damp, and dreary. Winter storms can make a mess of the valley October–April. Snow typically begins to fall in December, with a cold snap of below-zero temperatures often occurring in January. Winter conditions last through February, when the maple-sugaring season begins.

Many small-town sights, restaurants, and accommodations have variable hours in the off-season, and it's a good idea to call ahead to confirm hours of operation. Reservations are essential during the fall foliage season and when major festivals, car shows, or county fairs are in town. For outdoor adventures, wear layers, as temperatures can change rapidly with elevation and proximity to the river. Field guides, sports equipment, rain gear, sunscreen, and insect repellent will also come in handy.

Explore the Hudson River Valley

DAY TRIPS FROM NEW YORK CITY

If you find yourself in Manhattan with an extra day to spare, these easy day trips up the Hudson River offer a glimpse of what the valley has to offer.

TARRYTOWN AND THE ROCKEFELLER ESTATE

Plan ahead for this trip by pre-booking your preferred Kykuit tour online. Start your day at Grand Central Station and catch an early morning train on the Hudson Line north to Tarrytown.

Walk up Main Street and grab a cup of coffee at Coffee Labs. Take a cab or shuttle to the Kykuit Visitor Center in neighboring Sleepy Hollow. Check in for your tour of the Rockefeller Estate at Pocantico Hills.

After the tour, head to Stone Barns to see a working, sustainable farm in action, and order a light lunch at the Blue Hill Café.

Next stop is Sunnyside, Washington Irving's Romantic estate on the border between Tarrytown and Irvington. After the house tour, browse the museum shop and pick up one of Irving's books for the train ride home.

Return to the Tarrytown train station, and grab dinner nearby at Striped Bass or Sunset Cove, both in the Tarrytown Marina.

BOSCOBEL RESTORATION AND COLD SPRING VILLAGE

If you want to browse antique shops, tour a neoclassical mansion, or paddle around the river, stay on the train a couple stops farther north to Cold Spring station in Putnam County. Exit the station and stop at the visitor booth directly above to pick up a map and inquire about the shuttle to Boscobel, site of the annual Hudson Valley Shakespeare Festival.

Grab a freshly baked scone at the Foundry Café just up the street, then walk down to the riverside gazebo to take in the view of West Point and the surrounding cliffs across the river.

Hop on the shuttle to beautifully restored 19th-century Boscobel and admire the apple trees, river views, and collections of silver, china, and glassware inside. After, head down to the river's edge to walk or paddle the Constitution Marsh Wildlife Sanctuary, run by the National Audubon Society.

Catch the shuttle back to Cold Spring Village to browse the antique shops along Main Street. Stay for dinner at Cathryn's Tuscan Grill or the Cold Spring Café, or walk a few blocks north along Fair Street to enjoy views of the Hudson at Riverview. When the sun has set, it's time to catch the return train south to Grand Central.

DIA:BEACON

River views and the innovative restoration of an old factory make for an enjoyable day of modern art at this now popular Dutchess County museum. An added plus is the location within walking distance of the Beacon Metro-North train station. Catch an early morning train from Grand Central to Beacon and allow a few hours to explore the galleries. Plan ahead to time your visit with a museum event, such as a gallery talk or film screening. A café on-site serves light breakfast and lunch fare, or you can walk or cab over to Main Street for a more substantial lunch and more art galleries in the afternoon.

SIX-DAY RIVER TOUR

The ideal Hudson River Valley itinerary includes a little bit of everything—outdoor adventure, good food, history, and culture. This trip makes a circle from New York City, up the east side of the river and back down on the west.

THE LOWER HUDSON
Day 1

Travel by car to the Lower Hudson Valley to begin this trip with a day in and around **Tarrytown,** including a visit to the **Rockefeller Estate.** Book your preferred tour of Kykuit in advance, and plan to arrive at the visitors center for an afternoon tour.

If you arrive in the morning, visit **Sunnyside,** Washington Irving's former home, and then grab lunch at Sunset Cove at the Tarrytown Marina. From the **Kykuit Visitor Center,** head back into the Pocantico Hills to tour **Stone Barns,** a working farm and education center where you can also grab a bite to eat at the Blue Hill Café. Make a quick stop to admire the stained glass windows of the **Union Church,** which were designed by Matisse and Chagall as Rockefeller family memorials.

Finish the day by driving 30 minutes north along Route 9D to **Cold Spring** and check in to the Pig Hill Inn B&B or Kittleman House. Walk to dinner at Cathryn's Tuscan Grill, Le Bouchon, or Riverview.

THE HUDSON HIGHLANDS
Day 2

Today is dedicated to exploring the wilderness that surrounds the **Cold Spring Village.** Grab a scone at the Foundry Café and walk towards the gazebo at the bottom of Main Street. Pick up a trail map for **Hudson Highlands State Park** at the visitor booth above the train station, or stop by **Hudson Valley Outfitters** to inquire about kayak tours of the nearby **Constitution Marsh Preserve.** For more culture and less adventure, walk the grounds of **Boscobel Restoration** or tour **Manitoga** and the **Russel Wright Design Center.**

After your activity of choice, return to your hotel in Cold Spring in time for cocktails. Then head to Valley Restaurant at the Garrison for dinner or Stoneleigh Creek farther afield.

BEACON, HYDE PARK, AND RHINEBECK
Day 3

Start the day with a dose of modern art at **Dia:Beacon** in a restored factory at the river's edge. Follow Route 9D out of Cold Spring until it winds its way into **Beacon.** After the museum, drive across Route 9D and browse the art galleries along Main Street. Have lunch at Sukhothai or Café Maya before continuing the drive north to Hyde Park, where more history and gourmet eats await.

Catch the last tour of the day at FDR's home and library, or opt for a late afternoon stroll around the grounds of the Vanderbilt Estate. Check in to Belvedere Mansion or the 1766 Beekman Arms in Rhinebeck for the night, then head to the CIA campus for dinner at American Bounty, or stay in town for Italian at Gigi Trattoria.

THE CATSKILLS
Day 4

Today brings a scenic drive and the first glimpse of the mountains that inspired the Hudson River School of painters. Follow Route 9 north out of Rhinebeck heading toward the city of Hudson. Travelers in search of high-end antiques should explore the shops in town; others should proceed directly across the Rip Van Winkle Bridge into Greene County.

Stop for a late breakfast or early lunch in the fast-changing village of Catskill. On a nice day, follow Main Street all the way out to Catskill Point for up-close river views. An optional loop through the High Peaks region along Routes 23 and 23A leads to the mountain towns of Windham and Hunter. Otherwise, head south on Route 9W to Saugerties, which has more antiques, a historic lighthouse, and several tempting eateries to offer: Café with Love and Miss Lucy's Kitchen are two good bets.

Finish the day in Kingston with a walk through the historic Stockade District, followed by dinner downtown at Le Canard Enchaine or at Rondout Landing's Ship to Shore.

Follow Route 209 south out of Kingston to reach the Sparrow Hawk Bed and Breakfast in Stone Ridge or Captain Schoonmakers in High Falls for the night.

THE SHAWANGUNKS
Day 5

From Stone Ridge or High Falls, it's a short drive up to the Mohonk Mountain House or Lake Minnewaska, both with scenic trails for a leisurely walk or hike. Watch the rock climbers ascend perfectly pitched cliffs. On a hot day, go for a swim in crystal clear spring water. Later, head back to High Falls for lunch at Chef's on Fire below the Depuy Canal House, or continue into New Paltz for a quick bite to eat on Main Street.

Spend a second night in the area, and leave early the next morning for Newburgh and West Point.

WEST POINT
Day 6

Finish your river tour with a last dose of history and a boat ride along the Hudson. From the New Paltz area, it is about an hour drive south along Route 9W to West Point. Arrange a river cruise or campus tour in advance through West Point Tours, and check in at the visitors center and then enter West Point through the main gate. (Alternatively, you can skip West Point and book an all-day river cruise out of Haverstraw Marina with Hudson Highlands Cruises.)

After tour and cruise, head a few miles south to the traffic circle at the Bear Mountain Bridge, and cross back over to the east side of the Hudson. Enjoy a scenic drive over the Hudson Highlands heading south toward Peekskill. Call ahead for reservations at Monteverde at Oldstone Manor for an unforgettable last dinner in the Hudson Valley. If time permits, book a spa appointment before dinner and catch sunset over the river with a glass of chilled wine in hand.

ART AND ARCHITECTURE: WEEKEND GETAWAY

A handful of majestic estates line the Hudson River, representing several centuries of architectural and cultural trends. Many have been turned into interpretive museums that are open to the public. In many cases, the surrounding gardens are as beautiful—or more so—as the buildings themselves. This itinerary includes examples of American Renaissance, Georgian, Federal, Romantic, Greek Revival, and Gothic Revival architecture.

Day 1

Kykuit, the sprawling estate of the Rockefeller family, tops the list of must-see destinations for anyone interested in modern art and American Renaissance architecture. The three-hour Grand Tour is well worth the time investment; many visitors feel they could spend three days exploring the estate. Note, even the shortest tours take several hours, because the visitors center is located several miles away from the home and tours arrive by shuttle bus. When you've had your fill of Rockefeller history, head back into the hills to visit Stone Barns, a working farm and education center where you can tour the grounds and also grab lunch. On the drive back to Tarrytown, stop at the Union Church to admire stained glass windows designed by Henri Matisse and Marc Chagall for the Rockefeller family.

Head back into town and south along Route 9 to tour Sunnyside, the Romantic-style home of Washington Irving, America's first "man of letters." If you have time left over, squeeze in a visit to Lyndhurst, financier Jay Gould's former residence, built in the Gothic Revival style.

For dinner, head to Buffet de la Gare or Harvest on Hudson, in Hastings-on-Hudson. Choose luxury accommodations at Castle on the Hudson or something more moderate at the Marriott in Tarrytown, or drive two hours north to Rhinebeck, to get an earlier start on the next day's itinerary.

Day 2

Your day in Hyde Park begins with breakfast at the Apple Pie Bakery Café on the CIA campus. Next up is a tour of FDR's home and library, followed by a picnic lunch and house tour at the Vanderbilt Estate. In the afternoon, head to Rhinebeck for shopping or stop at a couple of wineries along the Dutchess Wine Trail. For accommodations nearby, choose the Belvedere Mansion or the 1766 Beekman Arms in Rhinebeck. Walk to dinner at Terrapin or Gigi Trattoria, or return to the CIA campus for a student-prepared meal at American Bounty or Caterina d' Medici.

Day 3

Continue the drive north to Columbia County to visit Montgomery Place and Clermont, the Georgian-style estate of Robert Livingston, Jr., in the morning. In the afternoon, head to Olana, the former home of Romantic landscape painter Frederick Church, and compare it to what you saw on Day One at Sunnyside. If time permits, hit the antique shops in Hudson and stay for dinner at Red Dot or Wunderbar. Return to your Rhinebeck hotel for the night, or change to Mount Merino Manor, closer to Hudson and the Rip Van Winkle Bridge.

WEEKENDS IN THE WILD

Fresh air and challenging terrain for a wide range of sports are two primary factors that draw visitors to the more remote parts of the Hudson River Valley. Whether you choose to hike, bike, or ski, you'll have plenty of choices for a memorable outdoor adventure.

CATSKILL ESCARPMENT TRAIL

Some 200 miles of trails traverse the Catskill Forest Preserve. High above the Hudson River Valley are Kaaterskill Falls and the Escarpment Trail, a magical wilderness setting where the Hudson River School of painters found inspiration and the Catskill Mountain House entertained prominent guests. The rugged 23-mile trail connects the towns of Haines Falls and Windham, changing 10,000 feet in elevation along the way. The highest peak along the trail is 3,940-foot Blackhead Mountain. Allow two days for a challenging overnight hike, or three days for side trips at either end of the hike.

Grab breakfast at Maggie's Krooked Café and stock up on supplies in Tannersville on Route 23A before heading to the trailhead at North Lake in Haines Falls. Summit Blackhead Mountain (3,940 feet) on day one, and aim to reach the Elm Ridge lean-to before sundown. Although camping is unrestricted below 3,500 feet, camp in established sites when possible.

Retrace your steps on the second day, and finish the trip with a drive through the mountaintop towns of Hunter and Windham, followed by a dinner of hearty German fare at Maassmann's Restaurant in Round Top.

SHAWANGUNK ADVENTURE WEEKEND

New Paltz is your home base for this weekend of hiking, swimming, and optional rock climbing in Minnewaska State Park. There are rare dwarf pines and peregrine falcons to see and gorgeous vistas to enjoy at every bend in the trail.

Make reservations for the weekend at the Minnewaska Lodge near New Paltz or Sparrow Hawk B&B in High Falls. Get an early start Friday, so you can avoid traffic and stroll downtown New Paltz before dinner at Beso or Main Course.

WINTER WONDER WEEKEND

Falling temperatures mean one thing to winter sports enthusiasts: the possibility of powder. Ski resorts in the Catskills and Adirondacks start making snow as soon as it will freeze, and then hope for a little help from Mother Nature as the season progresses. Whether you prefer the thrill of downhill or the serenity of the open trail, the greater Hudson Valley has much to offer December–March.

For downhill thrills, head to Windham, Hunter, or Belleayre in the northern Catskill

Mountains, where snow guns cover nearly 100 percent of the terrain. Choose the Eggery Inn (Tannersville), Hotel Vienna (Windham), or Scribner Hollow Lodge (Hunter)—all three cozy winter accommodations close to the slopes.

For more solitude on Nordic trails, choose the Capital-Saratoga region: John Boyd Thacher State Park near Albany and Lapland Lake near Saratoga Springs are good bets. Stay at the Morgan State House or 74 State in downtown Albany to mix urban amenities with your outdoor adventure, or the Adelphi Hotel on Broadway in Saratoga Springs.

FUN FOR FOODIES

Hudson Valley chefs take the concept of eating local to the extreme. And a love of fresh food prepared with a creative flare is a prerequisite for enjoying all that the Hudson River Valley has to offer. CIA graduates run kitchens in every county in the region. Eateries range from classic diners to contemporary American restaurants, and from game-inspired, farm-fresh menus to upscale Italian, French, and international cuisine. Ethnic foods are easier to find the farther south you go. Many towns now offer gourmet coffee shops, bakeries, and bagels too. To make food the focus of your trip, consider enrolling in a cooking class, or design your route to follow a wine trail.

COOKING CLASSES

The main campus of the nation's premier culinary college sits on 80 acres overlooking the river at Hyde Park. The Culinary Institute of America runs five restaurants, a bookstore, and courses for cooking professionals and enthusiasts. Its facilities include 41 kitchens and the largest collection of culinary books and reference materials of any library in the country. For serious training, enthusiasts can enroll in one of the CIA's Boot Camp programs.

Vintage Hudson Valley organizes culinary events at restaurants across the valley, including Le Chambord in Dutchess County, Valley Restaurant at the Garrison in Putnam County, and Equus in Westchester County. Other options for learning from the masters include classes with Chef Damon Baehrel of the Basement Bistro in Greene County.

FRESH PRODUCE

Every county in the region has its share of apple orchards, berry patches, organic farms, and cornfields. Flavors differ from one hillside to the next, in what locals like to call micro-terroirs. Farmers markets and farm stands are a popular pastime for locals and visitors alike.

The Hudson Valley specializes in a number of delicious fruits and vegetables. Fern-like fiddleheads appear on many menus in the early spring. For those who like to forage for their food, spring rains bring wild mushrooms, including morels and chanterelles. In summer, the local garlic harvest begins in Saugerties, and farm stands overflow with fresh-picked corn, tomatoes, and other vegetables. Strawberries and cherries ripen through June and July, and blueberries last July–September. You can pick apples July–November, and pumpkin patches do a steady business in September and October.

Greig Farm runs one of the most developed farm markets in the valley, including a garden shop, bakery, and winery. Columbia County's V. R. Saulpaugh and Sons has evolved from a green bean operation into a more diversified grower. Look for the stand along Route 9G in Germantown. Two more standout markets are the Nyack Farmers Market in Rockland County and Warwick Farmers Market in Orange County. And

Stone Barns is doing its part to define what it means to be a sustainable working farm. Meanwhile, the growing popularity of community-supported agriculture programs, which deliver the week's bounty directly to your doorstep, gives farmers a way to survive and area residents a connection to the land.

GOURMET RESTAURANTS

You'll find pockets of high-end cuisine across the region, with the highest concentrations of restaurants in Westchester, Dutchess, Ulster, and Columbia counties. Tarrytown, Cold Spring, Rhinebeck, Albany, and Saratoga Springs are known for their wide selection of gourmet eats.

A handful of venues are worth planning a trip around, by virtue of the outstanding cuisine they prepare and the unparalleled dining experiences they offer. Here is an abbreviated list of the best: Blue Hill at Stone Barns in Westchester, American Bounty on the CIA campus, Valley Restaurant at the Garrison, and The Basement Bistro in Greene County.

WINERIES

Hudson Valley grape growers introduced French-American hybrid grapes in the 1970s to please an increasingly sophisticated consumer base. The switch put the region on the New York State wine map, producing award-winning Italian-style whites, as well as pinot noirs and cabernet francs. The Dutchess Wine Trail includes Alison Wines, Clinton Vineyards, and Millbrook Winery & Vineyards and covers miles of pretty countryside. Meanwhile, the wineries themselves produce some of the highest-quality labels in New York State.

On the other side of the Hudson, the Shawangunk Wine Trail is a 30-mile loop connecting nine family-owned wineries. The trail runs along back roads between the New York State Thruway, I-84, and Route 17 between New Paltz in Ulster County and Warwick in Orange County. Some of the most popular stops include Rivendell Vineyards and Winery, Applewood Winery, and the Warwick Valley Winery & Distillery.

FALL FOLIAGE TOURS

Time a visit with the changing of the seasons to catch one of the most spectacular displays of color anywhere on the planet. The leaves begin to turn in mid-September and peak around Columbus Day in October, depending on temperature, rainfall, and elevation. The clear, crisp days of autumn offer prime conditions for hiking.

ON FOOT

The hardwood forests of the Catskill and Shawangunk ranges explode in shades of red, orange, and yellow.

Catskills Hike

One of the most difficult but rewarding fall hikes is a triple-summit over the Catskill High Peaks of Thomas Cole, Black Dome, and Blackhead Mountains. Windham or Hunter make equidistant launching points for the day.

You'll need two vehicles to complete this one-way hike. Park the pickup vehicle at the eastern end of Big Hollow Road, off Maplecrest Road/County Route 40 in the town of Jewett. Then drive to the eastern end of Barnum Road, also off Maplecrest Road/County Route 40, to begin the hike (6.1 miles one-way) on an old logging road. A mixed hardwood forest of oak, maple, and beech trees puts on the initial display. Dress in layers and be prepared for fast-changing weather conditions.

Shawangunks Hike

Fall colors are all the more striking against a pair of sparkling lakes in the Minnewaska State Park Preserve. For a moderate day hike on a network of carriage trails, park at the Wildmere lot off Route 44 and follow the red trail markers as you pass Lake Minnewaska. Pick up the Castle Point Carriageway (blue markers) on the west side of the lake. Enjoy the views of Gertrude's Nose from the trailside gazebo. After the hike, drive to High Falls for a casual dinner at Chefs on Fire.

BY CAR
The Taconic State Parkway

This tree-lined road offers changing scenery around every bend, with occasional vistas across the surrounding valley. The stretch from Route 55 north to Chatham is particularly beautiful in the fall and takes about an hour to drive. Along the way, Clinton Vineyards and Millbrook Winery make easy side trips.

Route 9W

Hugging the river's western shoreline, Route 9W passes through long stretches of hardwood forest between Newburgh and Coxsackie, with several commercial zones mixed in. Begin the day's drive at the Bear Mountain Bridge and make your way north, stopping for lunch and antique shopping in Saugerties. Allow about three hours of driving time to reach downtown Albany.

Route 23/23A

This is a good route for a late-season tour, as the elevation means color will peak a bit later than elsewhere in the valley. Begin the drive in the village of Catskill, after grabbing a cup of coffee at Retriever Roasters on Main Street. Follow Route 9W south to pick up Route 23A west. At Palenville, you'll begin to climb. Look for a trailhead on the right for Kaaterskill Falls if you want to hike; otherwise, continue the winding road uphill to Tannersville, where you can tour the Mountaintop Arboretum. At Hunter Mountain, stock up

for a picnic lunch at the Catskill Mountain Foundation Farm Market, then complete the loop by picking up Route 23 toward Windham and descending from the High Peaks region back to the village of Catskill.

Route 44

Pick up Route 44 from the Taconic Parkway heading east and follow it through Millbrook, taking the Millbrook Winery detour if time permits. Browse the shops in Millbrook, or continue east through Amenia to Millerton. In Millerton, park near the Harney & Sons tea company and walk part of the Harlem Valley Rail Trail. Afterwards, warm up with a cup of tea at the Harney & Sons Tea Tasting Room, which serves the local brew. Total driving time will be about an hour from the Taconic Parkway to the state line. Retrace your steps at day's end to have dinner at Millbrook's Café Les Baux.

Hawk's Nest

This drive begins in western Orange County, near the Delaware River. Exit I-84 at Port Jervis and pick up Route 97 north. It's about a two-hour scenic drive along the Delaware, past Minisink Battleground and Narrowsburg to Hancock, where you'll pick up Route 17 heading back east and south. Stop for lunch in Narrowsburg at Lander's River Cafe overlooking the river. When you reach Roscoe and Livingston Manor on Route 17, consider a visit to the Catskill Fly Fishing Museum on your way through Livingston Manor, then finish the day with dinner at Ianine's inside the DeBruce Country Inn along the Willowemoc River.

AERIAL VIEWS

Skydiving in the Hudson River Valley is the best around, and what better time to attempt a jump than during the leaf-peeping season? Operators include Saratoga Skydiving in the Capital Region and Skydive the Ranch in the Mid-Hudson.

REVOLUTIONARY WAR ROUTE

The outcome of the nine-year struggle for independence from the British hinged largely on who controlled the Hudson River. From the boycott of British tea to the turning point at Saratoga, many of the war's pivotal events took place in the surrounding valley. Today, a number of interpretive museums and historic sites preserve and commemorate various events and decisions that took place in those long years between 1774 and 1783.

The itinerary below identifies major Revolutionary War sights along the river, from south to north. Other options are to follow the Henry Knox Cannon Trail through Saratoga Springs, Albany, and Columbia County; or to trace the Washington-Rochambeau Revolutionary Route, through the lower Hudson Valley.

Day 1

This tour begins at the former home of Loyalist Frederick Philipse III, who was arrested by General George Washington in 1776, after signing the Declaration of Independence. Both the family residence, Philipse Manor Hall in Yonkers, and the Philipse Manor farming estate in Sleepy Hollow were confiscated by the state and later preserved as museums. Situated in the neutral zone, Van Cortlandt Manor hosted loyalists and patriots alike during the war.

An American victory at Stony Point Battlefield in 1779 boosted morale and severely damaged British forces. To reach this state historic site, cross the Hudson at the Bear Mountain Bridge and head south into Rockland County.

Retrace your steps north to the United States Military Academy at West Point, a training ground for army officers since 1802. The academy sits on the bluffs overlooking the narrow stretch of the river that was chained to keep the British out. You can begin your tour with a walk through the museum (outside the gate), which includes Washington's pistols among its exhibits. Next, book a bus or river tour at the visitors center and have lunch at the stately Thayer Hotel just inside the campus gate. Add half a day for a visit to Constitution Island.

Cold Spring Village makes a convenient stopover. Choose between two equally appealing bed-and-breakfast inns: the Pig Hill or Kittleman's; then dine at Cathryn's Tuscan Grill in town, or venture one town over to Valley Restaurant at the Garrison.

Day 2

The first Purple Heart was issued at the Hasbrouck family farmhouse, where Washington stayed for 16 months at the end of the war.

Washington's Headquarters in Newburgh became the first national historic site in the United States. His army camped at New Windsor Cantonment in Vails Gate, now also the site of the Purple Heart Hall of Honor. After touring these museums, plan a waterfront lunch at Newburgh Landing.

In the afternoon, visit Mount Gulian outside of Beacon, an 18th-century Dutch stone barn that once belonged to the Verplanck family and served as headquarters for Revolutionary War General Friedrich Wilhelm Augustus von Steuben.

In keeping with the historic theme, join the likes of George Washington, Philip Schuyler, Benedict Arnold, and Alexander Hamilton in spending the night at the 1766 Beekman Arms in Rhinebeck, where local townspeople gathered inside for safety while the British burned Kingston to the ground across the Hudson. In the evening, head to the Culinary Institute of America nearby to enjoy the menu of regional dishes at American Bounty.

Day 3

Today begins with a drive across the river to visit Kingston, a colonial city that the British burned to the ground. They landed at Rondout Battlefield, where periodic reenactments now take place. In Kingston's Stockade District, the Senate House hosted the first Senate of New York State in 1777. Grab a quick lunch nearby at Jane's Homemade Ice Cream, or drive to the waterfront for a seafood extravaganza at Mariner's Harbor.

Cross the river on the Kingston-Rhinecliff Bridge and make your way north to Clermont, colonial estate of the Livingston family. The British torched it in 1777, but the family promptly rebuilt the home during the war.

At day's end, head to Mount Merino Manor, a relatively new bed-and-breakfast near the city of Hudson. For dinner options in town, try Swoon, Red Dot, or Mexican Radio.

Day 4

Start the day with a drive across the Rip Van Winkle Bridge and a hearty breakfast at Ursula's Riverside Diner in Athens. Continue north along Route 9W to the Bronck Museum, where New Yorkers signed the Coxsackie Declaration of Independence in 1775. From there, it's about 25 miles north to Albany and the Schuyler Mansion, home of Major General Philip Schuyler and the place where British General Burgoyne was imprisoned after his defeat at Saratoga. Enjoy a formal lunch at Jack's Oyster Bar, or something more casual at any of the Lark Street eateries.

Complete the trip at the Saratoga National Historic Park, which commemorates the Battle of Saratoga. Here, you can follow a 10-stop auto tour that interprets the battle. Reserve an antique-filled room at the Adelphi Hotel right in town, and for dinner indulge in a basket of award-winning fried chicken at Hattie's Chicken Shack.

THE LOWER HUDSON

Not surprisingly, the Hudson Valley's most densely populated counties border New York City. Although no longer much of a getaway destination itself, the Lower Hudson Valley is packed with historic mansions and restored gardens at every bend in the road. John Jay, Frederick Philipse, the Vanderbilts, and the Harrimans all left their mark, but the grandest estate of all was the sprawling Rockefeller residence at Pocantico Hills near Tarrytown. As a legacy of these large estates, Westchester and Rockland counties were able to preserve wilderness areas that rival many upstate parks and preserves, even as they struggled to cope with rapid industrial and housing development. More than a dozen gardens are open to the public and easily accessible in a day trip from New York City.

These days, Donald Trump is building in White Plains, and the Clintons have put Chappaqua on the map. Both counties support diverse populations that represent the very highest and lowest income brackets, as well as many different nations and cultures. Local restaurants prepare menus you only expect to find domestically in New York City or San Francisco, including specialties from Brazil, China, India, and Japan, as well as Italy, Spain, and France. And unlike in other parts of the Hudson River Valley, night owls who visit the Lower Hudson have many choices for evening entertainment, from the Westchester Broadway Theater in Elmsford to the Performing Arts Center in Purchase and the Caramoor Center for Music and the Arts in Katonah.

The Tappan Zee Bridge connects the two

COURTESY OF HISTORIC HUDSON VALLEY/WWW.HUDSONVALLEY.ORG

HIGHLIGHTS

◖ **Sunnyside:** The Romantic home of author Washington Irving is set amidst rolling hills, a babbling brook, and the purple and white flowers of wisteria that climbs all the way up to the gabled roof (page 35).

◖ **Kykuit:** John D. Rockefeller built a six-story, 40-room mansion in the Pocantico Hills near Tarrytown, with breathtaking views of the Hudson River and Palisades across it (page 38).

◖ **Katonah Museum Mile:** Katonah is home to three first-rate museums, all located within a mile of each other: the Caramoor Center for Music and the Arts, the Katonah Museum of Art, and the John Jay Homestead (page 42).

◖ **Piermont Village:** Three miles south of the Tappan Zee Bridge, on a steep hillside between Route 9W and the riverbank, is the upscale village of Piermont, a haven for cyclists, foodies, and creative types (page 54).

◖ **Stony Point Battlefield State Historical Site:** Located on Haverstraw Bay is the site of a small but important victory in the American Revolution, with a riverside park and museum that includes the oldest lighthouse on the Hudson (page 57).

◖ **Harriman State Park:** The first section of the Appalachian Trail was cleared here in 1923; today, hikers can access several lakes, plus 200 miles of trails, inside the park (page 57).

LOOK FOR ◖ TO FIND RECOMMENDED SIGHTS, ACTIVITIES, DINING, AND LODGING.

counties at the widest part of the Hudson River, while the Bear Mountain Bridge spans the river at Westchester's northern border.

PLANNING YOUR TIME

Whether you want to add an easy day trip to a longer New York City stay or find a new stopover on your way to a regular weekend getaway farther north, Westchester and Rockland counties offer many choices for historic tours, outdoor entertainment, and fine-dining experiences. And the well-developed New York and New Jersey transit systems make it easy to leave the car behind.

If you have one day to explore the area, head to the gardens of the former Rockefeller estate at Kykuit, in Sleepy Hollow, and choose a restaurant for dinner in Tarrytown. Alternatively, plan to tackle a section of the 26-mile Old Croton Aqueduct by foot, bike, or horseback.

THE LOWER HUDSON

CONNECTICUT

NEW YORK

NEW JERSEY

Long Island Sound

Saugatuck Reservoir

Titicus Reservoir

Cross River Reservoir

Ward Pound Ridge Reserve

North Salem

Katonah

Bedford

North Stanford

Greenwich

Rye

New Rochelle

KATONAH MUSEUM MILE

Mt Kisco

Pleasantville

Rye Lake

PLAYLAND AMUSEMENT PARK

Somers

New Croton Reservoir

Kensico Res

NEUBERGER MUSEUM

White Plains

Yonkers

Mt Vernon

Shrub Oak

KYKUIT

Ossining

Croton-on-Hudson

Tarrytown

SUNNYSIDE

Irvington

Dobbs Ferry

PHILIPSE MANOR HALL

Bronx

Peekskill

Hudson River

Nyack

TAPPAN ZEE BRIDGE

Hastings-on-Hudson

PIERMONT VILLAGE

STONY POINT BATTLEFIELD STATE HISTORICAL SITE

Palisades Interstate Park

Stony Point

Lake De Forest

Oradell Lake

Mt Ivy

PALISADES

Lake Tappan

Paramus

HARRIMAN STATE PARK

Spring Valley

Suffern

GARDEN STATE PKWY

WEST POINT MILITARY RESERVATION

BEAR MOUNTAIN BRIDGE

SEVEN LAKES PKWY

Trail

Appalachian

Greenwood Lake

Darlington

Point View Reservoir

Wanaque Reservoir

Patterson

Passaic River

PUTNAM

WESTCHESTER

ROCKLAND

ORANGE

NASSAU

Long Island

TACONIC STATE PKWY

SAW MILL RIVER PKWY

MERRITT PKWY

5 mi

5 km

© AVALON TRAVEL

In Rockland County, head to the Piermont area for the perfect mix of entertainment, food, and outdoor recreation. Then drive north on Route 9W to visit a series of Revolutionary War sights and scenic river overlooks. Or forget the history lesson and get away from it all with a backcountry hike in Harriman State Park.

Longer itineraries allow you to visit multiple historic homes, such as Jay Gould's Lyndhurst and Washington Irving's Sunnyside, or to contemplate the works of art in one of several well-funded museums. Add half a day to sample the wild mushrooms at the Nyack Farmers Market or attend a White Plains Antique Show. Add another day to tour the gardens in Somers and Purchase. When planning an overnight visit, beware that choices in accommodations will be limited primarily to business hotels. If quaint and memorable lodging is a priority, consider visiting the Lower Hudson on a day trip from New York City or when passing through to parts north.

Westchester County

Bordering the Bronx, the southern edge of Westchester County is just 15 minutes from Manhattan by train. The county boasts the largest population and the highest population density in the Hudson Valley region—and a surprising blend of wealthy suburbs, ample green space, and historic sites. Yonkers, Mount Vernon, New Rochelle, Rye, and White Plains are the largest cities, and White Plains is the county seat.

The New York Assembly established Westchester County in 1683, and the first English settlements popped up in the eastern part of the county at Rye, Mamaroneck, Eastchester, and Bedford. The manor of Frederick Philipse, deeded through a royal grant, covered more than 52,000 acres between Yonkers and Tarrytown. Roads, taverns, and ferries were built in the 18th century, and by the end of the century, Westchester had become the wealthiest and most populous county in New York.

The American Revolution took its toll, however, through the battles of Pelham and White Plains. Westchester found itself stuck between the American headquarters, near Peekskill, and the British, in New York City. It took decades for local communities to rebound from the expense and disruption of war.

Westchester County became a commuter base as early as the 19th century, when rail travel made it possible to reach New York City in just a few hours. As transportation evolved from steamboat to rail to car, Westchester grew at a frenzied pace. Its river towns began to produce medicines, cars, beer, sugar, and elevators, among other goods. Expansion of the New York City watershed created more jobs and further accelerated growth. Today's population is more than 900,000 and counting. But along with the crowds came upscale shopping, first-rate cultural attractions, and outstanding international cuisine.

ALONG THE RIVER–ROUTE 9
Yonkers

Start a tour of Westchester's river towns from the West Side Highway in Manhattan and follow Route 9A north to Yonkers. This diverse city of 188,000 people is a major transportation hub and is the fourth-largest city in New York State. Its name derives from *jonkheer,* the Dutch word for "young nobleman," in reference to Dutchman Adriaen Van Der Donck, who built a sawmill where the tiny Nepperhan River (later renamed the Saw Mill River) empties into the Hudson. Four miles of frontage on the eastern bank of the Hudson offer beautiful views of the Palisades in New Jersey and Rockland County.

Legendary jazz singer Ella Fitzgerald was raised in Yonkers, and a statue of her greets passengers arriving at the train station. Nearby, where Main Street meets the river, is the hundred-year-old **Yonkers Recreational Pier,** newly renovated to hold community events and festivals.

Two notable museums are within walking distance of the train station. Two blocks east on Warburton Avenue is **Philipse Manor Hall** (29 Warburton Ave. at Dock St., 914/965-4027, www.philipsemanorfriends.org; noon–5 P.M. Tues.–Sat., 1–4 P.M. Sun., Apr. 1–Oct. 31; adults $4, seniors and students $3, under 12 free; on-site parking free). This Georgian mansion housed three generations of the Philipse family until loyalist Frederick Philipse III was arrested in 1776 and forced to flee to England. The building dates to 1682, and exhibits inside trace the history of Yonkers.

Also on Warburton Avenue, the **Hudson River Museum** (511 Warburton Ave., 914/963-4550, www.hrm.org; noon–5 P.M. Wed., Thurs., Sat., and Sun., noon–8 P.M. Fri., May–Sept.; adults $5, seniors $3, children ages 5–16 $3, under 5 free; Fri. 5–8 P.M. free) was founded in 1919 with a focus on Hudson River art, history, and science. Exhibits include landscape paintings from the Hudson River School of Painters, historic photographs, sculpture, and prints. After browsing the collection of 19th- and 20th-century art, enjoy river views from the museum café. Then learn about the natural history of the Hudson and the summer night sky inside the Andrus Planetarium.

Inside the Glenview Mansion, which is also part of the museum, six rooms are furnished in turn-of-the-20th-century style. The sitting room holds one of the highlights of a house tour: a delicately carved and inlaid sunflower pattern in the woodwork, representative of the rare American Eastlake interior style. In addition to these varied exhibits, the museum hosts an annual jazz series each summer.

Three River Towns: Hastings-on-Hudson, Dobbs Ferry, and Irvington

If you have one day to spend on the **Old Croton Aqueduct** (15 Walnut St., Dobbs Ferry, 914/693-5259, www.nysparks.state .ny.us), choose the section that connects the three river towns above Yonkers: Hastings-on-Hudson, Dobbs Ferry, and Irvington. Artists and commuters have made these towns their home, and the route leads to one delight after another—from historic homes and shady lanes to local parks and river views, with the Palisades always looming in the distance. Farmers markets, bookstores, antiques, and other shops provide good diversions from the trail. The Ossining aqueduct tunnel is open June–October by reservation only; the rest of the park is open sunrise-sunset year-round (see sidebar, *Old Croton Trailway State Historic Park,* for more information on this attraction).

The most famous resident of Hastings-on-Hudson began his career as an architect and later became a painter associated with the first generation of the Hudson River School. Like his fellow Romantic artists, Jasper Francis Cropsey (1823–1900) depicted the Hudson River, Catskill Mountain House, and Lake George, as well as other natural wonders in the northeast, in a series of colorful and fantastical landscapes. The **Newington Cropsey Gallery** (25 Cropsey Lane, Hastings-on-Hudson, 914/478-7990, www.newingtoncropsey .com; by appointment 1–5 P.M. Mon.–Fri.), located near the train station, contains an exhaustive collection of Cropsey's works, including oil paintings, watercolors, drawings, and architectural renderings. A guided tour of the gallery takes about 45 minutes. Also in town, the yellow 1835 **Cropsey Homestead** (49 Washington Ave., Hastings-on-Hudson, 914/478-1372, www.newingtoncropsey.com/ homestd.htm; 10 A.M.–1 P.M. Mon.–Fri., closed Dec., Jan., and Aug.; under 16 not admitted), called Ever Rest, has been furnished and decorated to reflect the 19th-century sensibility. The separate artist studio dates to 1885, and many of Cropsey's sketches and studies are on display inside the home and studio.

During the same time period, a 19th-century photographer and astronomer named John William Draper (1811–1882), who took some of the earliest pictures of the moon, built a federal-style farmhouse on 20 acres in Hastings. His two sons later built a famous observatory that hosted the likes of Thomas

THREE PERFECT DAYS IN WESTCHESTER COUNTY

So many sights, so little time. Can you fit it all in during one long weekend? With Tarrytown as a home base, this ambitious plan offers a good mix of art, history, and culture.

Day 1

Arrive via Westchester County airport or any New York City airport and transfer to the Tarrytown area via rental car or take the Metro-North Hudson Line to Tarrytown.

Book a tour of Kykuit, the Rockefeller Estate, in advance, for your first morning; then head to Tarrytown for lunch. In the afternoon, tour Lyndhurst, Jay Gould's Gothic Revival mansion. Check in to a Tarrytown hotel and enjoy an evening of dinner and entertainment at the Westchester Broadway Theatre in Elmsford.

Day 2

Tour the Caramoor Center for Music and the Arts and walk downtown Katonah. Have lunch in White Plains before shopping at the Westchester mall. Tour the PepsiCo Sculpture Garden or visit the Neuberger Museum of Art in Purchase. Head to Blue Hill at Stone Barns for dinner.

Day 3

Tour Washington Irving's Romantic estate, Sunnyside, then grab lunch at Sushi Mike's in Dobbs Ferry. Head to the Hudson River Museum in Yonkers as a last stop before your departure.

Edison and Samuel Morse. Today, the **Draper Observatory Cottage** (41 Washington Ave., Hastings-on-Hudson, 914/478-2249, http://hastingshistorical.org; 10 A.M.–2 P.M. Mon. and Thurs.) holds the Hastings-on-Hudson Historical Society, with an archive of books, maps, paintings, and other town memorabilia. After browsing the museums, enjoy a picnic and the riverside views at MacEachron Waterfront Park, next to the train station.

Much of the 2002 movie *Unfaithful,* starring Diane Lane and Richard Gere, was filmed in neighboring Dobbs Ferry, a town that locals affectionately call the Sausalito of the east, referring to its setting on a hillside overlooking the Hudson River. Settled by Irish, Italian, and other European immigrants during the Industrial Revolution, this town of 10,000 residents was named for a ferry service that operated in the 1700s. Journalist and railroad financier Henry Villard (1835–1900) joined the well-to-do here in 1879. Many of the original homes feature long-lasting Vermont slate roofs. A handful of art galleries are located along Main Street and Broadway.

Irvington takes its name from Washington Irving, but the town is better known as the home of the first African American millionaire and philanthropist, Madam C. J. Walker (1867–1919), who made her fortune selling hair and beauty products. Walker commissioned Vertner Woodson Tandy, considered the first licensed black architect in New York State, to build her dream home on Broadway in 1917. The resulting Italianate structure, called Villa Lewaro, featured river views from the dining room and hosted many black leaders of the time, from Langston Hughes to W. E. B. DuBois. Villa Lewaro is privately owned today by Helena and Harold Doley.

Tarrytown and Sleepy Hollow

Soon after he moved to the neighboring hamlet of Sleepy Hollow, John D. Rockefeller reportedly tried to purchase and shut down Tarrytown's only tavern. It was a rare instance where the Puritan business mogul was unable to impose his will on those around him, and Tarrytown remained a lively center for commerce and the arts.

In September 1780, three Tarrytown militiamen captured Benedict Arnold's partner in

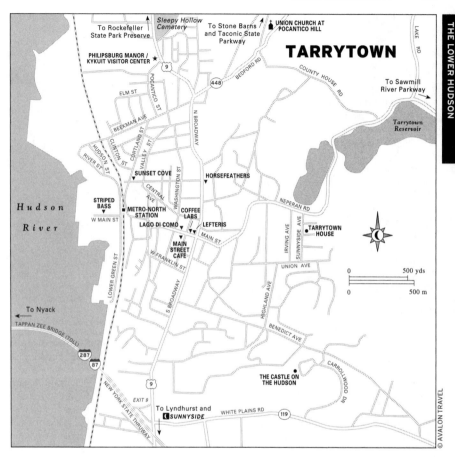

© AVALON TRAVEL

treason, British Major John André, and found in his boot copies of George Washington's plans for fortifying West Point. Andre was tried, convicted, and hung across the river in Nyack. A sign in Patriot's Park commemorates the arrest.

Today, a stroll along Main Street, with its coffeehouses and antique shops, is the perfect interlude between tours of the surrounding homes and gardens, and it is a convenient stop for nourishment while exploring the Old Croton Aqueduct. Route 9 turns into Broadway as you approach the center of town. Follow Main Street toward the river to find a public parking lot.

◖ Sunnyside

A few miles south, Sunnyside (West Sunnyside Lane, Tarrytown, 914/631-8200, www .hudsonvalley.org; 10 A.M.–5 P.M. Wed.–Mon. Apr.–mid-Oct., 10 A.M.–4 P.M. Nov.–Dec. and weekends in March; adults $9, seniors $8, children $5, under 5 free), the Romantic-era home of celebrated author Washington Irving, known as America's first man of letters, comes right out of the pages of a children's storybook. Set among rolling hills, a babbling brook, and the purple and white flowers of wisteria that climb all the way up to the gabled roof, Sunnyside captures the imagination in much the

© NIKKI GOTH ITOI

Romantic details of Washington Irving's Sunnyside reflect the writer's Dutch heritage.

same way that Irving's tales "Rip Van Winkle" and "The Legend of Sleepy Hollow" did.

After a life of international travel and diplomacy, Irving found this peaceful retreat near Tarrytown, a place he remembered well from his childhood. Irving purchased the future site of Sunnyside in 1835 and settled here a year later. After a brief stint as minister to Spain, he returned to Sunnyside to live until his death in 1859. John D. Rockefeller acquired the property in 1945 and opened it to the public two years later.

In Sunnyside, Irving happily mixed and matched architectural styles, according to the Romantic philosophy: Stepped gables and weather vanes reflect the writer's Dutch heritage, while steeply pitched rooflines, irregular window sizes, and a facade of cut stone were borrowed from the Scottish home of Sir Walter Scott, a contemporary of Irving's. Later, Irving added a Spanish-style tower to remind him of the time he had spent living in the country. The surrounding gardens and grounds were as important to the writer as the design of his home. In a letter sent in 1846, Irving wrote, "I understand my cottage is nearly buried alive among trees I set out, and overrun with roses and honeysuckles and ivy from Melrose Abbey, and my nieces implore me to come back and save them from being buried alive in foliage."

Today, guides in Victorian-era costumes welcome visitors into the enchanted home to experience a day in the life of the writer. A pair of Gothic Revival–style benches line the entrance to the home. Among the furnishings on display are Irving's desk and many of his books. In the kitchen, visitors can admire the cast-iron wood-burning stove, cast-iron pedestal sink, which featured both hot and cold running water, modern conveniences during Irving's time.

Nationally known and loved in his own lifetime, Irving wrote far more than the stories we remember today: Among his last works was an exhaustive biography of his namesake, George Washington. Visitors can tour the inside, walk the grounds, and picnic under the trees. Tours begin with a short film, and visitor services

COURTESY OF HISTORIC HUDSON VALLEY/WWW.HUDSONVALLEY.ORG

Sunnyside's rooflines were inspired by the Scottish home of Sir Walter Scott, Irving's contemporary.

include a café and museum shop stocked with books by and about Irving as well as some of his contemporaries.

Lyndhurst

The Old Croton Trailway connects Sunnyside to the adjacent Lyndhurst property, the former residence of financier Jay Gould (635 S. Broadway, Tarrytown, 914/631-4481, www .hudsonvalley.org; 10 A.M.–5 P.M. Apr.–Oct., 10 A.M.–4 P.M. Nov.–Apr.; grounds fee $4, adults $10, seniors $9, students 12–17 $4, under 12 free). Designed in 1838 by renowned architect Alexander Jackson Davis, the mansion, with its asymmetrical lines, reflects the Gothic Revival style. Gould was third to own the home, after New York City mayor William Paulding and businessman George Merritt.

The carefully planned gardens on 67 acres are as visually interesting as the ornate rooms inside. Also on the premises, Gould built the largest private conservatory in his day, while his daughter, Helen Gould Shephard, later designed the circular rose garden that still blooms

today. A popular way to arrive in summer is by boat from Manhattan (NY Waterways, 800/533-3779, www.nywaterway.com; adults $49, seniors $47, children $25, including transfers and site admission).

Philipsburg Manor

A tour of the three-story, white Philipsburg Manor (381 N. Broadway/Rte. 9, Sleepy Hollow, 914/631-8200, www.hudsonvalley.org; 10 A.M.–5 P.M. daily Apr.–Oct., 10 A.M.–4 P.M. Nov.–Dec. and weekends only in March; adults $9, seniors $8, children $5, under 5 free), at Upper Mills, is an interactive production, with theatrical guides dressed in colonial garb. It is also a sobering experience, designed to give visitors an appreciation for the manual labor required to run an international trading company in the 19th century. The Philipse family was one of the earliest and largest slaveholders in the northeast, and today's museum exhibits address the African American experience on the farm. The tour begins in the basement kitchen and former slave quarters, and then

COURTESY OF HISTORIC HUDSON VALLEY / WWW.HUDSONVALLEY.ORG

Philipsburg Manor in Sleepy Hollow

progresses through the house with a narrative that brings the enslaved perspective to life.

Philipsburg Manor is also the departure point for all tours to the Rockefeller Estate, Kykuit. A small café (10 A.M.–4 P.M. Mon. and Wed.–Fri., 9:30 A.M.–5 P.M. Sat.–Sun.; mains $5–9) sells basic breakfast fare, snacks, and paninis; the adjoining giftshop stocks a variety of relevant books and souvenirs. Across Route 9 from Philipsburg Manor is the **Sleepy Hollow Cemetery,** with the gravesites of Washington Irving, William Cullen Bryant, Andrew Carnegie, Walter Chrysler, William Rockefeller, and others. The property runs for several miles along Route 9, surrounding the **Old Dutch Church** and its historic burying ground.

◖ Kykuit

Land prices were at a historic low in 1893 when John D. Rockefeller bought his first 400 acres in the **Pocantico Hills** (po-CAN-tee-co, meaning "water rushing over rocks") north of Tarrytown. Stunning views of the Hudson River and surrounding hills and mountains drew the oil magnate to an area he described as "a place where fine views invest the soul and where we can live simply and quietly." The family's country estate expanded to 1,600 acres by the turn of the 20th century and 3,000 at its peak. Today, it remains an extraordinary place where visitors can absorb some history, admire a modern art collection, learn about local flora, and reflect on a bygone era.

Rockefeller built 75 homes and 70 miles of roads, all strategically placed to show off the surrounding views. He designed much of the landscape himself, and except for a central private area, he insisted that the grounds be kept open to the public, as long as visitors abided by his rules: no cars, no drinking, and no smoking. As the estate grew, Rockefeller paid handsomely to relocate a small college, a neighborhood of homes, and even a stretch of the New York Central Railroad to the outskirts of his property. A small farm supplied food for the family, and golf became Rockefeller's preferred pastime at Pocantico. He designed a 12-hole course and played year-round, rain or shine.

For the first decade, Rockefeller lived in and remodeled the modest home that had come with the property. When that residence burned down in 1902, the family built a hilltop mansion two miles from the Hudson called Kykuit (pronounced KYE-cut), which means "lookout." It was designed to maximize sunlight in winter. Conceived as an English country house, the structure evolved into a six-story, 40-room ordeal in the American Renaissance style. It was completed in 1913.

Rockefeller's son, Junior, commissioned the estate's garden design to architect William Welles Bosworth, who crafted one of the finest surviving examples of beaux arts gardens found anywhere in the United States. Among the unusual flora are a split-leaf maple and weeping cherry trees. Wisteria blooms in May. A hedge is trimmed to mirror the profile of Hook Mountain in the distance. A table and stools in the form of mushrooms are set back in an overhang. Made of rough-cut stone, the Grotto features a Guastavino tile ceiling and Moravian tile floor. In a characteristic installation, Junior's son, Nelson Rockefeller, added the yellow and green *Futuristic Flowers* by Italian artist Giacomo Balla.

In fact, it was Nelson Rockefeller who first added a sense of fun to the estate, introducing modern art, a card table, and bowling alley. His collection of modern art is a highlight of any Kykuit tour. A dozen tapestries by Pablo Picasso are hung in lower level galleries, and sculpture works by Alexander Calder and other 20th-century artists complement the formal Italian-inspired gardens and challenge golfers on the putting green. *The Bathers,* a series of six figures Picasso originally made of driftwood, were cast into bronze and set against a background of white pine near the brook garden and adjacent to the former tennis court. Having a bit of fun with the placement of the installation, Nelson Rockefeller decided to elevate the diver onto a platform.

Seven different walking tours—led by knowledgeable guides who cover art, plants, and architecture, as well as the family history—allow visitors to tailor their experience

to the areas of the estate that interest them most. The two-hour house and inner gardens tour is oriented toward first-timers. A three-hour Grand Tour includes more of the sculpture and gardens, as well as a tour of the second floor of the home. The first group of the day gets the best view of the river from inside the house; later in the day, other groups a few minutes ahead tend to block the views. Book online at www.historichudsonvalley.org (Pocantico Hills, Tarrytown, 914/631-1470, www.hudson valley.org; 9 A.M.–3:15 P.M. Mon. and Wed.–Fri., 9 A.M.–4 P.M. Sat.–Sun. May 12–Nov. 4; adults $20–38).

The only access to Kykuit (200 Lake Rd./ Rte. 448) is via shuttle bus from the visitors center at Philipsburg Manor. The adjoining **Rockefeller State Park Preserve** (Rte. 117, 1 mile east of Rte. 9, Tarrytown, 914/333-0102, www.friendsrock.org; 8 A.M.–sunset daily Apr.–Oct., weekends only Nov.–Mar.; $6 parking fee) is open year-round for hiking, fishing, horseback riding, and cross-country skiing.

Route 442 out of Sleepy Hollow leads to

visitor center at Stone Barns

Bedford and the **Union Church of Pocantico Hills** (Rte. 448/Bedford Rd., Sleepy Hollow, 914/631-2069, www.hudsonvalley .org; 11 A.M.–5 P.M. Wed.–Fri. and Mon., 10 A.M.–5 P.M. Sat., 2–5 P.M. Sun. Apr.–Dec.; admission $5). Take the Eastview exit from the Saw Mill River Parkway. This church features stained-glass windows designed by Henri Matisse and Marc Chagall, as Rockefeller family memorials. Matisse completed the design for a rose window, in honor of Abby Aldrich Rockefeller who founded the Museum of Modern Art in New York City, just days before he died in 1954. The series of one large and eight small windows, completed in 1965, are the only church windows Chagall ever created.

Stone Barns Center for Food and Agriculture

Just up the road from the Union Church, a nonprofit farm and educational center set on 80 acres has redefined what it means to eat local. Visitors to Stone Barns (630 Bedford Hills Rd., 914/366-6200, www.stonebarns center.org; 10 A.M.–5 P.M. Wed.–Sun.) can tour the vegetable gardens, pick their own eggs, and watch sheep graze the rolling hills. A 90-minute Insider's Tour is offered at 11 A.M. Friday and Saturday (adults $15, children 12 and older $9). Stone Barns also runs a farm market with fresh vegetables in season, plants, flowers, meats, eggs, and honey (from 1 P.M. Wed., Fri., and Sun.). Save time for lunch at the casual Blue Hill Café (914/366-9600; 10:30 A.M.–5 P.M. Wed.–Sun.; mains $5–8 and salads $12.25/lb.) or plan ahead for a gourmet dinner inside the farm's outstanding restaurant, Blue Hill at Stone Barns. A gift shop on the premises sells farm-themed goodies such as beeswax candles, gardening gifts, and books about growing green.

Ossining and Croton

Continuing north along Route 9, Ossining is best known as the location of **Sing Sing Prison,** which you can see from a small riverfront park near the train station. Ossining's Main Street is busy and attractive in a no-non-

sense sort of way, though a Bikram yoga studio suggests the town may be shedding its working-class image. The Old Croton Aqueduct runs straight though the middle of town. And just beyond, **Teatown Lake Reservation** (1600 Spring Valley Rd., Ossining, 914/762-2912, www.teatown.org; trails open year-round dawn to dusk, free admission and parking) is a nature preserve with 14 miles of secluded trails and environmental exhibits. The nature center is open 9 A.M.–5 P.M. Tuesday–Saturday and 1–5 P.M. Sunday.

The next river town, **Croton-on-Hudson,** is a major point of transfer for rail commuters coming to and from the northern counties. Croton also boasts the third-largest reservoir in the New York City Watershed. By the turn of the 20th century, New York City needed more water than the original aqueduct could provide, and work began anew. Irish, German, and Italian immigrants labored hard to build the dam that created the **New Croton Reservoir.** It measures nine miles long—touching the towns of Cortlandt, Yorktown, Somers, Bedford, and New Castle—and holds 19 billion gallons at full capacity. The dam is located on Route 19, off Route 9A north of the village of Croton.

At the junction of the Croton and Hudson Rivers and within walking distance of the Croton-on-Hudson train station, the fieldstone **Van Cortlandt Manor** (S. Riverside Ave., Croton-on-Hudson, 914/631-8200, www.hudsonvalley.org; 10 A.M.–5 P.M. Wed.–Mon. Apr.–Oct., 10 A.M.–4 P.M. weekends only Nov.–Dec.; adults $9, seniors $8, children $5, under 5 free) hides behind a row of hardwood trees. As the Dutch-style home of a prominent colonial family, the museum contains many original Georgian and Federal period furnishings. On the grounds outside, caretakers plant seasonal heirloom vegetable and herb gardens.

Peekskill

At the northern edge of Westchester County and just below the Hudson Highlands lies the city of Peekskill, yet another strategic location during the American Revolution that

OLD CROTON TRAILWAY STATE HISTORIC PARK

Yonkers is the southern terminus for the most unique outdoor space in all of Westchester County: the Old Croton Trailway State Historic Park. In the early 19th century, a thirsty New York City, plagued by fire and illness, turned to abundant upstate resources for a clean and ready supply of water. The Croton River delivered, and the city has feuded with rural upstate towns over rights to water ever since.

Engineers diverted the river through a 26.2-mile aqueduct to the Bronx. They built a stone tunnel 8.5 feet tall by 7.5 feet wide that sloped just enough to use the force of gravity. They then laid the length of it with brick, adding a stone shaft at every mile for ventilation. Completed in 1842 at a cost of $12 million, the Old Croton Aqueduct served the growing city well until the turn of the next century. When New York needed more, a replacement in 1905 tripled its capacity.

The oldest aqueduct in the New York City watershed is now a National Historic Landmark and a long corridor of a state park. It's also just the perfect length, surface, and terrain to prepare for a marathon. In fact, joggers hit the trail at dawn most days of the year. Historic mansions, riverside villages, and Hudson River views distract them from the work at hand, while the stone markers at every mile ensure they stay on pace.

You don't have to be an endurance athlete to appreciate the trail: Cyclists, walkers, cross-country skiers, and horseback riders of all levels enjoy the path and its ever-changing scenery. Access is convenient to most of the train stations along the Metro-North Hudson Line, including Hastings-on-Hudson, Dobbs Ferry, Irvington, and Greystone in Yonkers. Parking is available at the train stations and also at the Ossining Heritage Area Visitor Center. The community organization **Friends of the Old Croton Aqueduct** (www.aqueduct. org) publishes a detailed color map of the trail for $5.75.

---

later became a large manufacturing center and busy river port. After some tough years of decline, Peekskill is quietly attracting artists and small businesses again. Its **Flat Iron Gallery** (105 S. Division St., 914/734-1894, www.flatiron.qpg.com; 3–5 P.M. Tues.–Thurs., 3–7 P.M. Fri., 10 A.M.–5 P.M. Sat., noon–4 P.M. Sun.) specializes in contemporary fine art and handcrafted jewelry. This is a good place to look for Hudson River landscapes. In June, you can tour local artist studios in the downtown area. Guided and self-guided tours are available. Contact **Peekskill Open Studios** at 914/734-2367.

Peekskill's **Riverfront Green** is a good place to launch a kayak for a paddle around Peekskill Bay. **Blue Mountain Reservation** (Welcher Ave., 914/862-5275, www.westchestergov .com/parks; 8 A.M.–dusk daily year-round; parking $8) has a 3.5-mile mountain bike trail, as well as hiking and picnic grounds. Exit Route 9 at Welcher Avenue and head east to the park entrance.

CENTRAL WESTCHESTER COUNTY

Several old highways traverse the length of central Westchester County, following smaller rivers that empty into the Hudson: the Saw Mill River Parkway connects Manhattan's Upper West Side to the Taconic Parkway in Mount Pleasant; the Bronx River Parkway connects Mount Vernon to the Taconic at I-287; and the Hutchinson River Parkway runs from Pelham Manor to I-684. In the center of all the traffic is White Plains, a land of corporate headquarters, chain hotels, shopping gallerias, and business conference centers.

Named for the fog that hung over its wetlands when the first settlers arrived, White Plains has secured its place in history: It was the site of a major Revolutionary War battle, and George Washington set up a command from the 1720 **Jacob Purdy House** (60 Park Ave., White Plains, 914/328-1776, westchester tourism.com; by appointment only). Unless you seek upscale stores outside of New York

City, however, you'll find few sights that require a special trip.

Purchase

East of White Plains, near the Westchester County Airport, is an outstanding modern art museum, the **Neuberger Museum of Art** (735 Anderson Hill Rd., Purchase, 914/251-6100, www.neuberger.org; noon–5 P.M. Tues.–Sun.; adults $5, seniors $3, under 5 free, free admission on the first Sat. of the month). The museum is currently the 10th-largest university museum in the United States and the 8th-largest in New York State. In 1969, Purchase College, part of the State University of New York, received a generous donation of 20th-century American art. Roy R. Neuberger enabled the college to begin a collection that now features contemporary and African art, as well as its initial base of modern masterpieces. The permanent collection at the Neuberger Museum of Art includes works by Edward Hopper, Georgia O'Keefe, Jackson Pollack, and Mark Rothko. Occasional solo exhibitions feature artists who have had a significant impact on the contemporary art world but have not yet been recognized for their contributions.

In 2007, the museum began a redesign of its front entrance and visitor lobby and planned to introduce a new interactive tour with handheld audio-video devices. A café on-site is open weekdays noon–3 P.M. Take Exit 28 from the Hutchinson River Parkway.

While you're in the area, don't miss the chance to tour the **Donald M. Kendall Sculpture Gardens at PepsiCo Headquarters** (Anderson Hill Rd., Purchase, 914/253-2001). The company has placed 45 sculptures by 20th-century artists including Rodin on 168 landscaped acres. You can walk or drive the grounds free of charge, and maps are available at an information booth Memorial Day through Labor Day.

Pleasantville

In a quiet town off the Saw Mill River Parkway, Frank Lloyd Wright introduced the carport and radiant heat as key elements of his Usonian vision for the American residential neighborhood. Isolated examples of the functional suburban style are scattered across New York; however, the only full-scale cooperative that Wright developed is found in Pleasantville, north of where the Taconic State and Saw Mill River Parkways meet.

Pleasantville's **Usonia** was designed with 47 homes on about 100 acres of thickly wooded property. Wright used light, glass, and open designs to blur the lines between inside and out. Two of the homes are relatively easy to find today, but visitors must look from a distance, because both are private residences. Look for the Reisley House, at 44 Usonia Road. Exit I-684 at Route 120, then turn left onto Bear Ridge Road, and left again onto Usonia Road. The circular Friedman House is located around the corner, at 11 Orchard Brook Drive.

Chappaqua

For much of his 30-year tenure as founding editor of the *New York Tribune,* journalist Horace Greeley (1811–1872) owned a country home in Chappaqua. Today, the town is better known for high-profile residents Bill and Hillary Clinton.

A contemporary of Abraham Lincoln, Greeley was an influential writer and political figure who campaigned against slavery, hired Karl Marx as a European columnist, and ran for president against Ulysses S. Grant. To learn more about Greeley's life and works, visit the **New Castle Historical Society** (100 King St., 914/238-4666, www.newcastle-ny.org; 1–4 P.M. Tues.–Thurs., noon–4 P.M. Sat., and other times by appointment; donations encouraged), or pick up a copy of his autobiography, *Recollections of a Busy Life,* available in paperback from University Press of the Pacific.

🄲 Katonah Museum Mile

New York City's need for water left an indelible mark on the hamlet of Katonah. When city officials flooded the Cross River in the 1890s to add new capacity to the Croton Watershed System, they threatened to swallow the homes that had stood on its bank since the first Europeans arrived. A group of resolute townspeople pooled their resources and moved dozens of buildings to the opposite shore. They planned a simple grid, and the new town thrived as a place of commerce and leisure. As a result, present-day Katonah blends a Victorian look and feel with a modern sensibility.

This community of 5,000 people supports a remarkable group of cultural institutions, three of which make up the town's Museum Mile, along Route 22. The **Caramoor Center for Music and the Arts** (149 Girdle Ridge Rd., Katonah, 914/232-1252, www.caramoor.org, box office hours 10 A.M.–6 P.M. daily) began as the summer home of Walter and Lucie Rosen, both passionate musicians and patrons of the arts. The Rosens purchased the estate in 1928, and they had exquisite taste in furniture, tapestries, china, and jewels—many of which are on display in the 20 rooms that are open to the public today. They invited musicians to perform in the Old World setting of a Spanish courtyard, and over the years, their private concerts evolved into an annual summer festival. A tour of the house and gardens is intriguing, but to really experience the place, you must attend a performance.

North of Caramoor on Route 22, the **Katonah Museum of Art** (Rte. 22 at Jay St., Katonah, 914/232-9555, www.katonah-museum.org; 10 A.M.–5 P.M. Tues.–Sat., noon–5 P.M. Sun.; adults $3) is known for developing small, high-quality shows that often pair a well-known artist with an emerging local one. In this way, the museum draws a large following while giving exposure to newer works. Exhibits change frequently and have recently included prints by Richard Diebenkorn.

Katonah's third museum is a good place to dive into the early history of the nascent U.S. government. At the conclusion of a distinguished career, diplomat and negotiator John Jay retired to his family's farm in Katonah. A descendant of the Van Cortlandt family, Jay had worked with the Founding Fathers to ensure the future of the new republic. After a succession of international posts, George Washington appointed him first chief justice of the U.S. Supreme Court. His former resi-

dence is now the **John Jay Homestead** (Rte. 22, Katonah, 914/232-5651; 10 A.M.–4 P.M. Tues.–Sat., 11 A.M.–4 P.M. Sun.; adults $7, students and seniors $5, under 12 free), located on Route 22 between Katonah and Bedford Village. Katonah is at the junction of the Saw Mill River Parkway and I-684, or Exit 6 off I-684.

Cross River

Westchester County's largest park has been a wildlife sanctuary since 1924. Located east of Katonah at the junction of Routes 35 and 121, **Ward Pound Ridge Reservation** (Rtes. 35 & 121, Cross River, 914/864-7317, www.westchester.gov; dawn–dusk daily; admission $8) encompasses 4,700 acres of wildflowers, hiking trails, campsites, and picnic grounds, plus an interpretive **Trailside Museum and Wildlife Center** with Native American exhibits. Its Gallery in the Park offers four rotating exhibitions per year (9 A.M.–4 P.M. Mon.–Sat.).

Somers

IBM and Pepsico draw business travelers to the suburban town of Somers, but a couple of unusual sites are worth a peek if you happen to pass through. Apply the concept of heirloom vegetables to fauna, and you've got **Muscoot Farm Park** (Rte. 100, 914/864-7282; 10 A.M.–4 P.M. daily). Its rare farm-animal breeds and vintage-equipment exhibits on 777 acres portray the life of the American farmer in the early 20th century. In something of a cross between a petting zoo and a museum, the farm raises pigs, horses, sheep, and ducks. It is also a good place to look for wild butterflies. From Exit 6 on I-684, follow Route 35 west to Route 100. The entrance is a mile down the road, on the right.

Also in Somers is the eclectic **Museum of the Early American Circus** (Rtes. 100 and 202, 914/277-4977; 2–4 P.M. Thurs.; admission by donation), one of a couple dozen museums in the country dedicated to the history of this all-American pastime. Several of the town's residents—including one Hachaliah Bailey, of Barnum and Bailey fame—were instrumental

GARDENS OF WESTCHESTER COUNTY

© NIKKI GOTH ITOI

Johnny Jump-ups

Westchester County boasts some of the largest and most elaborate outdoor gardens in the Hudson River Valley. Here is a sampling of the very best:

- Caramoor Center for Music and the Arts, Katonah

- Hammond Museum & Japanese Stroll Garden, North Salem

- John Jay Homestead State Historic Site, Katonah

- Donald M. Kendall Sculpture Gardens at PepsiCo Headquarters, Purchase

- Kykuit, The Rockefeller Estate, Sleepy Hollow

- Luquer-Marble Memorial Wildflower Garden, Ward Pound Ridge Reservation, Cross River

- Lyndhurst Rose Garden and Fern Garden, Tarrytown

- Van Cortlandt Manor, Croton-on-Hudson

- Wildflower Island at Teatown Lake Reservation, Ossining

in developing the circus as we know it today. They imported some of the first exotic animals and built the first circus tent. The Somers Historical Society has documented their activities in a three-room museum on the 3rd floor of the old Elephant Hotel.

North Salem

Michael Bloomberg and David Letterman are among the well-to-do who vacation in rural North Salem, across the interstate from Somers and close to the Connecticut border. The **Hammond Museum and Japanese Stroll Garden** (28 Deveau Rd., 914/669-5033, www .hammondmuseum.org; noon–4 P.M. Wed.–Sat.; adults $5, seniors $4, under 12 free) blends Eastern and Western aesthetics to create an enchanting outdoor experience. Water lilies, a reflecting pool, and the red maple terrace take visitors back to 6th-century Japan. And a delightful combination of rock, sand, waterfalls, and evergreens stimulates the senses. Inside the Hammond Museum is a collection of Mandarin fans, as well as several hundred portraits taken by music and theater critic Carl Van Vechten. A miniature replica of Mount Fuji is also in the works. The museum has a café open noon–3 P.M. Thursday–Saturday.

THE LONG ISLAND SOUND

You can't exactly hear the surf crashing from Larchmont or Mamaroneck—and the water is generally too polluted for swimming—but Westchester is the only county in the Hudson Valley that boasts oceanfront property on Long Island Sound. Much of this area is congested with suburban sprawl, but if you're headed out to the Connecticut coast, a couple of sights may be worth a stop.

New Rochelle

Revolutionary writer and human-rights champion Thomas Paine (1737-1809) lived his later years and passed away in New Rochelle, and the town has preserved his former home and some of its original furnishings. A contemporary of Benjamin Franklin, who helped him get to America from England, Paine mastered the art of controversy in his writing. His "Common Sense" pamphlet challenged colonists to fight for independence. Upon returning to Europe midcareer, he wrote two well-known political treatises, *The Age of Reason* and *The Rights of Man*. The **Thomas Paine Cottage** (983 North Ave., www.thomaspaine.org) is open year-round to visitors.

Rye

Roughly a million visitors a year come to Rye's **Playland Amusement Park** (Playland Parkway, 914/813-7010, www.ryeplayland.org; noon–11 P.M. Tues.–Fri., noon–midnight Sat., noon–11 P.M. Sun. June–Aug., open weekends and some midweek days May and Sept. and occasionally in Oct.; $20 for 24 tickets), along a boardwalk on the Long Island Sound. The park has been entertaining thrill-seekers since 1928, and its art deco buildings are now recognized as a National Historic Landmark.

SPORTS AND RECREATION
Winter Sports

Despite its population density, Westchester maintains 17,000 acres of public parks for recreation throughout the year. Many of them are ideal for cross-country skiing after heavy winter storms. Take a loop around the lake on three miles of trails at **Cranberry Lake Preserve** (Old Orchard St., White Plains, 914/428-1005; 9 A.M.–4 P.M. Mon.–Fri. July–Aug., 9 A.M.–4 P.M. Tues.–Sat. Sept.–June). Some sections of the gently graded **Old Croton Aqueduct** are also skiable. Try Croton Dam Plaza in Croton or North Tarrytown, near Rockefeller State Park.

Hiking

Westchester wilderness lends itself more to a walk in the woods than a backcountry experience. But several large green spaces make it possible to get well away from the bustle of everyday suburban life. Many of Westchester's parks are open to residents only and require the purchase of a county parks pass (www .westchestergov.com/parks/parkpass.htm; $45 for one year). Both **Tibbetts Brook Park** (Midland Ave., Yonkers, 914/231-2865; 8 A.M.–

dusk daily) and **Sprain Ridge Park** (Jackson Ave., Yonkers, 914/231-3450; 8 A.M.–dusk daily; adults $5.75 with a required Westchester County Park Pass) have trails for hiking and biking. More than 230 species of migrating birds have been sighted at the **Marshlands Conservancy** (Rte. 1, Rye, 914/835-4466; nature center 9 A.M.–5 P.M.; Westchester County Parks Pass not required; free admission) on Long Island Sound.

Cycling

In addition to the parks above, Westchester County maintains a network of trailways for cyclists—paths that are mostly paved and closed to motorists. The **South County Trailway** is a 14.1-mile path that runs north to south in the southern part of the county. Pick up the northern end by the Eastview park-and-ride at Route 100C. The **North County Trailway** starts at the same park-and-ride and runs north for 21 miles. There is a relatively steep climb up from the Croton Reservoir. The **Bronx River Parkway** also closes to traffic for Bicycle Sundays, May–September. Blue Mountain Reservation (Welcher Ave., Peekskill, 914/862-5275; 8 A.M.–dusk daily year-round; parking $8) has a 3.5-mile trail designated for mountain biking. **TrailMasters Touring** (914/325-5916, www.trailmasterstouring.com) offers tours and clinics for riders of all levels.

Golf

New York City executives support some 50 public and private golf courses across the county. The newest course is the **Hudson Hills Golf Course** (400 Croton Dam Rd., Ossining, 914/864-3000; www.hudsonhillsgolf.com; weekends $115, weekdays $85, reduced rates with parks pass). Architect Mark Mungeam, who led the overhaul of Chicago's Olympia Fields Country Club for the 2003 U.S. Open, designed the course. You'll have to fight the city crowd for tee times.

The **Centennial Golf Club** (185 John Simpson Rd., Carmel, 845/225-5700, www.centennial golf.com; Sat., Sun. and holidays $135; Mon.–Thurs. $95, Fri. $125) offers a golf-cart GPS

system as a convenience to players. The Larry Nelson 7,100-yard course strictly enforces a pace-of-play policy, so if you waggle like Sergio and fall behind, you may be gently reminded to keep the game moving. Greens are fast but roll true. First-rate service compensates for the steep fees.

Dunwoodie Golf Course (Wasylenko Lane, Yonkers, 914/231-3490, www.westchestergov .com/parks/golf/dunwoodie.htm; weekends $54, weekdays $44, reduced rates with parks pass) is county-owned, and some patrons say it shows in the greens. The short 5,815-yard, par 70 course offers plenty of challenges, with elevation changes and a deep rough.

All 18 tees were recently renovated and expanded at **Maple Moor Golf Course** (1128 North St., White Plains, 914/995-9200; weekends and holidays $38, Mon.–Fri. $34, prices do not include cart, reduced rates with parks pass), also county-run. Some greens are slow on this 6,226-yard, par 71 course, but there's enough action to keep it interesting. Don't let the highway noise on the front nine distract you.

© NIKKI GOTH ITOI

river tour aboard the *M/V Commander*

Swimming and Boating

Kayak Hudson (Five Islands Park, New Rochelle, 888/321-4837, www.kayakhudson.com; 6 A.M.–6:30 P.M. Mon.–Wed., 6 A.M.–10 P.M. Thurs., 6 A.M.–11 P.M. Fri.) takes paddlers on guided trips on the Hudson River and Long Island Sound.

Hudson Highlands Cruises (Cornwall-on-Hudson, 845/534-7245, www.hudsonhighlands cruises.com; May–Oct.; adults $16–30) offers scenic and informative river tours aboard the 1917 *M/V Commander,* departing from Peekskill one Saturday and one Sunday each month. The three-hour cruise heads north under the Bear Mountain Bridge toward West Point. For alternate days and routes, check the schedule for departures from Haverstraw Marina in Rockland County (full-day tours) and West Point in Orange County (90 minutes, weekdays only).

Fishing and Hunting

Freshwater fishing in Westchester revolves around the reservoir system. With a New York Watershed permit, you can catch large bass and the occasional trout. Rent a canoe to open up the possibilities. **Mohansic Lake** (201 Hawley Rd., North Salem, 914/864-7310, www .westchestergov.com/parks) is a zoo on summer weekends, but it is known to have aggressive bass and large crappie. **Kensico Reservoir,** three miles north of White Plains, has rainbows, browns, and lakers up to about 15 or 20 pounds.

Yoga and Spa Treatments

The Mondeverde Spa (28 Bear Mountain Bridge Rd., Cortlandt Manor, 914/372-1212, www .monteverderestaurant.com; noon–7 P.M. Mon.– Tues., 10 A.M.–7 P.M. Wed.–Fri., 10 A.M.–5 P.M. Sat., Sun. by appointment) offers a full menu of treatments, from massage and facials to body wraps and custom programs. A one-hour massage costs $120–160. For the complete experience, reserve one of the two guest suites for an overnight stay (but be prepared for some sticker shock.) The spa also holds yoga classes in an outdoor studio overlooking the Hudson, and an indoor Yoga Barn.

ACCOMMODATIONS

Westchester has mastered the science of the business conference hotel. Although there are a few exceptions, for more choice in charming accommodations, you're better off heading north to Putnam County, or south to New York City.

$150-200

Close to Van Cortlandt Manor and two blocks from the village of Croton-on-Hudson, the **Alexander Hamilton House** (49 Van Wyck St., Croton-on-Hudson, 914/271-6737, www .alexanderhamiltonhouse.com; $135–225) is a Victorian affair, complete with a white picket fence. Eight rooms and suites have private baths, air-conditioning, and high-speed Internet; some have fireplaces and soaking tubs too. There is a two-night minimum on weekends.

Crabtree's Kittle House (11 Kittle Rd., Chappaqua, 914/666-8044, www.kittlehouse .com; $157) is first and foremost an outstanding restaurant, but its 12 moderately priced rooms are an added convenience if you plan to sample more than a taste from its enormous wine cellar. Rooms are decorated simply in pastels and floral linens, and with white trim and dark wood furniture.

Over $200

With 300 rooms set on 30 acres, the **Renaissance Westchester Hotel** (80 West Red Oak Ln., White Plains, 914/694-5400, www.marriott.com; $300–329) is a comfortable Marriott property that primarily hosts business travelers.

One of the priciest places to stay in the Hudson Valley region is the **Castle on the Hudson** (400 Benedict Ave., Tarrytown, 914/631-1980, www.castleonthehudson.com; $350–730). Built by the son of a Civil War general on a hilltop outside of Tarrytown, this ultra-luxurious inn features a 75-foot tower that is the highest point in Westchester County. Its rooms feature high ceilings and plenty of natural light. Elegant drapery and furnishings create a decidedly Old World atmosphere. Dinner at Equus Restaurant on-site will be an experience to remember, if only for the views and the bill.

Tarrytown House (49 E. Sunnyside La., Tarrytown, 800/553-8118; $259–359) is a full-service conference center set on 26 acres in two 19th-century mansions. More than 200 rooms and suites are designed to accommodate business travelers but also make for a pleasant weekend getaway. The 10 Georgian-era rooms in the King Mansion have the most character.

Built in 1760 by the Van Cortlandt family, **Monteverde at Oldstone Manor** (28 Bear Mountain Bridge Rd., Cortlandt Manor, 914/372-1212, www.monteverderestaurant .com; $626–966) has been lovingly restored as a restaurant and spa with two luxurious overnight guest suites upstairs. Deep reds and creams, hardwood floors, and antique French posters define the ambience in the rooms. Marble baths have steam showers and soaking tubs built for two. One room has a private room for spa treatments; the other has a wood-burning fireplace. Other amenities include wireless Internet, flat-screen TVs, comfy robes, queen-size beds, top quality linens, and goose down bed covers. Guests receive a welcome basket with fresh fruit and a complimentary bottle of wine, Champagne, or non-alcoholic sparkling cider. Combination packages are available including spa treatments, yoga classes, and dinner. Outside, the property includes 29 acres of lawn, gardens, and woods that border Hudson Highlands State Park and overlook the river. Monteverde is a popular venue for weddings and other group events.

FOOD

Restaurants are plentiful and diverse in Westchester, serving cuisines from Indian to Southwest. French and Italian themes are most common, and the county offers a number of casual cafés and local farm stands. That said, there are a lot of expense-account traps to avoid—unless, of course, you're on an expense account.

Along the River—Route 9

In an unlikely location near a Citgo gas station and a Toyota dealership, **Nyauta** (27 Meyer Ave., Yonkers, 914/476-1910) has affordably

priced Indian cuisine. Spices ground on the premises and homemade cheese and yogurt add a special touch. Also in Yonkers, Hunan Village is a top choice for gourmet Chinese.

Up the hill from the Hastings train station, tiny **(Buffet de la Gare** (155 Southside Ave., Hastings-on-Hudson, 914/478-1671; 6–9:30 P.M. Tues.–Sat. and noon–2 P.M. Thurs.–Fri.; dinner menu mains $26–34) serves a mouthwatering cassoulet, along with other French specialties such as venison, duck confit, and coq au vin. Down the hill from Buffet de la Gare, locals order burgers, beer, and standard pub fare at **Maud's Tavern** (149 Southside Ave., Hastings-on-Hudson, 914/478-2326, www .maudstavern.com; lunch noon–5 P.M. Wed.–Mon., dinner 5–10 P.M. Sun.–Thurs., 5–11 P.M. Fri.–Sat.; mains $11–20).

For outdoor dining on a warm summer eve, try **Harvest on Hudson** (1 River St., Hastings-on-Hudson, 914/478-2800, www.harvest2000 .com; dinner daily and lunch Mon.–Fri.). Set in an inviting Tuscan farmhouse, the restaurant prepares Mediterranean foods, including heirloom tomatoes from a garden on-site. The **Chart House** in Dobbs Ferry (1 High St., Dobbs Ferry, 914/693-4130, www.chart-house. com) has better river views and the usual surf and turf fare found at Chart House restaurants across the country.

Tarrytown's Main Street has a full menu of choices for casual and fine dining. The "Labs" in **(Coffee Labs** (7 Main St., Tarrytown, 914/332-1479; 6 A.M.–6:30 P.M. Mon.–Tues., 6 A.M.–8 P.M. Wed.–Thurs., 6 A.M.–10:30 P.M. Fri., 8 A.M.–10:30 P.M. Sat., 8 A.M.–7 P.M. Sun.; drinks $2–5) refer to Labrador retrievers, which the owners evidently adore. This is your stop for Fair Trade coffees and a great selection of teas. Try the Rooibos winter blend on a snowy afternoon.

Lefteris (1 North Broadway, Tarrytown, 914/524-9687, www.lefterisgyro.com; 11 A.M.–10 P.M. daily; mains $5–16) packs in the crowds at the corner of Main and Broadway. Neighboring shop owners use this busy Greek restaurant as a barometer for the business level on any given day. Sit outside and enjoy the traditional Greek salads and excellent people watching.

Continuing toward the river, **Main Street Café** (24 Main St., Tarrytown, 914/524-9770; lunch and dinner daily) attracts a mix of locals and out-of-towners with a diverse menu and outdoor seating along Main Street. You can walk to the Tarrytown Music Hall from family-run **Lago di Como** (27 Main St., Tarrytown, 914/631-7227, www.lagodicomo restaurant.com; noon–2:30 P.M. and 5–10 P.M. Tues.–Sat., 4–9 P.M. Sun.; mains $16–27) after a meal of northern Italian specialties.

At the docks in the Tarrytown marina, **Striped Bass** (236 W. Main St., Tarrytown, 914/366-4455, www.stripedbassny .com; noon–10 P.M. Mon.–Thurs., till 11 P.M. weekends; mains $11–26) offers a Caribbean menu and live jazz on weekends. Inside the Washington Irving Boat Club, **Sunset Cove** (238 Green St., Tarrytown, 914/366-7889, www.sunsetcove.net; lunch mains $9–12, dinner mains $18–30, Sun. brunch $22), is a popular stop for lunch after a Sunnyside tour. The restaurant takes reservations for tables inside and serves outdoor tables on a first-come, first-served basis. Order from the seafood raw bar, or choose a sandwich or pasta entrée for lunch.

Also centrally located is **Horsefeathers** (94 N. Broadway, Tarrytown, 914/631-6606, www .horsefeatherstarrytown.com; 11:30 A.M.–10 P.M. Mon.–Wed., 11:30 A.M.–11 P.M. Thurs.–Sat., 11:30 A.M.–9 P.M. Sun.), known for its literary decor and a tome of a menu, which is arranged by chapters and includes 100 types of beer. Burgers and pub fare prevail. Across from the Tarrytown Hilton Inn, **El Dorado West** (460 S. Broadway, Tarrytown, 914/332-5838) is a classic diner that's open late.

On a hilltop outside of town, **Equus Restaurant** (400 Benedict Ave., Tarrytown, 914/631-3646, www.castleonthehudson.com) may be the place to celebrate a special occasion. Part of The Castle at Tarrytown, the restaurant offers an outstanding, if pricey, wine list and a seasonal prix fixe menu consisting of four courses. Sunday brunch and high tea are good alternatives to a full lunch or dinner.

One of Westchester's newest experiments in fine-dining, **◖ Blue Hill at Stone Barns** (630 Bedford Rd., Pocantico Hills, 914/366-9600, www .bluehillstonebarns.com; 5–10 P.M. Wed.–Sun., till 11 P.M. Fri.–Sat., brunch 11 A.M.–2:30 P.M. Sun.; two courses $46, three courses $56, four courses $66), has taken the concept of seasonal cuisine up a notch, to wide acclaim. True to the Rockefeller vision of a self-sustained farm, the restaurant raises its own livestock, as well as herbs and produce, on the premises. Chef Dan Barber hails from the original Blue Hill in New York City and a genuine family farm in the Berkshires. Dinner and brunch are served in a converted dairy barn with window views designed to offer harried city people a chance to take in the quiet countryside. At Blue Hill, you'll choose your meal by its source: the greenhouse, the ocean, the pasture, etc. Even the toughest of critics say the food is simply awesome. Call ahead for a table, or wait it out for a seat at the bar.

For a more casual meal at Stone Barns, grab a wooden tray and settle at an outdoor table at the **◖ Blue Hill Café.** Espresso, iced tea, and Ronnybrook yogurt drinks will quench your thirst, while creative salads made of the freshest ingredients and homemade baked goods take the edge off your appetite. This may be the only café in the entire Hudson Valley to offer sea salt at its condiment counter. You can also bring a taste of Stone Barns home by purchasing the café's own spices, oils, and vinegars.

At **Zeph's** (638 Central Ave., Peekskill, 914/736-2159), Victoria Zeph prepares a creative menu that reflects an ever-changing variety of international influences, from French and Chinese to Moroccan, Caribbean, and Thai. The setting is a converted gristmill outside downtown Peekskill.

Sushi Mike's (142 Main St., Dobbs Ferry, 914/591-7553, www.sushimikes.com; 11:30 A.M.–3 P.M. and 4:30–10 P.M. Mon.–Fri., noon–11 P.M. Sat., 3–10 P.M. Sun.; mains $14–26) is a small Japanese restaurant on the corner of Main and Cedar in Dobbs Ferry. A block away **Sam's** (126-138 Main St. at Oak

St., Dobbs Ferry, 914/693-9724) is a friendly local Italian eatery.

Under the direction of Chef Neil Ferguson, who worked in the kitchens at Michelin three-star restaurants in Paris and London, the menu at **Mondeverde at Oldstone Manor** (28 Bear Mountain Bridge Rd., Cortlandt Manor, 914/739-5000, ext. 1, www.monteverderestaurant.com) emphasizes sustainably farmed, organic ingredients, some of which are grown in an herb garden on the premises. An appetizer of caramelized veal sweetbreads is served with a Bartlett pear puree and candied sage, while roasted Hudson Valley foie gras comes with a turnip puree, buttered radishes, and ham gastrique. Entrees of duck, lamb, and filet mignon round out the menu. On Friday and Saturday evenings, enjoy a seven-course tasting menu in the Chef's Garden ($75 per person, $105 per person with wine pairings).

Central Westchester County

Bengal Tiger (144 E. Post Rd., White Plains, 914/948-5191; lunch and dinner daily) and **Coromandel** (30 Division St., New Rochelle, 914/235-8390; noon–2:30 P.M. daily, 5–10 P.M. Thurs.–Sun., till 11 P.M. Fri.–Sat.) rank among Westchester's best for Indian-inspired fare.

Take a break from the shopping to dine at **P.F. Chang's China Bistro** (The Westchester Mall, 125 Westchester Ave., White Plains, 914/997-6100, www.pfchangs.com; mains $7–18), part of a national chain of upscale Chinese restaurants.

Finch Tavern (592 Rte. 22, Croton Falls, 914/277-4580; 11:30 A.M.–2:30 P.M. Tues.–Fri. and 5:30–10 P.M. Tues.–Thurs., till 11 P.M. Fri.–Sat., 11 A.M.–2 P.M. and 5–9 P.M. Sun.; mains $17–30) opened in 2002 in a historic home along Route 22 with a menu of fish, meat, and pasta dishes that are designed to highlight local flavors.

Locals praise **Iron Horse Grill** (20 Wheeler Ave., Pleasantville, 914/741-0717, www.ironhorsegrill.com; from 5 P.M. Tues.–Sat.; mains $25–29) for contemporary American dishes including breast of pheasant and tenderloin of venison. The 60-seat restaurant occupies a converted train station.

A stroll along Katonah's main thoroughfare reveals a handful of tempting places to eat. **Blue Dolphin Ristorante** (175 Katonah Ave., Katonah, 914/232-4791; lunch 11 A.M.–3 P.M. Mon.–Fri., 11 A.M.–3:30 P.M. Sat., dinner 5–9:30 P.M. Mon.–Thurs., 5–10 P.M. Fri.–Sat.; mains $13–20) prepares fresh daily seafood specials, making it a local favorite. Expect to wait for a table on weekends. Across from the train station, **Willy Nick's Café** (17 Katonah Ave., Katonah, 914/232-8030) has patrons raving about its blintzes and oversized waffles, consumed at steel-banded retro tables.

Crabtree's Kittle House (11 Kittle Rd., Chappaqua, 914/666-8044; lunch Mon.–Fri. noon–2:30 P.M., dinner daily from 5:30 P.M.; mains $24–29) has an unparalleled selection of wines, with more than 50,000 bottles in its cellar. Order a special bottle in advance to have it brought up to temperature or let sediment settle out. A creative American menu leads to some fabulous wine and food pairings. Try a half-bottle of Condrieu with the scallop appetizer.

Power business lunches take place at **Mulino's** (99 Court St., White Plains, 914/761-1818; 11:30 A.M.–11:30 P.M. Mon.–Thurs., till midnight Fri., 5 P.M.–midnight Sat.; $25–30), known more for its free starter plates than for standout northern Italian food. **Little Spot** (854 N. Broadway, White Plains, 914/761-1334; mains $5) is a roadside find, serving "freedom fries," split chili dogs, and milk shakes to rave reviews.

Fresh fish and reasonable prices bring in the crowds at **Eastchester Fish Gourmet** (837 White Plains Rd., Scarsdale, 914/725-3450, http://eastchesterfish.com; lunch 11:30 A.M.–2:30 P.M. Thurs. and Fri. only, dinner at 5 P.M. daily; mains $8–12). Expect a wait unless you show up early.

The Long Island Sound

La Panetière Restaurant (530 Milton Rd., Rye, www.lapanetiere.com; lunch Mon.–Fri., dinner daily; prix fixe $52–78) excels in the service department. The menu is Provençal, and the atmosphere defines elegant.

The Bayou Restaurant (580 Gramatan Ave., Mount Vernon, 914/668-2634, www.thebayourestaurantny.com; 11:30 A.M.–11 P.M. daily, till 1 A.M. Thurs.–Sat.; mains $13–20) prepares Cajun delights and live music performances.

ENTERTAINMENT AND EVENTS
Performing Arts

Built by music lovers for music lovers, the **Caramoor Center for Music and the Arts** (149 Girdle Ridge Rd., Katonah, 914/232-1252, www.caramoor.org) features classical and jazz performances in two theaters. The **Performing Arts Center** (735 Anderson Hill Rd., Purchase, 914/251-6200, www.artscenter.org; 10 A.M.–6 P.M. Mon.–Fri., 10:30 A.M.–5:30 P.M. Sat.–Sun.) holds 600 jazz, cabaret, and classical music events annually. You can catch Tony Bennett on a summer weekend or watch *The Wizard of Oz* with the kids.

Another popular evening venue is Elmsford's **Westchester Broadway Theatre** (1 Broadway Plaza, Elmsford, 914/592-2222, www.broadwaytheatre.com; $56–77), a dinner theater that produces musicals, comedy, and children's shows. Choose from matinee or evening performances. The standard dinner menu includes chicken marsala, prime rib, and roast pork loin.

Musicians from Dave Brubeck to Bruce Springsteen have performed on the stage of the 1885 **Tarrytown Music Hall** (13 Main St., Tarrytown, information 914/631-3390, www.tarrytownmusichall.org). A local nonprofit rescued the theater from near demolition in the 1970s, and although the building is showing its age outside, it continues to host concerts, plays, musicals, operas, dance performances, and recordings inside. In 2004, the theater began showing movies again, after a 27-year hiatus. For tickets, call 877/840-0457 10 A.M.–6 P.M. daily, or go to the box office up to two hours before a show.

Bars and Nightlife

Get your blues fix at **Isabel's Café** (61 Main St., Tarrytown). The owner has pulled bands off stage if he finds the music below par at this well-loved local establishment. The food is American with a Scandinavian slant. Call ahead for a table. **New Roc City** (33 LeCount Pl., Yonkers, 914/637-7575, www.newroccity.com; 11 A.M.–11 P.M. Sun.–Thurs., 11 A.M.–1 A.M. Fri., 10 A.M.–1 A.M. Sat., hours vary by event) has it all under one roof: ice rink, mini-golf, a multiplex theater with an IMAX screen, and even a grocery store.

Festivals

Caramoor International Summer Music Festival (149 Girdle Ridge Rd., Katonah, 914/232-1252, www.caramoor.org; July–Aug.) is a summer concert series with a wide range of productions from classical music to Latin jazz fusion. Many shows sell out, so check the website early for tickets.

Yonkers Hudson Riverfest (Yonkers Waterfront, Yonkers, www.yonkersriverfest.com) is a daylong environmental and multicultural festival held every September. Tens of thousands of visitors come each year. A new "ferry-go-round" provides ferry service to five communities for events, fireworks, and arts and crafts. Also on the river, the Clearwater Festival takes place in Croton each June (see the *Mid-Hudson* chapter for information).

Once a year, Historic Hudson Valley invites artists of all ages and abilities to work on the grounds of Sunnyside, Washington Irving's estate. **Artists on the Hudson** (914/631-8200 ext. 618, www.hudsonvalley.org; free admission) takes places in May. Also in May, Tarrytown's **Art in the Park** (914/531-8347; free admission) show includes local art and crafts with live music. In April, the Rivertowns Arts Council hosts an **Annual Artists' Studio Tour** that covers about 50 studios in Ardsley, Irvington, Hastings-on-Hudson, and Dobbs Ferry (914/476-2321, www.riverarts.org; free admission).

The Headless Horseman of Washington Irving's famous story, "The Legend of Sleepy Hollow," still rides at Philipsburg Manor the last weekend in October, inviting kids and the young at heart to celebrate Halloween. Legend Weekend Nights is $13 for adults and $9 for children. Contact Historic Hudson Valley (914/631-8200, www.hudsonvalley.org) for information.

SHOPPING

Westchester and shopping go all the way back to the Great Depression, when the first department store opened in White Plains. Today you can find it all, from antiques and flea markets to Neiman Marcus. If you're on a quest for unusual antiques, head to Bedford Hills, Cross River, Tarrytown, or Larchmont.

With more than 100 stores, the **Cross County Shopping Center** (6-K Mall Walk, Yonkers, 914/968-9570; 9:30 A.M.–9:30 P.M. Mon.–Sat., 9:30 A.M.–7:30 P.M. Sun.), in Yonkers, is one of the oldest and largest malls in the county, while **The Westchester** (125 Westchester Ave., 914/421-1333, www.the-westchester-ny.com), in White Plains, and **Vernon Hills Shopping Center** (700 White Plains Post Rd., 914/472-2000), in Eastchester, are among the most upscale.

The **Charles Department Store** (113 Katonah Ave., Katonah, 914/232-5200; 9 A.M.–6 P.M. Mon.–Fri., 9 A.M.–5 P.M. Sat.) is a throwback to the era of the family-owned department store. The store is managed by the grandsons of the founder and sells everything from shoes to coffeepots.

Antiques and Galleries

Good finds in Larchmont include **Dualities Antiques and Art** (2056 Boston Post Rd., Larchmont, 914/834-2773; 10 A.M.–5:30 P.M. Mon.–Sat.) and **Milestones Antiques and Collectibles** (2134 Larchmont Ave., Larchmont, 914/833-3133, www.milestones antiques.com; 11:30 A.M.–4:30 P.M. Tues.–Sat.). In Tarrytown, look for the **Tarrytown Antiques Center** (25 Main St., Tarrytown, 914/366-4613; noon–6 P.M. Tues.–Thurs. and Sun., noon–10 P.M. Fri.–Sat.) or **Belkind, Bigi Antiques,** just up the street (21 Main St., Tarrytown, 914/524-9626; 11:30 A.M.–5 P.M. Tues.–Sun.).

Yellow Monkey Antiques (Rte. 35, Cross River, 914/763-5848, www.yellowmonkey.com; 10 A.M.–5:30 P.M. Mon.–Sat., 10 A.M.–5 P.M. Sun.) has more than 7,000 square feet of showrooms that focus on British Pine antiques, shipped in large quantities from Europe. **The Eclectic Collector** (215 Katonah Ave., Katonah, 914/232-8700, www.theeclecticcollector. com; 10 A.M.–6 P.M. Mon.–Sat., noon–5 P.M. Sun., 10 A.M.–8 P.M. Thurs. in Dec.) sells contemporary, folk, ceramic, and glass works from more than 300 artists.

For a wide selection of fine jewelry, browse the shops in **Kohl's Shopping Center** (431 Boston Post Rd., Port Chester, 914/690-0107; 8 A.M.–10 P.M. Mon.–Fri., 8 A.M.–10 P.M. Sat., 9 A.M.–9 P.M. Sun.). Take Exit 21 from I-95 or Exit 11 from I-287.

More than a dozen antique shows take places year-round in Westchester County. Check www.westchestertourism.com for dates and locations. Hundreds of vendors set up outdoor booths at the **Yonkers Raceway Market** (9 A.M.–4 P.M. Sun. Mar.–Dec.) each Sunday. Goods for sale include new merchandise, as well as antiques and collectibles. From the New York Thruway, take Exit 2 northbound or Exit 4 southbound.

Riverrun Rare Book Room (12 Washington St., Hastings-on-Hudson, 914/478-1339; daily 11 A.M.–5 P.M.) is a haven for aficionados, with 200,000 titles in two stores and two warehouses. The collection includes signed books, vintage paperbacks, and modern first editions.

Inside a municipal building on Maple Avenue, **The Gallery at Hastings-on-Hudson** (7 Maple Ave., Hastings-on-Hudson, 914/478-4141; Wed.–Sun. noon–5 P.M.) produces rotating exhibits of art from Westchester County.

Peekskill's **Flat Iron Gallery** (105 S. Division St., Peekskill, 914/734-1894, www.flat iron.qpg.com; 3–5 P.M. Tues.–Thurs., 3–7 P.M. Fri., 10 A.M.–5 P.M. Sat., noon–4 P.M. Sun.) specializes in contemporary fine art and handcrafted jewelry. This is a good place to look for Hudson River landscapes. More Hudson River art is found at **The Art Barn** in Ossining (211 N. Highland Ave., Ossining, 914/762-4997, www.artbarnonline.com; 10 A.M.–6 P.M. Mon.–Sat., noon–5 P.M. Sun.).

Farm Stands

In Tarrytown, family-owned **Mint Premium Foods** (18 Main St., Tarrytown; 11 A.M.–10 P.M. Mon.–Sat.) carries gourmet cheeses, olive oils, and meats, as well as organic teas and honey. The **Tarrytown Farmers Market** (914/923-4837; 8:30 A.M.–2 P.M. Sat. only, June 2–Nov. 17) takes place at Patriot's Park off Route 9.

INFORMATION AND SERVICES

The **Westchester County Office of Tourism** (222 Mamaroneck Ave., White Plains, 800/833-9282, www.westchestertourism.com) also runs a tourism information center at Exit 9 off the Bronx River Parkway, near Leewood Drive. Local commerce chambers in these towns can also provide visitor information:

- Greater Ossining Chamber of Commerce (914/941-0009, www.ossiningchamber.org)

- Sleepy Hollow/Tarrytown Chamber of Commerce (914/631-1705, www.sleepy hollowchamber.com)

- Irvington-on-Hudson Chamber of Commerce (www.irvingtonnychamber.com)

- Dobbs Ferry Chamber of Commerce (914/478-9831)

- Hastings-on-Hudson Chamber of Commerce (914/478-0900)

- Yonkers Chamber of Commerce (914/963-0332, www.yonkerschamber.com)

GETTING THERE AND AROUND
By Bus

The **Bee-Line System** (914/813-7777) is a countywide bus service with more than 55 different routes and express service. Routes serve many of the county's recreational facilities and also provide connection to trains. The fare is $1.75 cash ($.85 for seniors or disabled travelers) on most routes, or $2 on the MetroCard ($1 seniors).

By Train

It's hard to avoid the **Metro-North** (800/638-7646) commuter line in Westchester. It was practically built to serve this county's suburbs, and today, there are 43 station stops on three lines providing continual service to Manhattan's Grand Central Station and points within the county. Tarrytown, Croton-on-Hudson, and all of Westchester's riverside towns are easily accessible via the Hudson Line.

By Car

You can rent a car at the **Westchester Airport** in White Plains (240 Airport Rd., Suite 202, White Plains, www.westchestergov.com/airport/airportinformation.htm). But be forewarned: Traffic is bad and getting worse in Westchester—both from cars passing through and those that belong to local residents. The Tappan Zee Bridge regularly backs up during the rush hour commute. Drive off-peak when you can and allow extra time to reach your destination at any time of day. Tune in to frequent metropolitan area traffic reports on the radio at AM 880 "on the eights" (1:08, 1:18, 1:28, etc.) and AM 1010 "on the ones" (1:01, 1:11, 1:21, etc.).

Rockland County

With the Hudson River, New Jersey, and Orange County as its borders, Rockland County is the smallest county in the state, outside of the five boroughs of New York City. Located just 16 miles from New York City, Rockland has protected almost a third of its 176 square miles from development, thanks in part to generous donations from the wealthy families who built the first mansions along its riverbank. The terrain encompasses approximately 30 miles of Hudson River frontage, plus Bear Mountain and Harriman State Parks, which contain most of the Ramapo Mountain Range.

Rockland County's first European settlers arrived to join the Native American population in the 17th century. Initially a part of Orange County, Rockland separated in 1798 because the Ramapo Mountains made it difficult for residents to reach the county courthouse in Goshen. Rockland communities endured two key battles during the Revolutionary War: British forces captured Fort Clinton at Bear Mountain in October 1777, but two years later, colonial forces overwhelmed the British at Stony Point. Benedict Arnold's partner in treason, British Major John Andre, was captured in Tarrytown across the river. In his possession were the plans for West Point that he had received from Arnold. Andre was taken to the village of Tappan for trial. A jury found him guilty, and he was hanged.

Like most of the neighboring Hudson River communities, Rockland grew around the industries of milling lumber, making bricks, harvesting ice, mining, and quarrying. In the 1920s, internationally accomplished artists and performers settled in the area, including painter and muralist Henry Varnum Poor, playwright Maxwell Anderson, and composer Kurt Weil. Artist Edward Hopper hailed from Nyack, along with actress Helen Hayes.

The opening of the Tappan Zee Bridge, Palisades Interstate Parkway, and New York State Thruway, all in the 1950s, ended Rockland's days as a rural getaway. The county began to absorb much of the sprawl from New York City, and business conference centers became plentiful. Fortunately, Rockland has managed to develop without compromising its treasured green space. Dozens of historic markers remind visitors of the churches, farms, cemeteries, and homes that hold a significant place in the American past. At the same time, numerous immigrant communities have helped create a vibrant scene for restaurants, performing arts, and museums. Several world-class shopping malls line the Route 59 corridor near Nanuet.

Four townships hold most of the county's historic and outdoor attractions: Clarkstown, Haverstraw, Ramapo, and Stony Point. New City is the county seat.

ALONG THE RIVER—ROUTE 9W

Rockland County begins about 10 miles north of the George Washington Bridge (I-95), a main artery out of New York City. From the bridge, the Palisades Interstate Parkway cuts diagonally across the county, and Route 9W hugs the riverbank. Near the New Jersey state line, the dramatic Palisades cliffs plunge into the river, creating a playground for geologists and rock climbers alike.

◖ Piermont Village

Rockland's major river crossing, the Tappan Zee Bridge (I-287), is the longest span across the Hudson, connecting Rockland residents to Westchester County and points east. With 85,000 cars a day passing through, the bridge is the busiest crossing in the region.

Three miles south of the Tappan Zee Bridge, on a steep hillside between Route 9W and the riverbank, is the upscale village of Piermont, where you can savor a high-style brunch at **Xaviars** (506 Piermont Ave., 845/359-7007; 6–9 P.M. Wed.–Sat., noon–2 P.M. and 5–8 P.M. Sun.; prix fixe $70–90 pp), paddle a canoe through 1,000 acres of marsh, and then return to town for an evening of live music. Piermont has long been a haven for creative types. Woody Allen's 1985 film *The Purple Rose of Cairo* was filmed here, as was *At First Sight* (1999), starring Mira Sorvino and Val Kilmer.

These days, many residents also commute daily into Manhattan and ride their Italian-made bicycles on the weekends. A row of lively bistros and boutiques takes up most of Piermont Avenue in the village center, where a mile-long pier juts out over the marsh and into the Hudson.

Initially built to handle steamboat traffic, and later, railroad commerce, the **Piermont Pier** became the site of a successful paper mill during the 20th century. During World War II, tens of thousands of U.S. troops boarded ships to Normandy from the pier, earning it the name "Last Stop USA." The soldiers received their last training and inspections at **Camp Shanks,** four miles west of the pier. The camp also housed German and Italian prisoners of war until the end of the conflict. It's hard to get a sense of the magnitude of the camp from the small museum that remains today. Exhibits inside a model barracks depict life during the war.

Today, the Piermont Pier is a public park that attracts anglers, walkers, and anyone in search of a cool breeze. Just south of the pier is **Tallman Mountain State Park** (Rte. 9W, Bear Mountain, 845/359-0544; admission $7), a favorite spot for viewing birds and wildflowers on land that once belonged to John D. Rockefeller's Standard Oil Company. Additional facilities include a public pool and tennis courts. Take Exit 4 from the Palisades Parkway to reach the Piermont area.

Tappan

Students of the Revolutionary War must pay a visit to several sites in the village of Tappan, a few miles southwest from Piermont. George Washington turned the Dutch colonial **DeWint House** (20 Livingston Ave., 845/359-1359; 10 A.M.–4 P.M. daily; free admission)—now a registered national landmark and the oldest building in Rockland County—into temporary headquarters during the trial of Major

John André, the British spy who was accused of conspiring with Benedict Arnold. The trial took place at the county courthouse, which stood on the Village Church Green, next door to the 1835 **Reformed Church of Tappan** that stands today.

Near a stoplight at the center of town is the **The Old'76 House,** built in 1755. Andre was held captive here until his execution. The building is now a restaurant and tavern.

Nyack

On the other side of the Tappan Zee Bridge lies the busier commercial center of Nyack (meaning Point of Land), part of the Clarkstown township. Home to a vibrant mix of artists, immigrants, and commuters (many of whom know each other by name), Nyack draws day-trippers out of the city with the **Edward Hopper House Art Center** (82 N. Broadway, Nyack, 845/358-0774, www.edwardhopper houseartcenter.org; 1–5 P.M. Thurs.–Sun.; donation requested), as well as dozens of galleries, shops, and restaurants. Most of the businesses are gathered around the intersection of Main Street (which slopes downhill toward the river), and Broadway, which runs parallel to it. Look for a visitor information booth near the Clock Tower, where Main Street crosses Cedar.

Realist painter Edward Hopper spent his childhood in a modest clapboard house on Broadway, a few blocks north of the main retail strip. After attending high school in Nyack, he moved to New York City but returned home frequently throughout his career. A small museum in the family home, now a restored New York State Historic Site, documents Hopper's life and displays works by local artists. In summer, jazz concerts are often held in the garden.

A short drive beyond the Edward Hopper House leads to a row of riverside mansions—many of them owned by celebrities, including Rosie O'Donnell—protected by imposing brick and stone fences. At the end of this exclusive neighborhood is **Nyack Beach State Park** (Broadway, 845/268-3020; open year-round; parking $6), where local residents come to walk, relax, and fish. A two-mile trail for jogging and biking follows the river north to Hook Mountain. Trains rumble in the distance, and to the south, you can see the Tappan Zee Bridge.

New City

Between Rockland Lake State Park and Haverstraw, Route 304 West leads to New City, where the **Historical Society of Rockland County** produces historical exhibits inside the **Jacob Blauvelt House** (20 Zukor Rd., New City, 845/634-9629, www.rocklandhistory.org; 1–5 P.M. Tues.–Sun.; admission $6). This two-story brick farmhouse was built in 1832 in the Dutch style. Six rooms and an 1865 carriage house are currently open to visitors. Exhibits cover a broad span of time and address a range of topics relevant to the local experience. Native American culture, Dutch bibles, Civil War diaries, 19th-century furnishings, the agrarian lifestyle, and former industries (such as making bricks, harvesting ice, mining, and quarrying) are all represented. Take Exit 10 from the Palisades Parkway.

Haverstraw Bay

Natural resources and innovation in the process of brick making positioned Haverstraw at the forefront of the construction industry through most of the 19th century. In 1771, clay was discovered in the Hudson offshore from Haverstraw, and the ability to mold bricks into a standard size allowed Rockland County to play a pivotal role in the building of New York City. At its peak before the advent of steel and the Great Depression, the local industry supported 42 independent brickyards. The **Haverstraw Brick Museum** (12 Main St., Haverstraw, 845/947-3505, www.haverstrawbrickmuseum .org; 1–4 p.m. Wed. and Sat.–Sun.; admission $2), open three afternoons a week, documents the history of the industry. A ferry to the Ossining Metro-North station departs from Short Clove Road.

◖ Stony Point Battlefield State Historical Site

Located on Haverstraw Bay is an all-important Revolutionary War site: the Stony Point Battlefield State Historical Site (Park Rd. off Rte. 9W, Stony Point, 845/786-2521, www2.lhric.org/ spbattle/spbattle.htm; 10 a.m.–5 p.m. Wed.– Sat.; free admission) is a riverside park and museum that includes the oldest lighthouse on the Hudson (1826). On the night of July 15, 1779, Brigadier General Anthony Wayne led a small group of colonial soldiers in a midnight assault on the British troops who had taken control of the point. In a textbook operation, Wayne's men waded silently through marsh and mud to catch the British by surprise. A small but important win, the victory restored morale among American troops.

It takes about 10 minutes to walk from the parking lot to the lighthouse, where visitors are rewarded with a view of Haverstraw Bay. Interpretive signs inside the park document the battle, and staff members occasionally dress up in colonial costumes to set the mood. There are two entrances to the park from Route 9W:

a historic marker indicates the southern turnoff, while the northern one is more difficult to spot.

THE RAMAPO MOUNTAINS

Rockland's greatest outdoor treasure is an enormous green space that straddles the border with Orange County, running southwest from the Bear Mountain Bridge almost to the New Jersey state line. Thanks in part to families like the Rockefellers, Vanderbilts, and Harrimans, more than 50,000 rugged acres are divided into two adjoining state parks: Harriman (46,000 acres) and Bear Mountain (5,000 acres).

◖ Harriman State Park

The first section of the Appalachian Trail was cleared here in 1923, and today, hikers can access 200 miles of trails and more than 30 lakes and reservoirs inside the second largest park in the New York state system. Seven Lakes Drive runs the length of Harriman State Park (Rte. 9W, Bear Mountain, 845/786-2701; admission $7) and provides access to the main recreation areas, including Lake Sebago, Lake Welch, Lake Tioran, and the Anthony Wayne Recreation Area.

Camping, swimming, and picnics are permitted. Wilderness accommodations include shelters, cabins, and campsites. There are two entrances to the park: from Route 17 in Sloatsburg or from the Palisades Parkway near West Haverstraw. Park only in designated areas. The park often fills to capacity on busy holiday weekends; a midweek visit affords more tranquility, but if you do arrive with the masses, you can quickly escape by heading into the backcountry.

Bear Mountain State Park

Formed in 1910 as a reaction against the proposed relocation of Sing Sing prison from Ossining, the smaller but well-developed Bear Mountain (Rte. 9W, Bear Mountain, 845/786-2701; dawn-dusk; parking $6) sees as many visitors per year as the most popular national parks. The sprawling parking lot gives an indication of how crowded the park can get on hot summer weekends.

NEW YORK STATE PARKS IN THE HUDSON RIVER VALLEY

In addition to the **Catskill Forest Preserve** – which spans parts of Greene, Ulster, Delaware, and Sullivan counties and consists of nearly 300,000 acres of public and private lands and 98 peaks over 3,000 feet – the Hudson River Valley has a great variety of more modest, yet beautiful state parks.

Albany County

- Black Creek Marsh State Wildlife Management Area
- Cole Hill State Forest
- Five Rivers State Environmental Education Center
- John Boyd Thacher State Park
- Knox State Wildlife Management Area
- Louise E Keir State Wildlife Management Area
- Partridge Run State Wildlife Management Area
- Peebles Island State Park
- Pine Bush State Unique Area
- Rensselaerville State Forest
- Scott Patent State Forest
- Thompsons Lake State Park

Columbia County

- Beebe Hill State Forest
- Harvey Mountain State Forest
- Hudson River Islands State Park
- New Forge State Forest
- Nutten Hook State Unique Area
- Olana State Historic Site
- Rogers Island State Wildlife Management Area
- Stockport Creek State Wetland Preservation Area

Delaware County

- Artic China State Forest

- Barbour Brook State Forest
- Beals Pond State Forest
- Bear Spring Mountain State Wildlife Management Area
- Bearpen Mountain State Forest
- Cherry Ridge Wild Forest
- Columbia Lake State Forest
- Dry Brook Wild Forest
- John Lennox State Demonstration Forest
- Kerryville State Forest
- Little Pond State Campground
- Michigan Hill State Forest
- Middle Mountain Wild Forest
- Murphy Hill State Forest
- Oquaga Creek State Park
- Plattekill State Forest
- Relay State Forest
- South Hill State Forest
- Steam Mill State Forest
- Tomannex State Forest
- Wolf Hollow State Wildlife Management Area

Dutchess County

- Clermont State Historic Park
- Depot Hill State Forest
- James Baird State Park
- Lafayetteville State Forest
- Margaret Lewis Norrie State Park (Mills-Norrie State Park)
- Ogden Mills & Ruth Livingston Mills State Park
- Roeliff Jansen Kill State Forest
- Stony Kill State Environmental Education Center
- Taconic Hereford State Forest
- Taconic Lake State Park

- Taconic State Park
- Taconic State Park - Rudd Pond Area
- Thompson Pond & Stissing Mountain
- Tivoli Bay State Unique Area
- Wassaic State Forest
- West Mountain State Forest

Greene County

- Ashland Pinnacle State Forest
- Bearpen Mountain State Forest
- Blackhead Range Wild Forest
- Colgate Lake Wild Forest
- Devils Tombstone State Campground
- Great Vly State Wetland Preservation Area
- Halcott Mountain Wild Forest
- Hunter Mountain Wild Forest
- Huntersfield State Forest
- Indian Head Wilderness
- Kaaterskill Wild Forest
- Mount Pisgah State Forest
- North South Lake State Campground
- Phoenicia Wild Forest
- Shandaken Wild Forest
- Vinegar Hill State Wildlife Management Area
- West Kill Mountain Wilderness
- Windham High Peak Wild Forest

Orange County

- Bear Mountain State Park
- Cherry Island State Wildlife Management Area
- Goose Pond Mountain State Park
- Harriman State Park
- Hawk Watch Trailway
- Highland Lakes State Park
- Knox Headquarters State Historic Site

- Kowawese State Unique Area
- New Windsor Cantonment State Historic Site
- Sterling Forest State Park
- Stewart State Forest
- Storm King State Park
- Washington's Headquarters State Historic Site

Putnam County

- Big Buck Mountain State Forest
- Bog Brook State Unique Area
- California Hill State Forest
- Castle Rock State Unique Area
- Clarence Fahnestock State Park
- Cranberry Mountain State Wildlife Management Area
- Hudson Highlands State Park
- Nimham Mountain State Forest
- Pudding Street State Forest
- White Pond State Forest

Rensselaer County

- Bennington Battlefield State Historic Site
- Berlin State Forest
- Capital District State Wildlife Management Area
- Castleton Island State Park
- Cherry Plain State Park
- Clermont State Historic Park
- Grafton Lakes State Park
- Lock 4 State Canal Park
- Petersburg Pass State Forest
- Pittstown State Forest
- Tibbetts State Forest

Rockland County

- Blauvelt State Park

(continues on next page)

NEW YORK STATE PARKS
IN THE HUDSON RIVER VALLEY (continued)

- Haverstraw Beach State Park
- High Tor State Park
- Hook Mountain State Park
- Minisceongo State Tidal Wetlands
- Nyack Beach State Park
- Palisades State Park
- Piermont Marsh State Tidal Wetlands
- Rockland Lake State Park
- Rockwood Hall State Park
- Stony Point Battlefield State Historic Site
- Tallman Mountain State Park

Sullivan County

- Bashakill State Wildlife Management Area
- Beaverkill State Campground
- Hickok Brook State Forest
- Lake Superior State Park
- Middle Mountain Wild Forest
- Mongaup Pond State Campground
- Mongaup Valley State Wildlife Management Area
- Neversink River State Unique Area
- Painter Hill State Forest
- Sundown Wild Forest
- Willowemoc Wild Forest
- Wolf Brook State Forest
- Wurtsboro Ridge State Forest

Ulster County

- Balsam Mountain Wild Forest
- Belleayre Mountain Ski Center
- Big Indian Wilderness

- Bluestone Wild Forest
- Bristol Beach State Park
- Dry Brook Ridge Wild Forest
- Great Vly Wildlife Management Area
- Hemlock Ridge State Forest
- Highwoods State Forest
- Indian Head Wilderness
- Kenneth Wilson State Campground
- Little Pond State Campground
- Minnewaska State Park
- Oak Ridge State Forest
- Overlook Mountain Wild Forest
- Phoenicia Wild Forest
- Shandaken Wild Forest
- Shawangunk Ridge State Forest
- Shawangunk State Forest
- Slide Mountain Wilderness
- Sundown Wild Forest
- Turkey Point State Forest
- West Kill Mountain Wilderness
- Willowemoc Wild Forest
- Woodland Valley State Campground

Westchester County

- Croton Gorge State Unique Area
- Franklin D. Roosevelt State Park
- John Jay Homestead State Historic Site
- Rockefeller State Park
- Titus Mill Pond State Tidal Wetland

Visit http://nysparks.state.ny.us/parks for information.

Near the entrance, a stone lodge overlooking Hessian Lake houses the **Bear Mountain Inn** (Bear Mountain, 845/786-2731, www.bearmountaininn.com; $89)—which was *the* place to stay in 1920s New York. Prospective guests had to complete an application and provide a personal recommendation for the privilege of spending the night. The price of $3.50 a day bought a room with all meals. The lodge is currently under renovation.

Behind the inn, Perkins Memorial Drive winds its way to the top of Bear Mountain and a commanding view of the highlands. Hikers can reach the summit in about three hours, starting at Hessian Lake. The **Bear Mountain Trailside Museum** (845/786-2701; www.hudsonrivervalley.com; 10 A.M.–4:30 P.M. daily; ages 13 and up $1, 6–12 $.50, under 5 free, parking $6) entertains kids with exhibits on black bears, beavers, coyotes, and other animals. Additional activities include swimming, paddleboats, ice-skating, and numerous seasonal festivals. Look for the entrance to Bear Mountain State Park on Route 9W, about half a mile from the traffic circle at the **Bear Mountain Bridge.**

Common wisdom said it would take the Bear Mountain Hudson River Bridge Company 30 years to build a span across the narrowest part of the Hudson—it would be the longest suspension bridge in its day. Engineers finished in 20 months, and the first crossing over the river opened to traffic in 1924. The Appalachian Trail crosses the river at this point, and many hikers stop to admire the views of the highlands from the span.

THE ROUTE 59 CORRIDOR

The old Nyack Turnpike, built to transport manufactured goods from the Ramapo Mountains to the Hudson River, is now a busy thoroughfare that connects the towns of Suffern, Spring Valley, and Nanuet to Nyack. Along Route 59 are several suburban communities with sprawling shopping centers.

On a more somber note, **The Holocaust Museum and Study Center** (17 South Madison Ave., Spring Valley, 845/356-2700, www.holocauststudies.org; 10 A.M.–4 P.M. Tues.–Thurs.; adults $5, students $3), in Spring Valley, displays documents, artifacts, and films as a powerful reminder of the tragedy. Particularly moving is the Children's Wall, built as a memorial to the youngest victims of the Holocaust.

Continuing along Route 59, you reach historic **Suffern** with a handful of shops and restaurants, as well as Rockland County's largest movie complex, the 1927 **Lafayette Theatre** (Rte. 59 & Washington Ave., Suffern, 845/369-8234; adults $12, under 12 and seniors $8). The **Suffern Railroad Museum** (Orange Ave., Suffern) is housed in the original Wells Fargo Express Mail Depot, which was restored in 1998. For a faster east-west route, take I-287, which runs parallel to Route 59.

SPORTS AND RECREATION

With two large state parks and several smaller green spaces, Rockland offers a surprising variety of possibilities for outdoor entertainment. You can do just about everything in Bear Mountain and Harriman State Parks: hike, bike, boat, camp, picnic, swim, fish, skate, ski, and play.

Winter Sports

When the Hudson ices over and snow blankets the highlands, cross-country skiers head to the two-mile trail at Nyack Beach State Park for a morning of exercise.

Hiking

Harriman State Park is a great place to hike in mid- to late-fall, since no hunting is allowed within its boundaries. A number of daylong routes, including the scenic Lichen Trail, lead to the summit of Surebridge Mountain. Claudius Smith's Den is another popular excursion into the wilderness. The hike begins at the Tuxedo train station (Orange County) along the red-dot trail and ends at the hideout of a Revolutionary War–era outlaw.

For an overnight hike, head to the Cornell trailhead near the Iona Island Bird Sanctuary off Route 9W, follow it to a ghost town called Doodletown, and camp at a shelter near Timp

Brook. Maps are available from the New York-New Jersey Trail Conference (156 Ramapo Valley Rd., Mahwah, NJ, 201/512-9348, www .nynjtc.org). Park only in designated lots for hikers and camp only in public camping areas.

Hook Mountain State Park (Rte. 9W, Nyack, 845/268-3020; dawn-dusk; admission $6) is well known as a place to watch hawks soar above the treetops. Enter through Rockland Lake State Park and follow signs to the executive golf course. As a courtesy, park away from the club house and look for a yellow mark on the curb next to the flag pole in the cul-de-sac. Proceed to the woods and follow the yellow-blazed trail to the blue blazed trail to the summit. Another entrance is found inside Nyack Beach State Park.

Cycling

Piermont's scenic roads are popular with cyclists, but beware of the steep fine for riding double file. Stop in to chat with the crew at **Piermont Bicycle Connection** (215 Ash St., Piermont, 845/365-0900, www.piermontbike. com; 9 A.M.–7 P.M. Thurs.–Tues.) and pick up maps and supplies before you ride. None of the shops in the area rent road bikes.

Golf

Spook Rock Golf Course (199 Spook Rock Rd., Ramapo, 845/357-6466; $55) has large, fast greens with tight fairways. The course consistently ranks in the top public courses in the state. **Rockland Lake State Park Golf Course** (Rte. 9W & Lake Rd, Congers, 845/268-7275; weekends $29, weekdays $24) is a 6,864-yard, par 72 course with 18 holes. A second nine-hole executive course has plenty of bunkers to keep golfers on their toes.

Swimming and Boating

Piermont Marsh is a unique aquatic habitat within walking distance of Piermont's shops and restaurants. The best way to explore it is by canoe or kayak, which you can rent from Captain Bill at **Paradise Boats** (845/359-0073, www.paradisecanoeandkayak .com; 9 A.M.–5 P.M. Sat., Sun., and holidays).

Look for a sign at the corner of Piermont and Paradise. September and October are the best months to go for a paddle.

Hudson Highland Cruises (Haverstraw Marina, West Haverstraw, 845/534-7245, www.hudsonhighlandscruises.com; prices vary) runs daylong scenic and informative river tours out of West Haverstraw, with additional departures and shorter tours from West Point and Peekskill.

ACCOMMODATIONS

Accommodations with personality are surprisingly hard to come by in Rockland County. Like Westchester, Rockland has mostly conference centers and chains, from Marriott and Holiday Inn to Best Western and Super 8. Travelers will be better off continuing on to Orange County to settle down for the night.

Under $100

An alternative to the aging Bear Mountain Inn is **Overlook Lodge** (Bear Mountain, 845/786-2731, www.bearmountaininn.com; $99), on the other side of Hessian Lake. Motel-style rooms are simply furnished with two double beds and private baths, and you can't beat the price.

FOOD
Along the River–Route 9W

You can't go wrong in Nyack when it comes to finding good food. **Lu Shane's** (8 N. Broadway, Nyack, 845/358-5556, www.lushanes.com; mains $20–27) has a raw bar and loud weekend jazz. **The King & I** (93 Main St., Nyack, 845/358-8588, www.king&inyack.com; noon–10:30 P.M. Mon.–Thurs. and Sun., noon–10:30 P.M. Fri.–Sat.; mains $7–10) has been serving curries and other specialties to locals for years.

Outstanding sushi prepared by a Vietnamese chef—and offered at Manhattan prices—sums up the experience at **Wasabi** (110 Main St. at Park St., Nyack, 845/358-7977, www.wasabi nyack.com; lunch noon–2:30 P.M. Tues.–Thurs., dinner 5–10 P.M. Tues.–Thurs., 5–11 P.M. Fri.–Sat., 4–9:30 P.M. Sun.).

Vertigo (91 Main St. between Broadway

and Cedar, Nyack, 845/358-3202, www.vertigo nyack.com; 5–10 P.M. daily; mains $23–38) is a trendy New American restaurant that turns into a nightclub after hours. Start with an order from the raw bar. The dinner menu includes lobster ravioli, pepper-crusted pork loin, and pistachio-crusted rack of lamb.

In Piermont, **Pasta Amore** (200 Ash St., Piermont, 845/365-1911; noon–9 P.M. Sun.–Thurs., till 10 P.M. Fri.–Sat.; mains $10–17) does pasta right, with river views and patio seating. **Romolo's** (77 Rte. 303, Congers, 845/268-3770, www.dineromolos.com; lunch Tues.–Fri. 11:30 A.M.–2:30 P.M., dinner 5–9:30 P.M. Tues.–Thurs., 5–10:30 P.M. Fri.–Sat., 3–8:30 P.M. Sun.; mains $13–28) gets high marks for classic Italian cuisine. Serving tavern cuisine, including a variety of steaks and seafood and even a chicken pot pie, **The Old'76 House** (110 Main St., Tappan, 845/359-5476, www.76house.com; mains $17–26) also has jazz on Saturday nights and a popular Sunday brunch.

THE HUDSON VALLEY'S BEST TAVERNS AND PUBS

You haven't experienced the Hudson Valley until you've settled into a cozy tavern for a cold beer and hearty meal. Here are some of the perennial favorites:

- The Colonial Tap Room at the Beekman Arms, Rhinebeck
- Jack's Oyster House, Albany
- Mahoney's Irish Pub & Restaurant, Poughkeepsie
- Maud's Tavern, Hastings-on-Hudson
- The Old '76 House, Tappan
- The Original Saratoga Springs Brewpub, Saratoga Springs
- The Western Hotel, Callicoon

The Ramapo Mountains

Just before the New Jersey state line, the **Mount Fuji Steakhouse** (296 Rte. 17, Hillburn, 845/357-4270, www.mtfujirestaurants .com; lunch noon–2 P.M. Mon.–Fri., dinner 5–10 P.M. Mon.–Thurs., 5 P.M.–midnight Fri., 4 P.M.–midnight Sat., 3–10 P.M. Sun.; mains $22–40) is perched on a hilltop above Route 17. Seating around a private hibachi station and servers tossing cleavers in the air make it the perfect venue to celebrate a birthday or a family reunion. You'll likely wait for a table, even with a reservation. Arrive in daylight to catch the mountain views.

At the southern end of Harriman State Park, the town of Sloatsburg has a handful of casual dining options. Conveniently located on the main route through Harriman State Park, **Miele's Deli & Restaurant** (23 Seven Lakes Dr., Sloatsburg, 845/753-2662; 11 A.M.–10 P.M. daily; mains $10–15) makes hot and cold sandwiches, as well as burgers and fried shellfish. **Characters** (formerly The Glenwood, 94 Orange Tpke., Sloatsburg, 845/753-5200; 11:30 A.M.–10 P.M. Sun.–Wed., 11:30 A.M.–11 P.M. Thurs.–Sat.; mains $8–10) prepares a comprehensive American menu of steaks, seafood, and chicken entrées.

In a pinch, you can also grab a quick bite to eat at the concession stand at Lake Welch State Beach in Harriman State Park. For a greater variety of dining options, Suffern, at the southern edge of the park along Route 59, is the next closest town.

The Route 59 Corridor

For a traditional Indian lunch buffet, try **Priya** (36 Lafayette Ave., Suffern, 845/357-5700, www.priyaindiancuisineny.com; 5–10 P.M. Tues.–Thurs., 5–10:30 P.M. Fri.–Sat., 1–9:30 P.M. Sun.; mains $13–23).

Marcello's Ristorante of Suffern (21 Lafayette Ave., Suffern, 845/357-9108, www .marcellosgroup.com; noon–2:30 P.M. and 5–9:30 P.M. Mon.–Sat., 3–8:30 P.M. Sun.; mains $17–30) is a white linen affair with a menu of true Italian specialties. Look for the burgundy awning. Across the street,

Caffe Dolce (24 Lafayette Ave., Suffern, 845/357-2066; 11:45 A.M.–10 P.M. Mon.–Sat., 3–8 P.M. Sun.) serves a more casual menu in a coffee and wine bar setting. The bar is open later than the listed dining hours.

Pasta Cucina (www.pastacucina.com; noon–10 P.M. Mon.–Thurs., noon–11 P.M. Fri., 5–11 P.M. Sat., 4:15–9 P.M. Sun.; mains $10–16) offers great value on family-style dining in three Rockland County locations: Suffern (8 Airmont Rd., Suffern, 845/369-1313), New City (261 S. Little Tor Rd., New City, 845/638-4729), and Stony Point (32 S. Liberty Dr., Stony Point, 845/786-6060).

ENTERTAINMENT AND EVENTS
Performing Arts
One of the most popular theater venues in Rockland County is Nyack's **Helen Hayes Theatre Company** (123 Main St., Nyack, 845/358-6333, www.hhtco.org). Performances include musicals, symphony, orchestra, and opera. Its Main Street location is close to a number of restaurants for pretheater dining. **Rockland Center for the Arts** (27 South Greenbush Rd., West Nyack, 845/358-0877, www.rocklandartcenter.org) holds classes, weekend performances, and interviews with performers.

Bars and Nightlife
Turning Point (468 Piermont Ave., Piermont, 845/359-1089, www.turningpointcafe.com) lures acclaimed jazz performers to a cozy space in Piermont Village. You can have dinner on the porch before the show. Alternatively, the art deco ⚫ **Freelance Café and Wine Bar** (506 Piermont Ave., Piermont, 845/365-3250, www.xaviars.com; lunch and dinner Tues.–Sun.; small plates $6–15, large plates $18–24), next door to Xaviars and owned by the same group, is the place to meet a friend for drinks. You'll have to wait for a table, because the café does not take reservations. **Hudson House of Nyack** (134 Main St., 845/353-1355; 11:30 A.M.–3 P.M. and 5:30–10 P.M. Tues.–Thurs., till 11 P.M. Fri.–Sat., 11 A.M.–3:30 P.M.

and 4:30–9:30 P.M. Sun., bar menu available between lunch and dinner; mains $14–19) also plays jazz on Thursday nights to accompany its New American menu.

Enjoy an evening of rarely shown documentaries at **Reality Bites** (100 Main St., Nyack, 845/358-8800, www.realitybites.net; 11:30 A.M.–10 P.M. Mon.–Fri., till midnight on weekends). Comic documentary filmmaker Steven M. Manin opened the theater and eatery in 2004 to show documentaries, unreleased films, and comic outtakes on three large plasma screens. Order "bites" for $1, or salads, sandwiches, and tapas for $7–10 while you watch. Check the website for a daily schedule of films.

Festivals
Suffern produces the **Native American Festival** (845/786-2701) at Harriman State Park each August. More than 1,000 artists, performers, and educators participate. The event culminates in a dance competition that draws competitors from across North and South America. The New York City Triathlon Club (April–Oct., www.NYTC.org/calendar/CFM for races and dates) also runs a summer race series at Harriman. Entrants must be over 18.

Bear Mountain State Park puts on a festive **Octoberfest** (845/786-2701), with music and dancing in the crisp fall air. The **Rockland Audubon Society** (www.rocklandaudubon.org) runs field trips for wildlife observation.

SHOPPING
Farm Stands
The weekly **Nyack Farmers Market** (845/353-2221, www.localharvest.org/farmers-markets/M5223; 8:30 A.M.–2:30 P.M. Thurs.), in the municipal parking lot at the corner of Main and Cedar Streets, is not to be missed. You can buy 20 different types of mushrooms from a single grower, plus the usual assortment of locally grown fruits and vegetables. Suffern, Spring Valley, and Haverstraw each have their own farmers markets during the growing season.

Antiques and Galleries

Art galleries and antique shops abound in Nyack and Piermont. In addition, the **Nyack Tobacco Company** (140 Main St., Nyack, 845/358-9300; 11 A.M.–8 P.M. Tues.–Sat., 11 A.M.–5 P.M. Sun.) carries one of the best selections of handmade cigars outside of New York City. Its cigars are stored in a digitally controlled humidor. Meanwhile, book lovers will find titles piled floor to ceiling in the **Pickwick Bookshop** (8 S. Broadway, Nyack, 845/358-9126; 9:30 A.M.–7 P.M. daily).

On the Route 59 corridor, the **Palisades Center** (1000 Palisade Center Dr., West Nyack, 845/348-1000; 10 A.M.–9:30 P.M., Mon.–Sat., 11 A.M.–7 P.M. Sun.) opened in 1998 as a four-level megamall with 250 stores, anchored by Lord & Taylor, Filene's, Target, H&M, and Williams-Sonoma.

INFORMATION AND SERVICES

The **Rockland County Office of Tourism** (18 New Hempstead Rd., New City, 845/708-7300 or 800/295-5723) is headquartered in New City. In Nyack, look for a visitor information booth by the Clock Tower at Main and Cedar.

GETTING THERE AND AROUND
By Bus

Several companies run buses in Rockland County: **Transit of Rockland** (845/364-3333) and the **Spring Valley Jitney** (845/573-5800) provide local service, while Shortline Bus and Adirondack Trailways connect to parts north.

By Train

Metro-North (800/638-7646) and **New Jersey Transit** (201/762-5100) offer rail service to Rockland County. A ferry runs between Haverstraw and the Hudson line station in Ossining (800/533-3779), and cabs are readily available in major towns, including Nyack. Stewart Airport is the best place to rent a car.

By Car

The Palisades Interstate Parkway (Exits 4–15) connects Rockland County to the George Washington Bridge, and the Garden State Parkway heads to New Jersey. I-287 crosses the Tappan Zee Bridge to Westchester County. You can get frequent metropolitan area traffic reports on the radio at AM 880 and AM 1010.

THE HUDSON HIGHLANDS

Between the towns of Peekskill in Westchester County and Beacon in Dutchess County—a 15-mile stretch—a solid granite mountain range called the Appalachian Plateau crosses the Hudson. Here, the river has carved a narrow and deep path through the range to form the Hudson Highlands, a dramatic landscape that resembles the signature banks of the Rhine. Storm King Mountain on the west and Breakneck Mountain on the east rise up on opposite shores near Cold Spring and West Point, giving Orange and Putnam counties some of the most beautiful vistas—and colorful history—of any county in the region.

It was here, in the narrowest part of the river, that American troops stretched an iron chain—each link measuring two feet long and weighing more than 140 pounds—across the entire width of the river. The goal, of course, was to prevent British ships from sailing north up the Hudson. Though it may well have been an effective deterrent, the chain was never tested because none of the British ships managed to advance as far as West Point after the chain was set.

A few miles north, where the river widens to form Newburgh Bay, tiny Pollopel Island has an abandoned Scottish-style castle and what remains of the former Bannerman's Island Arsenal, an unusual family business that dealt in military supplies. You can see what remains of the fortress from river cruises and kayak tours that pass close by; the state has also built a new dock with the intent of offering guided walking tours as soon as the buildings are deemed safe for visitors.

History and mysterious islands aside, the Hudson Highlands boast four sizable state

HIGHLIGHTS

West Point: This gold mine of American military history sits in one the most beautiful spots along the Hudson (page 70).

Storm King Art Center: This unique outdoor sculpture museum features works from well-known American and British artists (page 72).

Greenwood Lake: There's plenty of summer fun at this lake large enough for sailing and waterskiing (page 74).

Woodbury Common Premium Outlets: This sprawling complex of designer outlets draws shoppers from miles around (page 84).

Boscobel Restoration: The home of the annual Hudson Valley Shakespeare Festival is a restored neoclassical mansion called Boscobel (Beautiful Wood). From the wood-carved drapery on the balcony to the 18th-century silver, china, and glassware within, this historic site is a cultural treasure (page 86).

Cold Spring Village: The antique shops and restaurants in this town are conveniently located on the Metro-North commuter line (page 86).

LOOK FOR TO FIND RECOMMENDED SIGHTS, ACTIVITIES, DINING, AND LODGING.

parks through which a section of the Appalachian Trail passes, the Black Dirt onion growing region, and a lively summer scene around Greenwood Lake.

PLANNING YOUR TIME

Few travelers attempt to see the entire Hudson Highlands area in one trip. Weekend itineraries are best limited to one section. You might target several sights along the river, or plan to visit one of the expansive state parks. West Point, the Storm King Art Center, and Cold Spring Village are top destinations that can take from a few hours to a full day to explore. In summer, a day at Greenwood Lake followed by an evening of shopping and fine dining in Warwick make a good combination. Route 17 through western Orange County is a major access route to Sullivan County and the Catskill region.

Putnam County measures less than 20 miles north to south and is well worth a full day's visit. Cold Spring is the county's most popular destination, and a day passes quickly in and around the riverside town. With an early start at the Bear Mountain Bridge, you'll have time for brief stops at Manitoga, Boscobel Restoration, and Constitution Marsh Wildlife Preserve, followed by a walk and a meal along Cold Spring's

THE HUDSON HIGHLANDS

CONNECTICUT

NEW JERSEY

PA

Hudson River

THUNDER RIDGE SKI AREA

Pawling

The Great Swamp

Carmel

Brewster

Ward Pound Ridge Reserve

Cross River Reservoir

Katonah

West Branch Reservoir

Croton Falls Reservoir

Mahopac

Kensico Res.

Croton Res.

Rye Lake

DUTCHESS
PUTNAM

Billings

Poughkeepsie

Fishkill

Fahnestock Memorial State Park

COLD SPRING VILLAGE

BOSCOBEL RESTORATION

Hudson Highlands State Park

Newburgh

King SP

WEST POINT

WEST POINT MILITARY RESERVATION

Peekskill

Stony Point

Mt Ivy

Lake De Forest

Ossining

PUTNAM
WESTCHESTER

STORM KING ART CENTER

Schunnemunk Mtn

Central Valley

WOODBURY COMMON PREMIUM OUTLETS

Goose Pond Mountain State Park

Harriman State Park

Ramapo Mountains

Montebello

ORANGE
ROCKLAND

Appalachian Trail

Orange Lake

Montgomery

Washingtonville

Goshen

Minnewaska State Park

Pine Bush

Highland Lakes State Park

Middletown

GREENWOOD LAKE

Warwick

Pine Island

Wawayanda State Park

Clinton Reservoir

Shawangunk

ULSTER
ORANGE

SULLIVAN
ORANGE

Wamasink Lake

Yankee Reservoir

Rio Reservoir

Delaware River

Port Jervis

High Point State Park

5 mi

0   5 km

© AVALON TRAVEL

A SCENE ON THE BANKS OF THE HUDSON

Cool shades and dews are round my way,
And silence of the early day;
Mid the dark rocks that watch his bed,
Glitters the mighty Hudson spread,
Unrippled, save by drops that fall
From shrubs that fringe his mountain wall;
And o'er the clear still water swells
The music of the Sabbath bells.
All, save this little nook of land,
Circled with trees, on which I stand;
All, save that line of hills which lie
Suspended in the mimic sky-
Seems a blue void, above, below,
Through which the white clouds
come and go;
And from the green world's farthest steep
I gaze into the airy deep.

Loveliest of lovely things are they,
On earth, that soonest pass away.
The rose that lives its little hour
Is prized beyond the sculptured flower.
Even love, long tried and cherished long,
Becomes more tender and more strong
At thought of that insatiate grave
From which its yearnings cannot save.
River! in this still hour thou hast
Too much of heaven on earth to last;
Nor long may thy still waters lie,
An image of the glorious sky.
Thy fate and mine are not repose,
And ere another evening close,
Thou to thy tides shalt turn again,
And I to seek the crowd of men.

– William Cullen Bryant (1827)

Main Street. Serious antique shoppers will need more time, as will anyone who plans to hike the Hudson Highlands or paddle the river.

To add Clarence Fahnestock Memorial State Park and eastern Putnam County to the itinerary, follow Route 301 west out of Cold Spring through the towns of Kent, Carmel, and Brewster.

Scenic Drives

Route 9D in Putnam County, from Beacon to the Bear Mountain Bridge, winds its way through the dramatic Hudson Highlands. On the other side of the Hudson, Route 218 takes you over Storm King Mountain, with spectacular views of West Point and the Bear Mountain Bridge.

Orange County

New York's Orange County is everything that Southern Califonia's "OC" is not: From Washington's Headquarters to the annual Renaissance Faire in Sterling Forest, this Orange County takes its historical sites and traditions seriously. It is the home of the prestigious U.S. Military Academy at West Point and several related attractions, which draw some three million visitors a year.

The only county in the Hudson Valley region with frontage on both the Hudson and Delaware Rivers begins 50 miles north and across the river from New York City, encompassing 816 square miles of fertile fields, rolling hills, and quiet suburban communities. Orange County's largest commercial centers are Newburgh, Middletown, and Port Jervis. Goshen is the county seat.

ALONG THE RIVER–ROUTE 9W

Orange and Rockland Counties share a border at the Bear Mountain Bridge on the west side of the Hudson River. Several thoroughfares meet here in a traffic circle at the approach to the bridge: Route 9W runs along the riverbank, the Palisades Parkway heads south toward New Jersey, and Route 6 runs west to join Route 17 (The Quickway). Appalachian Trail hikers also pass through on their way to or from Harriman State Park. (The AT crosses the Hudson at the Bear Mountain Bridge.)

Fort Montgomery

A few miles south of West Point, you can view the remains of an old fort, from which American soldiers sought—unsuccessfully—to prevent the British from advancing up the Hudson during the Revolutionary War. A newly opened visitors center contains artifacts found in the area of the fort—from shoe buckles and cuff links to glasses and flatware. Visits begin with a short film about the site and its role in early American history. Contact Fort Montgomery through Bear Mountain State Park, 845/446-2134, http://nysparks.state.ny.us/sites/info.asp?siteID=36. Grounds are open daily dawn till dusk, and

the visitors center is open Wednesday–Sunday 9 A.M.–5 P.M. (adults $3, seniors/students $2, children 12 and under free).

West Point

A few miles north of the bridge, the Hudson flows through its narrowest and deepest stretch (more than 200 feet), creating the strategic military position of West Point. In revolutionary times, American forces strung a 40-ton chain 500 yards across the river to keep the British at bay. After the colonial victory, President Thomas Jefferson believed the young nation needed to build its own military capability and wean itself from dependence on foreign expertise. He signed the United States Military Academy into law in 1802.

The academy's first curriculum produced civil engineers, who went on to build much of the nation's transportation infrastructure. West Point established its reputation for military excellence during the Civil War, when graduates including Robert E. Lee and Ulysses S. Grant fought against each other during almost every

The West Point Museum houses weapons from 135 military conflicts.

FIVE THINGS TO DO ON YOUR VISIT TO WEST POINT

1. Tour the military museum
2. Attend a performance at Eisenhower Hall
3. Take a river cruise
4. Watch an Army vs. Navy football game
5. Enjoy the breakfast buffet at the Thayer Hotel

battle. Superintendents during the 20th century broadened the program to include academic, physical, and military education, and the first woman graduated from the academy in 1980.

Today, the academy runs guided bus tours daily, except on football Saturdays and holidays and during graduation week. The one-hour tour, led by **West Point Tours** (Highland Falls, 845/446-4724, www.westpointtours.com), begins at the visitors center, off the West Point Highway, where you can view a model cadet barracks room and gather information about the academy.

Behind the visitors center stands the **West Point Museum** (www.usma.edu/museum; 10:30 A.M.–4:15 P.M. daily), which houses four floors of warfare exhibits covering 135 military conflicts in the history of the United States. A large weapons display in the basement has a World War I tank, while the small weapons include axes, clubs, and swords that date all the way back to the Stone Age. Tours often stop at **Fort Putnam,** a key position in defending the fortress, with panoramic views of the river and campus. **Trophy Point** offers a postcard-perfect view of the Hudson Highlands.

Familiar names grace the monuments across the central part of the campus: Patton, Marshall, MacArthur, Eisenhower, Schwarzkopf. More than 2,000 names are inscribed on the massive granite shaft of the striking **Battle**

Monument (1897), designed by Sanford White, who also built and furnished the opulent Vanderbilt Estate in Hyde Park (see the *Mid-Hudson* chapter). Nearby, the **Old Cadet Chapel** (8:15 A.M.–4:15 P.M. daily), built in 1836, is one of the oldest buildings still used on campus.

Extended two-hour tours, offered twice daily June–October, include a stop at the **West Point Cemetery,** which holds graves that date back to 1782 and represent casualties of almost every war the academy's graduates have fought. Inquire about combination bus and river tours. The West Point Band plays on Sunday evenings in an outdoor amphitheater near the North Dock in West Point.

The Gothic **Thayer Hotel** (674 Thayer Rd., West Point, 845/446-4731, www.thethayerhotel.com; $175), built in 1926, overlooks the Hudson at the south entrance to West Point. It was named for Colonel Sylvanius Thayer, superintendent of West Point from 1817 to 1833. A $26 million face-lift in 1996 restored the hotel to its former glory. Portraits of military leaders decorate the walls in the formal dining room, which is popular for holiday gatherings.

Call before you intend to arrive at West Point, because the visitors center may cancel tours at any time. Photo identification is required for entry, and your vehicle will also be searched. Allow extra time if you are taking a cruise or attending an event. Exit the New York Thruway at Exit 16.

From the back lawn of the hotel, you can see **Constitution Island** (845/446-8676), the first place George Washington chose to fortify at West Point. Unfortunately, the British had the same idea and established a stronghold in 1777; the Americans won it back a year later. By the 1830s, the island fell into private hands. Henry Warner and his two daughters built a family estate, and for years the daughters invited cadets to the island to study the Bible. The Warners donated their house and gardens to the academy in 1908. Today's cadets complete many of their training exercises here.

Visitors must make a reservation to tour the 180-acre island. Boats depart from the South

Dock inside West Point, past the Thayer Hotel. The nonprofit Constitution Island Association runs a shuttle from the Cold Spring rail station on select Saturdays during the summer.

Cornwall-on-Hudson

After West Point, Route 9W winds its way north to the base of Storm King Mountain and the quiet hamlet of Cornwall-on-Hudson. Alternatively, follow Route 218 north for a spectacular drive over Storm King Mountain, with gorgeous views of the fjord-like highlands. The **Museum of the Hudson Highlands** (The Boulevard, Cornwall-on-Hudson, 845/534-7781, www.museumhudson highlands.org; noon–4 P.M. Sat.–Sun.), in Cornwall, hosts a variety of art and nature exhibits that explore the cultural and natural heritage of the area. The museum occupies two locations: At the Boulevard location near the river are the Ogden Gallery featuring local artists whose work focuses on the natural world, a gift shop, and occasional live animal exhibits. A mile and a half away on Route 9W is the 177-acre Kenridge Farm, an outdoor classroom of native flora and fauna.

◖ Storm King Art Center

The Quaker Avenue exit off Route 9W leads to the expansive sculpture gardens of the Storm King Art Center (Old Pleasant Hill Rd., Mountainville, 845/534-3115, www.skac.org; 11 A.M.–5:30 P.M. Wed.–Sun. Apr. 1–Nov. 3; adults $10)—a perfect site for a summer picnic. In this unique outdoor museum, you can walk along tree-lined paths and view larger-than-life sculptures against the dramatic landscape and ever-changing light of the Hudson Highlands. The collection represents British and American artists, both postwar and contemporary. Some of the sculptures were designed expressly for their sites in the 500-acre park. *The Arch,* one of Alexander Calder's "stabiles," measures 56-feet high. The *Joy of Life,* a monumental piece by Mark di Suvero, weighs 20 tons and stands 70 feet tall. Storm King is a popular place for organized singles' outings from New York City. The center of-

fers guided, self-guided, and audio tours. On Saturdays during the summer, the center stays open until 8 P.M.

Newburgh

Farther up the river at the intersection of Route 9W and I-84 lies Newburgh, a city that—like Poughkeepsie to the north—has struggled with its legacy as a manufacturing center. Jobs remain scarce, and many of the old buildings are run down, but underneath the layers of industrial age, the city retains a deep sense of history.

George Washington established Revolutionary War headquarters in the home of Jonathan Hasbrouck, a fieldstone fortress on a hill overlooking the river, and the building has been a national historic site since 1850. Guides in period dress lead groups through a half-hour tour of the house, which has been restored to reflect its setup as military headquarters. Before or after, you can walk through a separate interpretive museum exhibit to learn more about the Revolutionary War. Across the lawn and overlooking the river is a monument built in the 1880s to honor the peace treaty that ended the Civil War. Funds have been secured to make it safe for visitors to climb to the top of the structure, and museum management expects to have the new feature open by 2009. **Washington's Headquarters** is located at 84 Liberty St., Newburgh, 845/562-1195; 10 A.M.–5 P.M. Wed.–Sat., 1–5 P.M. Sun. Apr.–Oct., also 10 A.M.–5 P.M. Mon. summer only; adults $4, children $3.

The parking lot is somewhat tricky to find and although the surrounding neighborhood is cleaner than it's been in years, some drivers still may be intimidated. If you're coming from I-84, follow Route 9W/32 south until Broadway. Turn left on Broadway and go about 10 blocks. Turn right on Liberty Street and after a block, look for the fenced lawn on the left and an alleyway just before Washington Street that leads to a parking lot.

The 1839 **Crawford House** (189 Montgomery St., Newburgh, 845/561-2585, www .newburghhistoricalsociety.com; 1–4 P.M. Sun.

April–Oct.), once the residence of a shipping merchant, houses the Historical Society of Newburgh Bay and the Highlands. On display inside the classic revival building are 19th-century antiques and paintings.

In addition to many private restorations under way, Newburgh has revived a section of its waterfront by turning several abandoned factories into an attractive boardwalk with a handful of upscale restaurants and shops. People now arrive at **Newburgh Landing** (88 Pierces Rd., Newburgh, 845/565-3297) by the boatful on summer weekends, where a variety of cuisines and trendy bars are just steps away from a slip in the marina. Fake palm trees—and some real ones too—are all part of the experience. Serious partiers often sleep on their boats after a night of revelry at one of the nearby clubs.

From the water's edge, you can see the beginning of the narrow Hudson Highlands to the south. Several river cruises depart from the landing. To reach the Newburgh Landing, exit I-84 at Route 9W and turn left at the second light onto North Plank Road.

If you continue on Route 9W instead of heading to the landing, you'll soon reach the intersection of South Street and the edge of Newburgh's onetime gem of a green space: 35-acre **Downing Park** (Rte. 9W and 3rd St., Newburgh, 845/565-5559, visitors center open year-round with summer hours 11 A.M.–5 P.M. Wed.–Sun.), named for architect Andrew Jackson Downing and designed by the same Frederick Law Olmstead and Calvert Vaux who created Central Park in New York City. The resemblance is striking, except that this park is now surrounded by low-income housing instead

THE HUDSON HIGHLANDS

© NIKKI GOTH ITOI

monument at Washington's Headquarters, Newburgh

of multimillion-dollar high rises. The restored Downing Park Shelter House serves as the city's visitors center.

New Windsor Cantonement and the Purple Heart Hall of Honor

The history lesson continues a short drive from Newburgh, at the New Windsor Cantonement. George Washington's army stayed at the New Windsor Cantonement State Historic Site (Temple Hill Rd., Vails Gate, 845/561-1765), which offers musket and artillery demonstrations and a tour of a replica of the Temple of Virtue, where Washington delivered one of his most moving speeches to troops who were losing faith in the war. The thinking behind slanted bed frames, charcoal for toothpaste, and the wonders of hard bread are just some of the trivia you'll pick up on a tour of the Cantonement.

With the addition of the new National Purple Heart Hall of Honor (Temple Hill Rd., Vails Gate, 845/561-1765, http://nysparks.state .ny.us/heritage/purple_hrt.asp), the Cantone-

ment site now offers an appealing blend of old and new. A visit to the Purple Heart Hall of Honor is an interactive experience that makes full use of the latest audiovisual technology. There are high-definition films to watch and computer stations set up for visitors to find or add their loved ones. Although the hall is designed to honor all 1.7 million recipients collectively, museum staff bring individual stories to life through a series of Roll of Honor interviews recorded in an on-site video studio. An outdoor courtyard is set aside as ceremonial grounds for quiet reflection.

CENTRAL ORANGE COUNTY—ALONG ROUTE 17
⟨ Greenwood Lake

The Appalachian Trail enters New York State from New Jersey at Greenwood Lake, a long, narrow body of water that joins the two states. Surrounded by dense forest and mountains, the natural lake is shallow with a maximum depth of 57 feet and wetlands at each end. Visibility is generally good, except after heavy storms.

© NIKKI GOTH ITOI

THE HUDSON HIGHLANDS

ready for a ride on Greenwood Lake

A narrow local road hugs the eastern shore of the lake, and busy Route 210 heads into New Jersey on the western side.

The Erie Railroad brought the first wave of visitors to the lake in the 1870s, and Babe Ruth was a frequent vacationer. Year-round residences crowd the shoreline today, but several access areas are open to the public for swimming and boating.

From Greenwood Lake, Route 17A climbs over Sterling Mountain to the east, winding through a 19,000-acre state park that is the site of a small ski resort and the annual Renaissance Faire before meeting up with Route 17 and the New York Thruway at the town of Tuxedo.

Fifties-era billboards and diners like the battered Red Apple Rest line this stretch of Route 17. During the peak of the summer resorts, traffic leaving New York City poured through town en route to the western Catskills. Look for the entrance to **Harriman State Park** (Rte. 9W, Bear Mountain, 845/786-2701, http://ny sparks.state.ny.us/parks/info.asp?parkID=143; admission $7) on the east side of the highway.

A much larger neighbor to Bear Mountain State Park at the Rockland County line, Harriman boasts the oldest stretch of the Appalachian Trail, which was cleared in 1923 (see the *Lower Hudson* chapter).

Warwick

In the opposite direction from Sterling Mountain on 17A—just minutes from the New Jersey state line—lies Warwick, one of the most charming Victorian villages in Orange County. A handful of art galleries, antique shops, and gourmet restaurants line Main Street in a scaled-down but convincing imitation of New York City's SoHo district. The fun begins at **Port of Call** (40 Main St., 845/986-9500, www.portofcall.net; 10 A.M.–6 P.M. Mon.–Thurs., 10 A.M.–7 P.M. Fri.–Sat., 11 A.M.–5 P.M. Sun.), a 3,500-square-foot gallery that represents fine art, photography, and sculpture from local, national, and international artists.

From May through December, the surrounding farmland produces a constant supply of freshly harvested treats: vegetables and berries in summer; pears, apples, and pumpkins in fall; evergreen Christmas trees in winter. Not surprisingly, the town features one of the best farmers markets around. Nightlife is lively, especially in summer when several local cafés and galleries offer live music. Parking will challenge even the most seasoned urbanites on weekends.

Black Dirt Region

The township of Warwick encompasses much of the 14,000-acre Black Dirt Region, an agricultural anomaly formed by glacial activity some 12,000 years ago. Polish and German immigrants cleared fields in present-day Pine Island and Florida by hand in the 1880s and discovered that the soil was well suited to growing onions. The region still produces about a quarter of all the onions consumed in the United States. During the August harvest season, the sweet aroma seeps into the car the moment you enter the region.

© NIKKI GOTH ITOI

Black Dirt Region, near Pine Island

To reach the Black Dirt Region from Warwick, follow the Pine Island Turnpike (Route 1B) west to Pine Island, or Route 17A north to Florida.

Monroe

Back on Route 17, schoolchildren have been visiting the historic **Museum Village of Old Smith's Clove** (1010 Rte. 17M, 845/782-8247, www.museumvillage.org) in Monroe since the 1940s to learn about the wonders of colonial life, such as making wagons and candles. Walk from the red barn to the firehouse, weaver, and blacksmith in the shade of stately sugar maples. The museum is located behind a park-and-ride lot off Exit 129. Turns are well marked from the exit ramp. The museum is open April–June and September–November. Self-guided tours are $3, and tours led by costumed interpreters are $5.

Farther west, off Route 17M, is the craft village of **Sugar Loaf** (845/469-9181, www.sugarloafartsvillage.com; 11 A.M.–5 P.M. Wed.–Sun.), a collection of boutique shops selling handmade goods including ceramics, clothes, and soaps.

Harness racing fans head to Goshen for a tour of the sport's hall of fame. Housed in a 1913 Tudor stable, the **Harness Racing Museum & Hall of Fame** (240 Main St., Goshen, 845/294-6330, www.harnessmuseum .com; 10 A.M.–5 P.M. daily; admission varies each year) contains an extensive collection of Currier & Ives trotting prints, as well as photographs, trophies, and memorabilia. Interactive exhibits include a 3-D simulator and theaters.

WESTERN ORANGE COUNTY–I-84 TO THE DELAWARE RIVER

From the intersection with Route 17, I-84 heads southwest toward Middletown and Port Jervis at the southern end of the Shawangunk Mountains. The Neversink and Delaware Rivers meet here, a stone's throw from both New Jersey and Pennsylvania.

A one-time hub for road, rail, and canal transportation, Port Jervis was named for John Bloomfield Jervis, an engineer who built the D&H Canal and Croton Aqueduct. Although the name suggests a major shipping port, the river is better suited to canoes than freighters. Today, a population of 10,000 supports several small to midsized industrial businesses, and Port Jervis serves as a gateway to the Upper Delaware River in Sullivan and Delaware Counties. Beginning in the town of Sparrowbush, about five miles outside of Port Jervis, Route 97 twists and turns and climbs over the **Hawk's Nest** to present breathtaking views of New York, Pennsylvania, and the Delaware River in between. At a height of 150 feet above the river, the road has several lookouts, called bay windows, that were built into the original design. BMW, Saab, Honda, and other car companies have filmed commercials along this stretch of winding road.

SPORTS AND RECREATION

Although more developed than the Upper Hudson Valley, Orange County has preserved a number of open spaces that are ideal for a surprising variety of mountain and aquatic adventures.

Winter Sports

Orange County enjoys a mild climate compared to other parts of the Hudson Valley, receiving only a foot of snow on average each winter. But the Hudson Highlands and Ramapo Mountains create ideal terrain for beginner skiers, and several local ski areas offer weekend and evening entertainment for families. One of the four chairlifts at the **Sterling Forest Ski Area** (16 Sterling Lake Rd., Tuxedo, 845/351-2151, www.sterlingforest.com; 10 A.M.–5 P.M. Mon.–Fri., 9 A.M.–5 P.M. Sat.–Sun. Jan.–Feb., night skiing and riding till 10 P.M.; adults $39, juniors $29) crosses right over Route 17A. To the west of Greenwood Lake, also on Route 17A, is the smaller **Mount Peter Ski Area** (Rte. 17A, Warwick, 845/986-4940, www.mtpeter.com; adults $33, juniors $29), with three lifts.

Hiking

Backpackers can follow the **Appalachian Trail** from the New Jersey state line at Greenwood Lake (Orange County) across the Bear Mountain Bridge to the Dutchess County line near Kent (Putnam County). Along the way is the oldest section of the AT, completed in 1923 in Harriman State Park. Moderate elevation changes provide valley and lake views.

In the western part of Sterling Forest above Greenwood Lake, the 5.3-mile Sterling Ridge Trail leads to views of Sterling Lake and the Sterling Fire Tower, while the four-mile Indian Loop Trail, an offshoot of the AT, climbs to views of Route 17 and the surrounding valley.

Birdwatchers have several good choices to explore in Orange County: The **Bashakill Wildlife Management Area** (Rte. 209 South, Wurtsboro, 845/754-0743,) is a bird sanctuary on 2,000 acres of state-owned wetlands, forests, fields, and abandoned orchards. And the **Eagle Institute** (Barryville, 845/557-6162, www.eagleinstitute.org) conservation group offers guided tours of bald eagle habitats along the Delaware and Hudson Rivers. The Orange County Audubon Society maintains another

62-acre sanctuary near the Heritage Trail, **6 1/2 Station Road Sanctuary** (6 ½ Station Rd., Goshen, 845/744-6047).

Cycling

On the access road to Museum Village is a treasure of a bikeway, the 15-mile Heritage Trail, which follows the bed of the old Erie Railroad, connecting Monroe to Goshen. You can rent bikes (or snowshoes in winter) at **Bryan's Bikes** (240 Main St., Cornwall, 845/534-5230).

Golf

A round of golf at the **Mansion Ridge Golf Club** (1292 Orange Turnpike, Monroe, 845/782-7888, www.mansionridgegc.com/golf.cfm; $80–124) begins in the stone barn clubhouse and meanders through forest and across hills, with incredible views of the countryside. The championship course is the only Jack Nicklaus Signature Design course in New York State that's open to the public. Another good option is the **Central Valley Golf Club** (206 Smith Clove Rd., Central Valley, 845/928-6924, www.centralvalleygolfclub.com; dawn-dusk daily Apr.–Nov.; $26–36), where golfers play with the Ramapo Mountains as a scenic backdrop.

In western Orange County, head to **Eddy Farm Golf Course** (Rtes. 42 & 97, Sparrowbush, 800/336-5050; 7 A.M.–8 P.M. daily Mar.–Nov.; $18), an 18-hole course featuring spectacular views of both the Catskill Mountains and Delaware River. The entrance is conveniently located five miles from I-84 near Port Jervis.

Swimming and Boating

Orange County offers easy access to a host of aquatic activities. On the Delaware River, **Silver Canoe Raft Rentals** (37 South Maple Ave., Port Jervis, 800/724-8342, www.silvercanoe.com; 8 A.M.–7 P.M. daily Apr.–Sept.; $31–38) has canoes and kayaks for rent. Rates include transport and pickup. (See *Sullivan County* in *The Western Catskills* chapter for additional canoe and kayak outfitters in the area.)

THE HUDSON HIGHLANDS

APPALACHIAN TRAIL

CONNECTICUT
NEW YORK

East Branch Res

Titicus Reservoir

Cross River Reservoir

Ward Pound Ridge Res

West Branch Res

Anawalk Res

New Croton Reservoir

TACONIC STATE PKWY

Clarence Fahnestock Memorial State Park

Blue Mtn Res

Hudson River

Beacon

Cold Spring

NY STATE MILITARY RES, CAMP SMITH

Bear Mtn State Park

Stony Point

PALISADES INTERSTATE PKWY

Newburgh

WEST POINT MILITARY RESERVATION

Harriman State Park

NEW YORK THRUWAY

Goose Pond Mtn SP

Appalachian Trail

Greenwood Lake

Sterling Forest State Park

Highland Lakes SP

Goshen

Middletown

4 mi

4 km

N Y
N J

© AVALON TRAVEL

Adventurous scuba divers may consider an eddy dive in the Delaware River. Visibility is generally poor, but the sensation of drifting in a circle is something you won't experience when diving in the tropics.

Sailing and waterskiing are summer pastimes on Greenwood Lake. There are four marinas on the lake, and you can rent powerboats and personal watercraft at Long Pond Marina. A new public beach opened in 2004 on Windermere Avenue on the east shore. The **Greenwood Lake Triathlon** (www.american memorialtriathlon.com), held each year in mid-September, has become a popular race, drawing athletes from across the state.

Several marinas along the Hudson have boat ramps and services: **Highland Falls Marina** (72 Station Hill, Highland Falls, 845/446-2402; 9 A.M.–9 P.M. daily May–Oct.), within walking distance to West Point, has 44 slips and five moorings. In Newburgh, **Front Street Marina** (26 Front St., Newburgh, 845/661-4914, www .frontstreetmarina.com) puts you at the doorstep of all the new restaurants and shops on the Newburgh waterfront. This is a state-of-the-art marina with all the amenities, including an ATM, but no fuel.

River Cruises

Pride of the Hudson (845/220-2120) offers river cruises from Newburgh Landing. Boats depart on Thursday afternoons, Saturday afternoons and evenings, and Sunday evenings (adults $17) A two-hour Bannerman Island lecture cruise costs $18.

Fishing and Hunting

Largemouth bass, chain pickerel, and panfish are the most popular catches in Orange County's lakes and ponds. The **Bait Bucket** (313 Rte. 211 West, Middletown, 845/361-4774; 6 A.M.–7 P.M. daily) sells bait, equipment, and licenses and will happily point you to the best access points. **O&H Bait Shop** (48 Main St., Chester, 845/469-2566; 6 A.M.–6 P.M. daily) is another option for fishing supplies.

For a guided trip on the Delaware, contact **Reel 'Em In Guide Service** (13 Fall St., Port Jervis, 845/856-3009; reservations required) to book a half-day trip for one or two people on a custom-made driftboat. Ice-fishing trips are an option in January and February.

To stock up on gear, visit the newest and largest branch of **Gander Mountain** (Crystal Run Plaza, 100 N. Galleria Dr., Middletown, 845/692-5600; 9 A.M.–9 P.M. Mon.–Fri., 9 A.M.–10 P.M. Sat., 10 A.M.–7 P.M. Sun.), a sprawling destination store for gear-hungry outdoors lovers.

Aviation

For a romantic morning adventure, take a hot air balloon flight with **Above the Clouds** (Middletown, 845/692-2556, www.abovethe cloudsinc.com/BalloonRidesNewYork.htm; May–Oct., reservations required). Flights with **Fantasy Balloon Flights** (Middletown, 845/856-7103, www.fantasyfliers.com) depart from Randall Airport and include a glass of champagne. Private pilots can rent planes at **Freedom Air** (550 Dunn Lane, Montgomery, 845/457-3595; 9 A.M.–5 P.M. daily).

Horseback Riding

Horseback riding and lessons are available at the 230-acre **Borderland Farm** (340 South Rte. 94, Warwick, 845/986-1704, www.wolfs bane.com/borderland) or **Celtic Pines Farms** (135 Crawford St., Pine Bush, 845/361-3076), which also has a B&B on the premises. **Juckas Stables** (Rtes. 302 & 17, Bullville, 845/361-1429, www.juckasstables.com) has 117 acres of trails and English and Western riding lessons. Camping is available.

ACCOMMODATIONS

The best places to stay in Orange County are clustered near Greenwood Lake and Warwick, and along the river between West Point and Cornwall. Small bed-and-breakfast inns are by far the most common, with an assortment of chain hotels located along I-84.

$100-150

Four-poster or sleigh beds, fresh flowers, and bathrobes are among the special touches at **€ The Inn at Stony Creek** (34 Spank-town Rd., Warwick, 845/986-3660, www.inn stonycreek.com; $115–135). Canopy beds and working fireplaces set an elegant mood at the meticulously restored **€ Peach Grove Inn** (205 Rte. 17A, Warwick, 845/986-7411, www .peachgroveinn.net; $130–225). Its six rooms occupy a stately 1850 Greek Revival building tastefully furnished with 19th-century antiques throughout. The two downstairs rooms have whirlpool tubs and televisions. The back porch looks out over the original 285-acre property.

The **New Continental Hotel** (15 Leo Court, Greenwood Lake, 845/477-2456, www.new continentalhotel.com; $85–140) is a comfortable and affordable lakeside option. Its rooms have tiled private baths and lake views. Twin and double beds are available.

$150-200

Storm King Lodge (100 Pleasant Hill Rd., Mountainville, 845/534-9421, www.storm kinglodge.com; $150–175) offers four cozy rooms in a 19th-century lodge near Storm King Mountain. The Lavender and Pine rooms have fireplaces. Call ahead to schedule a massage appointment during your stay.

A piano room, library, and outdoor hot tub set the mood at the **The Glenwood House** (49 Glenwood Rd., Pine Island, 845/258-5066, www.glenwoodbb.com; $110–295). Its five comfortable rooms, with modern whirlpool baths, are set in an 1855 Victorian farmhouse.

West Point's **Thayer Hotel** (674 Thayer Rd., West Point, 845/446-4731, www.thethayer hotel.com; $175) has 151 modern but cozy rooms decorated in 19th-century Americana style. Guest rooms and suites inside the imposing granite building offer campus, river, or mountain views. Amenities include cable TV, high-speed Internet access, and a fitness center.

Over $200

A stay at the ultraromantic **€ Cromwell Manor** (174 Angola Rd., Cornwall, 845/534-7136, www.cromwellmanor.com; $165–370) includes a gourmet breakfast and afternoon tea. Its 1764 cottage delights with a collection of antiques.

Internet access is a plus for travelers who need to stay in touch with the real world.

Campgrounds

Oakland Valley Campground (399 Oakland Valley Rd., Cuddebackville, 845/754-8732 or 800/832-2254; May–Oct.; $25–40) has large wooded sites for tents, trailers, and motor homes. Amenities include water and electric hookups, flush toilets, firewood, cable TV, swimming pool, and free hot showers. **Otisville Campground** (298 Grange Rd., Otisville, 845/386-5104; open year-round) has tent sites next to a small pond, with wooded trails, telephone hookups, hot showers, and a laundry.

FOOD
Along the River – Route 9W

Centrally located **Painter's** (266 Hudson St., Cornwall-on-Hudson, 845/534-2109, www .painters-restaurant.com; lunch 11:30 A.M.–4 P.M. Mon.–Sat., dinner until 10 P.M. Sun.–Thurs., until 10:30 P.M. Fri.–Sat., brunch 10:30 A.M.–3 P.M. Sun.; mains $10–25) is a favorite eatery for summer dining from a menu with a mix of American, Mexican, Japanese, and Italian entrées. Save room for dessert. At West Point, the buffet-style champagne brunch in the Thayer Hotel is a memorable experience for a special occasion (10 A.M.–2 P.M. Sun.).

In Newburgh, early risers head to **Hudson Valley Coffee Roasters** (639 Broadway, Newburgh, 888/822-6333, www.hudsonvalley roasters.com) in an old factory on Broadway for a brew with more character than any Starbucks blend. Also on Broadway, enjoy the famous hot dogs at **Newburgh Lunch** (348 Broadway, Newburgh, 845/562-9660), but the chef will turn you down if you dare ask for the recipe.

A trio of related Italian restaurants serve Tuscan specialties in the Newburgh area: **Cena 2000** (50 Front St., Newburgh, 845/561-7676, www.cena2000.com; lunch noon–3 P.M. daily, dinner 5–10 P.M. Mon.–Thurs., 5–11 P.M. Fri.–Sat., 5–9 P.M. Sun.; mains $13–18) offers river views to match the cuisine. Neighboring **Café Pitti** (40 Front St., Newburgh,

WE ALL SCREAM FOR ICE CREAM

© NIKKI GOTH ITOI

the best ice cream in Orange County

Frozen summer treats are a competitive business throughout the Hudson Valley, ranging from soft-serve stands to family-run creameries. These top four stand apart from the crowd:

- Bellvale Farms Creamery, between Warwick and Greenwood Lake

- Happy Clown, near Hudson

- Heinchon's Old Farmhouse, Pawling

- Mabbettsville Creamery, between Millbrook and Amenia

picture windows facing the Hudson. And just when you think you've reached the end of the road at Newburgh Landing, you reach a large dirt parking lot and **Gully's** (2 Washington St., Newburgh, 845/565-0077; 11:30 A.M.–10 P.M. daily; mains $10–27), a two-story bar and restaurant on an old barge. The atmosphere is super casual, and the floor slopes with the tide. This is the place to order a bowl of steamers or a plate of surf and turf. On weekend nights, the upstairs bar stays open until the wee hours of the morning.

Central Orange County – Along Route 17

Locals pile in at **(Ye Jolly Onion** (Rte. 517, Pine Island, 845/258-4277, www.yejolly onioninn.com; 5–9 P.M. Wed.–Thurs., till 10 P.M. Fri.–Sat., noon–7:30 P.M. Sun.; mains $25–30), a Pine Island tradition, to sample a variety of dishes made from the local bounty. Vegetarians can enjoy the healthy fare at **Pure City Restaurant** (100 Main St., Pine Bush, 845/744-8888; 11 A.M.–10 P.M. Mon.–Thurs. and Sun., 11 A.M.–11 P.M. Fri.–Sat.; mains $6–13).

New restaurants are opening at a fast clip in the Warwick area. But **The Landmark Inn** (Rte. 94, North Warwick, 845/986-5444; dinner Tues.–Sun., lunch Tues.–Sat.; mains $18–24) remains a local favorite for casual American cuisine and evening cocktails. Out-of-towners head to the fancier **Chateau Hathorn** (33 Hathorn Rd., Warwick, 845/986-6099; 5–9 P.M. Wed.–Sat., 3–7 P.M. Sun.; mains $20–32) for French cuisine in an 18th-century mansion. **Ten Railroad Avenue** (10 Railroad Ave., Warwick, 845/986-1509; 11:30 A.M.–2:30 P.M. and 5–10 P.M. Wed.–Mon.; mains $7–12) serves a blend of Spanish and Italian cuisine and occasionally hosts live music performances. For another taste of Europe, visit neighboring **La Petite Cuisine** (20 Railroad Ave., Warwick, 845/988-0988; 10 A.M.–4 P.M. Tues.–Sat., 9 A.M.–4 P.M. Sun.).

At Greenwood Lake, the most popular choices for lakeside dining are **Emerald Point** (40 Sterling Rd., Greenwood Lake,

845/565-1444; 10:30 A.M.–9 P.M. daily; mains $9–12) serves antipasti, panini, and pizzettes under a bright yellow awning. And the upscale **(Il Cenâcolo** (228 S. Plank Rd., Newburgh, 845/564-4494) gets high marks for its ever-changing antipasti platters.

River Grill (40 Front St., Newburgh, 845/561-9444, www.therivergrill.com; lunch 11:30 A.M.–3 P.M. Mon.–Fri., noon–3 P.M. Sat., noon–2 P.M. Sun., dinner 5–9 P.M. Mon.–Thurs., 5–10 P.M. Fri.–Sat., 3:30–9 P.M. Sun.; mains $22–27) offers surf and turf, including a seafood paella special, in a dining room with

845/477-2275; noon–10 P.M. Mon.–Thurs., noon–11 P.M. Fri.–Sat., noon–9 P.M. Sun.; mains $15–24) and the **Breezy Point Inn** (620 Jersey Ave., Greenwood Lake, 845/477-8100, www.breezypointinn.com; lunch and dinner daily; mains $15–25), with a raw bar and German-influenced menu.

On the drive between Warwick and Greenwood Lake, don't miss the homemade ice cream and valley views at the hilltop ◖ **Bellvale Farms Creamery** (385 Rte. 17A, 845/988-1818, www.bellvalefarms.com).

ENTERTAINMENT AND EVENTS
Performing Arts
West Point's **Eisenhower Hall Theatre** (Eisenhower Hall Theatre Box Office, Bldg. 655, West Point, 845/938-4159, www.eisenhowerhall.com) is a top-notch venue for a range of performances, from *The Full Monty* musical to the Vienna Boys' Choir around the holidays.

Bars and Nightlife
These days, Newburgh Landing gets high marks for a lively—and sometimes downright

Tiki Bar at Blue Martini, Newburgh Landing

rowdy—nightlife. **Blue Martini** (50 Front ⌣⌣ Newburgh, 845/562-7111, 11:30 A.M.–10 P.M. daily) prepares more than 20 variations on the theme, with happy hour specials. The **Tiki Bar** has a fake red palm tree waving overhead.

For a more mellow scene, Warwick locals gather at the bar inside the **Landmark Inn.** Keep an eye out for live music performances at Warwick's wineries and cafés. **Applewood Winery** (82 Four Corners Rd., Warwick, 845/988-9292, www.applewoodorchards andwinery.com; 11 A.M.–5 P.M. Sat.–Sun.) produces chardonnay, cabernet franc, and hard cider. And **Warwick Valley Winery & Distillery** (114 Little York Rd., Warwick, 845/258-4858, www.wvwinery.com; 11 A.M.–6 P.M. daily) makes riesling and pinot noir wines, as well as apple and pear ciders and a variety of baked goods.

The family-owned, 1950s-era **Warwick Drive-In Theater** (Rte. 94, 845/986-4440; adults $7.50) is also packed on summer nights.

Festivals
Nothing quite tops the spirited rivalry of an Army vs. Navy football game at West Point. West Point Football Saturdays take place at Michie Stadium, with a parade, cannon salute, and cadet review to kick off the event. Ferry service is available from Tarrytown.

Cars line the sides of Route 17A over Sterling Mountain during the popular **Renaissance Faire** (Sterling Forest, Tuxedo, 845/351-5174, www.renfair.com/NY/index. php; 10 A.M.–7 P.M. Sat.–Sun. Aug.–Sept.; admission $19) each year. The **Orange County Fair** (100 Carpenter Ave., Middletown, 845/343-4826, www.orangecountyfair.com) takes place in Middletown each July.

In 2009, Newburgh will celebrate the Hudson Fulton Champlain Quadra Centennial. A committee began meeting well in advance to plan the festivities.

SHOPPING
Orange County has everything a shopper could desire, from mega-chains and discount outlets to one-of-a-kind boutiques. One of the

...nds is Sugar Loaf, a small vil-
...who craft handmade ceramics,
...her goods.

Woodbury Common Premium Outlets

Bargain hunters flock to the Woodbury Common Premium Outlets (498 Red Apple Court, Rte. 32, Central Valley, 845/928-4000, www.premiumoutlets.com; 10 A.M.–9 P.M. daily), at the edge of Harriman State Park (Exit 16 off I-87). Dozens of stores are arranged in a campuslike setting, making it less-than-ideal for rainy-day retail therapy. Look for significant discounts on name brands from Coach and Fendi to Banana Republic and Gap. Calvin Klein, Diesel, MaxStudio, and Ecco are among the newest additions to the complex. Beware, the long list of stores and often-deep discounts draw crowds on holiday weekends throughout the year. Shortline Bus offers daily service to the outlets, and several local hotels offer "shop and stay" packages.

Farm Stands

Orange County made national TV in February 2004 when the Food Network produced a Hudson Valley episode of *Food Nation with Bobby Flay,* featuring several local eateries. Among them was the **Quaker Creek Store** (757 Pulaski Highway, Goshen, 845/258-4570; 7 A.M.–7 P.M. Mon.–Fri., 7 A.M.–6 P.M. Sat.) in Pine Island, a must-try for homemade sausages and smoked meats made by a third-generation owner and CIA graduate. The family-run business has evolved from a 1940s sandwich shop to a gourmet treasure. Onion rings are made from the bounty that makes the region famous.

Chances are, you'll have to wait for a parking space at the **Warwick Valley Farmers Market** (South St. parking lot off Main St., Warwick, www.warwickinfo.net/farmers market; 9 A.M.–2 P.M. Sun. May–Oct.) Local businesses sell homemade pies and candies, as well as fresh-picked produce. The entire town of Warwick shuts down for the wildly popular **Applefest** every September.

Antiques, Galleries, and Boutiques

Main Street in Warwick has a wide range of antique dealers selling everything old, from toys to rugs to lace, as well as several contemporary boutiques. Most stores close by 6 P.M., although some stay open until 8 P.M. on Fridays.

Victorian Treasures (21 Main St., Warwick, 845/986-7616, www.victoriantreasures online.com; 10 A.M.–6 P.M. Mon.–Sat., noon–5 P.M. Sun.) specializes in Winnie-the-Pooh and other collectibles. And **The Eclectic Eye** (16-18 Railroad Ave., 845/986-5520, www.theeclecticeye.com; 9:30 A.M.–5 P.M. Sun., 11 A.M.–4 P.M. Mon., 11 A.M.–5 P.M. Tues.–Wed., 11 A.M.–6 P.M. Thurs., 11 A.M.–8:30 P.M. Fri.–Sat.) has furniture, rugs, and items the owner simply calls "worthies."

One of Warwick's top boutiques is **Frazzleberries** (24 Main Street, Warwick, 845/988-5080, www.frazzleberries.com; 10 A.M.–5:30 P.M. Mon.–Fri., 11 A.M.–6 P.M. Sat., noon–5:30 P.M. Sun.), known for cute country furnishings and festive seasonal displays. At check, the store was stocked with quilted bags and smelled like apples. Another tempting store is **Newhards** (39 Main St., Warwick, 845/986-4544), which stocks upscale kitchen equipment and supplies, including pottery and cookbooks. On Railroad Avenue, **Sweetbriar's** (26 Railroad Ave., Warwick, 845/986-5700, www.sweetbriars.com) makes designer candies, chocolates, and truffles.

INFORMATION AND SERVICES

A network of 10 tourist information centers serve Orange County visitors; several of them open seasonally. The **Orange County Tourism** (124 Main St., Goshen, 845/291-2136, www.orangetourism.org; 9 A.M.–5 P.M. Mon.–Fri.) office in Goshen can provide a wealth of information before or during a visit. The **Palisades Parkway Tourist Information Center** (between Exits 16 & 17, Palisades Interstate Parkway, 845/786-5003; 8 A.M.–6 P.M. daily April–Oct., 8 A.M.–5 P.M. Nov.–March) stocks a variety of trail guides and road maps. This is also the place to pick up your New York State fishing license.

GETTING THERE AND AROUND
By Bus

Adirondack Trailways stops in Newburgh, while Shortline Bus stops include Monroe, Middletown, Newburgh, Goshen, Chester, and Central Valley. Main Line Trolley Bus offers local service to Chester, Goshen, Harriman, Middletown, Monroe, and Woodbury Common. New Jersey Transit also runs bus service to Greenwood Lake and Warwick.

By Train

The Metro-North Port Jervis Line stops in western Orange County between Port Jervis and Suffern, with connecting service to Newark International Airport in New Jersey and Penn Station in New York City. Alternatively, Beacon station along the Hudson Line is a short cab or shuttle ride across the river from Newburgh. The Newburgh Beacon Shuttle bus connects the Beacon station, downtown Newburgh, and Stewart International Airport.

By Car

In the eastern part of Orange County, Route 17, I-87, and I-84 form a triangle that encloses many of the most popular attractions in the area. More than a dozen taxi services cover Orange County, including West Point, Monroe, Warwick, and Greenwood Lake—but only two service all points in the county: All Family Taxi (845/565-1616) and ASAP TXI (845/294-7433). Car rentals are available at Stewart International Airport (Avis, Budget, Enterprise, Hertz).

By Boat

The Newburgh-Beacon Ferry (www.mta.nyc.ny.us/mnr/html/raillink/newburghferry.htm; $1) connects the cities of Newburgh and Beacon on opposite sides of the Hudson and provides convenient access to the Metro-North train station in Beacon. Although it's primarily run for commuters, travelers who want to experience both the Dia:Beacon museum (See *Dutchess County* in the *Mid-Hudson* chapter) and Newburgh Landing may find the ferry service to be a good way to avoid driving.

Putnam County

Squeezed between the large and densely populated counties of Westchester to the south and Dutchess to the north are 231 square miles of the most dramatic landscape along the Hudson. On overcast days, a dreamy mist clings to the jagged ridgeline of the Hudson Highlands, producing a landscape reminiscent of a tale from the Brothers Grimm. Just 50 miles from Manhattan and easily accessible by rail, romantic Putnam County features two Victorian-era towns along the river, two large state parks, and hundreds of miles of wilderness trails. The county's many lakes and streams provide a vital source of freshwater for the New York City reservoir system.

Putnam does not have a Hudson River crossing of its own—its borders extend from just

above the Bear Mountain Bridge to a point south of the Newburg/Beacon Bridge—however, two Metro-North rail lines make Putnam an easy day trip from New York City. The Hudson Line stops in Garrison and Cold Spring along the river, while the Harlem line stops in Brewster. From Brewster, it's about a 90-minute ride to Grand Central.

In addition to the train tracks, a 20-mile stretch of the Appalachian Trail crosses diagonally through Putnam County, from the Bear Mountain Bridge and **Hudson Highlands State Park** in the southwest to Clarence Fahnestock Memorial State Park and the Dutchess County line in the northeast.

Anthony's Nose at the Bear Mountain Bridge makes a logical starting point for a

Putnam County tour. Follow Route 9D north from Westchester County or Route 301 east from I-84.

ALONG THE RIVER—ROUTE 9D
◖ Boscobel Restoration

Two rows of apple trees frame the view of the Hudson from the entrance to Boscobel (Beautiful Wood), a restored neoclassical mansion dating back to the 19th century. Named after an English manor, the home belonged to colonial loyalist States Morris Dyckman, a contemporary of Chancellor Robert Livingston.

The building originally sat on a 250-acre farm in Montrose, about 15 miles south of its present-day location. It was nearly lost to history when the federal government sold it to a demolition contractor in the 1950s for $35. Fortunately, a group of private citizens came to the rescue and moved the building, piece by piece, to a scenic bluff in Garrison.

The structure and details of the home create a light and airy feel that is unique among the Hudson Valley's riverside mansions. On the outside, wood-carved drapery, complete with bow ties and tassels, decorates the space between columns on the 2nd-floor balcony. Inside, Dyckman furnished Boscobel with exquisite silver, china, and glassware that he purchased in London in the late 18th century.

Home to a number of cultural events throughout the year, Boscobel Restoration (Rte. 9D, Garrison, 845/265-3638, info@boscobel .org, www.boscobel.org; 9:30 A.M.–5 P.M. Wed.–Mon. Apr.–Oct., 9:30 A.M.–4 P.M. Wed.–Mon. Nov.–Dec.; adults $12, seniors $10, under 6 free, grounds only adults $7, children $5) hosts the annual Hudson Valley Shakespeare Festival. The museum runs a free shuttle from the Cold Spring Metro-North station on designated weekends. Call for exact dates. Visitors must pay an entrance fee to wander the formal gardens and the mile-long Woodland Trail, but the variety of roses (more than 150 types) and the views of West Point across the river are well worth the donation.

Directly below Boscobel, the National Audubon Society operates the **Constitution Marsh**

Wildlife Sanctuary (Rte. 9D/Indian Brook Rd., Garrison, 914/265-2601). A short but steep and rocky path leads from the parking lot to a nature center and boardwalk that spans a large section of tidal marsh—an ideal setting for birdwatchers. The center offers guided canoe trips in summer months. The parking lot off Route 9D can accommodate only eight cars at a time, so be prepared to change plans if the sign says Full.

To the east of Route 9D in Garrison, Manitoga (Place of the Great Spirit of Algonquin) and the Russel Wright Design Center are a one-of-a-kind nature retreat and residence created by nationally acclaimed designer Russel Wright. With his unique and practical designs for the home, Wright championed easier living and pioneered lifestyle marketing. Beginning in 1942, he transformed an abandoned quarry and lumberyard in Garrison into a 75-acre masterpiece of ecological design, featuring native plants, stones, and streams. Dragon Rock, his experimental home, sits on a rock ledge, surrounded by four miles of trails that connect to the Appalachian Trail. Visitors can tour the home and grounds beginning at 11 A.M. daily (Rte. 9D, Garrison, 845/424-3812, info@ russelwrightcenter.org, www.russelwrightcenter.org; 9 A.M.–5 P.M. Mon.–Fri.; adults $15, children $5).

Another place to stroll in Garrison is the **Graymoor Spiritual Life Center** (Rte. 9, Garrison, 845/424-2111, www.graymoor center.org/), the headquarters of the Franciscan Friars of the Atonement. Open to the public, the grounds offer a serene vantage for scenic river views.

◖ Cold Spring Village

The timeless village of Cold Spring lies in the shadow of Storm King Mountain, which rises 1,000 feet across the Hudson at the narrowest and deepest stretch of the river. A haven for antique-lovers, Cold Spring's Main Street is divided into upper and lower sections that slope downhill toward an inviting gazebo at the river's edge—the site of many a marriage proposal. Adjoining it is the new Foundry

Dock Park, with access to the river. Pedestrians can cross the tracks via an underpass, but drivers must take a detour to the south to reach lower Main Street and the riverfront. An easy day trip for city dwellers, Cold Spring lures hikers, shoppers, and diners by the trainful. Treasures from vintage toys to designer jewelry await within walking distance of the station. There is a new visitors center booth located directly above the station, next to the Cold Spring Depot.

Nearby, the **Putnam County Historical Society** and **Foundry School Museum** (63 Chestnut St., Cold Spring, 845/265-4010, www.pchs-fsm.org; 11 A.M.–5 P.M. Wed.–Sun.; adults $5, seniors $2, children free;) is a popular field trip for area schoolchildren. Built in 1817 when America was reeling from the War of 1812 and the realization that it needed a domestic source of iron to defend its borders, the building contains a collection of tools, letters, blueprints, and decorative ironworks, such as the ornate

Washington Irving Bench. Other highlights include a famous painting by John Ferguson Weir called *The Gun Foundry* and the Civil War–era *Parrot Gun*.

Outdoor activities are readily accessible from Cold Spring: The most popular pastimes include paddling the river and the Constitution Marsh Wildlife Preservation and hiking trails in the 4,200-acre Hudson Highlands State Park.

Hudson Highlands State Park

Extending the length of Putnam County, from Westchester to Dutchess, Hudson Highlands State Park (Rte. 9D, Beacon, 845/225-7207, http://nysparks.state.ny.us/parks/info.asp?parkID=130; dawn–dusk daily) offers 25 miles of hiking trails that meander along the ridgeline of the Hudson Highland range. Views of the river here are among the best anywhere in the region.

Birdwatchers frequent 900-foot-high Anthony's Nose at the Westchester County line to watch hawks, eagles, and vultures hover over the Bear Mountain Bridge. A route to the summit of South Beacon Mountain, six miles round-trip, brings hikers to the highest point along the range. Look for the trailhead on Route 9D, four miles north of Cold Spring. For a more challenging hike (5.5 miles round-trip), try the Breakneck Ridge Trail, which begins north of the tunnel on Route 9D, two miles north of Cold Spring. This trail covers some of the steepest terrain and most striking views in the park; however, it can be dangerous during inclement weather. Choose a different route in wet or windy conditions.

As a symbol of its commitment to preserving open space along the river, the New York State government added 240

THE HUDSON HIGHLANDS

acres to this park in 2002. Camping, camp-fires, bikes, and motorized vehicles are not per-mitted within the park. Fishing and boating is, however, permitted along the shoreline.

Bannerman's Castle

As the river widens to form Newburgh Bay, a small island appears just north of Storm King Mountain and about four miles north of West Point. At less than seven acres, the island is made mostly of rock and sits about 1,000 feet from the river's eastern shore. (Though Bannerman Island lies technically within Dutchess County, it is most often viewed from Hudson Highlands itineraries.) It played a role in colonial history, first as part of a plan to stop the British from ad-vancing north along the Hudson, and later as a designated military prison that was built but never used.

The island's most interesting story, how-ever, is connected with a Scottish American entrepreneur named Frank (Francis) Banner-man VI, who collected and sold military goods

acquired at government auctions. When he needed a place to store ammunition from the Spanish American War, Bannerman's Island Arsenal came to be.

Bannerman acquired the island formerly known as Pollopel from the state of New York in 1900 and built a Scottish-style castle, complete with crenellated towers and turrets. The fortress housed the family business until 1967, when the Bannermans sold the island back to New York State. State officials had planned to open the is-land to visitors, but a fire in 1969 severely dam-aged many of the buildings, and the island has remained off-limits ever since, making it the subject of much speculation and mystery.

Today, what remains of the castle is man-aged by the Bannerman Castle Trust (www .bannermancastle.org), which recently received a $350,000 grant to stabilize structures on the island in preparation for opening it to the pub-lic. With a new dock on the North side, the trust was just about ready to begin walking tours at press time. You can get a glimpse of the island and its abandoned castle from a river

Bannerman Island

© NIKKI GOTH ITOI

cruise or kayak tour—but paddlers, beware of strong currents around the island.

CENTRAL PUTNAM COUNTY—ALONG THE TACONIC STATE PARKWAY
Clarence Fahnestock Memorial State Park

The white sand beach at Lake Canopus in central Putnam County arrived by truck from Long Island in the late 1970s. Today, the completed waterfront complex has everything beach-goers need, save the salty air. A concession stand sells burgers and hot dogs, and there are showers, picnic tables, a boat launch, and campsites.

The beach sits within Putnam County's second state park, Clarence Fahnestock Memorial State Park (1498 Rte. 301, Carmel, 845/225-7207; sunrise–sunset daily), which covers 10,000 acres extending from a few miles east of Cold Spring to beyond the Taconic State Parkway. Several lakes and ponds are suitable for boating and fishing.

Hikes on 42 miles of wooded trails range from easy to moderately strenuous. The Three Lakes Loop is a popular route that follows the bed of an old railroad line and meets up with the Appalachian Trail at the end. Along the way, hikers meander through forest, wetlands, and dense patches of mountain laurel (3.2 or 5.9 miles, depending on shortcuts). Mountain bikers and horseback riders have access to additional trails and bridle paths. Access the park from Route 301, which connects Route 9 along the Hudson River to the Taconic State Parkway.

Also inside the park, **Taconic Outdoor Education Center** (755 Mountain Laurel Rd., Cold Spring, 845/265-3773; year-round for group use by reservation) has wildlife exhibits and runs geology, aquatic ecology, astronomy, and outdoor skills programs for groups only. Guests stay in nine heated log cabins. In winter, the center has 15 kilometers of groomed cross-country ski trails, along with equipment rentals and lessons. A little farther east on Route 301, Cannabis Lake has more trails

for cross-country skiing. It's about a two-mile drive to the center from Route 301, and the turn-off is well marked.

EASTERN PUTNAM COUNTY—ALONG I-84
Brewster

Named for a local contractor, Walter Brewster, who built a station for the Harlem Line Railroad in the 1850s, this village thrived as an early thoroughfare between New York City and Danbury, Connecticut. Today, however, the town is a mixed bag of 19th-century homes and run-down storefronts.

Unique among regional museums, Brewster's **Southeast Museum** (67 Main St., 845/279-7500, www.southeastmuseum.org; 10 A.M.–4 P.M. Tues.–Sat.; admission free) documents a number of seemingly unrelated developments—from the arrival of the early American circus and the Borden Condensed Milk factory to the engineering of the Harlem Line Railroad and the Croton Reservoir—that took place in and around the town of Southeast. Located in a historic building in downtown Brewster, the museum also displays a collection of antique farm equipment, quilts, and other Americana in rotating exhibits throughout the year.

Carmel and Mahopac

On the shores of a small lake at the intersection of Route 6 and Route 301, Carmel (CAR-mel) has been the Putnam County seat since 1812. It is home to the second-oldest courthouse in New York State, a Greek Revival structure built in 1814.

Suburban Mahopac sits on the shores of Lake Mahopac, once a large resort community. Today, local residents water ski, sail, and fish the lake during summer months. The town has two marinas for launching and servicing powerboats.

Nearby in Kent is a more unusual sight: the peaceful **Chuang Yen Monastery** (Rte. 301, Kent, 845/225-1819), a Dharma education center featuring the largest Buddha statue in the Western hemisphere. The 37-foot Buddha Vairocana towers over thousands of smaller

THE HUDSON HIGHLANDS

statues inside the Great Buddha Hall, a pago-dalike structure that was built around the giant statue in the style of the Tang Dynasty era (A.D. 618–917). The Woo-Ju Memorial Library on the premises contains 70,0000 Buddhist reference texts in many different languages. A pleasant reading room faces Seven Jewels Lake and is open to the public.

SPORTS AND RECREATION

Putnam County offers a remarkable variety of outdoor activities, given its proximity to the urban sprawl of New York City. Much of the county's land and water is protected from development by the state park system. Trails are well maintained, and rental gear and professional instruction are readily available for a range of sports, including hiking, skiing, paddling, and horseback riding.

Winter Sports

In winter, Clarence Fahnestock Memorial Park becomes a playground for Nordic skiing, snowshoeing, ice skating, ice fishing, and snowmobiling. **Thunder Ridge Ski Area** (Rte. 22, Patterson, 845/878-4100, www.thunderridgeski.com; 10 A.M.–9 P.M. Mon.–Fri., 9 A.M.–9 P.M. Sat., 9 A.M.–5 P.M. Sun.; adults $35, juniors $22) is a family-run business with easy slopes that are ideal for beginners. The mountain runs a free shuttle from the Patterson train station during the peak season.

Hiking

Both Hudson Highlands and Clarence Fahnestock state parks maintain extensive trail systems for hikers, including well-traveled stretches of the Appalachian Trail. Water found on the trails within these parks is not safe to drink. Bring your own. Except for the designated camping area at Lake Canapus, camping and campfires are not permitted with the parks.

The **Putnam Trailway** follows the route of the old New York Central Railroad, connecting Mahopac to Carmel and Brewster. From 1881 until 1958, the Old Put ushered passengers

sailing near Cold Spring

THE AMATEUR GEOLOGIST

Unless you are a professional geologist, it's hard to imagine that a good part of the Hudson River Valley was once a tropical sea. Over the course of hundreds of millions of years, a continual process of uplift and erosion – and four different ice ages – shaped the mountains and rivers we know today. As a result, geological sites abound along highways, in state parks, and on mountaintops across the region, offering insight for both professional and amateur scientists into the natural forces that have defined the topography over time.

WHERE TO GO
Hudson Highlands

Head first to Harriman State Park in search of rocky exposures along trails in the western part of the park. You can reach the trails directly from the Metro North station in Tuxedo. Plan for several hours of hiking to reach the best views and geologic sites.

Nearby, swing through Bear Mountain State Park to view examples of resilient Storm King Granite. Then cross the Bear Mountain Bridge to view the roadcuts along Route 9D near Anthony's Nose.

Upper Hudson

Start with the road cuts along Route 23 between the towns of Leeds and Cairo in Greene County (New York State Thruway Exit 21) – a popular destination for college fieldtrips. Continue northwest to Kaaterskill Falls on Route 23A to get an idea of the power of water erosion. In the Albany area, the "Indian Ladder" is a striking 80-foot-high limestone cliff inside John Boyd Thacher State Park.

WHAT TO LOOK FOR

In the Hudson Highlands, you'll encounter glacier-scoured exposures of bedrock, granite gneiss (combinations of sandstone and shale) cut by small veins of quartz, and abandoned iron mines. In the Catskills, look for fossils of ferns, root systems, and marine life, as well as ripple marks in shale layers.

WHERE TO LEARN MORE

The U.S. Geological Survey (USGS) has published a thorough guide to New York geological sites online, as well as an overview of geological fundamentals at http://3dparks.wr.usgs .gov. In addition, see local geologist Robert Titus's *The Catskills: A Geological Guide* (Fleischmann's, NY: Purple Mountain Press, 1998).

THE HUDSON HIGHLANDS

between the Bronx and Brewster. Today, the tracks are a paved bike- and footpath. Many sections are still under construction.

Cycling

Putnam's annual **Tour de Putnam Cycling & Mountain Biking Festival** (845/225-0381, www.visitputnam.org/activities/tourdeputnam .html) takes place in late August. The races (15–100 miles) start and finish in Kent, covering miles of Putnam's pretty countryside.

Golf

Golfers can choose from four public golf courses in Garrison, Mahopac, and Carmel. The **Highlands Golf Club** (Rte. 9D, Garrison, 845/424-3727; Mon.–Fri.; $17) has river views.

Swimming and Boating

Putnam County offers aquatic activities on the Hudson and in several natural lakes located in its two state parks. For a sandy beach, head to Lake Canopus in Clarence Fahnestock State Park.

Hudson Valley Outfitters (63 Main St., Cold Spring, 845/265-0221, www.hudsonvalley outfitters.com; 11 A.M.–5 P.M. Mon.–Wed., 11 A.M.–6 P.M. Thurs.–Fri., 6 P.M. Sat., 9 A.M.–5 P.M. Sun.) runs beginner- to advanced-level kayak trips on the Hudson to Constitution Marsh, Bannerman Castle, and overnight destinations, as well guided hikes through the Hudson Highlands. The Constitution Marsh Wildlife Preserve offers guided canoe trips in summer months.

Another great place for paddlers to explore

is **The Great Swamp** (Patterson), which covers more than 6,000 acres of wetlands in Dutchess and Putnam counties. Wildlife sightings include 185 species of birds, turtles, beaver dams, and otters. Most of the land is privately owned and in danger of being developed over time; however, local and national environmental organizations are working to raise awareness of the sensitive habitat and the important role it plays in the New York City watershed. The Appalachian Trail traverses the swamp in Dutchess County near Pawling; paddlers can launch at Green Chimney's School (Doansburg Rd., at the Southeast/Patterson town line, 845/279-2995). Another, more challenging option is the Patterson Environmental Park (South St., Patterson, 845/878-6500).

Fishing and Hunting

Anglers head to the lakes to catch bass, perch, pickerel, and trout. Stillwater Lake in Fahnestock State Park is stocked with rainbow and brook trout each spring. Brown trout are common in the streams that feed the New York City Watershed. Thirteen miles of water are open to the public, and the season typically runs April 1–September 30. Regulations vary by location and are more protective in Putnam County than elsewhere in New York State. In designated areas, size limits may be higher, daily limits may be lower, and artificial lures may be required. Bow hunting for deer and wild turkey hunting are permitted in both states parks during limited seasons.

Horseback Riding

There are bridle paths in Clarence Fahnestock Memorial State Park, and **Hollow Brook Riding Academy** (890 Peekskill Hollow Rd., Putnam Valley, 845/526-8357, www.hollow brookriding.com) offers lessons to new and experienced riders.

ACCOMMODATIONS

Putnam County accommodations range from historic inns along the river to budget motels and chains closer to the interstate.

$150-250

At the bottom of Cold Spring's Main Street, the 1832 **Hudson House River Inn** (2 Main St., Cold Spring, 845/265-9355, www.hudsonhouse inn.com; $155–225) has 11 well-appointed guest rooms with private baths, television, and breakfast included. Some rooms have balconies with views of the Hudson River.

Formerly the home of a Marquise, the timeless **Plumbush Inn** (1656 Rte. 9D, Cold Spring, 845/265-3904, www.plumbushinn.net; $165–185) has several stylish rooms and an adjoining gourmet restaurant. This 1867 Victorian is showing its age on the outside, but the interior country decor is still cozy and inviting.

The lobby of the three-story **(** **Pig Hill Inn B&B** (73 Main St., Cold Spring, 845/265-9247, www.pighillinn.com; $150–250) doubles as an antique shop, and just about everything you see is for sale. All nine rooms are individually appointed in Victorian decor and now have private baths—some with marble tile and basins; several have poster beds, Jacuzzi tubs, and fireplaces or tiny woodstoves. A CIA grad serves breakfasts like brie waffles with poached pear sauce in a lovely atrium in the back of the inn.

A few doors downhill from the Pig Hill is a newer, small bed-and-breakfast, **Kittleman House** (45 Main St., Cold Spring, 845/265-3697, kittlemanhouse@aol.com; $175–195). Owner Kathleen Kittleman has relocated her successful Albany bed-and-breakfast to the 18th century Cold Spring home where she raised her own family and opened for business in May 2007. Three newly renovated and spacious guest rooms have a bright and cheery feel, with French colors and accents. Guests choose from a menu of three breakfast dishes each day, and Kathleen prepares wine and cheese at 5 P.M. daily.

Garrison's romantic **Bird and Bottle Inn** (1123 Old Albany Post Rd., Garrison, 845/ 424-2333 or 800/782-6837, www.thebird andbottleinn.com) began as a restaurant in a 1761 farmhouse and then expanded into a four-room inn as well. Fireplaces, four-poster beds, and antique furnishings set the mood.

Campgrounds

The best place to pitch a tent in Putnam County is the shores of Lake Canopus in Clarence Fahnestock Memorial State Park (1498 Rte. 301, Carmel, 845/225-7207).

FOOD

Putnam County restaurants excel in blending farm-fresh ingredients with international cuisine to please the cosmopolitan palette.

Along the River—Route 9D

Kick off a day of antiquing with a fresh-baked scone at the **Foundry Café** (55 Main St., Cold Spring, 845/265-4504; mains $5–10). Continuing down Main, **Cathryn's Tuscan Grill** (91 Main St., Cold Spring, 845/265-5582, www.tuscangrill.com; lunch noon–5 P.M., dinner 5–10:30 P.M. daily, Sun. brunch noon–3 P.M.; lunch mains $10–18, dinner mains $15–25) is another longtime favorite for an upscale Italian lunch or dinner. **Brasserie Le Bouchon** (76 Main St., Cold Spring, 845/265-7676; noon–10 P.M. daily; mains $15–25) is a popular bistro with garden seating in warm weather.

The **Cold Spring Depot** (1 Main St., Depot Square, Cold Spring, 845/265-5000, www. coldspringdepot.com; 11 A.M.–10 P.M. daily; mains $13–22), at the foot of Main, draws a crowd for its patio seating and separate clam bar. A Dixieland band plays live music on weekends. Tucked away on a side street by the depot is a small gray building that houses **Perry's Ice Cream,** a real find on a hot summer day.

The **Cold Spring Café** (129 Main St., Cold Spring, 845/265-9471; 8 A.M.–4 P.M. daily; mains $5–10) doubles as an art gallery. Located toward the upper end of Main Street in Cold Spring, the cafe has a cheery country feel inside, with a low ceiling, pine floors, white wainscoting, and sage green table clothes. Admire the art on display or the pansies growing in window boxes while you wait for you breakfast or lunch. Choose from staples like a classic chef's salad, piled high with julienned chicken and ham, two kinds of cheese, crisp lettuce and cucumbers, plus an assortment of vegetables. There are eight tables in the main dining room, plus a few in a smaller back room.

A short walk from Main Street, **Riverview** (45 Fair St., Cold Spring, 845/265-4778, www.riverdining.com; lunch and dinner Tues.–Sun.; mains $15–22, cash only) features an

THE HUDSON HIGHLANDS

© NIKKI GOTH ITOI

Riverview Restaurant, Cold Spring

enclosed terrace that offers views of the Hudson and a simple Italian menu, including a variety of individual pizzas. In business since 1941, the restaurant is located next to a large municipal lot for easy parking.

During the summer Shakespeare festival at Boscobel, the **Plumbush Inn** (1656 Rte. 9D, Cold Spring, 845/265-3904, www.plumbush inn.net; lunch and dinner daily; mains $22–29) is popular with theatergoers. The inn is known for its Continental menu, outstanding desserts, and formal and attentive service. Enjoy two intimate dining rooms with fireplaces in winter or a table on the porch in summer. Reservations are required.

Hudson House River Inn (2 Main St., Cold Spring, 845/265-9355, www.hudsonhouseinn .com; lunch 11:30 A.M.–3:30 P.M. Fri.–Sat., 11 A.M.–3 P.M. Sun., dinner 5–9 P.M. Mon., Wed., Thurs., Sun., 5–10 P.M. Fri.–Sat.; mains $22–30) is the place for an old-world dining experience. Executive chef Lukas E. Wagner hails from the Culinary Institute and serves a varied menu, from jambalaya pasta to New Zealand rack of lamb. The restaurant is affiliated with two Dutchess County eateries: Hudson's Ribs & Fish and Union House, both in Fishkill. A prix fixe Sunday brunch begins with a bloody Mary or mimosa and costs $23.

Another CIA-trained chef reigns at **Valley Restaurant at The Garrison** (2015 Rte. 9 at Snake Hill Rd., Garrison, 845/424-3604, www .thegarrison.com; April–Nov. Fri.–Sat.; mains $20–30), a golf and spa resort nestled among the Hudson Highlands. The American and Continental menu at the **Bird & Bottle Inn** (1123 Old Albany Post Rd., Garrison, 845/424-2333 or 800/782-6837, www.thebirdandbottleinn .com; brunch 11:30 A.M.–3 P.M. Sat.–Sun., dinner 6–10 P.M. Thurs.–Sat., and 4–8 P.M. Sun.) has been a Garrison mainstay for years.

The best margaritas around are to be found at **Guadalajara** (2 Union St., Briarcliff Manor, 914/944-4380, guadalajara@mxr.com; 11:30 A.M.–10 P.M. Mon.–Thurs., till 11 P.M. weekends; mains $13–22) in a mustard-yellow stucco building. Tile floors and bright colors complete the ambience inside. On the menu are tempting chiles rellenos, taquitos al carbon, tostadas, and bistec. Servers prepare guacamole at the table. Enjoy live music on Fridays and Saturdays.

Eastern Putnam County– Along I-84

A relative newcomer to Putnam County's restaurant scene, **Stoneleigh Creek** (166 Stoneleigh Ave., Croton Falls, 845/276-0000, www.stoneleighcreek.com; noon–2 P.M. and 5 P.M. till close Tues.–Sun.; mains $18–28) opened in 2000 to serve the fly fishers who frequent a nearby stretch of the Croton River. Given its out-of-the-way location at the Westchester County line, this country bistro surprises first-time guests with starters of fried oysters and grilled quail, and mains that include rib eye, duck breast, and an unusual seafood cassoulet. Reservations are recommended on weekends.

You can't miss Brewster's **Red Rooster Drive-In** (Rte. 22, Brewster, 845/279-8046; daily) for burgers, fries, shakes, and ice cream. For an evening of house-cured gravlax, grilled antelope medallions, or roasted baby pheasant, head to **The Arch** (Rte. 22N, Brewster, 845/279-5011, www.archrestaurant.com; $66 prix fixe dinner, $36 brunch). For spicier fare, try **Jaipore Royal Indian Cuisine** (280 Rte. 22, Brewster, 845/277-3549, www.fineindian dining.com; noon–3 P.M. and 5–10 P.M. daily; mains $13–20), located in an 1856 mansion that was once a speakeasy. Known locally for its lunch buffet, the restaurant has several dining rooms, including an outdoor porch and patio.

Locals stop for burgers and hot dogs at **Forrest's Side Street Café** (Rte. 22, Patterson), near Pawling and the Dutchess County line, where a friendly couple serves food from a converted truck on the west side of Route 22.

ENTERTAINMENT AND EVENTS
Performing Arts

The theater event of the summer in Putnam County is the **Hudson Valley Shakespeare**

Festival (845/265-9575, www.hvshakespeare
.org). Performances take place under a tent at
Boscobel Restoration. Locals also adore the
Philipstown Depot Theatre (Lower Station
Rd., Garrison, 845/424-3900, www.philips
towndepottheatre.org) at Garrison Landing.

Festivals

Dozens of dealers participate in the **Cold
Spring Antiques Show** (97 Main St., Cold
Spring, 845/265-4414, www.coldspring
antiqueshow.com) held each June in Mayor's
Park on Fair Street.

Bars

Sports fans can view 22 TVs and a most impressive collection of memorabilia at **The Stadium**
(1308 Rte. 9, Garrison, 845/734-4000, www
.stadiumbarrest.com; 11:30 A.M.–9:30 P.M.
Sun.–Thurs., till midnight Fri.–Sat., bar stays
open till 3 A.M.). Unique treasures represent
the essential all-American pastimes: football,
baseball, basketball, and hockey, including
two Heisman trophies, Mickey Mantle's Triple
Crown award, and more. The restaurant serves
pub fare 11:30 A.M.–10 P.M., and the bar stays
open late with 16 beers on tap.

SHOPPING
Farm Stands

The Hudson Valley's orchards aren't far
away from Putnam County. Brewster (municipal parking lot at Rte. 22 & Rte. 6; Sat.
10 A.M.–2 P.M.) and Cold Spring (former
hospital lot, 845/265-3611; May–Oct. Sat.
7:30 A.M.–2 P.M.) host two of the most popular farmer's markets around.

Antiques and Galleries

Antique shoppers must head to Cold Spring
for a day of retail adventure. Several blocks
of shops line Main Street, with window displays of vintage toys, coins, jewelry, and home
furnishings. Among them, **Serious Toyz**
(82 Main St., Cold Spring, 845/265-6543
or 866/653-8699. www.serioustoyz.com;
noon–6 P.M. Thurs.–Mon.) buys and sells an
assortment of collectible toys, including tin,

**WHERE TO TAKE
THE KIDS**

- Children's Museum of Science and
  Technology, Troy

- Museum Village of Old Smith's
  Clove, Monroe

- New Windsor Cantonement, Valatie

- Old Chatham Sheepherding
  Company, Chatham

- Petrified Sea Gardens,
  Saratoga Springs

- Splashdown Water Park, Fishkill

- Stone Barns Center for Food and
  Agriculture, Pocantico Hills

- Taconic Outdoor Education Center,
  Cold Spring

- Washington's Headquarters, Newburgh

THE HUDSON HIGHLANDS

pressed steel, die cast, plastic, and character
toys. **Joseph's Fine Jewelry** (171 Main St.,
Cold Spring, 845/265-2323) handles coins and
currency, as well as antiques and jewelry. The
Cold Spring Antique Center (77 Main St.,
Cold Spring, 845/265-5050, www.coldspring
antiquecenter.com) is located just a few doors
up from the Pig Hill Inn.

The **Country Goose** (115 Main St., Cold
Spring, 845/265-2122) is the place to find a gift
for the kids. A friendly British proprietor has
everything from Ugly Dolls to Groovy Girls,
plus an assortment of candles, coffee, and other
knicknacks. She also prepares country gift bas-
kets for a loyal clientele. Most stores close by
6 P.M., with some open later on weekend evenings. Many are also closed on Tuesdays.

Mahopac's **Kitch 'n' Kaffe** (985 Rte. 6,
Mahopac, 845/621-3535, www.kitch-n-kaffe
.com; 9 A.M.–8 P.M. Mon.–Fri., 9 A.M.–6 P.M.
Sat., 10 A.M.–6 P.M. Sun.) sells high-end cooking
equipment and ingredients, in addition to offering cooking classes for home chefs. In Carmel,

watch glassmaker **John Burchetta** at work in his 100-year old barn (Burchetta Glass Studio & Gallery, 1544 Rte. 6, Carmel, 845/225-1430, www.burchetta.com; 10 A.M.–5 P.M. daily).

INFORMATION AND SERVICES

The **Putnam Visitors Bureau** (110 Old Rte. 6, Bldg. 3, Carmel, 800/470-4854, www.visit putnam.org) is headquartered in Carmel, and its website contains detailed information on major destinations and sights in the county. The **Brewster Chamber of Commerce** (31 Main St., 845/279-2477, www.brewsterchamber .com) is located near the Southeast Museum. You can also pick up maps and brochures at the new Cold Spring visitors center, located directly above the train station.

GETTING THERE AND AROUND
By Bus

Putnam Area Rapid Transit covers major towns throughout the county with five lines

(845/878-RIDE or 845/878-7433; $1.25 one-way), but the Metro-North rail lines are a more reliable way to get around. A trolley is available for transportation to Boscobel and Garrison Landing (845/878-7433). A ride costs just $.10, and you can flag the trolley down anywhere you see one. Inquire at the Cold Spring visitor booth above the train station.

By Train

Two Metro-North rail lines serve Putnam County: the Hudson Line stops in Garrison and Cold Spring along the river, while the Harlem Line runs to Brewster on its way from Grand Central Station to Dover Plains in Dutchess County. Taxis are generally available from the stations.

By Car

The easiest way to see Putnam County is by car, and the fastest routes are I-84 and the Taconic State Parkway. On busy weekend days in Cold Spring, look for free parking in a large municipal lot on Fair Street.

THE MID-HUDSON

Above the Hudson Highlands, the river widens once again, and the surrounding terrain forms rolling hills, babbling brooks, and expansive orchards. Fenced horse farms, fields of wildflowers, and ranks of wood stacked for winter heat are common pictures along the scenic back roads of these two counties. Dutchess and Ulster counties share 40 miles of coastline along this stretch of the Hudson, with three points of connection: the Newburgh-Beacon, Mid-Hudson, and Kingston-Rhinecliff Bridges. A strong focus on the arts, abundant gourmet dining opportunities, and a variety of outdoor attractions draw visitors for weekends and longer stays—and are reviving places like Beacon, Poughkeepsie, and Kingston—once-prosperous towns that had fallen into a tailspin since the decline of manufacturing along the river.

Cultural highlights in the Mid-Hudson region include the Frances Lehman Loeb Art Center at Vassar College, the Dia:Beacon museum, and the prestigious Culinary Institute of America. To complement the gourmet cuisine, a handful of wineries on both sides of the river produce award-winning chardonnay, pinot noir, merlot, and cabernet franc wines.

Several large state parks, including the southern region of the Catskill Preserve, offer leaf peepers a prime setting for viewing the spectacular display of fall colors. If you aren't afraid of heights, head to the Shawangunk Ridge in Ulster County for a day of rock climbing. And if you are inclined to stay at sea level, there are miles of country roads to explore by bicycle and numerous streams and creeks that offer prime conditions for fly-fishing.

© JASON EGLIT

HIGHLIGHTS

◖ **Dia:Beacon:** Dutchess County's newest contemporary art museum draws art aficionados out of New York City for a refreshing change of pace. Expansive single-artist galleries flooded with natural light hold paintings, sculptures, and installations from the 1960s to the present (page 100).

◖ **Vanderbilt Estate:** The 50-room home of Frederick and Louise Vanderbilt exhibits a variety of interior design influences, from renaissance to rococo. A carved wooden ceiling in the formal dining room is one of many European antiques found by designer Stanford White (page 106).

◖ **Culinary Institute of America:** Set on a picturesque riverside campus, the CIA trains aspiring professionals and enthusiasts in the

art of fine cuisine. Tour the grounds at sunset before eating in one of the five public restaurants on campus (page 107).

◖ **Rhinebeck:** Rhinebeck stands out as an upscale enclave in an otherwise rural county. Victorian, Colonial, and Greek Revival buildings line several blocks of boutique stores, country inns, and gourmet restaurants (page 107).

◖ **Huguenot Street:** Named for the French Huguenots who came to America to escape persecution, Huguenot Street in New Paltz features a block of stone dwellings now more than 300 years old (page 130).

◖ **Minnewaska State Park Preserve:** Ulster County's gem of a park covers 12,000 acres of the Shawangunk ridge with a sparkling glacial lake (page 132).

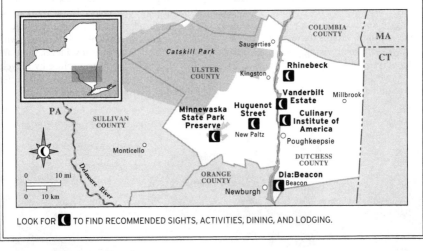

LOOK FOR ◖ TO FIND RECOMMENDED SIGHTS, ACTIVITIES, DINING, AND LODGING.

PLANNING YOUR TIME

By far the most popular destination in the region is the bustling college town of New Paltz and the surrounding countryside. You can walk the town center in a few hours, but to absorb the alternative vibe, you'll want at least a couple of days. Plan a hike or a bike ride and then enjoy a meal at one of the area's outstanding eateries. Climbers will want to spend the week.

Poughkeepsie and Kingston, the largest cities in the area, are not destinations per se; however, you won't be wasting your time if you stop to stroll or dine along their historic waterfronts. History buffs may want to make a special trip to tour the many preserved sites.

In northern Dutchess County, a 60-mile loop begins at the train station in Poughkeepsie and follows Route 44 east to Millbook, then

Route 22 n
west to th
hugs the
drive
ing

THE MID-HUDSON

© AVALON TRAVEL

rth to Millerton, and Route 199 Hudson River. From there, Route 9 riverbank back to Poughkeepsie. The nould take two to three hours, depend- on stops.

Ulster is a large county, and there are several options for scenic driving routes. One approach is to begin at the Mid-Hudson Bridge and follow Route 9D north to Kingston. Then take Route 28 west to Mount Tremper. A short loop along Route 212 heading northeast takes you through Woodstock and Saugerties and eventually back to Route 9W. Or you can continue along Route 28 to Belleayre Mountain and Delaware County beyond. Closer to Kingston, Route 209 south off Route 28 goes to New Paltz and Minnewaska State Park. Allow about half an hour to drive from New Paltz to Kingston on local roads, and an hour to cross the county from east to west.

Dutchess County

Scenic Dutchess County offers a telling mix of restored historic landmarks and nearly deserted manufacturing centers, bedroom communities, and progressive towns that attract weekenders by the thousands. A sampling of its historic riverside mansions should anchor every first-time visitor's itinerary. The county seat, Poughkeepsie, was designated the New York State capital in 1777 for about a decade. IBM set up shop in the 1950s, and despite the massive layoffs of the early 1990s, the company remains the county's dominant employer.

Poughkeepsie and Dover Plains mark the northern ends of the Metro-North commuter lines. But while the southern half of Dutchess County has succumbed to the congestion of suburban sprawl, the northern part retains an idyllic charm.

ALONG THE RIVER—ROUTE 9
◖ Dia:Beacon

A flight along the Hudson in search of a new museum space resulted in the creation of a major new cultural attraction for Dutchess County, and a positive influence on the surrounding town. Michael Govan, director of New York City–based Dia Center for the Arts, reportedly spotted the 75-year-old printing plant from the air and immediately chose the site to house the museum's permanent collection. The result is an enormous contemporary art museum, Dia:Beacon (3 Beekman St., Beacon, 845/440-0100, www.diabeacon

.org; 11 A.M.–6 P.M. Thurs.–Mon. Apr.–Oct., limited winter hours; adults $10, students $7), with constantly changing exhibits, which draw art aficionados out of New York City for a refreshing change of pace. Spacious single-artist galleries flooded with natural light hold paintings, sculptures, and installations from the 1960s to the present. Don't miss Richard Serra's *Torqued Ellipses* on the lower level. The towering pieces look especially dramatic at sunset, when they catch the light streaming in through frosted-glass windows. Outside, the West Garden presents sweeping river views.

Beacon

The Dia museum is located outside the small city of Beacon, which began to show the early signs of revival in the 1990s with the restoration of a stretch of East Main Street, now the city's antique district. Its 16,000 residents are nestled between Mount Beacon (which one can hike in under an hour), a recent extension of the Hudson Highlands State Park, and the eastern bank of the Hudson. Today, nearly the entire 1.5-mile street has been developed, from Route 9D to Wappingers Creek—with only a few older buildings remaining in the middle stretch. More than 100 artists have opened studios in town, plus there are galleries, cafes, shops, and restaurants to explore, and even an upscale pet store, Pilates studio, and boutique wine shop. Real estate prices have soared as the town builds a new profile.

BEACON

THE MID-HUDSON

© AVALON TRAVEL

One historic sight that has been maintained over the years is the 1709 **Madame Brett Homestead** (50 Van Nydeck Ave., Beacon, 845/896-6897 or 845/831-6533; tours by appointment 1–4 P.M.), another George Washington haunt and Dutchess County's oldest dwelling. Visitors can tour 17 rooms filled with antiques, artwork, and seven generations' worth of Brett family memorabilia. On the National Historic Register, the **Howland Culture Center** (477 Main St., Beacon, 845/831-4988, www.howlandculturalcenter.org) houses the Beacon Historical Society and hosts art exhibits, performances, and other events.

Farther north on Route 9D, the **Mount Gulian Historic Site** (145 Sterling St., Beacon, 845/831-8172, www.mountgulian.org; 1–5 P.M. Wed.–Sun.; adults $5, children $3) appears at the end of a row of modern townhouses. The 18th-century Dutch stone barn and 44 acres of gardens descending to the riverbank belonged to the Verplanck family and served as the headquarters of influential Revolutionary War General Friedrich Wilhelm Augustus von Steuben, a German volunteer who led the Americans to a critical victory at Freehold, New Jersey, in 1778.

Beacon has also become a hub of environmental activity, with the opening of the **Beacon Institute for Rivers and Estuaries** (199 Main St., Beacon, 845/838-1600, www.thebeaconinstitute.org), formed to study and protect rivers, estuaries, and watersheds such as the Hudson River. Folk singer Pete Seeger, owner of the Hudson River sloop *Clearwater*, lives in town, and the soon-to-be-complete **Long Dock Beacon** (Beacon Building, 427 Main St., Suite 201, Beacon, 845/831-1182, www.longdockbeacon.com), a new commercial development in progress on waterfront land owned by The Scenic Hudson Land Trust, will include a 140-room hotel, plus several restaurants, shops, and public facilities.

Fishkill and Wappingers Falls

Two miles east of Beacon, the signature steeple of the **First Reformed Church** (55 Main St., Fishkill) marks the village center of Fishkill (Fisherman's Creek), a major hub of wartime activity during the American Revolution. The church dates to 1731 and served as both a New York State government meeting place and a prison. Today, the town primarily hosts business travelers en route to IBM.

One mile south of town at the freeway interchange of I-84 and Route 9, the **Van Wyck Homestead Museum** (Rtes. 9 & I-84, Fishkill, 845/896-9560; 1–4 P.M. Sat.–Sun.) stands out among the surrounding group of chain hotels. Army officers and heads of state convened here during the American Revolution. The barracks and blacksmith shop that once surrounded the home are lost to history, but the town historical society continues to restore the inside with original documents and period furnishings. Visitors are welcome.

Stony Kill Farm Environmental Center (79 Farmstead Lane, Wappingers Falls, 845/831-8780; 8:45 A.M.–4:30 P.M. Mon.–Fri., 9:30 A.M.–4:30 P.M. Sat., 1–4 P.M. Sun.), run by the New York Department of Environmental Conservation, is a good place to stop for a picnic and a refresher in environmental science. Look for one of two entrances off Route 9D (Exit 11 from I-84). A tree-lined driveway leads to the Manor House and surrounding gardens. Inside, a visitors center houses an extensive library with titles on a wide variety of nature topics, including acid rain, wildlife management, and environmental literature.

Visit the Common Ground Farm on the property to learn about the model of community-supported agriculture (CSA). Historic buildings associated with the farm include a 19th-century barn and farmhouse and an 18th-century Dutch stone house.

Several interpretive trails, ranging from 0.5 to 2.5 miles long, lead walkers though evergreen and hardwood forests, across fields, and around ponds. Brochures for self-guided tours are available at each trailhead. The center holds special events throughout the year, including maple sugaring demonstrations, wildflower walks, and programs for children.

Poughkeepsie

Poughkeepsie has suffered the fate of postindustrial contraction worse than most. In a textbook case of urban decay, the majority of the city's middle class residents fled the city center for the suburbs during the late 20th century, leaving once-beautiful homes boarded up and constructing a six-lane arterial in their wake. When IBM slashed its workforce by two-thirds in the early 1990s, scores of small businesses went under, and the local economy never fully recovered. Though this city of 30,000 has a few historical gems, well-meaning locals continue to steer travelers north to Rhinebeck for a decent night's sleep.

That said, there are signs a long overdue recovery may be in the works: riverfront festivals—such as the Caribbean Day Parade and Festival (845/220-2227) and the Oldies & Rock 'n' Roll Festival (845/463-0409)—are drawing crowds again, and new eateries are breathing life into the city, one renovation at a time. Poughkeepsie has reopened its Main Street to car traffic to draw retail businesses back, and the old department storefronts are getting new tenants and a fresh coat of paint. The old Poughkeepsie Railroad Bridge is now a pedestrian bikeway. And the Bardavon 1869 Opera House continues to stage first-rate theater performances. With the influence of Vassar College, New York City commuters, and the Culinary Institute of America, Poughkeepsie has an appealing mix of culture and diversity. Like Newburgh to the south and Kingston to the north, its recovery hinges on making the waterfront an attractive place for residents and visitors alike.

Poughkeepsie's Main Street begins at Waryas Park under the Mid-Hudson Bridge and runs east-west between the two legs of the arterial

© NIKKI GOTH ITOI

downtown Poughkeepsie

(Routes 44/55) until it reaches the town of Arlington. The Hudson River Sloop *Clearwater* and its sister vessel, *Mystic Whaler,* dock here when they are in the area, as Poughkeepsie is the headquarters for the nonprofit environmental organization that runs them. Modeled after the Dutch vessels that sailed the Hudson in the late 18th century, *Clearwater* was conceived in the 1960s as a call to action to clean up the river before it was too late. In a unique classroom setting, *Clearwater* volunteers educate local residents about the importance of environmental awareness and conservation. Since 1966, the watchdog organization has battled GE on the dumping of PCBs into the river, prosecuted Clean Water Act offenders, and pioneered the model of encouraging environmental advocacy through a hands-on sailing experience.

Moving away from the riverfront, a number of historic sites are clustered in the downtown area near Academy Street. The **Clinton House** (549 Main St., Poughkeepsie, 845/471-1630; 10 A.M.–3 P.M. Tues.–Fri.) holds the offices and library of the Dutchess County Historical Society. This stone building hosted the New York State government briefly in 1777 and was rebuilt after a fire in 1783. The society also runs neighboring **Glebe House** (635 Main St., Poughkeepsie, 845/454-0605, www.theglebe house.org; 1–4 P.M. Wed.–Sun.; adults $5), a restored home dating back to 1767.

The **Bardavon 1869 Opera House** (35 Market St., Poughkeepsie, 845/473-5288, box office 845/473-2072, www.bardavon.org) escaped demolition in the mid-1970s to become listed on the National Historic Register. With its original pipe organ (a 1928 Wurlitzer Theatre Organ), and an interior dome that dates to 1920, the Bardavon is one of the oldest surviving theaters in the United States. Legendary performers from Mark Twain to Frank Sinatra have appeared on its stage. Today, the theater hosts the Hudson Valley Philharmonic and a full schedule of musical, dance, film, and theater productions by contemporary artists.

Samuel B. Morse became a household name in the 1840s when he developed the first commercial telegraph, sending the famous words

"What hath God wrought" across the line. With money earned from the venture, Morse bought **Locust Grove** (2683 South Rd., Poughkeepsie, 845/454-4500, www.morse historicsite.org; 10 A.M.–3 P.M. daily; adults $9, children $5), a 100-acre property south of the Mid-Hudson Bridge that is now a National Historic Landmark. The Italianate villa houses an informative exhibit on telegraph technology, as well as American and European furniture and many of Morse's own paintings. The surrounding woods and gardens are open to the public year-round.

Vassar College

Between downtown Poughkeepsie and Arlington is the ivory tower of Vassar College, a top-ranked liberal-arts school that draws students from across the country and around the world. Vassar's attractive campus is spread over 1,000 acres with some 200 varieties of trees interspersed among inviting lawns. English brewer Matthew Vassar founded the college in 1861 in an effort to provide young women with courses in science, math, art history, and music that rivaled the best men's schools in the country. Vassar remained single-sex until 1969, when the first coed class was admitted.

Vassar prides itself on being first among U.S. colleges to have established its own art gallery. Today, the **Frances Lehman Loeb Art Center** (124 Raymond Ave., Poughkeepsie, 845/437-7745, fllac.vassar.edu; 10 A.M.–5 P.M. Tues.–Sat., 1–5 P.M. Sun.; free admission) holds a varied permanent collection, from ancient Egyptian sculptures of marble and red granite to contemporary American paintings. The museum stays open late on Thursday evenings, till 9 P.M. Enter the gallery near the main gate on Raymond Avenue.

East of Vassar College, where Route 55 meets the Taconic Parkway, is **James Baird State Park** (845/452-1489, sunrise–sunset daily) with an 18-hole golf course, tennis courts, picnic areas, and hiking trails. Its wooded trails are popular with local runners, while families use the playground and attend programs at the nature center on summer weekends.

Back at the river's edge, Matthew Vassar's former home is now the **Springside National Historic Site** (185 Academy St., Poughkeepsie, 845/471-0183, dawn–dusk), preserved as the last standing design of landscape architect Andrew Jackson Downing. Most of the estate's 44 acres belong to a private condominium complex now, but visitors can view the restored gatehouse and wander along old carriage roads. Look for the entrance on Academy Street, on the west side of Route 9.

Hyde Park

Hyde Park offers a strong lineup for students of history and fine cuisine. For starters, the **Franklin D. Roosevelt Home National Historic Site** (Rte. 9, Hyde Park, 845/229-9115 or 877/444-6777, www.nps.gov/hofr/index.htm; buildings open 9 A.M.–5 P.M. daily; adults $10, 15 and under free; grounds open dawn–dusk daily, no fee), where the four-term president lived all his life, houses FDR's presidential library and museum. Exhibits inside chronicle the president's and first lady's achievements. Visitors can also tour **Top Cottage** (7097 Albany Post Rd. Rte 9, Hyde Park, 845/229-9115, www.nps.gov/hofr/hofrhome.html; 10 A.M.–5 P.M. Thurs.–Mon.), the hilltop retreat where FDR met with international heads of state. Trails on 300 acres lead to the river's edge.

Eleanor Roosevelt spent many quiet years at the unassuming Val-Kill Cottage after FDR's death. Today, the **Eleanor Roosevelt National Historic Site–Val-Kill** (Rte. 9G, Hyde Park, 845/229-9115, www.nps.gov/archive/elro/home.htm; 9 A.M.–5 P.M. daily May–Oct., Thurs.–Mon. Nov.–Apr.; admission $8) welcomes visitors with guided home tours and 180 acres of beautifully landscaped grounds.

Between Hyde Park and Rhinebeck along Route 9 stands a tribute to the Gilded Age: the former residence of Ogden Mills—a financier and philanthropist—and Ruth Livingston Mills, a descendent of the Livingston family that first settled much of Columbia County. The home began as a 25-room Greek Revival

© NIKKI GOTH ITOI

Hyde Park Railroad Station

in 1832. Subsequent renovations by the same architectural firm that built the Vanderbilt estate turned it into a massive 65-room estate adorned with exquisite furnishings from Europe, Greece, and Asia. The property was handed over to the State of New York in 1938 to become the **Staatsburg State Historic Site** (Old Post Rd., Staatsburg, 845/889-8851, www.staatsburgh.org; 11 A.M.–4 P.M. Sat.–Sun. Jan.–Mar., 10 A.M.–5 P.M. Tues.–Sat., noon–5 P.M. Sun. Apr.–Oct., noon–5 P.M. Sun. Nov., please call for holiday schedule in Dec.; adults $5, seniors students $4, 12 and under free).

If trains are your guilty pleasure, save time to visit the **Hyde Park Railroad Station** (34 River Rd., Hyde Park, 845/229-2338; www .hydeparkstation.com; noon–5 P.M. Sat.–Sun. and holidays; adults $5, children $4) before leaving the area. Built in 1914, the station was restored by the Hudson Valley Railroad Society and holds a treasured place on the National Register of Historic Places. Follow River Road from Route 9 in Hyde Park.

Vanderbilt Estate

A tour inside the Vanderbilt Estate (Rte. 9, Hyde Park, 845/229-9115 or 877/444-6777, www.nps.gov/vama; 9 A.M.–5 P.M. daily; adults $8, 15 and under free) will also send you straight back to the days of robber barons, railroad monopolies, and American capitalism run amok. A fine product of the Gilded Age, the 50-room home of Frederick and Louise Vanderbilt exhibits a variety of interior design influences, from renaissance to rococo. A carved wooden ceiling in the formal dining room is one of many European antiques found by designer Stanford White.

Though they only spent a few weeks a year at the estate, the Vanderbilts enjoyed entertaining guests, who arrived by boat, rail, or private car. Thirteen rooms on the third floor were reserved as quarters for the maids of lady visitors. Outside, the property remains as beautiful today as it did a century ago. Local residents meet here on weekends to play Frisbee and picnic on the lawn. Contemporary artists often set up canvases to paint the river and surrounding landscape. The grounds are open 7 A.M.–sunset and there is no use fee. The Hyde Park Trail system connects the Roosevelt and Vanderbilt estates along the river. Inquire at any of the homes for a trail map. If you plan to visit more than one of these historic homes, consider a combination ticket for $22.

C Culinary Institute of America

Since 1970, Hyde Park has been home to the oldest culinary college in the U.S., the prestigious Culinary Institute of America (Rte. 9, Hyde Park, 845/451-1588, www.ciachef.edu; tours 10 A.M. and 4 P.M. Mon., 4 P.M. Wed., 4 P.M. Thurs.; $5, reservations required). Set on a picturesque riverside campus, formerly the site of a Jesuit seminary, the CIA trains aspiring professionals and enthusiasts in the art of fine cuisine. Its facilities include 41 kitchens and the largest collection of culinary books and reference materials of any library in the country. Among the school's best-known graduates is Anthony Bourdain, author of the bestseller *Kitchen Confidential* and executive chef of Les Halles in New York City.

Tour the grounds at sunset before dining in one of the five public restaurants on campus. Better yet, enroll in one of the CIA's Boot Camp programs, which are multi-day intensive courses geared toward cooking enthusiasts. Classes cover a variety of rotating topics, such as French cuisine, baking, and healthy cooking. Tuition is steep at $1,500.

C Rhinebeck

Continuing north on Route 9, Rhinebeck stands out as an upscale enclave in an otherwise rural region. Victorian, Colonial, and Greek Revival buildings line several blocks of boutique stores, country inns, and gourmet restaurants expanding out from the intersection of Routes 9 and 308. (Route 9 is called Mill Street south of Route 308, and Montgomery Street north of Route 308; Route 308 is also called Market Street.)

At the center of all the activity is the **1766 Beekman Arms** (Rte. 9, Rhinebeck, 845/876-7077, www.beekmanarms.com), re-

portedly the oldest continuously operat in the United States. Indeed, colonial hi and political intrigue ooze from every creak the floorboards. George Washington, Philip Schuyler, Benedict Arnold, and Alexander Hamilton are among the most famous overnight guests. Local townspeople gathered inside for safety while the British burned Kingston to the ground across the Hudson.

As Rhinebeck grew into a commercial crossroads, the inn became a popular venue for political and cultural discussion. FDR even delivered several victory speeches from the front porch. The inn has expanded over the years, but much of the original building remains intact, including the oak beams and pine plank floor. The place is worth a peek, whether or not you plan to stay the night.

Next door to the Beekman Arms, FDR

TAURANTS

e Culinary Institute of America
se to their alma mater. More
than a dozen restaurants in the greater Hudson Valley are owned and operated by CIA alumni. Visit www.ciachef.edu/visitors/hp/alumnirestaurants.asp for the latest updates.

96 MAIN RESTAURANT AND BAR
96 Main St.
Poughkeepsie, NY
845/454-5200
Alumnus: Thomas Karcherski, 2001
Approximate distance from CIA: 4 miles

BARCLAY HEIGHTS BED & BREAKFAST
158 Burt St.
Saugerties, NY
845/246-3788
Alumnus: Justine Adelaide Smythe,
1992/1997
www.outstandinghospitality.com
Approximate distance from CIA: 29 miles

BRASS MONKEY BISTRO
150 Osborne Hill Rd.
Fishkill, NY
845/897-3055
Alumni: Janine & Todd Gray, 1996
www.brassmonkeybistro.com
Approximate distance from CIA: 14 miles

CAFE TAMAYO
91 Partition St.
Saugerties, NY
845/246-9371
Alumnus: James Tamayo, 1981
www.cafetamayo.com
Approximate distance from CIA: 30 miles

CALICO RESTAURANT & PATISSERIE
9 Mill St.
Rhinebeck, NY
845/876-2749
www.calicorhinebeck.com
Alumnus: Anthony Richard Balassone, 1981
Approximate distance from CIA: 13 miles

CORTLANDT COLONIAL RESTAURANT AND BALLROOM
5714 Albany Post Rd.
Cortlandt Manor, NY
Alumnus: Evan (Evangelos) Liaskos, 2000
www.ccrr.com
Approximate distance from CIA: 40 miles

CREW RESTAURANT & BAR
2290 South Rd.
Poughkeepsie, NY
Alumnus: Scott Holtzhouser, 2000
Approximate distance from CIA: 5 miles

GERSKY'S RESTAURANT AND CATERING
898 Rte. 6
Mahopac, NY
845/621-0696
www.gerskys.com
Alumnus: Joel M. Comiskey, 1980
Approximate distance from CIA: 40 miles

HILLSIDE MANOR RESTAURANT & CATERERS
240 Blvd. Rte. 32
Kingston, NY
845/331-4386
Alumnus: Deno M. Demosthenes, 1980
Approximate distance from CIA: 31 miles

JOHN'S HARVEST INN
633 Rte. 17M
Middletown, NY
845/343-6676
Alumnus: John Patrick Botti, 1982
Approximate distance from CIA: 46 miles

MARCEL'S
Rte. 9W
West Park, NY
845/384-6700
Alumnus: Michael James Hoysradt, 1978
Approximate distance from CIA: 30 miles

MRS. NESBITT'S FIRESIDE CAFE
FDR Presidential Library
Henry Wallace Visitors Center
4079 Albany Post Rd.
Hyde Park, NY
Alumnus: Scott Holtzhouser, 2000
Approximate distance from CIA: 2 miles

PERFECT ENDINGS - DESSERTS
Retail/Wholesale Bakery
Route 202 and Lovell St.
Somers, NY
Alumnus: Christine King, 2001
Approximate distance from CIA: 40 miles

PIPPY'S AT THE SQUARE
2 Delafield St. (at Mt. Carmel Square)
Poughkeepsie, NY
845/483-7239
Alumnus: Lou Fusaro, 1997
Approximate distance from CIA: 5 miles

PLUMBUSH INN
1656 Rte. 9D
Cold Spring, NY
845/265-3904

Alumnus: Mohsen Alam El Din, 1990
Approximate distance from CIA: 25 miles

THE POSTAGE INN
838 Rte. 32
Tillson, NY
845/658-3434
www.thepostageinn.com
Alumnus: James Gerard Jerkowski, C.E.C., 1986
Approximate distance from CIA: 20 miles

SILVER SPOON CATERING
200 East Main St.
Mt. Kisco, NY
Alumnus: Craig Pellis, 1991
Approximate distance from CIA: 50 miles

TWIST RESTAURANT
4290 Albany Post Rd.
Hyde Park, NY
845/229-7094
Alumnus: Benjamin Mauk, 2000/2002
www.letstwist.com
Approximate distance from CIA: 2 miles

UMBERTO'S OF MAMMA MARISA
2245 South Rd. (Rte. 9)
Poughkeepsie, NY
845/462-5117
www.umbertos.org
Alumnus: Alberto Annunziata, 1991
Approximate distance from CIA: 10 miles

THE WOULD RESTAURANT
120 North Rd.
Highland, NY 12528
845/691-9883
www.thewould.com
Alumnus: Claire Winslow, 1985
Approximate distance from CIA: 8 miles

THE MID-HUDSON

oversaw construction of the **Rhinebeck Post Office** (6383 Mill St.) through the Works Progress Administration (WPA). The building was designed to commemorate the first house in Rhinebeck. Inside, a series of murals chronicle the town's history. The **Dutch Reformed Church** (16 Albany Post Rd., Hyde Park, 845/229-5354), across Route 9 from the post office, was built in 1808.

Surrounding the town of Rhinebeck are idyllic family farms and grand country estates. **Wilderstein** (330 Morton Rd., Rhinebeck, 845/876-4818, www.wilderstein .org; noon–4 P.M. Thurs.–Sun., group tours by reservation), a riverside mansion located south of town on Route 9, has a five-story round tower that juts upward from its center, offering views of an equally dramatic landscape. With ties to the prominent Beekman and Livingston families, this fanciful Queen Anne country home began as an Italianate villa in the mid-19th century. Carefully planned trails, vistas, and lawns around the property reflect the Romantic-era aesthetic.

North of town, the Dutchess County Fairgrounds holds antique car shows and the annual Dutchess County Fair. Amtrak services the train station in Rhinecliff, three miles to the west.

Red Hook

The sleepy town of Red Hook received its name when early Dutch explorers ventured up the Hudson to find red sumac and Virginia creeper in full bloom. The Dutch called it Red Hoek (Red Peninsula), and the name has stuck ever since. A modern-day bedroom community, Red Hook encompasses the Village of Tivoli and hamlet of Annandale-on-Hudson on the banks of the river, as well as Bard College and the Village of Red Hook to the east. A small commercial district fans out from the intersection of Routes 9 and 199, with a John Deere store, CVC pharmacy, Stewarts, and a few casual eateries.

At **Alison Wines & Vineyards** (231 Pitcher La., Red Hook, 845/758-6335, www.alison wines.com; 11:30 A.M.–5 P.M. Mon.–Thurs.,

11:30 A.M.–5:30 P.M. Fri.–Sun.), winemaker Rick Lewitt makes a point of demystifying the wine-tasting experience. He greets nearly every visitor who walks in the door, offering tastings and informative barrel tours. Lewitt is a Westchester County native and a Bard College graduate who left a career in journalism to pursue a passion for wine. With Long Island already crowded and expensive, and the Finger Lakes too far away from New York City, he settled on the Hudson Valley. He apprenticed in Oregon to learn pinot noir, and locally at Millbrook Winery, before setting up shop in a dairy barn on the old Grieg Farm in Red Hook. Alison Vineyards specializes in pinot noir and hopes to harvest grapes from two unusual varietals in the near future: Aligote, from France, and Dornfelder, from Germany's Ahr Valley.

A rocker on the North Porch is the best seat in the house at **Montgomery Place** (River Rd., Annandale-on-Hudson, 845/758-5461, www .hudsonvalley.org; 10 A.M.–5 P.M. Sat.–Sun. May–Oct.; adults $7, seniors $6, children $4, grounds only $4). Nestled among 434 acres of woodlands with views of the Catskill Mountains across the Hudson, Montgomery Place is a stunning riverside estate conceived in the Federal style. Located in Annandale-on-Hudson, the home has been restored with period furnishings and enchanting gardens. The home was temporarily closed for renovations in 2007.

Many of the undergraduate students at **Bard College** (Rte. 9G, Annandale, 845/758-6822, www.bard.edu) have views of the Hudson and Catskill Mountains from their dorms. An affiliate of Columbia University, the liberal-arts school is set on 500 acres of lawns and woodlands. A variety of music and performing arts programs are open to the public year-round.

CENTRAL DUTCHESS COUNTY–ROUTES 44 AND 22
Pawling

Routes 22 and 55 meet at Pawling, in the southeastern corner of Dutchess County. Named after Colonel Henry Beekman's daughter, Catherine Pawling, the town has been a crossroads of commercial activity since colonial days. Pawling's early settlers were Quakers, as documented by the display of artifacts in the **Quaker Museum, Akin Free Library** (2nd Fl., Quaker Hill, Pawling, 845/855-9316; 2–4 P.M. Sat.–Sun.). The 1764 Oblong Friends Meeting House served as a temporary hospital for George Washington's troops in 1778. And Washington set up headquarters in the John Kane House. Inside is a replica of the village from the year 1948, complete with moving trains.

Today, Pawling attracts New York City commuters, Appalachian Trail hikers, and celebrities seeking privacy. Keep an eye out for permanent resident James Earl Jones if you pass through town.

Millbrook

Once known for celebrity residents and exclusive hunting, fishing, and horseback riding clubs, Millbrook seems to be quieter these days—though it is still the kind of place where restaurants raise their menu prices on weekends, figuring the Fortune 500 CEOs and Hollywood types who own second homes in the area can pay a little more for their burgers. In summer, the village's preserved Greek Revival homes hide behind a canopy of oak and maple trees. Several boutiques and restaurants are worth a visit, but there is only one place to stay right in town; others options are located a few miles away.

Innisfree Gardens (Tyrrell Rd., Millbrook, 845/677-8000; www.innisfreegarden.com; 11 A.M.–5 P.M. Sat.–Sun., 10 A.M.–4 P.M. Wed.–Fri. May 7–Oct. 20; admission Wed.–Fri. $3, Sat.–Sun. $4) is popular with locals and visitors alike. Petronella Collins, president of the Innisfree Foundation, has called the park "a textbook of tips for the home gardener." Inspired by ancient Chinese gardens, the 200-acre property applies Chinese ideas of design and motion to a decidedly American landscape. The result is a spectacular display of flora ranging from lotus blossoms to daffodils. Visitors can picnic on the grounds, walk the trails, or simply find a secluded place to while away the afternoon.

The scenic rural roads that surround Millbrook's town center are ideal for running and cycling. A popular route is to follow the Dutchess Wine Trail, which isn't exactly a trail, but a joint marketing effort of several local vineyards, located on different roads in different towns. While it's a far cry from the Silverado Trail in California's Napa Valley, the roads connecting Alison Wines, Clinton Vineyards, and Millbrook Winery & Vineyards cover miles of pretty countryside. Meanwhile, the wineries themselves produce some of the highest-quality labels in New York State.

Millbrook Winery & Vineyards (26 Wing Rd., Millbrook, 800/662-9463, www.mill brookwine.com; 11 A.M.–6 P.M. daily) introduced French hybrid grapes to the region and makes an outstanding chardonnay. A few miles away, **Clinton Vineyards** (450 Shultzville Rd., Clinton Corners, 845/266-5372, www.clinton vineyards.com; noon–6 P.M. Thurs.–Mon. summer, noon–4:30 P.M. Fri.–Sun. winter) is known for its seyval blanc.

On a hilltop overlooking Millbrook Winery & Vineyards stands **Wing's Castle** (717 Bangall Rd., Millbrook, www.wingcastle.us, 845/677-9085; noon A.M.–5 P.M. Wed.–Sun. May 31–Sept. 1., weekends only Sept.–Dec. 20; $8 adults, $6 children), the kind of place one might expect to find in Baja California. Made of stones and pipes and salvaged appliances—materials too solid and functional to be thrown away—this private home gets high marks for resourceful and eclectic design. Owners Peter and Toni Wing invite visitors from Memorial Day to Christmas.

The Harlem Valley

Continuing northeast from Millbrook, Route 44 enters the scenic Harlem Valley, which follows the west side of the Taconic Range and the Connecticut border from Pawling to Pine Plains. The land here is sparsely populated, with only a few thousand residents per town, and much of it is permanently protected from development. Taconic State Park, Stissing Mountain Forest, and the Harlem Valley Rail Trail are a few of the outdoor attractions.

From the west, Route 44 winds downhill to meet Route 22 at the rural town of Amenia and the **Troutbeck Inn and Conference Center** (515 Leedsville Rd., Amenia, 845/373-9681 or 800/978-7688, www.troutbeck.com). Named in 1765 for its counterpart in England, Troutbeck was founded by literary-minded farmers who knew the likes of Emerson and Thoreau. The original stone house is surrounded by sycamore trees and flower gardens. In the early 20th century, Sinclair Lewis, Earnest Hemingway, and Theodore Roosevelt were frequent guests of Troutbeck's second owners, Joel and Amy Spingarn. Joel Spingarn was instrumental in the founding of the NAACP and served as the organization's second president. Although the inn no longer attracts the same kind of movers and shakers—today's guests are primarily conference and wedding attendees—it still offers fine cuisine and quaint accommodations in a tranquil setting.

South of Amenia on Route 22 is Wassaic and the terminus for the Harlem Valley Line of the Metro-North commuter rail. The ride to Grand Central Station takes about two hours, with a transfer in Southeast.

Next stop is the **Webatuck Craft Village** (Rte. 55, Wingdale, 845/832-6601, www.hunt countryfurniture.com/webatuck), on Route 55 off Route 22 near Wingdale, where resident artists work in copper, tin, clay, glass, and wood. The village consists of half a dozen buildings, and visitors shop here for one-of-a-kind handmade items, from furniture and stained-glass windows to ceramics and vintage toys.

Millerton

A scenic location in the Harlem Valley, close proximity to the Housatonic River in Connecticut, and a bevy of antique stores have

Main Street, Millerton

turned Millerton into one of the latest Hudson Valley hotspots. The well-known Harney & Sons tea company recently moved its headquarters from neighboring Salisbury, Connecticut, to Millerton; several restaurants and shops have opened their doors to greet visitors who wander into town while enjoying the scenic country roads.

SPORTS AND RECREATION
Winter Sports

Cross-country skiing is permitted on the golf course at Baird Park and along the Harlem Valley Rail Trail. The **McCann Ice Arena** (Mid-Hudson Civic Center, 14 Civic Center Plaza, Poughkeepsie, 845/454-5800, www.midhudson civiccenter.com) offers public skating sessions year-round.

Hiking

A 30-mile stretch of the Appalachian Trail passes through the hills of Dutchess County, connecting the towns of East Fishkill, Dover Plains, Beekman, and Pawling along the way. Several well-marked access areas have trailside parking. In Stormville, find one on Route 52, three miles east of the Taconic State Parkway. In Poughquag, the area is at the intersection of Routes 55 and 216 or Depot Hill Road, off Route 216. In Pawling, it's on Route 22, north of town. Note that mountain bikes are not allowed on the trail.

Additional areas for hiking include the **Pawling Nature Preserve** (Quaker Lake Rd., Pawling), on 1,000 acres, and Poughkeepsie's **Bowdoin State Park** (85 Sheafe Rd., Wappingers Falls, 845/297-1224), on 300 acres near the riverfront.

Cycling

Whether you are riding off-road or on, Dutchess County offers terrain to suit all levels, from casual to aggressive. The scenery alternates between rolling hills, charming villages, and Hudson River views. The **Mid-Hudson Bicycle Club** (www.midhudsonbicycle.org) organizes area rides through the summer and fall. And coming soon: a Hudson River crossing, just for bikes. The old Poughkeepsie Railroad Bridge, closed since 1974, is scheduled to open to foot and bike traffic within a couple of years.

A section of the scenic **Harlem Valley Rail Trail** (51 South Center St., Millerton, 518/789-9591, www.hvrt.org) begins in Amenia and crosses through Millerton near the Harney & Sons tea company. The path follows the tracks of the old New York and Harlem Railroad and is paved for foot and bike traffic. The **Wassaic State Forest** (Rte. 22, Wassaic, 845/831-8780) on Route 22 is another tranquil place to get away from it all.

Golf

Golfers have a dozen or more courses to choose from in Dutchess County. Foremost among them is the swanky **Branton Woods Golf Course** (178 Stormville Rd., Hopewell Junction, www.brantonwoodsgolf .com, 845/223-1600 or 877/833-8559; $90–130), a semiprivate course located in Hopewell Junction. But the best course for the money in Dutchess County is **The Links at Union Vale** (153 N. Parliman Rd., Union Vale, 845/223-1000, www.thelinks atunionvale.com; 6:30 A.M.–dark daily; Mon.–Thurs. $38, Fri.–Sun. $52, cart rental $13 per player). Another good option is the **Beekman Country Club** (11 Country Club Rd., Hopewell Junction, 845/226-7700, www.beekmangolf.com; opens at 6 A.M. Sat.–Sun., at 7 A.M. Mon.–Fri.; weekends $65, weekdays $46, seniors $36).

Swimming and Boating

Kids love to slip and slide down the tubes at **Splash Down Park** (2200 Rte. 9, Fishkill, 845/896-6606; 10 A.M.–7 P.M. daily May–Sept.; adults $25, children under 42 inches $20).

Kayakers can paddle lakes, ponds, creeks, and of course the Hudson River in Dutchess County. **Hudson Valley Pack & Paddle** (45 Beekman St., Beacon, 845/831-1300, www .hvpackandpaddle.com; 10 A.M.–5 P.M. Mon.–Sat., noon–5 P.M. Sun.) rents kayaks and canoes April through November. Rates are $45/

THE MID-HUDSON

day for a single kayak and $60/day for a double kayak or two-person canoe. Look for the shop on the west side of Route 9D, just before the turn for the train station. For a Hudson River tour, you can launch nearby at Dennings Point in Beacon.

Another reputable shop, **The River Connection** (9 West Market St., Hyde Park, 845/229-0595 or 845/242-4731, www.the-river-connection.com), offers water sports instruction, as well as equipment sales and rentals. Certified instructors lead trips from various launch points along the river, including Norrie Point (Staatsburg), Tivoli, Croton Point, and Poughkeepsie ($100 pp). Experienced paddlers may join the guided day trips from Athens to Saugerties, Saugerties to Norrie Point, and Cold Spring to Annsville Creek, which make up the annual Great Hudson River Paddle (ages 16 and up only, $100 pp).

Fishing and Hunting

Anglers have a number of streams, lakes, and ponds to choose from, as well as the Hudson River itself. Outside of Millbrook, **Orvis Sandanona** (311 Sharon Tpke./Rte. 44A, Millbrook, 845/677-9701, www.orvis .com/sandanona; Apr.–Oct.) offers fly-fishing lessons and instruction in the English Churchill method of shooting clays. The club hosts a September Vintager's Side by Side Championship.

Aviation

Aviators must plan a weekend visit to the **Old Rhinebeck Aerodrome** (Stone Church Rd., Rhinebeck, 845/758-8610, www.oldrhinebeck .org; museum hours 10 A.M.–5 P.M. daily May 12–Oct. 31; adults $20 weekends, $10 weekdays), which hosts weekend air shows during summer and fall, complete with vintage fashion shows. The museum's collection of antique aircraft includes working models dating back to the early 20th century.

Blue Sky Balloons (19 Teller Ave., Beacon, 888/999-2461, www.blueskyballoons.com; sunrise–sunset daily; $195 per person) offers morning and evening tours.

Cooking Classes

Fleisher's Upstairs (47 East Market St., 2nd floor, Rhinebeck, 845/876-7507 www.grass fedmeat.net/Fleishers) is a satellite location of a Kingston institution: Fleisher's Grass-fed & Organic Meats (307 Wall St., Kingston), which supplies restaurants like Blue Hill at Stone Barns in Westchester County, Café Tamayo in Saugerties (Ulster), and Swoon in Hudson (Columbia). Recent classes ($35 pp) have included: Know What Your Dinner is Eating Before You Eat Your Dinner, Debunking Wine Myths, and The Art of Cooking Meat.

You can also learn to make spring rolls, curries, and other Thai specialties on Monday evenings at Sukhothai Restaurant in Beacon (845/790-5375; 6–8:30 P.M. Mon., $50 pp).

Yoga Workshops and Spa Treatments

The Rhinebeck campus of the nationally known **Omega Institute for Holistic Studies** (150 Lake Dr., Rhinebeck, 800/944-1001, www.eomega.org) offers wellness weeks ($395), yoga retreats, and spiritual programs throughout the year.

ACCOMMODATIONS

Business travelers congregate around corporate headquarters in southern Dutchess County, while the more distinctive inns are found in the northeastern part of the county. Book early around major events. Hotels are known to fill up as far as a year in advance.

$100-150

A midpriced option that's close to area wineries is the six-room **Red Hook Inn** (7460 S. Broadway, Red Hook, 845/758-8445, www.theredhook inn.com, $125), built in 1824. Lace curtains let in plenty of natural light. Hardwood floors, antique furnishings, and floral bedspreads complete the decor. Note, the inn no longer serves lunch, dinner, or Sunday brunch.

A Cat in Your Lap (62 Old Rte. 82, Millbrook, 845/677-3051, www.acatinyourlap.com; $100–125) is a rustic affair, with two rooms in the main house, built in 1840, and two studio suites with fireplaces in a converted 1890s barn. Hostess Madelyn Berensmann serves a country-style breakfast on weekends and a lighter breakfast midweek.

$150-200

Botsford Briar B&B (19 High St., Beacon, 845/831.6099; $145–195) was Melanie Griffith's house in the 1994 film *Nobody's Fool.* The owner used to host quilting retreats in this 1889 Victorian. The home features wicker furniture on the front porch, original hardwood floors, lace curtains, English faucets, and mixed furnishings. Rooms are named for flowers. The top floor room has a river view and enclosed porch; the downstairs Gentleman's Parlor has a cozy fireplace for winter getaways. The B&B is located across Route 9D from Main Street, near the Beacon train station.

Across from the Vanderbilt Estate in Hyde Park, the **Journey Inn** (1 Sherwood Pl., Hyde Park, 845/229-8972, www.journeyinn.com; $130–190) is a bed-and-breakfast with six individually decorated rooms. A multicourse breakfast is part of the package. European soaps add a fine touch, and you can get wireless Internet throughout. Also close to the CIA, and run by a graduate and beekeeper, **The Willows Bed & Breakfast** (53 Travis Rd., Hyde Park, 845/471-6115, www.willowsbnb.com; $135–165) occupies a restored 1765 colonial farmhouse. Two air-conditioned rooms appointed in country style come with a breakfast that takes homemade to a new level.

Millbrook's **Porter House** (17 Washington Ave., Millbrook, 845/677-3057, www.porterhousebandb.com; $140–225) is popular with members of the Orvis fly-fishing center and parents of boarding school students. It has three cozy suites and two rooms in a beautiful 1920 stone house. A bevy of famous people have stayed at the modern **Inn at the Falls** (50 Red Oaks Mill Rd., Poughkeepsie, 845/462-5770 or 800/344-1466, www.innat thefalls.com; $170), as evidenced by the wall of signed photographs in the lobby. Built at the edge of Wappingers Creek, the inn caters primarily to business travelers. A sunny atrium

and porch for breakfast compensate for rooms that are on the dark side.

You won't forget an overnight stay at the über-historic ◖ **1766 Beekman Arms** (6387 Mill St, Rhinebeck, 845/876-7077, www.beekman delamaterinn.com; $100–250). Ask for one of the 13 rooms in the main house, where the ceilings are low and the floors creak with every step. It's been more than a decade since the last major renovations, but the rooms are holding up well. For more modern accommodations, the inn has a total of 13 buildings and 74 rooms. Forget about getting a reservation when the auto shows come to town. Repeat visitors reserve every room on the premises more than a year in advance.

Owner and innkeeper Barbara Lanman renovated an 1860s home in the Queen Ann style and opened the **Pawling House Bed and Breakfast** (105 W. Main St. at Dykeman St., Pawling; $175–225) in late 2007. Its four guest rooms have private baths, and the Village of Pawling location is close to restaurants, shops, and the train station.

Over $200

Marble baths, French antiques, and ornate silk fabrics set the Gilded Age tone at **Belvedere Mansion** (10 Old Rte. 9, Stattsburg, 845/889-8000, www.belvederemansion.com; $225–275), a riverside getaway located between Hyde Park and Rhinebeck. Rooms in the neoclassical mansion, restored in 1993, are $275. Individually decorated rooms in the Carriage House have king-size beds for $150–175. Smaller rooms, called Cozies ($75–95), are a good way to get affordable lodging at an upscale venue. Suites in the new Hunting Lodge cost $250–450.

If your ideal weekend getaway is all about the room and board, Dover Plains has the romantic **Old Drovers Inn** (Rte. 22, Dover Plains, 845/832-9311, www.olddroversinn.com; $190–420). There is a two-night minimum, but the cost includes dinner for two and full breakfast. A Relais & Chateaux property, the restaurant and four guest rooms are set on 12 acres in an early 18th-century home. An international clientele has replaced the cattle drivers of the early days, but the traditional American cuisine is every bit as hearty (mains $20–39).

At the edge of the village of Millbrook, the ◖ **Millbrook Country House** (506 Sharon Turnpike/Rte. 44A, 845/677-9570; www.mill brookcountryhouse.com; $200–275) blends American Colonial architecture with 18th-century Italian decor. Journalist Lorraine Alexander and her husband Giancarlo Grisi moved from a Mediterranean town in Italy to open the bed-and-breakfast in 2002. The elegant furnishings and linens in their four guest rooms reflect the tastes of experienced world travelers. Behind the house is a white-picket-fenced flower and herb garden.

Le Chambord (2737 Rte. 52, Hopewell Junction, www.lechambord.com) has been a longtime favorite for elegant affairs. Set in an 1863 mansion, the inn has nine beautifully decorated rooms in the main building, and 16 more in a newer wing—all large with high ceilings and white tiled baths. Chef Lenny Mott prepares classic French fare for lunch and dinner (mains $25–36).

Campgrounds
Ideal for a family car-camping trip, **Wilcox Memorial Park** (Rte. 199, Stanfordville, 845/758-6100; $20–25 for nonresidents) has two small lakes with fishing, boat rentals, and swimming, Memorial Day–Labor Day. Kids can safely explore miles of trails by foot or on bikes. The park is open 9 A.M.–4 P.M. Monday through Friday January 1–April 15 and November 1–December 31, 9 A.M.–7 P.M. daily April 16–September 30, and 9 A.M.–6 P.M. daily in October.

FOOD
Dutchess County eateries range from classic diners and contemporary American bistros to game-inspired, farm-fresh menus, and the occasional international treat.

Along the River–Route 9
The restaurant scene has blossomed in Bea-

con in recent years, thanks to the influx of Dia:Beacon visitors and a new community of resident artists. In between gallery visits, stop for pad Thai, green curry, or other Thai specialties at ◖ **Sukothai** (516 Main St., Beacon, 845/790-5375, www.sukothainy. net; 11:30 A.M.–9:30 P.M. Tues.–Thurs. and Sun., 11:30 A.M.–10:30 P.M. Fri.–Sat.; lunch mains $9, dinner mains $13–18). This restaurant serves the most authentic Thai cuisine in the area. Follow Main Street all the way past the Howland Cultural Center and look for the restaurant across from the abandoned factory on Wappingers Creek. There are a few sidewalk tables outside, and a pleasant air-conditioned dining room inside. Another option for outstanding ethnic fare recently moved north from Cold Spring: **Café Maya** (294 Main St., Beacon, 845/838-4901; 11 A.M.–10 P.M. Mon.–Thurs., 11 A.M.–11 P.M. Fri.–Sat., 11 A.M.–9 P.M. Sun.; mains $10–20) is one of two new Dutchess County Mexican restaurants run by Luis Pinto, a native of the Yucatán peninsula. The menu reflects dishes from this region, including huachinango (red snapper) and cochinita pibil (pork steamed in banana leaves). Guacamole is made at your table. Pinto has a second restaurant, Maya Café in Fishkill (448 Rte. 9/Van Wyck Lake Rd., 845/896-4042).

Alternatively, you might stay for dinner at **Tonique** (240 Main St. btw Elm and Walnut, Beacon, 845/831-0003, www.toniquerestaurant .com) a much-loved New American newcomer run by the same chef who opened Le Bouchon in Cold Spring. Service—and quality Italian dishes—comes with a smile at the family-oriented **Brother's Trattoria** (465 Main St., Beacon, 845/838-3300; 11 A.M.–3 P.M. and 5–10 P.M. daily; mains $13–18).

The Piggy Bank (448 Main St., Beacon, 845/838-0028, www.piggybankrestaurant .com; 11 A.M.–9 P.M. Mon.–Thurs., 11 A.M.–10 P.M. Fri., noon–10 P.M. Sat., noon–9 P.M. Sun.) is a local favorite for burgers and southern-style barbecue. You can stock up for a picnic or eat in the café at **Homespun Foods** (232 Main St., Beacon, 845/831-5096;

HUDSON VALLEY WINERIES

Enterprising Hudson Valley farmers planted the first French American hybrid grapes in the 1970s, and the quality and popularity of their wines have been rising steadily ever since to meet the demands of increasingly sophisticated local consumers. Today, the Hudson Valley is the smallest of four major wine regions in New York State, with about 20 producers. (The others are Long Island, the Finger Lakes, and Great Lakes regions.) Among the newcomers is Dutchess County's Alison Wines & Vineyards.

According to Alison Wines & Vineyards winemaker Rick Lewitt, site selection is key to producing wines in this region. His winery is at the top of the commuter belt, where grape growers have to compete with real estate developers who will offer farmers $15,000 an acre for their apple orchards.

Unlike the hot, dry climate that nurtures California zinfandel, merlot, and cabernet sauvignon grapes, cooler temperatures in the Hudson Valley are well suited for growing the types of grapes you find in Burgundy, Germany, and northern Italy: chardonnay, aligote, dornfelder, and pinot noir. The resulting wines are earthy, crisp, and clean with a moderate alcohol content.

Grape	European Growing Region	Hudson Valley Wineries
Aligote	Burgundy (France)	Alison Wines (planted)
Dornfelder	Rhinehessen and Pfalz (Germany)	Alison Wines (planted)
Pinot noir	Burgundy (France)	Alison Wines, Millbrook Winery
Seyval blanc	French-American hybrid	Clinton Vineyards
Tocai friulano	Friuli (Northern Italy)	Millbrook Winery

THE MID-HUDSON

8 A.M.–5 P.M. Mon.–Wed., 8 A.M.–7 P.M. Thurs.–Sun.).

Near the intersection of Main Street and Route 9D, **Muddy Cup Coffee** (129 Main St., Beacon www.muddycup.com; 6 A.M.–10 P.M. Mon.–Thurs., 6 A.M.–11 P.M. Fri., 7 A.M.–11 P.M. Sat., 8 A.M.–10 P.M. Sun.) is the latest outpost of a popular Hudson Valley chain. Across from the Muddy Cup is **Jane's Ice Cream** (Main St., Beacon, www .janesicecream.com; 9 A.M.–6 P.M. daily), a satellite of the Kingston-based wholesaler. **Cup and Saucer Tea Room** (165 Main St., Beacon, 845/831-6287, www.cupandsaucertea room.com; 11 A.M.–5 P.M. Thurs.–Mon., till 9 P.M. Fri.–Sat.; mains $7–10) serves high tea 4–6 P.M. Sundays for $37.50 per person.

Moving north, entrées at **Hudson's Ribs and Fish** (1099 Rt. 9, Fishkill, 845/297-5002, www.hudsonsribsandfish.com; 5–10 P.M. Mon.–Thurs., 5–11 P.M. Fri., 4–11 P.M. Sat., 2–9 P.M. Sun.; mains $16–28) come with a piping hot popover on the side. Several Italian restaurants are worth a visit in this part of the county: **Il Barilotto** (1113 Main St., Fishkill, 845/897-4300 www.ilbarilottorestaurant .com; 11 A.M.–2:30 P.M. and 5–10 P.M. Mon.–Sat., till 11 P.M. Fri.–Sat.; mains $17–28) has a broad selection of wines by the glass to accompany its reliable Italian menu. **Aroma Osteria** (114 Old Post Rd., Wappingers Falls, 845/298-6790 www.aromaosteriarestaurant .com; 11:30 A.M.–2:30 P.M. and 5–10 P.M. Tues.–Sat., till 11 P.M. Fri.–Sat., 4–9 P.M. Sun.; mains $16–25), run by the same owners, ranks among the best Italian eateries in the region. In a busy commercial district near the Home Depot, always crowded **Longobardi's Restaurant** (1201 Rte. 9, Wappingers Falls, 845/297-1498) serves some of the best Italian food in the area.

Le Chambord (2737 Rte. 52, Hopewell Junction, www.lechambord.com; lunch 11:30 A.M.–2:30 P.M. Mon.–Fri., dinner 6–10 P.M. Mon.–Fri., 6–11 P.M. Sat., 3–9 P.M. Sun.; mains $14–35) prepares classic French dishes in a formal setting. Tournedos, chateaubriand, venison, and sea scallops are featured dishes. Just to the north, one of the only restaurants on the lower part of the Taconic Parkway is **Muscoot North** (Carpenter Rd., Hopewell Junction, 845/226-8495, www.muscoot.com; 5–9 P.M. Tues. and Sun., 5–10 P.M. Wed.–Sat.; mains $14–18), a popular hangout for commuters on Friday nights.

As in Beacon, there are many more opportunities for dining out in Poughkeepsie these days—many of the newcomers are located in an attractive new plaza next to the Poughkeepsie train station called Dooley Square. Shepherd's pie, corned beef and cabbage, and fish and chips anchor the menu at **Mahoney's Irish Pub & Restaurant** (35 Main St., Poughkeepsie, 845/471-3027, www.mahoneysirishpub.com; 11 A.M.–10 P.M. Sun.–Thurs., 11 A.M.–11 P.M. Fri.–Sat.; mains $13–20), but you can also order American fare instead.

The **River Station** (25 Main St. or 1 Water St., Poughkeepsie, 845/452-9207; $16–24) serves dependable surf and turf on a pleasant outdoor terrace that overlooks the Hudson. A few blocks away, **Aurora Café** (145 Mill St., Poughkeepsie, 845/454-1900) serves delicious Italian pastries made on the premises.

Nearby, overlooking the river, **Shadows** (176 Rinaldi Blvd., Poughkeepsie, 845/486-9500, www.shadowsonthehudson.com; mains $12–33) is a mammoth brick dining and events complex. Shadows caters to a business crowd during weekday lunch hours and turns into a trendy nightclub on weekends. There is a 14-foot HD video wall behind the main bar, and open seating all around and outside on the shaded terrace. You'll likely catch views

of the Mid-Hudson Bridge from your table, but don't expect a cozy romantic feel. Surf and turf defines the menu, but you can also choose from a list of filling sandwiches and salads. The bistro steak salad, for example, comes with marinated portobello mushrooms sliced on top. Lobster mac 'n' cheese is one of the more creative entrées on the pasta list. Shadows is open 11:30 A.M.–10 P.M. Monday–Thursday with late-night snacks and cocktails served till midnight, 11:30 A.M.–11 P.M. Friday–Saturday with late-night snacks and cocktails served till 2 A.M., and 11 A.M.–10 P.M. Sunday with the lounge open until 11 P.M.

In a pale yellow building near the YMCA downtown, **Busy Bee Café** (138 South Ave. at Reed Pl., Poughkeepsie, 845/452-6800; lunch 11:30 A.M.–2:30 P.M. Tues.–Fri., dinner 5:30–9 P.M. Tues.–Thurs. and 5:30–10 P.M. Fri.–Sat.) draws lunch and dinner crowds for creative New American fare.

Ask a group of locals to name the best diner in town and you'll spark a heated debate. **The Palace Diner** (294 Washington St., Poughkeepsie, 854/473-1576, www.thepalacediner.com; 24 hours daily; mains $16–19) gets the best marks for food. The **Arlington Diner** (251 Dutchess Tpke, Poughkeepsie, 845/452-1554) is a convenient standby that closes at midnight, while the **Acropolis Diner** (829 Main St., Poughkeepsie, 845/452-6255) gets bonus points for serving around the clock. The **Daily Planet** (1202 Rte. 55, LaGrangeville, 845/452-0110; 5 A.M.–midnight daily, till 1 A.M. Fri.–Sat.; mains $11), near Arlington High School, is a relative newcomer that has been slowly stealing market share.

Saigon Cafe (6A LaGrange Ave., Poughkeepsie, 845/473-1392, lunch noon–2 P.M. Mon.–Fri., dinner 5–10 P.M. daily; mains $12) serves passable Vietnamese pho in a small but air-conditioned space just off the Vassar College campus. Nearby, the **Beech Tree Grill** (1-3 Collegeview Ave., Poughkeepsie, 845/471-7279 www.beechtreegrill.com; 5–10 P.M. Mon., 11:30 A.M.–3 P.M. and 5–11:30 P.M. Tues.–Sat., 11:30 A.M.–3 P.M. and 5–11:30 P.M. Sun.; mains $15–18) has a decent wine and beer list, with an inviting bar and a dinner menu of hearty pub fare.

In a strip mall near the Dutchess County Airport, **Violet Creek** (1820 New Hackensack Rd., New Hackensack Plaza, Poughkeepsie, 845/463-3633; 11 A.M.–9 P.M. Tues.–Thurs., 11 A.M.–9.30 P.M. Fri.–Sat., 10 A.M.–4 P.M. Sun.; mains $15–22) serves American fare such as filet mignon and lamb chops in a casual setting; the restaurant is run by the former chefs of the Dutchess Golf & Country Club.

Poughkeepsie's growing Latino population has added to the opening of several dependable Mexican restaurants around town. One of the most authentic is **Taco Land** (3 Spackenkill Rd., Poughkeepsie, 845/463-3477, www.taco landmexicancafe.com; 10 A.M.–10 P.M. Sun.–Thurs., 10 A.M.–11 P.M. Fri.–Sat.; mains $5–13), located near the fire station and across from the IBM main plant on Spackenkill Road.

Between Poughkeepsie and Hyde Park is an award-winning French restaurant that's been open since 1980. Run by a chef originally from Normandy, **Le Pavillon** (230 Salt Point Tpke., Poughkeepsie, 845/473-2525, www.lepavillon restaurant.com; 5:30–9:30 P.M. Tues.–Sat.; mains $18–20) specializes in escargot, coq au vin, slow-cooked rabbit, and crispy sweetbreads—all offered at very reasonable prices.

CIA sophomores run the kitchens in five campus restaurants (Culinary Institute of America, 1946 Campus Dr., Hyde Park, www.ciachef.edu). Main dishes at **American Bounty** (845/471-6608; 11:30 A.M.–1 P.M. and 6–8:30 P.M. Tues.–Sat.; mains $21–27) feature regional cuisine such as grilled filet mignon, roasted pork tenderloin, and a New England seafood sampler. The reasonably priced ⬛ **Apple Pie Bakery Café** (1946 Campus Dr., Roth Hall, 845/905-4500; 8 A.M.–6:30 P.M. Mon.–Fri.; mains $5–7) is a favorite among local residents. Also at the casual end of the scale is **St. Andrews Café** (845/471-6608; lunch and dinner Mon.–Fri.; mains $17–20) for contemporary American fare. The Asian-influenced menu includes Korean-style short ribs and grilled marinated tuna with soba noodles. The elegant **Ristorante Caterina de Medici** (Colavita Cen-

ter for Italian Food and Wine, 845/471-6608; lunch and dinner Mon.–Fri.; mains $15–24) serves Italian specialties under a Venetian chandelier. For a more casual dining experience, ask to be seated in the Al Forno Dining Room. Finally, **Escoffier Restaurant** (Roth Hall, 845/471-6608, lunch mains $18–25, dinner mains $25–32) excels in classic French cuisine, from Provençal to Parisian delights. The à la carte menu, inspired by the late chef Auguste Escoffier, features entrées such as braised veal cheeks, monkish tournedos, and poached chicken breast with truffle consommé. When making reservations, note that CIA restaurants are only open when the school is in session.

Catch sunset over the river from the 100-seat dining room of **Belvedere Mansion** (10 Olde Rte. 9, Staatsburg, 845/889-8000, www .belvederemansion.com; 5:30–8:30 P.M. Thurs.–Sun.; mains $24–30), serving a menu of New American cuisine in a formal setting. This cigar-friendly restaurant takes pride in its selection of after-dinner drinks, which include single malt scotches, brandies, ports, and dessert wines.

In Rhinebeck, start the day with a mouthwatering French pastry at **Calico Restaurant** (6384 Mill St., Rhinebeck, 845/876-2749, www.calicorhinebeck.com; bakery opens at 8 A.M., lunch 11 A.M.–2:30 P.M., dinner from 5:30 P.M. Wed.–Sat., brunch 11 A.M.–2:30 P.M. Sun.; pastries $4, lunch mains $8–10, dinner mains $18–24), or enjoy a full meal later in the day.

Housed inside an old church in the center of town, ⬛ **Terrapin** (6426 Montgomery St., Rhinebeck, 845/876-3330, www.terrapin restaurant.com; 5–9:30 P.M. Mon.–Thurs., 5 P.M.–10:30 P.M. Fri.–Sat., 5–9 P.M. Sun.; mains $18–28) remains a hotspot for creative New American cuisine, including a grilled double-thick pork chop with rhubarb demi-glace, rack of spring lamb, Peking duck, and several vegetarian entrées. Its sister establishment, Terrapin Red, is a cozy bar and bistro that's open daily for lunch and dinner. On the same block, the refreshing blend of Italian, Mediterranean, and Hudson Valley dishes at ⬛ **Gigi**

© NIKKI GOTH ITOI

Terrapin, Rhinebeck

Trattoria (6422 Montgomery St., Suite 1, Rhinebeck, 845/876-1007, www.gigitrattoria .com; 11:30 A.M.–2:45 P.M. and 4:30 P.M. till close Tues.–Sun.; mains $15–27) has impressed travelers from all around the country, and weekend residents and visitors fill the place night after night. Another graduate of the CIA turns out flatbread pizzas, creative pastas, and a range of hearty second courses.

Tiny **Le Petit Bistro** (8 E. Market St., Rhinebeck, 845/876-7400, www.lepetitbistro .com; dinner Thurs.–Mon.) consistently ranks among the top French restaurants in the entire Hudson Valley. Whether you order sea scallops, English Dover sole, frogs' legs, duck, or steak au poivre, the meal will come perfectly prepared.

Tucked away on a side street, newcomer **Sabroso** (22 Garden St., Rhinebeck, 845/876-8688, www.sabrosoplatos.com; from 5:30 P.M. Wed.–Mon.; mains $18–28) adds Nuevo Latino cuisine to a long list of fine dining options in Rhinebeck. This is place to order ceviche, plantains, paella, and a range of foods inspired by the flavors of Peru, Ecuador,

and the rest of Central and South America. Choose indoor or patio dining.

Pete's Famous Restaurant is a popular local breakfast diner chain with locations in Rhinebeck (34 E. Market St., 845/876-7271; 6 A.M.–9 P.M. daily), Hyde Park (4200 Albany Post Rd., 845/229-1475) and on Hooker Avenue in Poughkeepsie, near Vassar College. The diners are open for breakfast, lunch, and dinner, and mains average $10. **Bread Alone** (45 E. Market St., Rhinebeck, 845/876-3108, www.breadalone.com; 7 A.M.–5 P.M. daily) has opened a Rhinebeck location as well, serving its legendary breads, pastries, and sandwiches.

Outside of town, **Diaspora** (1094 Rte. 308E, Rhinebeck, 845/758-9601, www.diaspora cuisine.com; 5–10 P.M. Wed.–Thurs. and Sun., till 11 P.M. Fri.–Sat.; mains $14–20) gets high marks for innovative Greek cuisine, including seafood and lamb dishes. Enjoy a three-course prix fixe menu on Wednesdays and Thursdays, or a full dinner Friday–Sunday.

Red Hook boasts a few casual eateries: At the corner of Routes 9 and 199, across from the Merit Bookstore, **J&J Gourmet Catering** has window display of old cans and tins from brands like Ritz Crackers, Life Savers, Coca-Cola, Hershey's, and Maxwell House. Inside is a gourmet deli that makes homemade soups and sandwiches. **Lucy's Tacos** on the same side of Route 199 as the bookstore, serves tasty Mexican fare. And on the same block, farther east, **Mercado** is known for a changing menu of somewhat unconventional Italian food.

South of town, there's barbecue and more barbecue to be found at **Max's Memphis Barbecue** (136 S. Broadway/Rte. 9, Red Hook, 845/758-6297; 5–10 P.M. Tues.–Sun.).

At the northern edge of the county, Bard College students frequent **Santa Fe** (52 Broadway off Rte. 9G, Tivoli, 845/757-4100, www .santafetivoli.com; mains $12–17) for tacos and burritos, margaritas and mojitos.

Central Dutchess County– Routes 44 and 22

Pawling residents know 【 **McKinney & Doyle** as simply, The Bakery (10 Charles

Colman Blvd., Pawling, 845/855-3875; lunch 11:30 A.M.–3 P.M. Tues.–Fri., dinner 6–9:30 P.M. Wed.–Sat., 5–9 P.M. Sun., brunch 9 A.M.–3 P.M. Sat.–Sun.; lunch mains $8–15, dinner mains $20–27). Enter through the bakery and admire all the treats behind the glass counter. Then grab a booth or table in the adjoining air-conditioned restaurant, which has brick walls and worn wood floors. Creative lunch mains include a meat loaf sandwich served on rye with grilled melted cheese, a crab cake burger, rough chop Cobb salad, or roasted turkey cranberry with crisp fried asparagus on top. The bakery is open daily.

Baklajava Coffee Shop & Bakery (10 E. Main St., Pawling, 845/855-1325, www.baklajava.com) puts a different spin on baked goods. Its muffins, scones, and cookies are winning customers around town. During the summer months, teens build strong arm muscles scooping homemade ice cream at **Heinchon's Old Farmhouse** (Rte. 22, Pawling; noon–10 P.M. early May–Labor Day). The family's dairy farm has been in business since the 1920s.

Just north of Pawling in Wingdale, **(Big W's Roadside Bar B Que** (1475 Rte. 22, Wingdale, 845/832-6200, www.bigwsbbq.com; mains $7–14) does dry rub right. This is the place to stop for slow-smoked spareribs, pulled pork, and beef brisket, but plan to get there early, as the restaurant often runs out of ribs by 8 P.M. The owner likes to show off the 1.5-ton tank smoker.

Whether you order a croque monsieur, a bowl of steamed mussels, or *le steak frites,* Millbrook's **(Café Les Baux** (152 Church St., Millbrook, 845/677-8166 www.cafelesbaux .com; noon–3 P.M. and 5–9 P.M. Wed.–Thurs. and Sun.–Mon., till 10 P.M. Fri.–Sat.; mains $7–24) ranks as one of the best French Bistros around. Open since 2002, the bistro serves lunch and dinner in a warm and cozy dining room located in the center of town.

Babbett's Kitchen, a relatively new bakery and café, is giving incumbent **Slammin' Salmon** (under new ownership) a run for the breakfast and lunch crowd. Locals line up for ice cream at the **Mabbetsville Creamery** on Route 44 between Millbrook and Amenia.

Just outside of town another longtime Millbrook eatery recently changed hands: Allyn's Restaurant is now **Charlotte's** (4258 Rte. 44, Millbrook, 845/677-5888; 5–9:30 P.M. Wed.–Thurs., 5–10:30 P.M. Fri., 11:30 A.M.–10:30 P.M. Sat., 11:30 A.M.–9:30 P.M. Sun.; mains $20–28), serving New American fare in a converted 200-year-old church.

On the way to Millbrook from the Taconic Parkway, **La Puerta Azul** (2510 Rte. 44, Salt Point, 856/677-2985, www.lapuertaazul.com; 11:30 A.M.–11 P.M. daily) is a beautifully designed Mexican restaurant oddly located in a strip mall plaza on the drive from the Taconic Parkway to Millbrook. Chef Ramiro Jimenez, a native of Acapulco, Mexico, oversees an authentic menu of fish, chicken, and meat dishes, including duck with mole negro sauce, Veracruz-style tilapia, and a slow-smoked rib eye steak with cumin sauce. No expense was spared on the interior design of the restaurant: it's worth a visit just to see the stylish restrooms.

Continuing up the Taconic State Parkway, the **Fireside Bar and Grill** (1920 Salt Point Tpke., Salt Point, 845/266-3440; from 4 P.M. Tues.–Sun.; mains $9–22) serves 25-ounce beers in frosted mugs. It's been around for generations and has a friendly staff that serves tasty baby back ribs, barbecue, tri-tip, and prime rib on weekends.

The ever-popular **Four Brothers Pizza** has locations in Amenia (Rte. 22, 845/373-8178) and Dover Plains (Rte. 22, 845/877-3662).

For travelers en route to Connecticut, several good restaurants hide out in Millerton, in the northeast corner of Dutchess County: For starters, you can taste the local brew along with lunch at the **(Harney & Sons Tea Tasting Room** (13 Main St., Railroad Plaza, Millerton, www.harney.com; 10 A.M.–5 P.M. Mon.–Sat., 11 A.M.–4 P.M. Sun.) after a walk on the Harlem Valley Rail Trail, which passes right through town. Connoisseurs rave about the garden ambience and friendly service, not to mention the incredible selection of fine teas. New England in New York defines the atmosphere inside the Victorian **Hamilton Inn** (67 Main St., Millerton, 518/789-9399, www.thehamiltoninn.com;

THE MID-HUDSON

© NIKKI GOTH ITOI

Harney & Sons Tea Tasting Room, Millerton

lunch 11:30 A.M.–3 P.M. Fri.–Sun., dinner 5:30–9:30 P.M. Sun.–Thurs., 5:30–10 P.M. Fri.–Sat.; mains $15–25). The menu features surf and turn staples, such as crab cakes, angus burgers, and chicken Français.

The **Irving Farm Coffee House** (44 Main St., Millerton, 518/789-2020, www.irvingfarm .com) serves its own espresso, roasted in a converted 19th-century carriage house nearby. You can also order wine, beer, and light snacks besides the usual menu of frothy coffee drinks.

ENTERTAINMENT AND EVENTS
Performing Arts

The 1869 **Bardavon Opera House** (35 Market St., Poughkeepsie, 845/473-2072, www.bard avon.org) is one of the top performing-arts venues in Dutchess County. It hosts the Hudson Valley Philharmonic and a full schedule of musical, dance, film, and theater productions by contemporary artists.

At the other end of the architectural spectrum, the **Fisher Center for the Performing Arts** (Rte. 9G, Annandale, 845/758-7900, fishercenter.bard.edu, box office 10 A.M.–5 P.M. Mon.–Fri.) is housed in a modern, stainless-steel building on the Bard College campus. Its innovative shows include orchestra, chamber, and jazz music, as well as modern theater, dance, and opera. The **Bard Music Festival** (Rte. 9G Bard College, Annandale-on-Hudson, 845/758-7900, summerscape.bard.edu) focuses on a single composer each year.

The Rhinebeck Theatre Society and other local groups perform at the **Center for the Performing Arts at Rhinebeck** (Rte. 308, Rhinebeck, 845/876-3080, www.centerfor performingarts.org; box office 11 A.M.–5 P.M. Tues.–Fri., 1–5 P.M. Sat.). Also in Rhinebeck, **Upstate Films** (6415 Montgomery St., Rte. 9, Rhinebeck, 845/876-2515, www.upstatefilms .org; $7.50 regular, $6 seniors 62 and over, $4.50 members & children under 16) has been showing indie films since 1972. Regulars can't resist the homemade treats at the candy counter.

Bars and Nightlife

Poughkeepsie's proximity to New York City means that well-known performers come to town

Upstate Films, the place for indie film in Rhinebeck

on a fairly regular basis. Most popular among the city's nightclubs is **The Chance** (6 Crannell St., Poughkeepsie, 845/471-1966, www.thechance complex.com), which plays live music. The Chance is part of an entertainment complex that includes four different clubs all in one building. The others are Club Crannel Street, The Loft (for DJ music), and the Platinum Lounge.

Bananas Comedy Club (Best Western Inn, 2170 Rte. 9, Poughkeepsie, 845/462-3333, www.bananascomedyclub.com; Fri. admission $12, Sat. $15) is the place to go for a good laugh. At 10:30 P.M., Fishkill's Il Barilotto restaurant transforms into a Manhattan-style night club called **IB Notte** and stays open till 2 A.M.

Near Vassar College, the former Dickens restaurant is now an Irish pub. The **Dubliner** (796 Main St., Poughkeepsie, 845/454-7322) serves delicious Irish food and plays live music several nights a week.

In Rhinebeck, the gorgeous wood-paneled **Colonial Tap Room** at the Beekman Arms (6387 Mill St., Rhinebeck, 845/876-1766) offers a cozy and historic atmosphere for enjoying a cold draft beer. Alternatively, the **Rhinebeck Wine & Liquor Store** (41 E. Market St., Rhinebeck, 845/876-6264) offers free tastings 4–7 P.M. on Friday and Saturday.

Festivals

Summer in Dutchess County brings one food, wine, auto, and art festival after another. The **Hudson Valley Food & Wine Festival** (River Rd., Annandale-on-Hudson, 845/758-5461) takes place at Montgomery Place in June. Kids get excited when the **Dutchess County Fair** (Rte. 9, Dutchess County Fairgrounds, Rhinebeck, 845/876-4001 www.dutchessfair .com) comes to town in August. Two of the largest antique car shows in the Northeast are also held at the fairgrounds: The **Hudson River Valley Antique Auto Association's Annual Car Show & Swap Meet** (Rte. 9, Dutchess County Fair Grounds, 845/876-4001, www .dutchessfair.com) arrives in May, and the **Good Guys Classic Rods Auto Show** (Rte. 9, Dutchess County Fairgrounds, Rhinebeck) takes place in September.

Wineries from the Hudson Valley and across New York State gather at Grieg Farm

THE MID-HUDSON

each September for the **Hudson Valley Wine Fest** (Dutchess County Fair Grounds, 845/876-4001, www.hudsonvalleywinefest .com; one-day tasting $30, weekend tasting $50), a weekend of gourmet food, crafts, wine seminars, cooking demos, and live music.

The Beacon Arts Community Association organizes a monthly event, **Beacon Second Saturday** (845/546-6222, www.beaconarts .org), during which galleries and shops stay open until 9 P.M. Building on the success of the event series, another local nonprofit began hosting **Open Doors @ Beacon Studios** (211 Fishkill Ave., Beacon, 845/838-4243, www .beaconstudios.org; 1–5 P.M.), also on the second Saturday of the month, at the Old Beacon High School.

Pawling hosts a triathlon each May that draws competitors from around the Tri-State area.

Spectator Sports

For an evening of all-American fun, head to **Dutchess Stadium** (Rte. 9D, Wappingers Falls, 845/838-0094; admission $5–9) to watch the Hudson Valley Renegades play minor league baseball. Tickets are easy to come by, and fireworks often follow the games.

SHOPPING

A busy commercial zone crowds Route 9 from Fishkill to Hyde Park, with one shopping mall after another. Head for the hills to avoid the chains. **La Vie en Rose** (111 Fraleigh Ln, Red Hook) sells vintage clothing from the 1800s to the 1960s.

Voted best handbag store in the Hudson Valley by the local press, **Citrus Handbags** (141 Church St., Millbrook, 845/677-9660) also has a unique selection of clothing, jewelry, headbands, and ribbon watches, and Bette Midler is an occasional customer. If you're in the market (and have the budget) for a one-of-a-kind beaded and jeweled dress, **Rowena Gill** (59 Front St., Millbrook, 845/677-3770, www.rowenagill.com; 10 A.M.–4 P.M. Tues.–Fri., 10 A.M.–12:30 P.M. Sat.) is the designer for you. Stop by her showroom to see these exquisite works of art. And while you're in town,

stock up on gourmet foods for a picnic or buy a gift basket for your host at **Keeper's Market** (Franklin St., Millbrook).

Rhinebeck has a handful of boutique shops: **Periwinkle's** (Mills St./Rte. 308, Rhinebeck) sells Sally Spicer handbags, Yankee Candles, and the usual assortment of kitchen and bath accessories. A few doors closer to the intersection with Route 9, **Summer Moon** (14 Mills St., Rhinebeck) carries everything from Tibetan player flags to Dr. Hoska skincare products and Putumayo World Music. **Kiddely Divvy** (Garden St., Rhinebeck, 845/876-7959) is a children's boutique with clothing, toys, books, and gifts—everything from Ugly Dolls to slinkies. The store is open 10 A.M.–5 P.M. Wednesday–Friday, 10 A.M.–6 P.M. Saturday, and noon–4:30 P.M. Sunday.

Stop by the handy **Cabin Fever Outfitters** (6423 Montgomery St., Rhinebeck, 845/ 876-6005, www.cabinfeveroutfitters.com) for any gear you left behind. The **Rhinebeck Bicycle Shop** is on Garden Street, open 10 A.M.–5 P.M. Monday and Wednesday, 10 A.M.–6 P.M. Tuesday, Thursday, and Friday, and 10 A.M.–4 P.M. Saturday.

In Red Hook, **Basic French** (5 East Market St., Red Hook, 845/758-0399) is your typical Francophile boutique with French-milled soaps, Petit Bateau baby clothes, and the like.

Wine

Beacon's **Artisan Wine Shop** (180 Main St., Beacon, www.artisanwineshop.com) has the chilled white wine you need for a riverside picnic after a Dia:Beacon visit. The **Rhinebeck Wine & Liquor Store** (41 E. Market St., Rhinebeck, 845/876-6264) carries labels from near and far and offers free tastings 4–7 P.M. on Fridays and Saturdays. You can also purchase locally made wines at the individual winery tasting rooms.

Farm Stands

The after-work stop for fresh veggies at a local farm stand is a way of life for Dutchess County residents. True connoisseurs can tell from the first bite if their corn was picked in the morning or afternoon. You can often find these stands at major local intersections, such as at Routes 9 and 9G near Rhinebeck. If you have more time on your hands, pick your own produce at an orchard like **Fishkill Farms** (222 E. Hook Cross Rd., Hopewell Junction, 845/897-4377), which has been growing apples for 75 years. At **Montgomery Place Orchards** (Back River Rd., Annandale-on-Hudson, 845/758-6338; 9 A.M.–6 P.M. Mon.–Sat., 9 A.M.–4 P.M. Sun.), you can combine your picking with a tour of the historic Montgomery Place mansion.

Family-run **Adams Fairacre Farms** (765 Dutchess Turnpike/Rte. 44 Poughkeepsie, 845/454-4330, www.adamsfarms.com; 8 A.M.–9 P.M. Mon.–Fri., 8 A.M.–7 P.M. Sat.– Sun.) began as a roadside stand in 1932, selling homegrown fruits and vegetables to Poughkeepsie residents. Today, the company is a local phenomenon with 650 employees operating three large retail spaces in Poughkeepsie, Kingston, and Newburgh. In addition to fresh produce, Adams sells gourmet cheese, breads, coffee, and meats, including many locally made products. Expect long lines on weekends. **Greig Farm** (223 Pitcher La., Red Hook, 845/758-6561, www.greigfarm.com; 8 A.M.–7 P.M. daily) has evolved from a standard apple-picking operation to a year-round marketplace and bakery.

The **Millbrook Farmers Market** takes place 9 A.M.–1 P.M. Saturday, May–October. Beacon has a farmers market on Sundays at the riverfront 11 A.M.–4 P.M.

Dykeman Farm (West Dover Rd., Wingdale) grows sweet corn and tomatoes and offers pick-your-own pumpkins in the fall. Northeast of Amenia, the **McEnroe Organic Farm Market** (Rte. 22/44, Northeast) offers organic produce in season, plus pick-your-own herbs and flowers.

Pick up fine teas and accessories for friends back home at the Harney & Sons Tea Shop in Millerton.

Antiques and Galleries

Every town in Dutchess County has its share of antique finds. Twenty-five of them are found under one art deco roof at Red Hook's **Annex Antiques Center** (23 E. Market St.,

Red Hook, 845/758-2843; 11 A.M.–5 P.M. daily). Watch artisans at work in half a dozen shops along the Ten Mile River at the **Webatuck Craft Village** (Rte. 55, Wingdale, www.huntcountryfurniture.com/webatuck). Handmade crafts include blown glass, pottery, and objects made of copper, tin, and wood. Most of the shops are open 10 A.M.–5 P.M. daily except Tuesday.

Hudson Beach Glass 162 Main St., Beacon, 845/440-0068, www.hudsonbeachglass .com; 10 A.M.–6 P.M. Mon.–Sat., 11 A.M.–6 P.M. Sun.) carries jewelry, vases, bowls, and other glass works created by several local artists. It is one of the only glassworks galleries of its size in upstate New York. The **Van Brunt Gallery** (460 Main St., Beacon, 845/838-2995, www .vanbruntgallery.com; 11 A.M.–6 P.M. Thurs.– Mon.) specializes in "edgy, emotional" works by regional artists.

Bookstores

Booklovers will find both big chains and independent treasure chests across the county. For example, **Merritt Bookstore** (57 Front St., Millbrook, 845/677-5857, www.merrittbooks .com; 9 A.M.–6 P.M. Mon.–Sat., 10 A.M.–5 P.M. Sun.) sells new fiction and nonfiction, with a second location in Red Hook (corner of Route 199 and Route 9, 845/758-2665; 10 A.M.–6 P.M. Mon.–Thurs., 10 A.M.–7 P.M. Fri.–Sat., 10 A.M.–5 P.M. Sun.). The recently renovated **Book Cove & Antique Center** (Charles Colman Blvd., Pawling) in Pawling doubles as an antique center. In Beacon, **World's End Books** (474 Main St., Beacon, 845/831-1760) has a delightful selection of new and used titles, many covering New York history and travel.

INFORMATION AND SERVICES

The **Dutchess County Tourism Promotion Agency** (3 Neptune Rd., Suite M-17, Poughkeepsie, 845/463-4000, www.dutchesstourism .com) can provide a wealth of information on places to see across the county. Several of the smaller towns have visitors centers as well: **Rhinebeck Chamber of Commerce**

(19 Mill St., Rhinebeck, 845/876-5904, www .rhinebeckchamber.com; 10 A.M.–4 P.M.Wed.– Sat., noon–4 P.M. Sun.) and **Red Hook Area Chamber of Commerce** (P.O. Box 254, Red Hook, 845/758-0824, www.redhookchamber .org; 9:30 A.M.–12:30 P.M. Mon.–Fri.).

GETTING THERE AND AROUND
By Bus
Shortline Bus (800/631-8405) provides daily service to Poughkeepsie, Hyde Park, and Rhinebeck from New York City, Long Island, and New Jersey. **Adirondack Trailways** (800/858-8555, www.escapemaker.com/adirondacktrailways) also runs buses between Poughkeepsie and New York City. The Dutchess County Loop Bus System (14 Commerce St., Poughkeepsie, 845/485-4690) covers major destinations, including Dutchess County Community College, Marist College, and the Poughkeepsie Train Station. In Poughkeepsie, a city bus system with six lines services all parts of the city.

By Train
Amtrak and **Metro-North** offer frequent connections to the Poughkeepsie Train Station, and taxis are usually waiting. On weekdays, the parking lot overflows with commuter vehicles. Amtrak also stops in Rhinecliff to the north. And the Metro-North Hudson Line stops in Beacon to the south, while the Harlem Line services Pawling, Dover Plains, and Wassaic.

By Car
The most direct routes through Dutchess County are the Taconic State Parkway and Route 22. Route 9 follows the Hudson River through the most densely populated areas of the county. I-84 runs east–west, connecting motorists to I-87, the New York State Thruway. Avis and Hertz have rental car offices off Route 9, near the IBM complex in Poughkeepsie. Budget, Enterprise, and Sears also have rental facilities in the area. Each major town in the county has at least one taxi service.

Ulster County

The Esopus Indians were the first people to settle mountainous Ulster County. European invasion began with a Dutch trading post in 1614, and a series of battles with the Native American population ensued for the next few decades. A group of French Huguenots arrived in 1663, fleeing religious persecution on the continent. One hundred years later came the British, who would burn Kingston—the county seat—to the ground during the Revolutionary War.

Ulster's early industries were the production of cement and bluestone; its communities also prospered as the terminus for the Delaware and Ulster Canal, which delivered coal from mines in Pennsylvania to the Eastern Seaboard.

Covering more than a thousand square miles of riverfront, foothills, and two distinct mountain ranges, modern-day Ulster County is a haven for rock climbers and general outdoor enthusiasts. The state university at New Paltz and nearby Minnewaska State Park attract a young and active crowd that supports an abundance of cafés, bookstores, restaurants, and gear shops. Farther west lie Woodstock, the Esopus River for tubing, and a few of the summer boarding houses that were popular in the 1960s.

Ulster boasts the highest peak in the Catskills: Slide Mountain, which rises 4,180 feet above the town of Oliverea. The Ashokan Reservoir, completed in 1917 in a major engineering feat, supplies more than half of New York City's water.

ALONG THE RIVER–ROUTE 9W
One of the oldest and prettiest spans across the Hudson, the Mid-Hudson Bridge, connects southern Ulster County to downtown Poughkeepsie. Since 1999, pedestrians have

been allowed to cross it on foot, bicycle, or in-line skates. To get to the walkway, follow Havelin Drive off Route 9W to a small park that connects to the bridge.

Ten miles south of the Mid-Hudson Bridge, **Gomez Mill House** (11 Millhouse Rd., Marlboro, 845/236-3126, www.gomez.org; 10 A.M.– 4 P.M. Wed.–Sun.; adults $7.50, seniors $5, students $2) boasts a multicultural past that reaches all the way back to the time of the Spanish Inquisition. Luis Moses Gomez, a Sephardi or descendant of the Jews who settled Spain and Portugal in the Middle Ages, fled persecution in the early 18th century and built a trading post in Marlboro in 1714. Subsequent owners of the fieldstone home were Patriots of the American Revolution, farmers, writers, artisans, and environmentalists. Today, the building is the oldest surviving Jewish homestead in North America. Tours of the inside are available, and the museum holds cultural events and lectures through the summer season.

Slabsides Burroughs Sanctuary

Naturalist John Burroughs wrote hundreds of essays over the span of his career, many of them from a log cabin tucked away in the woods near present-day West Park. A student of Whitman and Thoreau, Burroughs treasured the simple things in life: books, friends, and above all, nature. Of a summer hike in the southern Catskills, he wrote, "An ideal trout brook was this, now hurrying, now loitering, now deepening around a great boulder, now gliding evenly over a pavement of green-gray stone and pebbles; no sediment or stain of any kind, but white and sparkling as snow-water, and nearly as cool."

A visit to the Burroughs retreat, called Slabsides (Burroughs Dr., West Park, 845/ 384-6320), will bring out the nature writer in any traveler. The John Burroughs Association, formed soon after Burroughs died in 1921, maintains the grounds of the 180-acre Slabsides Burroughs Sanctuary and opens the 1895 cabin to the public twice each year, on the third Saturday in May and the first Saturday

in October. Allow about 20 minutes to walk from the parking lot to the cabin.

Kingston

As the third most important Dutch trading post (after New Amsterdam/Manhattan and Fort Orange/Albany), Kingston played a pivotal role in the establishment of New York State. But early settlers paid dearly for their independence: during the American Revolution, the British retaliated against the colonists by burning the city to the ground. The tragedy left its mark, and no story is repeated more often as one tours the Hudson Valley's historic sights.

Like Saugerties to its north, Kingston developed around a strategic watershed: where the Rondout Creek meets the Hudson River. Settlers traded cement, bricks, and bluestone, and Kingston served as a transportation hub during the steam and rail eras. Today, greater Kingston is a sea of huge retail stores with some interesting pockets of culture and history. A variety of architectural styles have been preserved, from Federal, Georgian, and Greek Revival to Romanesque, Italianate, neoclassical, and art deco. Two areas are of interest to the traveler: the Stockade Historic District and the revitalized Rondout Village.

Colorful brick facades of mauve, orange, and lima-bean green line Wall Street inside the old stockade, originally built to keep Native Americans out. Many of the homes in this district are private residences, but a few are open to the public. A gorgeous Federal home at the corner of Main and Wall streets was saved in the late 1930s by Fred J. Johnston, an antique and restoration specialist. Johnston deeded the home and collection of 18th- and 19th-century furnishings to a local nonprofit organization, and the building is open to the public.

Up the street stands the Old Dutch Church, dating back to the 18th century. George Clinton, the first governor of New York and vice president to Jefferson and Madison, is buried here. Hoffman House, at the north end of Front Street, is a Dutch colonial structure dating back to 1679. A pair of entrepreneurs renovated the building in the mid-1970s and turned it into a restaurant.

In 1777, a group of local political leaders gathered in Kingston to draft the New York State constitution. The first senate convened at 312 Fair Street, now the **Senate House State Historic Site** (296 Fair St., 845/338-2786; 10 A.M.–5 P.M. Mon., Wed., Sat., 11 A.M.–5 P.M. Sun.; adults $4, seniors $3, under 12 free). A historical exhibit contains paintings by Kingston's own John Vanderlyn.

For a guided tour of the Stockade District homes and the Senate House, contact 1658 Stockade District Walking Tours (63 Main St., 845/339-0720; adults $3, children $2). Tours are offered the first Saturday of the month May–October starting at 2 P.M., or by special appointment. Stop by the Tourism Information Caboose on Washington Avenue (800/331-1518) to pick up a self-guided brochure. Take New York Thruway Exit 19 to reach downtown Kingston.

When you leave the Stockade District, follow Broadway to its end at the edge of the Rondout Creek, where a handful of upscale restaurants, including the new Mariner's Harbor, have revitalized Rondout Village, a cluster of restored brick buildings near the Route 9W crossing. In summer, you can dine in one of the landing's trendy eateries and finish the evening with a stroll along the waterfront.

The **Hudson River Maritime Museum** (50 Rondout Landing, 845/338-0071, www.ulster .net/~hrmm; 11 A.M.–4 P.M. Fri.–Mon. May–Oct.; adults $5, seniors and children $4) opens here each spring with the annual Kingston Shad Festival. A restored 1898 steam tug named Mathilda takes up most of the museum's yard. Inside are a 100-year-old shad boat and a number of model ships. A collection of paintings, prints, photos, blueprints, and artifacts document the maritime history of the river—from sloops and iceboats to steam engines and tugs—and the industries it has supported throughout the years.

A short boat ride across the creek will get you to the **Rondout Lighthouse** (50 Rondout Landing, 845/338-0071, www.hudsonlights .com/rondout.htm), which dates to 1913 and is the largest on the river. Period furnishings and memorabilia trace the history of the lighthouse and its keepers. A $10 fee for adults includes admission to the museum. Tours are available weekends from Memorial Day to Labor Day on Saturdays, Sundays, and holiday Mondays.

For a taste of life during the railroad era, visit the **Trolley Museum** (89 E. Strand St., 845/331-3399, www.tmny.org; noon–5 P.M. Sat.–Sun. Memorial Day–Columbus Day; adults $4, seniors $3, children (2–12) $3, under 2 free) at Rondout Landing and take a short ride along the original tracks of the Del-

aware and Ulster Railroad. The trolley stops at Kingston Point Park on the Hudson River. Exhibits inside the museum trace the history of rail transportation, and visitors can watch restorations in progress in the workshop below.

Saugerties

The Esopus Creek empties into the Hudson at Saugerties. Water rushing out of the mountains once powered a mill that led the town to the forefront of the paper industry. Recognition on the National Register of Historic Places has put Saugerties on the map once again, with an eight-block stretch of 18th- and 19th-century homes, antique shops, and top-notch restaurants that draw a growing number of travelers.

The restored **Saugerties Lighthouse** (168 Lighthouse Dr. off Mynderse St., 845/ 247-0656, www.saugertieslighthouse.com) built in 1869, is a half-mile walk from the town center along a nature path that can be flooded at high tide. Now a two-room bed-and-breakfast, the house is furnished in 1920s-era style. Guided tours are available 2–5 P.M. Memorial Day–Labor Day ($3 donation).

Plan to arrive on a weekend afternoon, with time to browse the **Hope Farm Press and Bookshop** (252 Main St., 845/246-3522, www.hopefarm.com; 10 A.M.–6 P.M. Mon.–Sat.) before catching some live music at the **Chowhound Café** (112 Partition St., 845/ 246-5158).

Tucked away on a narrow country lane between Saugerties and Woodstock is a vestige of the bluestone era. Over four decades, sculpture artist Harvey Fite turned an abandoned quarry behind his house and studio into a six-acre sculpture garden that's open to the public on weekends throughout the summer. A small gallery on-site holds a collection of quarryman's tools. Look for the turnoff to **Opus One** at The Red Onion restaurant on Route 212.

Modern-day flower children gathered at nearby **Winston Farm** in July of 1999 to recreate the good times of the original Woodstock Music Festival (held not in Woodstock, but in nearby Delaware County). The property

© JASON EGLIT

Rondout Lighthouse

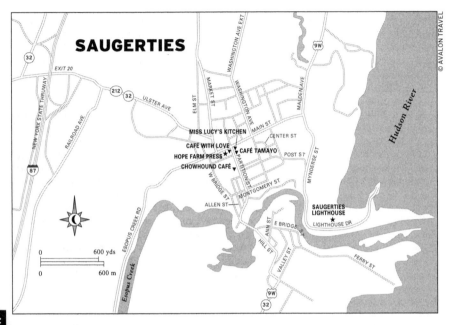

SAUGERTIES

© AVALON TRAVEL

is privately owned, and you must ask permission to pay a visit.

NEW PALTZ AND SURROUNDINGS

More than any other community in the Hudson Valley, New Paltz offers travelers a healthy dose of alternative culture. In 2004, Mayor Jason West brought the town to the center of a national debate when he began marrying same-sex couples on the heels of the highly publicized unions in San Francisco. Within walking distance from the town center, the SUNY New Paltz campus fosters a vibrant student community.

New Paltz has deep roots in protecting groups who face discrimination. The town owes its name to a group of French Huguenots from Mannheim, Germany—part of a region called Die Pfalz—who came to the New World in 1677 to escape religious persecution. These early settlers built homes above the Wallkill River on present-day Huguenot Street.

A short walk uphill from Huguenot Street

puts you on Main Street in striking distance of most of the shops and restaurants in town. The **Wallkill Valley Rail Trail** crosses Main Street just below Route 32, making this an ideal stopover for walkers or cyclists following the length of the trail from Wallkill to Rosendale. Drivers should take Exit 18 from the New York Thruway to reach New Paltz. Expect traffic jams and difficult parking on summer weekends.

◖ Huguenot Street

Several of the six original stone buildings on this street have survived more than three centuries of evolution in the community. The original structures of the Bevier-Elting, Jean Hasbrouck, and Abraham Hasbrouck Houses were built in the 1680s, and these homes are preserved as they would have looked in the 18th century. The 1799 LeFevre House was built in the Federal style, and the museum has furnished it with 19th-century accoutrements. The Deyo House is designed to portray an 1890s aesthetic, while the colonial Freer House was remodeled in the 1940s.

THE MID-HUDSON

The Huguenot Historical Society runs guided tours from its visitors center in the DuBois Fort (18 Broadhead Ave., New Paltz, 845/255-1660, www.hhsnewpaltz.org; 10 A.M.–4 P.M. Tues.–Sun.) Tours run 50 or 90 minutes and cost $10 for adults, $9 for seniors and students, and $5 for children, with reduced rates for the abbreviated tour.

The organization also maintains **Locust Lawn** (Rte. 32, Gardiner, 845/255-1660, www.huguenotstreet.org; tours 11 A.M.–4 P.M. Sat.–Sun.; adults $7, seniors $6, children and students $3, under 6 free), an 1814 Federal mansion that belonged to the prominent Hasbrouck family. A collection of family memorabilia is on display inside.

The Shawangunk Ridge

Between New Paltz and the Catskill Mountains lies another mountain range with its own geologic history, the Shawangunk Ridge. The result of a continental collision, the exposed sedimentary rock of the Shawangunks offers amateur and professional geologists an accessible, living laboratory to study the formation of the Appalachian Mountains—an eroded range that once stretched as high as the Himalayas.

The Shawangunk Ridge runs from the town of Rosendale all the way to New Jersey and Pennsylvania. From the spotted salamander to the black bear, it supports a delicate habitat for dozens of endangered plants and animals, among them the dwarf pitch pine, which grows on bedrock, and the peregrine falcon. Shale cliffs and dramatic overhangs also form ideal pitches for serious rock climbers, who know the area affectionately as The Gunks. Indeed, they arrive by the hundreds on clear summer days, with ropes, harnesses, and chalk in tow.

Three protected wilderness areas cover a

large portion of the Shawangunk Ridge: Minnewaska State Park Preserve, the Mohonk Preserve, and Sam's Point Preserve.

◖ Minnewaska State Park Preserve

Acquired by New York State in 1987, Minnewaska State Park Preserve (Rte. 44/55, New Paltz, 845/255-0579, www.nysparks.com; open year-round for day-use; $7 per vehicle) encompasses 12,000 acres with a main entrance at Lake Minnewaska, off Route 44/55. Though the elevation here is about 2,000 feet, the scrubby pines, precipitous cliffs, and sparkling water might trick you into thinking you are above 10,000.

Hikers have a full menu of options within Minnewaska, from easy two-mile routes to challenging 10-mile loops. You can actually follow the ridgeline by foot from the Appalachian Trail at the New Jersey state line all the way to Wurtsboro and the Bashakill Preserve, in Sullivan County. Climbers will want to head to the Peter's Kill Escarpment, a good alternative to the crowds at the Mohonk Preserve. Bicycles are allowed on the carriage paths only, not on the trails.

In addition to the Lake Minnewaska parking lot, Minnewaska has parking and trailheads at Peter's Kill to the east and Awosting to the west. A word of caution: to protect the fragile ecosystem, the park service limits the number of visitors allowed in Minnewaska at once. On summer weekends, the lots often fill immediately after opening. It's a good idea to arrive with a backup plan in mind, such as exploring the Wallkill Valley Rail Trail. Note that Minnewaska is a day-use park only; there are no overnight accommodations, and visitors must pack out all trash.

Outside of Minnewaska on Route 44/55 is the unassuming town of Gardiner, which finds itself at the center of a crossfire between real estate developers and environmentalists. The private owners of 2,600 acres that make up the Awosting Reserve next to Minnewaska mean to build a community of 350 luxury homes, complete with a new golf course and sewage treatment plant. Conservationists argue the development would threaten the habitat of some two dozen endangered species, while obstructing the views from trails in the adjoining state parks. But for now, the plans are stalled in a sea of red tape, and the Shawangunk Trail remains unharmed.

Mohonk Preserve

Adjoining Minnewaska to the north is the Mohonk Mountain Preserve (1000 Mountain Rest Rd., New Paltz, 845/255-1000, www.mohonk .com), set aside by the environmentally conscious Smiley family. Climbers flock here to choose from 1,000 different routes through world-class crags and crevices. Hikers have another 65 miles of trails to explore. Follow Route 199 from New Paltz to find the Mohonk visitors center. Climbers will want to continue past the center to the West Trapps trailhead. Parking lots fill quickly on weekend mornings. Entrance fees are $8 for hikers and $10 for climbers and cyclists.

At the intersection of Minnewaska and Mohonk lies the **Mohonk Mountain House** (1000 Mountain Rest Rd., New Paltz, 845/255-1000, www.mohonk.com), whose story begins with 280 acres of land, a 10-room inn, and a pair of Quaker twins. In the late 19th century, Albert and Alfred Smiley built rival country inns on the ridgeline, which grew to accommodate hundreds of guests at a time. A network of carriage paths connected the properties and provided the ideal setting for quiet contemplation. One of the original buildings burned down, but to this day, the historic Mohonk Mountain House, on the shores of Lake Mohonk, is owned and run by descendants of the Smiley family.

In its heyday, this sprawling hotel entertained a slew of famous guests, among them John Burroughs, Andrew Carnegie, and Theodore Roosevelt. Mohonk is no longer the remote and elegant wilderness getaway it was in the 19th century, but the property remains as beautiful as ever and continues to draw a steady crowd of tourists. Today, it serves as a popular venue for weddings and corporate events.

South of Minnewaska is the 4,600-acre **Sam's Point Preserve** (Sam's Point Rd., Cragsmoor, 845/647-7989; 8 A.M.–8 P.M. year-round; $7 parking fee), created in 1997 to protect the rare ridgetop dwarf pine barrens that define the landscape. Trails lead to numerous valley vistas, and the moderately strenuous 7.6-mile hike to Verkeerderkill Falls takes about five hours round-trip. Follow Route 52 to Cragsmoor.

Rosendale

Surrounding New Paltz are several smaller but equally charming towns: Route 32 north takes you to Rosendale, home of the internationally acclaimed Rosendale Cement Company, whose "natural cement" limestone was used in nearly every major construction project undertaken in the 19th century: Rosendale cement found its way into the Brooklyn Bridge, the wings of the U.S. Capitol, the pedestal of the Statue of Liberty, the Washington Monument, Grand Central Terminal, and even the Panama Canal.

bridge over the Wallkill River near High Falls

Geologists head to Rosendale's abandoned mines for clues about the past. The **Widow Jane Mine** (688 Rte. 213, 845/658-9900), run by the Century House Historical Society, is a rare horizontal mine that is open to the public. Since its operational days ended, the mine has been used to grow mushrooms and trout, and as a venue for musical performances.

The society also operates the former estate of farmer-turned-businessman A. J. Snyder, an 1809 home that's listed on the National Register of Historic Places. A tour of the **Snyder Estate** (668 Rte. 213, 845/658-9900, www .centuryhouse.org; 1–4 P.M. Wed., Sat., and Sun. May–October, or by appointment; adults $3, children $1) covers the house and mine, as well as a visit to the Delaware and Hudson Canal and a look at the old cement kilns.

High Falls

About 15 minutes from New Paltz by car, High Falls is the kind of place where locals give you funny looks when you try to get a cell phone signal. Tucked away in the Shawangunk Mountains, on the south shore of the swift-flowing

Rondout Creek, High Falls has found a niche in accommodating the spillover of weekenders from New Paltz. Many residents here started as weekenders, evolved into part-time commuters, and eventually moved in for good. A two-block stretch of businesses includes a handful of charming stores and eateries, including the exclusive **Depuy Canal House** (Rte. 213, 845/687-7700, www.depuycanalhouse.net; brunch 9 A.M.-noon Sat. and 9 A.M.–2 P.M. Sun., dinner 5–10 P.M. Fri.–Sat. and 4–9 P.M. Sun.; dinner mains $32–44).

It was a cold January day in 1825 when the founders of the Delaware and Hudson Canal Company began their company's public offering with a show and tell on Wall Street: the burning of anthracite coal. In the midst of the War of 1812, the country faced its first energy crisis and needed an alternative to bituminous coal, which the British had been supplying. Pennsylvania coal offered an alternative; the challenge was getting it from inland hills to coastal settlements.

The offering succeeded and thus began

THE MID-HUDSON

the construction of the Delaware and Hudson Canal. Built by Irish immigrants on the heels of the Erie Canal (by the same architect), it measured 108 miles long, 4 feet deep, and 32 feet wide. Along the way, the canal passed through 108 locks and crossed 137 bridges. At its terminus, it had to drop 70 feet to sea level in Rondout Creek—a series of five locks did the trick.

Today, the **D&H Canal Museum** (Mohonk Rd., 845/687-9311, www.canalmuseum.org; 11 A.M.–5 P.M. Mon., 11 A.M.–5 P.M. Thurs.–Sat., 1–5 P.M. Sun.; adults $4, children $2, families $7), housed in the former St. John's Episcopal Church, is a National Historic Landmark with lock demonstrations and a collection of documents and artifacts that trace the history of canal and railroad transportation.

Traveling Route 209 from High Falls toward Kingston, you pass through Marbletown, where the Ulster County Historical Society maintains a stone farmhouse with an exhibit of 18th- and 19th-century furniture and farming tools (2682 Rte. 209, Marbletown, 845/338-5614; 1–5 P.M. Wed.–Sun. June–Sept.). Five generations of Davenports have farmed the land in neighboring Stone Ridge. Today, the family's farm market, greenhouse, and pick-your-own crops are a favorite local destination.

Hurley

The next town on Route 209 is Hurley, settled in 1661. When the British set Kingston in flames in November 1777, settlers fled here for safety. The township lost several of its original villages to the flooding of the Ashokan Reservoir in 1907.

Hurley's Main Street features a cluster of privately owned stone houses built during the 17th, 18th, and early 19th centuries. The **Hurley Heritage Society Museum** (52 Main St., 845/338-1661, www.hurleyheritagesociety .org; 10 A.M.–4 P.M. Sat., 1–4 P.M. Sun.; admission $3) can arrange a guided tour that begins with the 1853 Dutch Reformed Church and includes a burial ground with headstones dating back to 1715.

THE SOUTHERN CATSKILL MOUNTAINS–ROUTE 28

Ashokan Reservoir

Route 28 West out of Kingston leads to the Ashokan Reservoir, the southern Catskill Mountains, and many of the old resorts that made the region world famous. Completed in 1915, the second-oldest reservoir in the New York City watershed (Croton is the oldest) holds 123 billion gallons in a man-made lake that covers 253 square miles. Nine villages were flooded in its making, and an entire cemetery of revolutionary war graves were dug up and relocated.

Woodstock

Follow the turnoff for Route 375 to reach the bustling mountain town of Woodstock, a one-time artists' colony with deep roots in folk and rock music. (Bob Dylan was a longtime resident.) Unlike some of the Hudson Valley's river towns, Woodstock has not reinvented itself overnight to appeal to a new demographic. Its busy cafés and art galleries give the impression of a genuine place with a passion for the arts.

Present-day Woodstock attracts a creative and outdoor-oriented crowd, including many New York City escapees. Uma Thurman and David Bowie are occasionally seen around town. As the daughter of singer Levon Helm (The Band), blues singer Amy Helm has continued to uphold the town's musical tradition with Ollabelle, a new sextet whose contemporary music blends gospel, blues, bluegrass, and country styles. Woodstock is also one of the few towns in the region that has several inviting accommodations within walking distance of its shops and restaurants.

A popular day hike from Woodstock is the **Overlook Mountain Fire Tower** (34 Wardwell Lane, 845/679-2580) at 3,150 feet elevation. On clear days, the summit rewards hikers with a sweeping view of the Hudson River to the east. The trail (2.4 miles one-way) passes the remains of the Overlook Mountain House, another of the Catskills' 19th-century inns. Listen for the rattle of the endangered timber rattlesnake along the way. To reach the trailhead from Woodstock, follow Rock City Road from Route 212 and cross Route 33, where the name changes to Meads Mountain Road. The trailhead is about 1.5 miles up the mountain.

Across from the trailhead, one of Woodstock's old inns, the former Mead Mountain House, is now a Tibetan Buddhist monastery called the **Karma Triyana Dharmachakra** (352 Meads Mountain Rd., 518/679-5906, www.kagyu.org/ktd/index.php; office@kagyu.org; 1:30–3 P.M. Sat.–Sun.). It may be the only monastery in the world located in a 19th-century farmhouse. Visitors can tour the main shrine room, which contains one of the largest Shakyamuni Buddha statues in North America. A library and bookstore are also open to the public.

After the Ashokan Reservoir and just minutes from Woodstock, a cluster of new buildings stand out on Route 28 like the set of a Hollywood film. Centered on a converted 1841 barn in the hamlet of Mount Tremper, they are the shops and restaurants of **Catskill Corners,** an upscale commercial plaza that seems out of place in the otherwise bohemian countryside. The main attraction for those passing through is a giant kaleidoscope.

Phoenicia

Farther along Route 28 is Phoenicia and the Catskill Mountain Railroad, which offers rides along the Esopus Creek. A better way to tour the creek, however, is by inner tube. On hot summer days, visitors line up at several rental shops in town to rent tubes that will float them down the gentle creek.

Train aficionados will want to check out the **Empire State Railway Museum** (Ulster & Delaware Railroad Station, 845/688-7501; www.esrm.com; 11 A.M.–4 P.M. Sat.–Sun. Memorial Day–Columbus Day; admission by donation), which houses artifacts, photographs, and films that document the history of rail travel in the area.

Slide Mountain

A few miles past Phoenicia in the town of Shandaken, Route 42 turns north to Greene County. And soon after, in Big Indian, comes the turn for Route 47 or Oliverea Slide Mountain Road. This road leads to Frost Valley and the base of Slide Mountain, at 4,190 feet. It's an eight-mile drive along Route 47 to the Winnisook Club and the Slide Mountain parking lot.

Naturalist John Burroughs spent long hours contemplating the highest peak in the Catskills. In an essay about the southern Catskills, he wrote that the peak looked like the back and shoulders of a gigantic horse: "The horse has got his head down grazing; the shoulders are high, and the descent from them down his neck very steep; if he were to lift up his head, one sees that it would be carried far above all other peaks, and that the noble beast might gaze straight to his peers in the Adirondacks or the White Mountains."

Burroughs spent many years fishing the streams that drained the mountain and camping on all sides of the peak before he attempted a summit. On approaching Slide at last from a spruce grove on the north side, he wrote, "The mountain rose like a huge, rock-bound fortress from this plain-like expanse. It was ledge upon ledge, precipice upon precipice, up which and over which we made our way slowly and with great labor, now pulling ourselves up by our hands, then cautiously finding niches for our feet and zigzagging right and left from shelf to shelf."

It's much easier to access Slide Mountain today, but the hike remains one/of the most difficult in the Catskill Preserve. A strenuous five-mile route from the parking lot leads to the top. There are no views from the summit proper, but from a ridge that connects Slide to neighboring Wittenberg, you can see all but one of the thirty-four Catskill peaks that rise above 3,500 feet (Thomas Cole peak is obscured by Hunter Mountain). Allow 4–5 hours to complete the hike.

Belleayre Ski Center

Past the turnoff for Oliverea, Route 28 begins to climb until it reaches the base of the Belleayre Ski Center (Rte. 28, Highmount, 845/254-5600 or 800/942-6904, www.belleayre.com; 9 A.M.–4 P.M. daily) in Pine Hill. With ideal terrain for intermediate skiers, Belleayre is located within the "forever wild" Catskill Preserve. Skiers began carving turns down its slopes as early as the 1930s, and in 1949, the New York State Department of Environmental Conservation cleared a network of trails and opened the area to the public. Today, Belleayre sponsors outdoor and cultural programs year-round, including the renowned **Belleayre Music Festival** in summer.

SPORTS AND RECREATION
Winter Sports

With an annual base of 75 to 165 inches of snow and the highest skiable peak in the Catskills, Belleayre offers the most varied terrain for downhill skiers and snowboarders in Ulster County. It is especially popular with families. In addition, the mountain boasts the only snowcat skiing in the Catskills and grooms 9.2 kilometers of cross-country ski trails. Adult tickets cost $48 on weekends and $39 midweek, with multi-day discounts. Lifts run 9 A.M.–4 P.M. daily.

Beginners or families with young kids may prefer the considerably smaller **Sawkill Family Ski Center** (167 Hill Rd. off Sawkill & Jockey Hill Rd.; Kingston, 845/336-6977, www.sawkill

BELLEAYRE MOUNTAIN STATISTICS

· Base: 2,025 feet
· Summit: 3,429 feet
· Vertical: 1,404 feet
· Trails: 38
· Lifts: 8
· Skiable acres: 171
· Snowmaking: 96 percent
· Snow report: 800/942-6904

ski.com, 10 A.M.–4 P.M. Sat.–Sun. and holidays, late June–Labor Day,; adult full day $35, half day $30, one-hour tubing $13) or **Roamer Mountain Park** (355 Woodland Valley Rd., Phoenicia, 845/688-5553; 10 A.M.–5 P.M. Dec.–Mar.) for snow-tubing in Phoenicia.

The **Frost Valley YMCA** (Frost Valley Rd., Claryville, 845/985-2291, www.frostvalley.org) in the shadow of Slide Mountain, provides access to 35 kilometers of cross-country ski trails, including several cable bridge crossings. Strung high above a swift-flowing creek, these "bridges" are made of three single cables in an inverted triangle: one for your feet and the other two for your hands. Choose a different route if you are at all afraid of heights. Ideal for groups, Frost Valley has cabins on the premises with hot showers and flush toilets. Some are in better shape than others. Meals are included with your stay, and reservations are required.

For the most extensive network of cross-country ski trails, head to Minnewaska State Park. The Mohonk Preserve and Mohonk Mountain House also groom trails for skiers. Rent your gear on the way in at **Rock & Snow** (44 Main St., New Paltz, 845/255-1311, www.rocksnow.com).

Hiking

Hikers will find endless miles of beautiful terrain in the Shawangunks, at Minnewaska, Sam's Point, and Mohonk Preserve (65 miles of trails). Note, there is no camping in Minnewaska. And other than a hot dog stand that occasionally sets up at the top of the Minnewaska parking lot, food and water are not readily available near the trailheads. Stock up on supplies before you head into the park.

For a moderately challenging day hike near Woodstock, head to the base of Overlook Mountain, on Meads Mountain Road (www.catskilltowers.com). For a more strenuous route, head west to climb the highest peak in the range: Slide Mountain. John Burroughs called Slide a "shy mountain" because it was difficult to spot until he got very close, and even on the ascent, it was difficult to find the peak.

Cycling

New Paltz is a mecca for avid cyclists. Surrounding country roads have terrain to match all levels: flat fields, rolling hills, and steep climbs. Stop by the **Bicycle Depot** (15 Main St., New Paltz, 845/255-3859, www.bicycle depot.com; 10 A.M.–6 P.M. Mon., Wed., Fri., Sat., 11 A.M.–7 P.M. Thurs., 10 A.M.–5 P.M. Sun.) at the bottom of Main Street for route advice. This is also one of the only shops in the area that rents decent road bikes. The gear is in good condition and prices are reasonable.

Mountain bikers can choose between gentle rail trails and more aggressive single track. Woodstock and New Paltz both have convenient access to trail heads. The **Wallkill Valley Rail Trail** is a favorite route for trail riding, jogging, and walking. This 12-mile trail connects the towns of New Paltz, Rosendale, and Gardiner. All trail signs have maps on the back.

Try **Overlook Mountain Bikes** (93 Tinker St., Woodstock, 845/679-2122; 10 A.M.–6 P.M. Thurs.–Mon., 11 A.M.–5 P.M. Sun.) or **Catskill Mountain Bicycle** (3 Church St., New Paltz, 845/255-3859) for maps and gear. **Table Rock Tours and Bicycle Shop** (386 Main St., Rosendale, 845/658-7832; 11 A.M.–7 P.M. Wed. and Fri., 11 A.M.–8 P.M. Thurs., 11 A.M.–5 P.M. Sat., noon–5 P.M. Sun.) offers one- and two-day bike tours of Ulster County.

Golf

More than a dozen golf courses are scattered along the base of the Shawangunks in Ulster County. One of the prettiest, **Apple Greens Golf** (161 South St., 845/883-5500, www.applegreens .com; $24), is set on an apple orchard. It also offers one of the best deals in the area for 18 holes. The **Shawangunk Country Club** (38 Country Club Rd., Ellenville, 845/647-6090, www.sha-wangunkcountryclub.com; $25) has nine holes on a hilly course that's built around a large pond.

Swimming and Boating

Ulster County offers access to several unusual water sports: For starters, a day of drifting along the Esopus Creek is practically a mandatory activity for anyone who lives within a

© JASON EGLIT

cruising Rondout Creek

day's drive of Phoenicia. Time your visit on the one day a month when the water is released, and you'll be in for a real adventure. **F-S Tube and Raft Rental** (Main St., Phoenicia, 845/688-7633) offers transportation and rentals. **Town Tinker Tube Rental** (Bridge St., Phoenicia, 845/688-5553, www.towntinker .com; 9 A.M.–6 P.M. daily; $25/day full gear rental) offers tubing courses for beginners and experts. It takes about two hours to travel 2.5 miles along the river.

Planning a trip to the Caribbean and need to get certified to dive? Spend two weekends with **Deep-Six Underwater Systems** (14 Deerpath Drive, New Paltz, 845/255-7446 or 888/901-5780, www.deep-six.com; 9 A.M.– 5 P.M. Mon.–Sat.) and you'll be good to go. Training dives take place at Diver's Cove in Lake Minnewaska, where the Mid-Hudson Diving Association has set up a bench and drying racks for fellow divers.

Lake Minnewaska is hands-down the most beautiful place to swim in Ulster County. In summer, the surface temperature climbs to a refreshing 75 degrees. Visibility is not as good as it once was (10–12 feet on average), but underwater cliffs and a maximum depth of 72 feet make for an interesting dive in a safe environment. Expect a thermocline at about 30 feet.

If you prefer to stay on top of the water, set sail for an evening of water, wine, and cheese with the **Great Hudson Sailing Center** (Dock St., Kingston, 845/429-1557, www.greathudson sailing.com; 10 A.M.–5 P.M. daily). The center offers guided sails, lessons, sales, and rentals. A 16-hour sailing course on two consecutive weekends makes a great active getaway ($400 per person, $360 for a second person).

Two additional operations launch boats from Rondout Landing: **Hudson Rondout Cruises** (Rondout Landing, Kingston, 845/338-6515) go from the Kingston Lighthouse south to the Esopus Meadows Lighthouse. Inquire about dinner and brunch cruises. **North River Cruises** (Rondout Landing, Kingston, 845/247-3524, www.northrivercruises.com) has a boat called *Teal* that is available for private charters.

Fishing and Hunting

Anglers primarily use nymphs and streamers to fish the lower Esopus, since it gets less water pressure than the Delaware, Willowemoc, and Beaverkill. As a tailwater, the Esopus offers the best conditions late in the season. Access the stream near Boiceville.

Fly-fishing with Bert (P.O. Box 153, Tillson, 845/658-9784, bdflycaster@aol.com) offers fly-fishing instruction and guide services on the Catskills' trout streams in May, June, and September. **Ed's Fly-Fishing & Guide Services** (69 Ridge Rd., Shokan, 845/ 657-6393, tailwaters@hvc.rr.com) is another option near the Ashokan Reservoir. **Osprey Marine** (12 Butterville Rd., New Paltz, 845/255-8737, captain@ospreymarine.com, www.ospreymarine.com; June–Oct.) runs fishing charters on the Hudson River out of Kingston when the striped bass run in spring.

Aviation

Learn to glide at the **Mountain Wings Hang Gliding Center** (150 Canal St., Ellenville, 845/647-3377, www.serioussports.com/mtn wings), where an introductory program costs $135. The course is certified by USHGA (United States Hang Gliding Association) and includes one day of training with videos and a simulator, followed by supervised flights.

If you'd rather have someone else handle the controls, call **River Aviation** (1161 Flatbush Rd., Kingston, 845/336-8400) for an aerial tour of the river and dramatic views of the Shawangunks. Flights depart from the Kingston-Ulster airport.

You can jump from 13,500 feet and freefall to 6,000 with **Skydive the Ranch** (45 Sandhill Rd., Gardiner, 845/255-4033, www.sky divetheranch.com; $189 per jump including gear; $89 additional for a video of the skydive). Repeat visitors can complete all 13 levels of the Instructor Assisted Freefall (IAF) skydiver training program. Group rates are also available.

Rock Climbing

When the weather cooperates, climbers descend on the Mohonk Preserve (West Trapps trailhead; admission $10) to scale several of the 1,000 world-class pitches in the preserve. A good alternative to climbing in the Mohonk Preserve is the Peter's Kill Area (Rte. 44/55, New Paltz, 845/255-0752, www.nysparks.com; open at 9 A.M. daily; $5/day) in Minnewaska State Park. Located five miles west of the junction of Routes 299 and 44/55, and one mile east of the main park entrance, Peter's Kill boasts some of the best bouldering anywhere in the northeast. You'll climb on quartz conglomerate cliffs found a half-mile walk from the parking lot. A range of single-pitch climbs will suit various levels. The area has a daily limit of 70 climbers.

Before you go, pick up a helmet, shoes, chalk, and a climbing harness at **Rock & Snow** (44 Main St., New Paltz, 845/255-1311, www.rocksnow.com; 9 A.M.–6 P.M. Mon.–Fri., 8 A.M.–8 P.M. Sat., 8 A.M.–7 P.M. Sun.) Brush up on your skills at **The Inner Wall** (234 Main St., New Paltz, 845/255-7625, www.theinner wall.com; 5–9 P.M. Wed. and Fri., 3:30–9 P.M. Tues. and Thurs., noon–7 P.M. Sat.–Sun.; $8–12), an indoor climbing gym.

High Angle Adventures (178 Hardenburgh Rd., Ulster Park, 800/777-2546, www.high angle.com) offers a range of classes, including classes for women, lead training, and transition courses from indoor to outdoor environments. Locals also recommend **Mountain Skills** (Stone Ridge, 845/781-8950, www.mountainskills. biz; single climber $260, two climbers $185 each, three climbers $160 each, four climbers $125 each) for climbing instruction.

You can also rent climbing shoes and camping equipment at the **Eastern Mountain Sports** (EMS) store (4124 Rte. 44/55, Gardiner, 845/255-3280, www.emsclimb.com; 8:30 A.M.–5 P.M. daily) at the intersection of Routes 299 and 44/55. Unlike other EMS locations, this one is a designated Climbing Specialty Store that offers classes, rental gear, and repair services. Note that the center does not rent harnesses, helmets, ropes, or protective gear.

Spa Treatments

Buttermilk Falls Inn and Spa (220 North Rd., Milton, 845/795-1310, www.buttermilk fallsinn.com) offers a full menu of spa treatments, including aromatherapy massage, hot stone massage, reflexology, and a variety of facials. A one-hour massage costs $85–95.

A new 30,000-square-foot spa at the Mohonk Mountain House has 200 windows overlooking Lake Mohonk and the hotel's 2,200-acre mountaintop estate. The spa was built with environmental conservation in mind: excavated stone was recycled into walls and fireplaces, a geothermal system regulates temperature inside, and a 2,000-square-foot garden terrace functions as a green roof. Choose from a menu of 50 treatments, including the signature Mohonk Red massage, which incorporates indigenous Mohonk Red witch hazel into the treatment, or the Shawangunk Grit exfoliation, which involves fine quartz grains from the surrounding cliffs. A private couples treatment room has a fireplace. Visit www.mohonk.com or call 800/772-6646. The spa is open year-round.

Another place to indulge in a luxurious spa treatment is the **Emerson Resort and Spa** (146 Mt. Pleasant Rd., Mt. Tremper, 877/688-2828 or 845/688-2828, www.emerson resort.com) near Woodstock. Fifty-minute treatments range $90–105. The Emerson Signature Massage involves warm ginseng-infused oil and two therapists.

ACCOMMODATIONS

Ulster accommodations conjure images of historic mountain houses, rustic country inns, and wooded campgrounds. There are surprisingly few places to stay in downtown New Paltz, but many quaint bed-and-breakfast inns dot the surrounding countryside.

Under $100

True to its reputation as a university town, New Paltz has one of the few hostel accommodations in the Hudson River Valley region. Stay from one night to two weeks at the **New Paltz Hostel** (145 Main St., New Paltz, 845/255-6676, www.newpaltzhostel.com; $27–87), within walking distance to public

THE MID-HUDSON

transportation, university buildings, and stores and restaurants of downtown New Paltz. The hostel closes during the day between 10 A.M. and 4 P.M.

$100-150

Private porches and a central location are defining features of **The Inn at Orchard Heights** (20 Church St., New Paltz, 845/255-6792, www.innatorchardheights.com; $110–160). Owners Janet and Darryl Greene offer five rooms in their 1888 Queen Anne Victorian. Some are on the small side and not all have private baths, but you can't beat the location for convenience.

Another affordable option within walking distance to Rondout Landing is the **Rondout B&B** (88 West Chester St., Kingston, 845/331-8144, www.rondoutbandb.com; $75–115). Four well-kept guest rooms are in a turn-of-the-20th-century home. Two have private baths, and the other two share a bath and sitting room.

Wood paneling and stone fireplaces lend a rustic feel to rooms and cabins at the **Woodstock Lodge** (20 Country Club Lane, Woodstock, 800/383-5567, www.woodstocklodge.com). Enjoy the outdoor pool in summer, and warm your toes by the tavern fireplace in winter. Walk to Woodstock shops and restaurants, or enjoy a meal at Marion's Country Kitchen on-site.

Closer yet to the action are nine basic but affordable rooms in the **Twin Gables** (73 Tinker St., Woodstock, 845/679-9479, www.twingableswoodstockny.com; $100–130), which has been open more than 50 years. Some rooms have private baths, while others share.

$150-200

A picturesque stream meanders through the property at **Captain Schoonmakers** (913 Rte. 213, High Falls, 945/687-7946, www.captainschoonmakers.com; $150–200). The inn is a 1760 stone house; rooms are located in the carriage house with private balconies and air conditioning. The owners are animal lovers, and a posse of cats and dogs roam the grounds at all times.

A hundred-year-old Bechstein grand piano takes center stage at the ❰ **Sparrow Hawk Bed and Breakfast** (4496 Rte. 209, Stone Ridge, 845/687-4492, www.sparrowhawkbandb.com; $139–195) and a concert pianist plays during breakfast. Set among a stand of black locust trees just off busy Route 209, the inn is located 15 minutes from downtown New Paltz. Owners Betsy and Howard Mont have created a romantic escape in their 1770 brick colonial. Cozy—and immaculate—guest rooms feature air-conditioning and high-quality linens; a gourmet breakfast of homemade frittatas starts the day right.

Weekend reservations are difficult to secure at the two-room **Saugerties Lighthouse** (168 Lighthouse Dr., off Mynderse St., Saugerties, 845/247-0656, www.saugertieslighthouse.com; Apr.–Oct. $160, Nov.–Mar. $135, breakfast included). Accommodations are rustic, with a shared bath and limited electricity.

In the southern Catskills, the **Enchanted Manor of Woodstock** (23 Rowe Rd., Woodstock, 845/679-9012, www.enchantedmanorinn.com; $165–250) is set on eight acres. Each of the five rooms has a private bath (one is a standalone cottage). Guests can swim in the saltwater pool, relax on the deck, or soak in the hot tub. One of the owners is a licensed massage therapist (treatments $85/hr.), and the inn offers outdoor yoga during the summer.

For Victorian ambience in a mountain setting, reserve a room at ❰ **The Wild Rose Inn** (66 Rock City Rd., Woodstock, 845/679-8783, www.thewildroseinn.com; $150–275). Its five floral-themed rooms all have private baths and have hosted the likes of Uma Thurman, Ethan Hawke, and Chevy Chase. The owners serve a gourmet continental breakfast each morning, and you can walk to shops in town.

Over $200

One of the most inviting places to stay anywhere in the Hudson Valley sits at the edge of the Shawangunks with views of sheer cliff walls right outside the window. Built in 2001, the ❰ **Minnewaska Lodge** (Rte. 44/55, Gardiner, 845/255-1110, www.minnewaskalodge.com; $200–220) has 26 modern but cozy rooms with a fitness center and a spacious, ground-floor breakfast room. Data ports are a plus for those traveling with a computer. Trails lead right from the back porch, and the restaurants and shops of New Paltz are just six miles away.

The historic **Mohonk Mountain House** (100 Mountain Rest Rd., New Paltz, 845/255-1000 or 800/772-6646; $179–735) reportedly spent more than $30 million on a new spa and other renovations in 2006–2007. Rates include buffet-style breakfast and lunch and a four-course dinner, as well as afternoon tea and cookies. Jackets are still required for dinner service, but once-strict alcohol policies have been relaxed. Rooms, suites, and cottages represent a variety of styles. Some create the feeling of a cozy mountain lodge, while others feature elaborate Victorian fabrics. Optional extras include balconies, fireplaces, or views. Televisions are available in some public areas.

The Inn at Stone Ridge/Hasbrouck House (3805 Rte. 209, Stone Ridge, 845/687-0736, www.innatstoneridge.com; $195–425) has five suites in a handsome 18th-century Dutch Colonial set on 150 acres of woods and gardens between New Paltz and Kingston. Rooms are decorated in warm tones and country quilts.

Once a 17th-century trading post, **◖ Buttermilk Falls Inn and Spa** (220 North Rd., Milton, 845/795-1310, www.buttermilk fallsinn.com; $225–425) now caters to a different kind of traveler: Thirteen individually decorated guest rooms in three carriage houses have fireplaces, private baths, cable TV, high-speed Internet, and air-conditioning. Most important, all have river, garden, or pond and field views. The owners maintain 70 acres of riverside trails that meander through woods, fields, and gardens. Breakfast includes such treats as freshly baked croissants, and guests may also enjoy afternoon tea service. Spa packages are available.

Soon after it opened the first time in 2003, the **Emerson Resort and Spa** (146 Mt. Pleasant Rd., Mt. Tremper, 877/688-2828 or 845/688-2828, www.emersonresort.com; $190–220) was severely damaged by a fire and had to be rebuilt. The new resort opened in 2007 with 26 luxury guest suites that blend Silk Road decor with mountain ambience. All have soaking tubs, flat-screen TVs, in-room wine refrigerators, private decks, and fireplaces. The adjoining **Emerson Lodge** is geared toward families with suites of varying sizes. Also in the Mt. Tremper complex are an award-winning spa, upscale country store, and a New American/Asian fusion restaurant called Phoenix.

Campgrounds

Campers have all kinds of options in Ulster County. **Yogi Bear's Jellystone Camp-Resort** (50 Bevier Rd., Gardiner, 848/255-5193, www.campjellystone.com; April 28–early Oct.) is a large but well-run operation with two locations, Lazy River in Gardiner and Birchwood Acres in Woodridge. Amenities include canoe rentals, showers, and swimming pools.

The **Saugerties/Woodstock KOA Kampground** (882 Route 212, Saugerties, 800/562-4081 or 845/246-4089, www.koa .com; Apr.–Oct.) has 90 sites, a camp store, children's play area, dumping station, flush toilets, showers, laundry room, wireless Internet, swimming pool, and fishing. Cabins are available, and you can bring your pooch along too.

FOOD

Ulster County holds some culinary surprises, as well as a number of mainstay establishments.

Along the River–Route 9W

By many accounts, the **Raccoon Saloon** (1330 Rte. 9W, Marlborough, 845/236-7872; 11:30 A.M.–9:30 P.M. Sun.–Thurs., till 10:30 P.M. Fri.–Sat.) serves the best burger in the region, if not more broadly speaking. Tucked away on a hill in a suburban neighborhood, **The Would** (120 North Rd., Highland, 845/691-9883, www.thewould.com; dinner nightly; mains $18–26) occupies the site of a 1920s-era summer resort and is worth a special trip for a memorable New American meal.

Creekside **Mariner's Harbor** (1 Broadway/

10 PLACES FOR A SUMMER PICNIC

- BashBish Falls
- Boscobel Restoration
- Harlem Valley Rail Trail
- Lake Minnewaska
- Kaaterskill Falls
- Saratoga Performing Arts Center
- Storm King Art Center
- The grounds at Vanderbilt Mansion
- Washington Irving's Sunnyside estate
- The shores of the Willowemoc River

Rondout Landing, Kingston, 845/340-8051, www.marinersharbor.com; 4–10 P.M. Tues.–Sat.; mains $15–28) got a fresh coast of paint inside and remains a mainstay for seafood dinners. On the same block are several newer establishments: The **Downtown Café** (1 West Strand, Kingston, 845/331-5904, www.downtowncafekingston.com; 9 A.M.–9 P.M. Sun., 10 A.M.–10 P.M. Mon.–Thurs., 10 A.M.–11 P.M. Fri.–Sat.; dinner mains $18–25) has an extensive wine list and an open dining area with a vintage storefront exterior. Main dishes on the dinner menu include thin-crust pizzas, handmade pasta, yellowfin tuna, veal scallopine, and chicken puttanesca. Italian-born chef-owner Graziano Tecchio opened the restaurant in 1998. **El Coqui Latin Jazz Café** (21 Broadway, Kingston, 845/340-1106, noon–10 p.m. Sun.–Thurs., Fri.–Sat. till midnight; mains $10–25) serves Puerto Rican specialties. A CIA grad oversees the surf and turf menu at **Ship to Shore** (15 W. Strand St., Rondout Landing, Kingston, 845/334-8887, www.shiptoshorehudsonvalley.com; breakfast, lunch, and dinner daily; dinner mains $14–30). Enjoy live jazz on Saturday evenings.

In Kingston's Stockade District, pop into **Jane's Homemade Ice Cream** (305 Wall St., Kingston, 845/338-8315) for a milk shake or quick lunch. For fine dining, **Le Canard Enchaine** (276 Fair St., Kingston, 845/339-2003, www.le-canardenchaine.com; 5–10 P.M. Mon.–Sat., 10 A.M.–10 P.M. Sun.; mains $21–30, prix fixe lunch $15) is an authentic French bistro serving classics like cassoulet and reasonably priced wines.

Additional options for global cuisine include dependable Tex-Mex at the **Armadillo Bar and Grill** (97 Abeel St., Kingston, 845/339-1550, www.armadillos.net; dinner Tues.–Sun., lunch Sat.–Sun.; mains $14–17) and Chinese fusion at **China Rose** (608 Ulster Ave., Kingston, 845/338-7443). There is another restaurant of the same name across the river in Rhinecliff (1 Shatzell Ave., 845/876-7442), now under separate ownership.

CIA graduates Rickie and James Tamayo opened **Café Tamayo** (89 Partition St., Saugerties, 845/246-9371, www.cafetamayo.com; from 5 P.M. Wed.–Sun.; mains $12–20) in 1987 to heartfelt applause. Antique fans, plaster on canvas ceilings, and a gorgeous hand-carved bar set the mood, while crispy duck confit tempts the palette. Also in Saugerties, **Café with Love** (85 Partition St., Saugerties, 845/246-1795, www.cafewithlove.com; 8:30 A.M.–5 P.M. Thurs.–Mon.; mains: $5–10) is a good spot for breakfast with wireless Internet. And **Miss Lucy's Kitchen** (90 Partition St., Saugerties, 845/246-9240, www.misslucyskitchen.com; noon–3 P.M. and 5–9 P.M. daily, till 10 P.M. Fri.–Sat.; dinner mains $17–24) serves hearty American dinners, such as a country-style veal stew, made of local ingredients.

New Paltz and Surroundings

New Paltz has it all when it comes to food: sushi, Mediterranean, haute cuisine, and cheese. For breakfast or a quick bite to eat at lunchtime, head to **The Bakery** (13A N. Front St., New Paltz, 845/255-8840, www.ilovethebakery.com; 7 A.M.–8 P.M. daily; mains $4–8). Soups and sandwiches change daily, and there

© JASON EGLIT

creekside dining

are a handful of tables in a courtyard outside. Service is slow, but the baked goods are worth the wait.

New York City chef Jacques Qualin and his wife Leslie Flam have turned an old German tavern into a slice of Paris at ◖ **The French Corner** (3407 Cooper St., Stone Ridge, 845/687-0810, www.frcorner.com; dinner from 5 P.M. Thurs.–Sun., brunch 11 A.M.–2 P.M. Sun.; mains $24–32). You might begin the evening with a champagne cocktail, move on to the veal chop, and finish with a tart featuring locally picked fruit.

At the end of Main Street in New Paltz is the **Gilded Otter Brewing Company** (3 Main St., Rte. 299, New Paltz, 845/256-1700, www.gildedotter.com; 11:30 A.M.–10 P.M. Mon.–Thurs., till 10:30 P.M. Fri.–Sat., 10 A.M.–8 P.M. Sun.; mains $12–18), with a good selection of wursts and schnitzels and freshly brewed beers to wash them down. The bar stays open till 2 A.M.

Gadaleto's Seafood (246 Main St., Cherry Hill shopping center, New Paltz, 845/255-1717, http://gadaletos.com; 11 A.M.–9 P.M. Sun.–Thurs., 11 A.M.–10 P.M. Fri.–Sat.; mains $13–25) is a local institution that supplies many area restaurants with their fresh catch. Consumers can sample the goodies at the raw bar or place an order for fish and chips or crab cakes. Be prepared to wait; the casual restaurant can get crowded, and service tends to be slow.

Closer to the center of town, one of New Paltz's old movie theaters was converted into a giant pub-style restaurant in 2003. **Barnaby's** (Rte. 32/N. Chestnut St., New Paltz, 845/255-2433; 11 A.M.–10 P.M. Sun.–Thurs., 11 A.M.–11 P.M. Fri. and Sat.; mains $6–18) prepares hearty steaks, burgers, seafood, and salads.

Located just steps away from the Walkill Valley Rail Trail, the **Cheese Plate** (10 Main St., Suite 302, New Paltz, 845/255-2444) is the perfect place to stop for a picnic. The owner is a Dutchess County native and Manhattan escapee who offers an outstanding selection of local and imported cheeses, from Sprout Creek Farm across the river to the Pyrenees of Spain and France. Next door, the **Mudd Puddle Café**

(10 Main St. #312, New Paltz, 845/255-3536, www.muddpuddlecoffee.com; 9:30 A.M.–5 P.M. Wed., 9:30 A.M.–6 P.M. Thurs., 9:30 A.M.–7 P.M. Fri.–Sat., 9:30 A.M.–5 P.M. Sun.–Mon.) roasts its own coffee and serves homemade soups and sandwiches. The $5.45 "best deal" includes a cup of soup and half panini. Also near the trail, **La Stazione** (5 Main St., New Paltz, 845/256-9447; 11:30 A.M.–10:30 P.M. Mon.–Thurs., 11:30 A.M.–11 P.M. Fri. and Sat., 1–10 P.M. Sun.) takes its name from the train station it converted into an eatery. Student servers staff the dining room, and the menu consists of reasonably priced Italian dishes.

A landlocked location is no obstacle to culinary creativity at **Neko Sushi** (49 Main St., New Paltz, 845/255-0162), where the chef presents an artistic variety of raw fish and maki rolls each evening. Two doors up, **Yanni Restaurant & Café** (51 Main St., New Paltz, 845/256-0988; 11:30 A.M.–11 P.M. daily; mains $8–12) offers a late-night menu of gyros, Greek salad, spanikopita, and other specialties to a clientele of students and weekend tourists. Greek TV is an added highlight. Dine amidst the historic stone buildings of Huguenot Street at **Locust Tree** (215 Huguenot St., New Paltz, 845/255-7888, www.locusttree.com; dinner from 5 P.M. Wed.–Sun., brunch 11 A.M.–3 P.M. Sun.; mains $16–23, brunch prix fixe $15), which serves northern European cuisine.

High Falls claims one of the region's most exclusive fine-dining establishments in the **DePuy Canal House** (Rte. 213, High Falls, 845/687-7700, www.depuycanalhouse.net; 5:30–9 P.M. Thurs., till 10 P.M. Fri.–Sat., 4–9 P.M. Sun., brunch 11:30 A.M.–2 P.M. Sun.; mains $32–44; reservations required). Guests can choose a three-, four-, or seven-course menu ($75), which features game dishes, such as a rabbit hunter's soup or venison medallions served rare with a maitake-mushroom risotto. Head to the more casual **Chefs on Fire** (Rte. 213, High Falls, 845/687-7778; 4–9 P.M. Mon. and Wed., 11 A.M.–10 P.M. Thurs.–Fri., 9 A.M.–10 P.M. Sat.–Sun.; mains $6–12), downstairs, to refuel after climbing the Shawangunks.

If the southwestern food at **The Egg's Nest** (Rte. 213, High Falls, 845/687-7255, www.theeggsnest.com; 11:30 A.M.–11 P.M. daily, till midnight Fri.–Sat.; mains $5–10) doesn't leave a memorable impression, the funky decor certainly will. Toasters hang from the ceiling, and tinfoil is stuck on the walls. Indeed, everything about the place is intentionally mismatched. Enjoy the huge portions, and save room for dessert.

Steaks anchor a menu that features local ingredients at the charming **Inn at Stone Ridge** (Rte. 209, Stone Ridge, 845/687-0736, www.innatstoneridge.com; mains $17–30), which has both formal and casual dining options. Preparations include au poivre, gorgonzola sauce, and braised mushrooms. For an unusual appetizer, consider the truffled Black Angus steak tartare with a fresh quail egg. The tavern menu includes panini, burgers, and quesadillas (mains $8–15).

Southern Catskill Mountains–Route 28

Between Saugerties and Woodstock, a colorful decor and central bar complement a menu of Cajun jerk chicken, ahi tuna, Thai mussel stew, and churrasco-style grilled meats at **New World Home Cooking** (1411 Rte. 212, Saugerties, 845/246-0900, www.newworldhomecooking.com; dinner 5–10 P.M. Mon.–Thurs., 5–11 P.M. Fri.–Sat., 4–10 P.M. Sun., lunch 11:30 A.M.–2:30 P.M. Sat., 11 A.M.–2:30 P.M. Sun.; dinner mains $15–27).

Located in an 1830s farmhouse, **Red Onion** (1654 Rte. 212, Woodstock, 845/679-1223; www.redonionrestaurant.com; 5–10 P.M. Thurs.–Tues.; mains $16–23) serves international fare and a Sunday brunch at half a dozen tables arranged around a cozy bar.

For a casual meal and a memorable experience, try a homemade muffin at ◖ **Bread Alone** (22 Mill Hill Rd., Woodstock, 845/679-2108, www.breadalone.com; 7 A.M.–6 P.M. daily), a European-style organic bakery and café with additional locations in Kingston, Rhinebeck, and Boiceville. The owner, Daniel Leader, is a CIA graduate who traveled from Paris to the Pyrenees to learn what gives European breads their hearty flavor. He now produces 15 tons of fresh bread per week from twin ovens that were custom-built by a Parisian oven mason. At headquarters in Boiceville, you can take an impromptu tour of the bakery while you sip a frothy cappuccino.

Another breakfast mainstay, famous for its variety of pancakes, lies farther west in Phoenicia. **Sweet Sue's** (49 Main St., Phoenicia, 845/688-7852; 7 A.M.–3 P.M. Thurs.–Mon.; mains $7–12) is the perfect place to start or end a day of tubing on the Esopus River.

Celebrity sightings are common among the trendsetters who dine creekside at **The Bear** (295 Tinker St./Rte. 212, Bearsville, 845/679-5555, www.bearcafe.com; 5–10 P.M. Sun.–Thurs., 5–11 P.M. Fri.–Sat.; mains $18–30). Entrées range from grilled tofu to filet mignon and from Caesar salad to a half-pound hamburger.

Across the parking lot is your best chance for good Chinese at **The Little Bear** (Rte. 212, Bearsville, 845/679-8899; mains $9–12, weekday lunch specials $5–6).

An owner-chef from the Rhine River region of Germany prepares European-style dishes, many inspired from her native country, at **Marion's Country Kitchen** (Risiley Rd., off Rte. 375, Woodstock, 845/679-3213, www.marionscountrykitchen.com; 5:30–10 P.M. Wed.–Sun., lunch 11 A.M.–2:30 P.M. Sun. only; mains $13–20).

Ten minutes from Woodstock by car, at **The Phoenix Restaurant** (Emerson Resort & Spa, Mt. Tremper, 146 Mt. Pleasant Rd., 845/688-7700, www.emersonresort.com/the phoenix; mains $22–28), the emphasis is on presentation (square plates and tall food) of dishes that blend Indian and Thai flavors with the local bounty.

ENTERTAINMENT AND EVENTS
Performing Arts
Come summer, the **New Paltz Summer Repertory Theatre** (SUNY New Paltz Samuel Dorsky Museum of Art, Theatre, Music, Festivals; 75 S. Manheim, New Paltz, 845/257-3872, www.newpaltz.edu/summerrep) performs at the SUNY New Paltz campus. Its Shakespeare Under the Stars show is a popular feature every year.

In Woodstock, the **Colony Café** (22 Rock City Rd., Woodstock, 845/679-5342; from 7 P.M. Thurs.–Tues.) stages music concerts and poetry readings inside a historic dinner theater.

Bars and Nightlife
New Paltz and Kingston's Rondout Landing present the most options for nightlife. About a dozen bars line a short stretch of Main Street in New Paltz, a town that allows its watering holes to stay open until 4 A.M. Many, though by no means all, of them are student hangouts. Open-mic Wednesdays are a popular feature at **Oasis** (58 Main St., New Paltz, 845/255-2400). **Bacchus** (4 S. Chestnut St., New Paltz, 845/255-8636, www.bacchus newpaltz.com), near the corner of Main and Chestnut, keeps 300 beers on hand to accompany a menu of Southwestern fare. Students and local residents alike enjoy the late-night appetizer menu until 11 P.M. Sunday–Wednesday and until 1 A.M. Thursday–Saturday.

Buffalo wings and a dozen TVs are a hit at **McGillicuddy's Restaurant & Tap Room** (84 Main St., New Paltz, 845/256-9289; 11 A.M.–4 A.M. daily; Fri.–Sat. night cover $3–5), which also has a pool table and dance floor.

P&G's Restaurant (91 Main St., New Paltz, 845/255-6161, www.pandgs.com; 9 A.M.–4 A.M. Mon.–Sat., noon–4 A.M. Sun.), affectionately known as "pigs," is a New Paltz institution among students and alumni. Nightly specials include $2 pitchers of Newcastle beer and a menu of casual pub fare.

The legendary **Country Inn** (1380 County Road 2, Krumville, 845/657-8956), in a southern Catskill hamlet, changed hands in 2003 when founder Larry Erenberg retired, but it's business-as-usual under new management. Choose from hundreds of beers among a crowd of locals and travelers.

Saugerties locals gather at the **Chowhound Café** (112 Partition St., Saugerties, 845/246-5158, www.thechowhoundcafe.com; 11 A.M.–10 P.M. Wed.–Sun., brunch 11 A.M.–3 P.M. Sat. and 10 A.M.–3 P.M. Sun.; mains $10–23) on weekend afternoons to down a burger and listen to live jazz in a super casual setting. Besides the reliable burger and Caesar salad, the menu features Latin American specialties, including a churrasco steak.

Festivals

The **Belleayre Music Festival** draws a large crowd of music lovers to the Catskills each summer. Popular with kids in October is the **Headless Horseman Hayride & Haunted House** (778 Broadway, Ulster Park, 845/339-2666, www.headlesshorseman.com) on Route 9W between Highland and Kingston. The attraction is open during the last two weekends in September and every weekend in October. Reservations are required.

The **Woodstock Film Festival** (www.wood stockfilmfestival.com) celebrated its fifth anniversary in October 2004. The festival draws a number of leading filmmakers and critics to watch a selection of the industry's newest and boldest independent films.

The hundred-year-old **Ulster County Fair** (Libertyville Rd., 845/255-1380, www.ulster countyfair.com; $12 admission) takes places in August each year, with music, amusement rides, and fireworks. The fairgrounds are located two miles outside of New Paltz.

SHOPPING
Farm Stands

While in the Saugerties area, be sure to sample a taste of the hardneck garlic that grows nearby. Darker in color than the more common softneck garlic that grows in California's Gilroy, hardneck garlic is better suited to colder climates. July is the harvest season. And during the last weekend in September, **Gippert Farm** (266 Churchland Rd., Saugerties, 845/247-9479; June–Sept.) hosts the annual Hudson Valley Garlic Festival (www .garlicgoddess.com), now in its 15th season. Hundreds attend to try the local variety. Some say it's more bitter than what you buy at the grocery store; others disagree. See for yourself.

Davenport Farms (3411 Rte. 209, Stone Ridge, 845/687-0051, www.davenportfarms .com) operates a popular farm market, greenhouse, and pick-your-own field on Route 209 in Stone Ridge. To pick your own strawberries, head to **Kelder's Farm** (5755 Rte. 209, Kerhonkson, 845/626-7137, www.kelderfarm .com; 10 A.M.–8 P.M. daily) in early June.

Antiques and Galleries

There are literally dozens of antique shops and art galleries across Ulster County, many of them clustered around Saugerties and Rosendale. The **Woodstock School of Art** (2470 Rte. 212, Woodstock, 845/679-2388, wsart@ulster.net) holds auctions and exhibitions during summer months. The **Center for Photography at Woodstock** (59 Tinker St., Woodstock, 845/679-9957, www.cpw.org; noon–5 P.M. Wed.–Sun. Mar.–Dec.) shows contemporary works in a small gallery. It also runs workshops, auctions, and lectures.

A number of home furnishing stores have opened in High Falls and Stone Ridge, selling both new and old pieces. **Lounge Furniture** (8 2nd St., High Falls, 845/687-9463) has couches, area rugs, lighting, and other accents.

Most of the 30 antique shops in Saugerties are located within the eight-block commercial area on Main, Market, and Partition streets. At **Saugerties Antiques Gallery** (104 Partition St., Saugerties, 845/246-2323), owner Pat Guariglia caters to other dealers with a two-floor showroom of European and American antiques. **Partition Street Antiques** (114 Partition St., Saugerties, 845/679-7561, www.partitionstreet antiques.com; 11 a.m.–5 p.m. Thurs.–Mon.) collects a range of American furniture styles, including rattan, bamboo, and Mission oak.

Bookstores

Anyone with more than a passing interest in New York State history should plan a visit to Saugerties to browse the extensive collection of titles in the **Hope Farm Press and Bookshop** (252 Main St., Saugerties, 845/246-3522, www .hopefarmbooks.com; 10 A.M.–6 P.M. Mon., noon–4 P.M. Sun.). Owner Richard Frisbie houses two sister bookshops in one location—the larger sign over the door says Booktrader, which is a general-interest bookstore, and a smaller sign in the window reads Hope Farm Press & Bookshop. It's open 10 A.M.–6 P.M. daily except Sundays and most holidays, when it's open noon–4 P.M.

A fitting addition to Woodstock's alternative scene, 20-year old **Mirabai Books** (23 Mill Hill Rd., Woodstock, 845/679-2100, www.mirabai.com; daily 11 A.M.–7 P.M.) stocks a unique collection of metaphysical books and music, all related to inspiring, transforming, and healing.

Though it seems a little out of place, the fanciest shopping in Ulster County is found at **Emporium at Emerson Place** (5340 Rte. 28 at Mt. Pleasant Rd., Mt. Tremper, 845/688-5800; 10 A.M.–7 P.M. daily). Gourmet foods, aromatherapy products, country furniture, and home decor are all on display.

Wineries

Like Dutchess County, Ulster has a handful of wineries producing a range of varietals. You can hit each of them by driving a 30-mile loop called the Shawangunk Wine Trail (845/255-2494, www.shawangunkwinetrail.com). Better yet, ride a bike. This group of nine family-owned wineries are scattered along the back roads connecting the New York State Thruway, I-84, and Highway 17 between New Paltz and Warwick in Orange County. A trail map is available online and at any of the member wineries. One of the closest stops to downtown New Paltz is **Rivendell Vineyards and Winery** (714 Albany Post Rd., New Paltz, 845/255-2494, www.rivendellwine.com; 10 A.M.–6 P.M. daily).

INFORMATION AND SERVICES

The Kingston Heritage Area Visitor Centers, located at 20 Broadway and 308 Clinton Avenue (845/331-7517 or 800/331-1518, www.ci.kingston.ny.us; 9 A.M.–5 P.M. Mon.–Fri., also 11 A.M.–5 P.M. weekends May–Oct.) can provide information about Kingston's past and present. This is the place to pick up brochures, maps, and schedules of events.

Alternatively, look for the Kingston Tourism Caboose in the traffic circle off I-87 Exit 19 (845/340-3766). In Saugerties, stop by the McDonald's on Route 212, I-87 Exit 20 (845/246-5816). A tourist information center at Belleayre Mountain also has a wealth of information for travelers (800/431-4555, www.belleayre.com).

GETTING THERE AND AROUND
By Bus

Ulster County Area Transit (845/340-3333) serves major towns and rural areas across the county. Routes and schedules are available online at www.co.ulster.ny.us/ucat. In addition, **Adirondack Trailways** (800/858-8555) runs connector services to and from other destinations in the region.

Kingston has its own reliable public transportation system called **CiTiBus** (845/331-3725, www.ci.kingston.ny.us/CityGovt/Agencies.html#Citibus; $1), with three city routes. The closest train station is at Rhinecliff directly across the Hudson River.

By Car

Car rentals can be found at the Stewart and Albany airports. **Blue Mountain Limousine** is another way to get to and from the airport (845/246-4404). Taxis are also available at the airports, bus terminals, and at the Rhinecliff train station. Kingston gets congested by Ulster County standards, and the narrow streets downtown can be disorienting. But with a little patience, it's easy enough to find your way around.

THE MID-HUDSON

THE WESTERN CATSKILLS

In the days before air-conditioning, the promise of lively entertainment, kosher food, and a cool mountain breeze lured hundreds of thousands of families out of the sweltering New York City heat and into the perennial weekend traffic jam on slow and winding Route 17. Their destination was the Western Catskills, where a handful of grand resorts delivered wholesome family fun.

During the 1950s and '60s, dozens of stand-up comedians launched their careers in this land of bungalows and boarding houses. George Burns, Rodney Dangerfield, and Don Rickles all performed in the Borscht Belt—at places like Gossinger's the Concord, the Nevele, and Kutshers.

But just as these resorts had reached their prime, affordable jet travel intervened, and travelers began to skip the Catskills in favor of more exotic destinations.

It's been more than 20 years since Gossinger's resort closed its doors. At its peak, the 1,200-acre resort served 150,000 guests a year. All that remains of the original property today is a golf course, although there are plans to rebuild something new. Meanwhile, the last of the family-owned resorts, Kutshers, was up for sale at last check.

And yet, even as the old guard fades quietly into history, a new wave of visitors have arrived to take their place. After several decades of neglect and decline, the Catskills are once again in vogue. The market for second homes is booming, and once-forgotten towns like Andes and Livingston Manor are getting makeovers seemingly overnight as artists, chefs,

© NIKKI GOTH ITOI

HIGHLIGHTS

🌙 **Sivananda Ashram Yoga Ranch:** A retreat at this secluded country yoga center includes time for contemplation and relaxation, as well as daily yoga practice. Sign up for a single class, a weekend retreat, or a monthlong teacher-training program. Nature trails meander across the wooded property, and meals come from an organic garden onsite (page 153).

🌙 **Catskill Fly Fishing Center and Museum:** Located in the heart of some of the country's best fly-fishing, the museum celebrates the art and sport of the catch (page 155).

🌙 **Roscoe:** They call it Trout Town U.S.A. for a good reason. A haven for anglers and outdoor enthusiasts of all kinds, Roscoe lies at the junction of the Beaverkill and Willowemoc Rivers, on land that provoked many a battle between the Iroquois and Algonquin nations (page 155).

🌙 **Upper Delaware Scenic and Recreational River:** This winding stretch of Route 97 begins near the Orange/Sullivan county line and leads to breathtaking views of New York, Pennsylvania, and the Delaware River (page 156).

🌙 **Callicoon:** Anglers and leaf peepers congregate in Callicoon along the Delaware River, a stone's throw from Pennsylvania and the Delaware County line (page 158).

🌙 **Catskill Scenic Trail:** This 19-mile rail trail begins in Grand Gorge off Route 23 and runs west to Bloomsville (page 169).

LOOK FOR 🌙 TO FIND RECOMMENDED SIGHTS, ACTIVITIES, DINING, AND LODGING.

THE WESTERN CATSKILLS

Morris

Oneonta

Rockdale

NEW YORK

Deposit

Hancock

PENNSYLVANIA

Long Eddy

Summit

North Blenheim

CATSKILL SCENIC TRAIL

Stanford

Hobart

Mt Utsayantha

Grand Gorge

Bloomville

South Kortright

Dehli

Walton

Andes

Halcottsville

Pepacton Reservoir

Margaretville

Oliverea

Downsville

152

Catskill Park

Winnisook

DELAWARE

ULSTER SULLIVAN

GREENE ULSTER

Catskill Mountains

ROSCOE

CATSKILL FLY FISHING CENTER AND MUSEUM

Livingston Manor

Willowemoc

Neversink Reservoir

Rondout Reservoir

Lackawack

CALLICOON

Liberty

SIVANANDA ASHRAM YOGA RANCH

Jeffersonville

Woodburne

Minnewaska State Park

Fosterdale

Bethel

Lake Superior State Park

Monticello

Wanasink Lake

Wurtsboro

Swinging Bridge Reservoir

Yankee Res

Narrowsburg

Mongaup Reservoir

BASHAKILL WILDLIFE MANAGEMENT AREA

Rio Reservoir

Highland Lakes State Park

SULLIVAN ORANGE

Shawangunk

Middletown

Lake Wallenpaupack

Minisink Battleground Memorial State Park

Minisink

Delaware River

Pond Eddy

Port Jervis

UPPER DELAWARE SCENIC AND RECREATIONAL RIVER

0   10 mi
0   10 km

BROOME DELAWARE

CHENANGO DELAWARE

OTSEGO

SCHOHARIE DELAWARE

© AVALON TRAVEL

and other creative types make their way north to enjoy a simpler, more sustainable way of life. They come for the hiking and the fly-fishing, good eats and yoga retreats. Even the farmers are getting by, in part due to the spread of community-supported agriculture programs.

The heady days of the Borscht Belt may never take shape again, but the area remains charming as ever—with scenic back roads, historic covered bridges, and babbling brooks all within a few minutes' drive from the Quickway.

PLANNING YOUR TIME

Although sleepy Sullivan and Delaware counties do not directly border the Hudson River, they make a natural extension to many Hudson Valley itineraries. The busiest seasons in the western Catskills correspond to peak fishing conditions: April–June and September–October. In July and August, many inns fill with parents visiting their children at local summer camps. Hunters arrive in November, and most towns are quiet January–March.

It takes less than an hour to drive the length of the Quickway (Route 17) from Wurtsboro to Rockland, but there are many back roads to explore along the way. A weekend stay allows time for both sightseeing and recreation. Most Sullivan County itineraries center on a specific activity, such as fishing, yoga, or antique shopping. Head here to enjoy the serenity of a quiet morning on the Beaverkill or to visit a selection of the three dozen shops along the Sullivan County Antiques Trail.

Popular itineraries in Delaware County include self-guided barn and farm stand tours, daylong bike rides, and multi-day hikes and canoe trips. No major highways cross the county, and it takes about three hours to drive the perimeter. Add a half-day stop to pick your own fresh berries or bid on rare antiques in a country auction.

Sullivan County

Home to many of the family resorts that made the Catskills famous during the early to mid-20th century, Sullivan County stretches from the Orange and Ulster county lines in the east to the Delaware River and state of Pennsylvania to the west, covering a total area of about 1,000 square miles. The northern part of Sullivan County lies within the Catskill Preserve, but the terrain is more hilly than mountainous, with many of the same exposed rock ledges that characterize other parts of the Catskill region.

With a low population density (though not as low as Delaware County), Sullivan County supports a diverse ecosystem, including a growing number of bald eagles that make an annual winter appearance. Abundant trout in two famous rivers, the Willowemoc and Beaverkill, attract diehard fly-fishers, while two large reservoirs at Neversink and Rondout send freshwater to New York City, 90 miles

to the southeast. Despite its outdoor treasures, Sullivan County is best known as the site of the original 1969 Woodstock Music Festival, a three-day extravaganza that took place in the town of Bethel.

Sullivan County separated from Ulster County in 1809, borrowing its name from the controversial Revolutionary War General John Sullivan. In 1779, Sullivan led a devastating attack against the remaining Native American settlements in New York and Pennsylvania. He later became the first governor of New Hampshire.

Early Dutch settlers in Sullivan County built tanneries, bluestone quarries, sawmills, and gristmills to compensate for the lack of arable land. Irish and German immigrants later arrived to build a canal and two railroads connecting Pennsylvania and its stores of natural resources to New York City. Novelist and local resident Stephen Crane popularized Sullivan County

SULLIVAN COUNTY FARM STANDS

CALLICOON
11 A.M.-2 P.M. May through December
Holiday Market-early December
Callicoon Creek Park, Audley Dorrer
   Drive near bridge over Delaware River
   to Pennsylvania
www.visitcallicoon.com

JEFFERSONVILLE
2-6 P.M. June through September
Route 52 (Main Street) across from the
U.S. Post Office
www.jeffersonvilleny.com

LIBERTY
3-6:30 P.M. May through November
Holiday Market-early December
In the Municipal Lot on Darbee Lane
   near The First National Bank of
   Jeffersonville
www.greaterlibertychamber.com

ROSCOE
10 A.M.-2 P.M. May through October
In the Municipal Parking Lot on
   Stewart Avenue
www.roscoeny.com

in the 1890s with a series of *Sullivan County Sketches*. Around 1900, the Jewish Agricultural Society began to encourage Jewish farmers to move to Sullivan County from New York City. But when the new residents found the land difficult to farm, they supplemented their income by turning their farmhouses into boarding houses. Thus began the Borsch Belt and its history of famous resort hotels, most of which have faded into history.

Today, Sullivan County consists of 15 townships and no large cities. Monticello is the county seat.

ALONG THE QUICKWAY
Wurtsboro

Real estate values are climbing here as people move in from suburban areas to the east and south, but Wurtsboro still moves at the comfortably slow pace of a rural community. A string of inviting shops and cafés lines a two-block stretch of Sullivan Street, off Route 209.

Aviation enthusiasts will want to meet the pilots at the family-run **Wurtsboro Airport** (Rte. 209, 845/888-2791; 9 A.M.–5 P.M. daily), one of the oldest soaring sites in the country. A low ridge of the Catskills passes through the town, creating the ideal updraft for flying sans motor. In fact, pilots have soared as far as Georgia in one day from this tiny airstrip. A sailplane ride begins with an exhilarating tow on the runway. Most flights pass over the **Bashakill Wildlife Management Area** (Rte. 209 South, Wurtsboro, 845/888-5381, www.the bashakill.org) outside of town, a prime location for viewing bald eagles. The airport is located on Route 209, two miles north of town. Call to schedule a tour or lesson.

Monticello

Sullivan County's largest township and government headquarters, Monticello is the next major stop on the Quickway. Many of the storefronts along Broadway are showing signs of age and neglect, but the imposing **Sullivan County Courthouse** (414 Broadway), made of sandstone in 1909, is a notable exception. Aside from a handful of food and gas options, the only attractions that call for a longer stop are the **Monticello Raceway** (Rtes. 17 & 17B, www.monticello-raceway.com) and the **Mighty M Gaming Casino** (204 Rte. 17B, 866/777-4263, www.monticellogamingan-draceway.com), which opened in June 2004. Its investors battled authorities for several decades to secure permission to open the casino.

For rail travelers, Monticello is located a half hour from the Middletown train station on the Port Jervis Line. Several hotels provide transportation to the racetrack. Take Exit 104 off Route 17.

MONTICELLO

MONTICELLO RACEWAY/
MIGHTY M GAMING
CASINO

★ SULLIVAN COUNTY
COURTHOUSE

0   600 yds

0   600 m

© AVALON TRAVEL

Kiamesha Lake and Fallsburg

Follow Route 42 northeast out of Monticello to reach Kiamesha Lake, a popular fishing destination, where smallmouth bass, perch, and panfish are the most common catches. The lakeside **Concord Resort & Golf Club** (Concord Rd., Kiamesha Lake, 845/794-4000 or 888/448-9686, www.concordresort.com; $30–95) is still undergoing a $500 million face-lift that began in 2000.

At the **Shree Muktananda Ashram** (371 Brickman Rd., South Fallsburg, 845/434-2000, ext. 2202, www.siddhayoga.org/shreemuktan andaashram.html; opens 9 A.M. daily), in the next town over, students of Siddha yoga congregate for a healthy dose of spiritual development and renewal. In recent decades, the center has turned three abandoned hotels into a vibrant community. Day visitors are welcome to participate in meditations, hatha yoga classes, and meals. A large temple dedicated to Bhagawan Nityananda, spiritual founder of the Siddha yoga discipline, is also open to the public. If you visit the grounds, respect the modest dress code and quiet atmosphere of the center.

Continuing along Route 42, the weathered buildings that line the streets of Fallsburg were once rows of pristine stucco hotels drawing visitors all the way from the Atlantic coast. Tough times have lingered in the area since the advent of air-conditioning and airplane travel, and the largest employers are now three county prisons in neighboring Woodbourne. That said, local residents are taking steps to revive their quiet town. The unsightly remains of hotels and bungalows abandoned long ago are gradually disappearing. And a new overlook at the Neversink River offers visitors a place to enjoy the falls that provided waterpower for the mills and tanneries that sustained the town in its earlier days.

🄲 Sivananda Ashram Yoga Ranch

Every Friday after work, a group of harried city dwellers gathers at a busy yoga center in Manhattan for a ride to a weekend escape at the Sivananda Ashram Yoga Ranch (Budd Rd., Woodbourne, 845/436-6492, www.sivananda .org/ranch) in northern Sullivan County. A

THE WESTERN CATSKILLS

getaway here promises ample time for relaxing and rejuvenating. The shuttle leaves Fridays at 6 P.M. from the Sivananda Yoga Vedanta Center at 243 W. 24th St. in Manhattan and returns by 6 P.M. Sunday; roundtrip fee is $50.

Located 12 miles north of Monticello in Woodbourne, the yoga center occupies 77 acres of secluded countryside. Wooded areas surround open lawns and a pond. Guests can participate in a single class, a weekend retreat, or a month-long teacher-training program. The day begins with breathing and meditation exercises. Asana sessions take place at 8 A.M. and 4 P.M. daily. After yoga practice, guests can walk the nature trails or enjoy the wood-fired sauna. Volunteers prepare meals from a large organic garden and greenhouse. Accommodations are shared rooms in either a turn-of-the-20th-century farmhouse or a 1920s-era hotel. Camping is also allowed. Call ahead for transportation from the bus terminal in Woodbourne. Rates are $70–95 per person per night depending on type of accommodations, and $50 for a full day of classes, $25 half day, and $12 for one class.

Hurleyville

Route 104 out of Monticello leads to Hurleyville, where you can take a walk through history at the **Sullivan County Historical Society Museum** (265 Main St., Hurleyville, 845/434-8044; 10 A.M.–4:30 P.M. Wed.–Sat., 1–4:30 P.M. Sun.) Built in 1912, the building housed the Hurleyville Schoolhouse until 1945. Exhibits include a vintage general store and post office, as well as a collection of textiles from the turn of the 20th century.

Route 17B to Bethel

Dairy farmer Max Yasgur put the unassuming town of Bethel in the global spotlight when he agreed to host the 1969 Woodstock Music Festival—a soggy, three-day extravaganza that turned green pastures to slop, private homes into soup kitchens, and schools into makeshift hospitals.

The idea for a rock concert near Bob Dylan's home in Woodstock began as a late-night conversation in a Manhattan apartment and became within a few short months the largest music event in history. Hundreds of thousands attended, among them Ken Kesey and the Merry Pranksters. They grooved to the hottest sounds of the day, including Jefferson Airplane, Creedence Clearwater Revival, The Who, The Grateful Dead, and the closing act, Jimi Hendrix. Cars en route to Bethel jammed the New York Thruway and created a 10-mile backup a full day before the event began.

Cable TV executive Alan Gerry purchased the former Yasgur Farm in the late 1990s and announced plans to invest $46 million to create the **Bethel Woods Center for the Arts** (200 Hurd Rd., Bethel, 866/781-2922, www.bethelwoods.us). After a long legal battle, the Gerry Foundation broke ground in the summer of 2004 and produced its first season in 2006. The center features a 4,800-seat copper-roofed pavilion, 7,500-square-foot stage, and lawn seating for 12,000. Performances include classical, pop, rock, and country music.

Liberty to Livingston Manor

Back on the Quickway, Liberty's town center has a few antique shops and a Greek Revival Methodist church. To the east, the **Neversink Reservoir** (Neversink, 845/985-2524; daily), completed in 1953, holds 34.9 billion gallons of water and covers 93 square miles in the northeastern corner of Sullivan County. Its northern section lies within the Catskill State Park. The reservoir is open to fishing for brown trout, smallmouth bass, pickerel, panfish, and landlocked salmon. Follow Route 16 east from the Quickway.

Beyond Neversink, the privately owned **Grahamsville Historic District** (Rte. 55, Grahamsville) on State Route 55 consists of six Gothic Revival, Italianate, and Greek Revival structures on 200 acres. Outside of town, the **Kalonymus Escarpment,** a National Natural Landmark created by glacial activity, may pique the interest of amateur geologists. The **Rondout Reservoir** in Grahamsville is an observation point for bald eagles.

East of the Quickway along Route 82 lies the

hamlet of DeBruce, where New York State operates one of its 12 fish hatcheries. The **Catskill Hatchery** (Mongaup Rd., Livingston Manor, 914/439-4328 8:30 A.M.–4 P.M. Mon.–Fri., 8:30 A.M.–noon Sat.–Sun.) specializes in raising brown trout. Some 115,000 pounds of fingerlings and yearlings leave the hatchery each year, from a base of two million eggs. The state places the trout in rivers, streams, lakes, and ponds to support recreational fishing and to restore native species to damaged environments.

Aside from the flurry of renovations under way in its town center, Livingston Manor might still be the kind of place where the milk arrives daily at your doorstep. During the railroad era, the town once known as Purvis had the only Y-shaped track in the area for turning trains around. The town became a transportation hub as a result. A pair of wagon wheels marks the beginning of Main Street, and the swift-flowing Willowemoc Creek runs parallel to it, with an attractive schoolhouse on the opposite shore. Fly-fishing conditions are just about ideal here, and every other storefront sells fishing gear.

These days, Livingston Manor is a town in transition. A group of progressive investors out of New York City recently purchased several buildings in an effort to turn the town into a vibrant community for the arts. Although the investment brings the prospect of new jobs, some locals bristle at the threat of change.

◖ Catskill Fly Fishing Center and Museum

A few miles farther up the Willowemoc is the Catskill Fly Fishing Center and Museum (1031 Old Rte. 17, Livingston Manor, 845/439-4810, www.cffcm.net; 10 A.M.–4 P.M. daily Apr.–Oct., 10 A.M.–1 P.M. Tues.–Fri., 10 A.M.–4 P.M. Sat. Nov.–Mar.), a beautiful facility on 55 acres. A one-lane wooden bridge leads to the parking lot, and you can often see fly-fishers casting right in front of the museum.

These waters were the stomping ground of the late Lee Wulff, celebrated angler, conservationist, and writer. His words appear on a plaque inside the museum: "Over my many years of fishing, I have learned that angling's problems are never solved. They rise anew with each new pool and each new day. Fishing, especially fly fishing, has problems, solutions, challenges and rewards, which have always captured my imagination and stimulated my creativity." His wife, Joan Wulff, continues to run the **Wulff School of Fly Fishing** (7 Main St., Livingston Manor, 800/328-3638, www .royalwulff.com) nearby in Roscoe.

The exhibits in this well-funded museum will interest most outdoor enthusiasts, whether or not they care to learn how to tie a fly. Vintage rods and reels depict the sport in its early days. A wall of materials used in tying flies includes fox hair and a rare feather that comes from specially bred chickens. An old fashioned Cortland line-braiding machine in the back corner still works.

Watch the pros tie their delicate flies on Saturdays April–October. The center offers courses on stream ecology and angling, fly tying, and rod building. A blue sign on the west side of Old Route 17 marks the entrance to the center.

Covered Bridges

Most visitors enjoy crossing Sullivan County's rivers, even if they don't want to catch the fish that live in them. Early settlers in the area constructed bridges over the Beaverkill and Willowemoc using native hemlock trees, and three historic covered bridges have survived to the present day: **Covered Bridge State Park** (Livingston Manor) outside of Livingston Manor, **Beaverkill State Park** (845/439-4781, Roscoe) in Lewbeach (Route 154), and Willowemoc (Route 84). When he wasn't performing in New York City, composer Irving Berlin lived and wrote music in the hamlet of Lewbeach, beginning in 1938. Former CBS anchorman Dan Rather reportedly owns property in Beaverkill.

◖ Roscoe

The land around Roscoe, at the western edge of Sullivan County, once marked the disputed border between the Iroquois and Algonquin nations. Today the town is better known as a haven for anglers and outdoor enthusiasts, and store owners kindly ask patrons to leave their studded wading shoes at the door. The Beaverkill and Willowemoc Rivers meet in Roscoe, a.k.a. Trout Town U.S.A., at a place called Junction Pool, which is recognized as the birthplace of dry fly casting. Opening day of trout season (April 1) draws a crowd of fishing enthusiasts each year, from distinguished instructors and fly tyers to renowned New York City chefs.

More developed than the surrounding hamlets, Roscoe has a number of reputable tackle shops, inns, and restaurants, most of them in a row along Stewart Street. Shortline Bus offers weekend packages to Roscoe from Port Authority in New York City.

ALONG THE DELAWARE–ROUTE 97
◖ Upper Delaware Scenic and Recreational River

Exit 53 off I-84 puts you at the intersection of Route 97 and the start of the Upper Delaware Scenic and Recreational River (Rte. 97, 845/252-7414, www.upperdelaware.com), a national park that extends 73 miles from the New York/New Jersey state line through Sullivan County and into the southern part of Delaware County. It takes about three hours to drive the length of the park.

Conceived in the early 1930s as a scenic and commercial route, Route 97 connects Port Jervis in Orange County to Hancock in Delaware County, with the majority of the highway running through Sullivan County. This winding road is New York's equivalent to the West Coast's Highway 1. It climbs over hills and crosses ravines, featuring many turnouts and picnic areas along the way. Route 97 enters Sullivan County at Mongaup, just after the Hawk's Nest section of the road in Orange County. Brown Scenic Byway signs depict a river and road with green on both sides.

At 410 miles in length, the Delaware is the longest free-flowing river in the northeast. Its East Branch originates in the natural springs

of the Catskills, while the West Branch begins in Schoharie County, near Pennsylvania. The rocky terrain of the western Catskills forms Class I and Class II rapids along some stretches. Before the era of rail travel, the Delaware and Hudson Canal served as a vital connection between the two commercial rivers. For anglers, the Delaware is home to scores of trout, bass, walleye, eel, and shad.

Take a detour from Route 97 at the town of Pond Eddy (Route 41), about five miles past the Hawk's Nest, to head north to Glen Spey and the **St. Volodymyr Ukrainian Church** (Glen Spey, 845/856-5500). Like its counterpart in Greene County, this architectural wonder was built without a single nail.

Minisink Ford

Sullivan County's only Revolutionary War skirmish took place at Minisink Ford in July 1779, when a group of 120 colonists were defeated by a combined force of Native American and Tory soldiers. Today, the site is listed on the National Register of Historic Places. **Minisink Battleground Memorial State Park** (County Rd. 168, Minisink Ford; opens 8 A.M. daily) encompasses 57 acres of woodlands, with walking trails and an interpretive center that recounts both the political and the natural history of the site.

Also at Minisink Ford is the oldest suspension bridge in the country, the Delaware Aqueduct or **Roebling Bridge.** Built by John A. Roebling, the same engineer who designed the Brooklyn Bridge, this historic bridge dates back to 1848, when it was constructed to support the Delaware and Hudson Canal. Though the bridge has been converted to carry cars instead of coal, the original cables still hold it in place.

The Eagle Institute

Although winter is not the most popular season to visit the Delaware River, it is the best time to catch once-endangered bald eagles in action. A small group of eagles are year-round residents along the Delaware, while a larger population migrates from Canada, spending mid-December through mid-March in the warmer climate.

The nonprofit Eagle Institute (Rte. 97, Barryville, 845/557-6162, www.eagleinstitute .org), based in Barryville, runs guided field trips and other educational programs. Popular observation points include: **Mongaup Falls Reservoir** (Forestburgh), off Route 42 (not to be confused with Mongaup Pond in northeastern Sullivan County) and **Rio Reservoir** in Forestburgh. The institute has a winter field office just across the Roebling Bridge from Minisink Ford (176 Scenic Dr., Lackawaxen PA, 570/685-5960).

Novelist Stephen Crane reportedly penned *The Red Badge of Courage* from his cabin in nearby Forestburg.

Narrowsburg

The Delaware River reaches its deepest point, 113 feet, at Narrowsburg, where the earliest colonial settlers arrived in the 1770s, during the French and Indian War. The **Fort Delaware Museum of Colonial History** (Rte. 97, Forestburgh, 845/252-6660; 10 A.M.–4 P.M. Sat. and Mon., 11 A.M.–4 P.M. Sun.), run by the New York State Department of Education, recreates the pioneers' way of life and is a popular destination for local schoolchildren. Over the years, Narrowsburg has developed a vibrant community of artists and a number of cultural attractions. Several art galleries and theaters draw year-round visitors.

From Narrowsburgh, Route 52 leads away from the river toward Cocheton Center, Kenoza Lake, Jeffersonville, and eventually Liberty. Along the way is a historic bridge made of stone instead of timber. While many covered bridges have been preserved, the only original stone bridge with three arches remaining in the U.S. crosses the Callicoon Creek in the town of Kenoza Lake. It was built in 1872 and is now known as **Stone Arch Bridge Historic Park** (Rtes. 52 & 52A, Kenoza Lake, 845/794-3000).

Hanging geraniums and crisp new American flags greet visitors on Main Street in Jeffersonville, the next town along Route 52.

© NIKKI GOTH ITOI

cornfields along Route 52

© NIKKI GOTH ITOI

Stone Arch Bridge over the Callicoon Creek

Settlement here coincided with the arrival of the New York and Erie Railroad in the 1830s, but a fire destroyed most of the original buildings in 1918. A number of Victorians have been recently restored, including one that houses the **The Blue Victorian** (4874 Main St., Jeffersonville, 845/482-5544, www.the bluevictorian.com; 10 A.M.–5 P.M. daily) art gallery at the intersection of Route 52 and Maple Avenue. The heiress to the Hearst family fortune, Patty Hearst, spent part of her famous 1974 captivity in the Jeffersonville home of Symbionese Liberation Army accomplice Nicki Scott.

◖ Callicoon

If you stay on Route 97 and continue north toward Delaware County, you'll reach the hamlet of Callicoon (Wild Turkey), where the only remaining single-screen movie theater in Sullivan County, built in 1948, is still open for business. Although it was first settled in the 1600s, no building here is older than 1888 because of a fire that leveled the town.

SPORTS AND RECREATION
Winter Sports

Sullivan County has one small downhill ski area that's ideal for youngsters, or anyone who's just starting to get the hang of the sport. **Holiday Mountain** (99 Holiday Mountain Rd., Monticello, 845/796-3161, www.holidaymtn .com) in Monticello has snowmaking facilities to cover all 14 of its trails.

For Nordic skiers, many of Sullivan County's hotels and inns maintain their own trails. The towns of Fallsburg, Liberty, and Thompson open trails to the public. Ice fishing and snowmobiling are also popular winter activities.

Hiking

For many years, the 108-mile-long D&H Canal carried coal, cement, bluestone, and other industrial materials from Pennsylvania to New York City. Built by Irish and German immigrants over the course of three years, the canal played an instrumental role in the growth and development of the Atlantic seaboard. The advent of the railroad retired the canal from

AMERICAN GINSENG

The Chinese weren't the only ones to discover the healthful effects of wild ginseng. Native Americans discovered the plant in the Catskills long before the Dutch settlers arrived, and local residents have been consuming it in teas, lotions, and tonics ever since.

In Chinese medicine, ginseng roots are believed to energize and rejuvenate the body and enhance immunity. Although most of the world's supply is now cultivated in China and Korea, the highest-quality ginseng grows wild under the shade of deciduous trees like the sugar maple.

In the mid-1990s, Bob Beyfuss at the Cornell Cooperative Extension of Green County began an experiment – to teach local farmers how to simulate the wild growth of ginseng in their own backyards, the Catskill Mountains. Earning a price of $500 or more per pound, the root offered struggling farmers a way to supplement their meager income.

Wild ginseng is difficult to find and identify. Few who know it well are willing to share their secrets. But those who care to sustain its presence in the Catskills spread the seeds of a plant before they harvest its root. The plant is protected by law in New York State and may only be picked September 1-November 30.

service, but today you can walk, bike, or ski some 20 miles of it. The restored sections, however, are not yet all connected.

Willowemoc Wild Forest, in the southwest corner of the Catskill Preserve, is another good place to get away from it all. Located 18 miles north of Liberty and nine miles northeast of Livingston Manor, its 14,800 "forever wild" acres include trails maintained for hiking, skiing, biking, and snowmobiling. About 15 miles of paths are reserved for hikers only. The terrain is gentle, with rolling hills instead of tall peaks. Four trailheads departing from Neversink and Rockland have parking nearby. Campfires and primitive camping are allowed, but there are no facilities.

Privately run **Eldred Preserve** (1040 Rte. 55, Eldred, 845/557-8316, www.eldredpreserve .com) is a year-round fishing and hunting resort on 3,000 acres off Route 55. Facilities include three stocked fishing ponds and a sporting-clay range, and the resort runs fishing tournaments in summer. Services include guided trips, corporate events, a pro shop, and motel-style accommodations in log-cabin buildings.

The National Park Service maintains the challenging three-mile **Tusten Mountain Trail** (Rte. 97, 8:30 A.M.–6 P.M. daily), between Barryville and Narrowsburg near the Ten Mile River. The route reaches 1,100 feet at its highest point.

Cycling

Sullivan County Bike Club (845/794-3000, ext. 5010, weekly Apr.–Oct.), **Cinder Track Bicycles** (36C Main St., Livingston Manor, 845/439-4590, http://cindertrackbicycles.net), and **Mike Fraysee's Sports Resort** (573 High Rd., Eldred, 800/994-3335, www.mikefraysse sports.com) offer guided cycling tours.

A Bike Peddler Corp. (41 Stewart Ave., Roscoe, 607/498-4188; 8 A.M.–4 P.M. daily) rents bikes and sells maps and gear.

Barryville-based Lander's River Trips (see *Swimming and Boating*) recently added new Fuji mountain bikes to its list of rental services (full day $28, half day $16). **Pearson Park** (Walnut Mtn., Liberty, 845/292-7690; 8 A.M.–dusk daily), on Walnut Mountain, features 265 acres of novice to expert terrain, including challenging single-track riding.

Golf

Sullivan County offers several championship golf courses with moderate greens fees and inspiring views of the Catskills. The 7,650-yard, world-class course at the Concord Golf Resort ranks among the best courses in the country, according to *Golf Digest* (Concord Rd., Kiamesha Lake, 888/448-9686, www.concordresort.com; weekends $55–95, weekdays $35–45).

Swimming and Boating

Mongaup Pond is actually a 12-acre lake, the largest body of water inside the Catskill State Park that is not a New York City reservoir. A variety of fish live in the lake, and visitors can swim, fish, and paddle in its refreshing waters. Boat rentals are available through the Mongaup Pond State Campground (Exit 96 off Rte. 17, DeBruce Rd., Livingston Manor, 845/439-4233; daily fee $14). Camping is permitted mid-May–Columbus Day.

For a day at the beach, head to 1,400-acre **Lake Superior State Park** (Rte. 55, Bethel, 845/794-3000; 9 A.M.–dusk daily).

Several outfitters run trips along the Delaware: **Kittatinny Canoes** (3854 Rte. 97, Barryville, 845/557-8611 or 800/356-2852, www.kittatinny.com; 8 A.M.–7 P.M. daily mid-Apr.–Oct.) has canoes, rafts, kayaks, and tubes for trips ranging from calm to white water. **Whitewater Willie's** (37 South Maple Ave., Port Jervis, 845/856-2229 or 800/233-7238, www.whitewaterwillies.com; Apr.–Sept.) is another reputable operation with reasonable prices.

Mongaup Pond has a swimming beach with lifeguard supervision. Rowboats and canoes are allowed on the lake (rentals available), but not motorboats.

Lander's River Trips (5666 Rte. 97, Narrowsburg, 800/252-3925, www.landersrivertrips.com; rentals $19–37), family-run since 1954, runs 10 bases along the Upper Delaware River, with rafts, canoes, and kayaks for rent. Camping and packages are available.

Fishing and Hunting

Fly-fishing was first introduced to the U.S. in Sullivan County, and the tradition draws a majority of Sullivan County visitors today. You can learn to tie flies at one of several area schools, such as the renowned Wulff School of Fly Fishing. Or drop in for a workshop at the Catskill Museum of Fly Fishing. Trout season opens April 1, and the shad run peaks in May on the Delaware River. In addition, the county and state stock hundreds of lakes and streams. The **Beaverkill Angler** (Main St., Roscoe, 8:30 A.M.–5 P.M. daily) has everything you need for a day of casting in the river. Leave your studded shoes at the door.

Guides and gear are available at a number of additional operations in Trout Town U.S.A.: **Catskill Flies Fly Shop & Fishing Adventures** (6 Stewart Ave., Roscoe, 607/498-6146; 8 A.M.–5 P.M. daily) leads trips and rents equipment. You can sleep and fish with **Baxter House B&B and River Outfitters** (Old Rte. 17, Roscoe, 607/498-5811, www.baxterhouse.net). A half day of wade fishing runs $175 for one or two people, full day $245. Driftboat trips are $200 half day and $295 full day. Modest accommodations are available in six recently renovated rooms ($45–125).

Local fisherman Anthony Ritter runs driftboat trips along the Upper Delaware River through **Gone Fishing Guide Service** (20 Lake St., Narrowsburg, 845/252-3657, www.gonefishingguideservice.com; daily Apr.–Nov.). Catches include shad, trout, smallmouth bass, and walleye.

Other local guides include Stefan Spoerri out of Narrowsburg (845/252-7309) and Bill Fraser with Upper Delaware Outfitters out of Hankins (845/887-4853, www.upperdelawareoutfitters.com). Stop in at the **Catskill Delaware Outdoor Store** for fishing and hunting supplies and licenses, as well as current river conditions (34 A. Dorrer Dr., Callicoon, 845/887-4800; daily 8 A.M.–6 P.M.).

Aviation

Learn to fly (with or without an engine), or just take an aerial tour at the private **Wurtsboro Airport** (Rte. 209, Wurtsboro, 845/888-2791, www.wurtsboroairport.com; 9 A.M.–5 P.M. daily). There are grass and paved runways. A taxi service is available for rides into town. Other local facilities include Monticello Airport and Sullivan County International Airport.

ACCOMMODATIONS
Under $100

◖ **The Reynolds House** (1934 Old Rte. 17, Roscoe, 607/498-4422, www.reynoldshouseinn.com; $75) is an excellent value option for cozy accommodations in a central location.

© NIKKI GOTH ITOI

Western Hotel, Callicoon

Each room in this three-story inn has a private bath with a very small shower. Dark wood and floral prints define the look and feel. The breakfast room has a fireplace and kitchenette. The inn caters to hunters and fishers, as well as parents of children at local summer camps.

Just off Route 97, near an eddy in the Delaware River, the **Narrowsburg Inn** (176 Bridge St., Narrowsburg, 845/252-3998, www.narrows burginn.com; $65–135) has been in business since 1840. Current owners Tom and Rose Prendergast took over in 1996. Seven basic guest rooms share three baths, and one suite has a private bath.

The five-acre meadow surrounding the **Old House on a Hill** (295 Lt. Brender Hwy., Ferndale, 845/292-3554, www.oldhouseonahill .com; $75–105) invites guests to read a book and enjoy the summer breeze from a weathered Adirondack chair. Once the servants' quarters for a large hotel complex, the 1860 farmhouse has been restored as a B&B that serves a European-style breakfast. Original wainscoting from floor to ceiling makes the

four guest rooms dark, but light-colored linens help to compensate.

The first building you notice when you roll into Callicoon is the Victorian **Western Hotel** (22 Upper Main St., Callicoon, 845/887-9871; $97), a pale yellow building with white trim. Built in 1852, the inn offers six guest rooms upstairs and a cozy downstairs tap room, with antique furnishings throughout. Carpeted rooms feature air conditioning, private baths, and king-size beds. The restaurant serves American Continental fare for dinner Thursday through Tuesday from 5:30 P.M. till close.

$100-150

As a hundred-year-old boarding house, **Sunrise House B&B** (193 North Branch Rd., Jeffersonville, 845/482-3778, www.sunrisehousebandb. com; Apr.–Dec.; $110–175) has four comfortable rooms on a 45-acre property.

$150-200

Another Jeffersonville option is **Griffin House**

THE WESTERN CATSKILLS

(27 Maple Ave., Jeffersonville, 845/482-3371, www.griffin-house.com; $139–159) in a large Victorian. A six-course gourmet dinner is available with advance reservation.

Villa Roma (356 Villa Roma Rd., Callicoon, 845/887-4880 or 800/533-6767, www .villaroma.com; Apr. 1–Jan. 1), a resort and conference center, manages to blend some of the old-fashioned Catskill resort flavor with a host of modern amenities. A variety of vacation packages include meals and entertainment as well as accommodations.

Over $200

Enjoy a peaceful getaway beside a private lake at the **Inn at Lake Joseph** (162 Saint Joseph Rd., Forestburgh, 845/794-1948, www.lake joseph.com; $170–385). Its gorgeous Redwood room has 18-foot ceilings, and the Tudor room has high ceilings and a deck with over 700 square feet of living space.

Relative newcomer **Ecce Bed and Breakfast** (19 Silverfish Rd,. Barryville, 845/557-8562 or 888/557-8562, www.eccebedandbreakfast.com; $200–250) opened in 2004 in a former private home perched on a bluff above the Delaware River. The B&B is located conveniently close to the Bethel Woods Center for the Arts. Its five rooms have private baths (some with whirlpool tubs). Decks offer views of the surrounding mountains.

Campgrounds

Beaverkill Campground (Berrybrook Rd., Roscoe, 845/439-4281 or 800/456-2267; mid-May–Labor Day; $12) has 108 sites along the Beaverkill with hot showers. On the Delaware, **Indianhead Campground** (Barryville, 800/874-2628, www.indianheadcanoes.com; $10 per person) has wooded campsites with fire rings, right next to the river.

FOOD

While not as sophisticated as the cuisine found closer to the Hudson, Sullivan County has a few good standbys for hearty country cooking.

Along the Quickway

Catch a Willowemoc trout and have it pre-

pared at **Ianine's** (982 DeBruce Rd., DeBruce, 845/439-3900, www.debrucecountryinn.com; 8 A.M.–10 A.M. and 7–10 P.M. daily) inside the DeBruce Country Inn. Its Dry Fly Lounge is open 5–10 P.M. daily.

Wurtsboro has several tempting places for nourishment. The friendly ◖ **Uncommon Grounds** café (108 Sullivan St., Wurtsboro, 845/888-2121) makes a legitimate iced coffee and features evening jazz for a $5 cover. A few doors up the street, **The Potager** (116 Sullivan St., Wurtsboro, 845/888-4086) is a bright yellow Victorian set back from the road. Inside are a large garden center and a café serving Northern Italian fare.

In Livingston Manor, **Papa Tony's Tree Hut** (Old Rte. 17, Livingston Manor, 845/434-4611; 10:30 A.M.–8 P.M. Mon.–Thurs., 10:30 A.M.–10 P.M. Fri.–Sat., noon–6 P.M. Sun. May–Sept.) will treat you right with a hearty meatball sub or slice of pizza.

Along the Delaware–Route 97

Order breakfast all day at the **Whistle Stop Café** (119 Kirk Rd., Narrowsburg, 845/252-3355, www.whistlestopcafe.net; 6:30 A.M.–8 P.M. Sun.–Thurs., 6:30 A.M.–9 P.M. Fri.–Sat.; mains $3–6). The dining room at family-oriented **Lander's River Café** (20A. Dorrer Dr., Callicoon, 845/887-6800, www .landersrivercafe.com; 7 A.M.–9 P.M. daily; mains $3–7) overlooks the Delaware River.

The **Narrowsburg Inn** (176 Bridge St., Narrowsburg, 845/252-3998, www.narrows burginn.com; Wed.–Sun. summer, Sat.–Sun. spring and fall) offers a menu of tavern staples.

Chef Michael Werneke cooks New American fare at **Michael's Delaware Valley Grill** (1768 Forestburgh Rd., Glen Spey, 845/856-6900, www.michaels-ny.com; 5:30–10 P.M. Mon.– Thurs., 5–11 P.M. Fri.–Sat., 4–9 P.M. Sun.).

Callicoon boasts the most upscale dining in Sullivan County. Filet mignon with bourbon sauce and blackened yellowfin tuna anchor a menu of country-style entrees at **The 1906 Restaurant** (41 Lower Main St., Callicoon, 845/887-1906, www.1906restaurant .com; 5–10 P.M. daily; mains $15–30). Booth seating and a notable wine list complete the dining experience. **The Club at Villa Roma** (356 Villa Roma Rd., Callicoon, 845/887-4880 or 800/533-6767, www.villaroma.com; Apr. 1–Jan. 1) serves Italian American cuisine in a pleasant dining room with views of the resort's golf course. And ◖ **Matthew's on Main** (19 Lower Main St., Callicoon, 845/887-5636; 11 A.M.–10 P.M. daily in summer; 11 A.M.–10 P.M. Thurs.–Tues. the rest of the year) has outdoor tables with a view of the Delaware River.

River views are a draw at **Eagle's Nest Restaurant** (58 Eagle's Nest Rd., Bloomingburg, 845/733-4561; 5:30–9 P.M. Wed.–Sun. Apr.–Dec.). Healthy foods abound at the **East Ridge Organic Diner & Country Store** (11722 Rte. 97, Hankins, 845/887-5751; 5 A.M.–9 P.M. daily).

ENTERTAINMENT AND EVENTS
Bars and Nightlife
The biggest entertainment venue in Sullivan County is the **Mighty M Gaming Casino** (204 Rte. 17B, Monticello, 866/777-4263, www.monticellogamingandraceway.com), which opened in 2004 at the Monticello Raceway.

Festivals
The ultimate place to celebrate opening day of the trout season is the Junction Pool in Roscoe. Crowds of locals and fly-fishing enthusiasts gather on the often icy rocks to watch celebrity "first casters" kick off the season. The annual Two-Headed Trout Dinner is held Saturday night at the Rockland House. Another annual outdoor event is **Eaglefest** (School Auditorium, Narrowsburg, 845/252-6509, www.narrowsburg.org), timed to coincide with the bald eagle migration from Canada in January.

SHOPPING
Sullivan County shops carry antiques and a wide variety of handmade country goods, from marmalade to greeting cards. **Canal Towne Emporium** (107 Sullivan St., Wurts-boro, 845/888-2100, www.canaltowne.com; 10 A.M.–5 P.M. daily) is a cavernous gift shop filled with gourmet foods (some locally produced and some from afar), as well as candles, bath products, and other country accents for the home.

Antiques
Start a hunt for treasured antiques at **Ferndale Antiques** (52 Ferndale Rd., Ferndale, 845/292-8701, www.ferndaleantiques.net; 10 A.M.–5 P.M. daily July–Aug., 10 A.M.–5 P.M. Thurs.–Sun. and Mon. holidays Sept.–June), among the largest shops in the county, with 13 rooms on four floors of an 1894 mansion. Specialties include Depression-era glassware, as well as furniture, paintings, toys, kitchenware, lighting, and accessories. Take Exit 101 off Route 17. At the store, pick up a free copy of the **Sullivan County Antiques Trail** map, which began with 21 participating shops across the county and was scheduled to double in size in 2004.

The summer flea market at the Monticello Raceway is another popular venue for finding old-fashioned treasures. Farther along Route 17, **Liberty Antique Warehouse Auctions** (Rte. 17 Quickway, Liberty, 845/292-7450, www.libauction.com) holds regular auction events.

One of Wurtsboro's oldest homes—an 1825 canal house—is the storefront for **Hamill's Antiques** (81 Sullivan St., Wurtsboro, 845/888-5356, 11:30 A.M.–5 P.M. daily). Shop for antique paintings, sculptures, jewelry, and chandeliers. On summer weekends, cars jam the roadside parking lot of **Memories** (Rte. 17, Parksville, 845/292-4270 or 800/222-8463, www.memoriesantiques.com; 10 A.M.–5 P.M. daily), between Exits 97 and 98 on Route 17. Six showrooms with thousands of home furnishings, lighting, and other antiques are the draw.

In addition to a full array of antiques wares, **The Blue Victorian** (4874 Main St., Jeffersonville, 845/482-5544, www.thebluevictorian.com; 10 A.M.–5 P.M. Mon.–Sat., 10 A.M.–3 P.M. Sun.) has dedicated a gallery to the work of local artists. The shop occupies a beautifully restored Victorian that was once the home of the town physician.

Browse collections of clothing, pottery, Depression-era glass, prints, mirrors, and more at the **Antique Center of Callicoon** (26 Upper Main St., Callicoon, 845/887-5918; 11 A.M.–4 P.M. Thurs., Fri., Mon., 10 A.M.–4 P.M. Sat., 11 A.M.–3 P.M. Sun. Jul.–Aug.; 10 A.M.–4 P.M. Sat.; 11 A.M.–3 P.M. Sun. Sept.–Jun.).

Farm Stands

In this land of dairy farms and boutique growers, it's difficult to narrow the list of farm stands to manageable length. Callicoon's **Apple Pond Farming Center** (80 Hahn Rd., Callicoon Center, 845/482-4764) is one of the standouts. **Silver Heights Farm** (216 Eggler Rd., Jeffersonville, 845/482-3608) grows heirloom vegetables, herbs, and flowering plants. The **Sullivan County Area Farmers Market** (845/292-6180, www.sullivancountyfarmers markets.org/market_schedule.html) takes place in four locations: Callicoon, Liberty, Monticello, and Roscoe. Hours vary by location.

Knaub's Farm Antiques & Gifts (1168 County Rte. 23, Narrowsburg, 845/252-3781; 9:30 A.M.–7 P.M. Sat., 10 A.M.–4 P.M. Sun. May–Dec.) is a combination antique shop, gift shop, and roadside farm stand.

INFORMATION AND SERVICES

The Sullivan County Visitors Association (100 North St., Monticello, 845/794-3000, www.svca.net) operates information booths at Rock Hill, Livingston Manor, and Roscoe during the busy fishing season. Look for the red caboose off Route 17 at DeBruce Road.

GETTING THERE AND AROUND

Sullivan County is easily accessible from Stewart International Airport and New York City transportation hubs. **Shortline Bus** (800/631-8405) provides service from Port Authority in New York City to Monticello, with frequent express service and connections to smaller towns like Roscoe. Many resorts provide shuttle transportation from Monticello. Car rentals are available through independent companies (no major chains) in Fosterdale and Monticello: **Fosterdale Rent-a-Car** (1166 County Road 114,, Cocheton, 845/932-8538, www.17bcars.com; 8:30 A.M.–8:30 P.M. Mon.–Sat., till 2 P.M. Sun.; $39–52 per day) and **Marty's** (4461 Rte. 42, Monticello, 845/794-5025; 8 A.M.–9 P.M. daily).

Taxi services in Monticello and Bloomingburg serve all major airports. Note that Route 17 is becoming an interstate, I-86.

Delaware County

It's hard to imagine two worlds more opposed than the exclusive Hamptons of Long Island and the fertile hills of rural Delaware County. And yet, scores of former beachgoers are trading their ocean view for a fixer-upper and a pair of cross-country skis.

The reason? Property that's beautiful, affordable, and within a two-hour drive of New York City. Roughly the size of Rhode Island, Delaware County is the third-largest county in New York State and has the lowest population density (33.2 persons per square mile) of any county in the Hudson Valley and Catskill re-

gion—a figure that almost triples in summer. Encompassing the headwaters of the Delaware River, the area is known for an abundance of freshwater and unparalleled hunting and fishing.

Early European settlers arrived in present-day Delaware County in the 1780s by traveling the Catskill Turnpike. This first route to the western frontier was a dirt road with periodic tollgates that connected the Village of Catskill in Greene County to the Susquehanna River in Unadilla.

New York State recognized Delaware County

DELAWARE COUNTY FARM STANDS

DELANCEY
Kaufman Farm & Catskill Mountain Maple
Cabin Hill Road
607/746-6215

HALCOTTSVILLE
Pakatakan Farmers Market
Kelly Round Barn, Route 30
845/586-4177

HAMDEN
Lucky Dog Farm
35796 State Highway 10
607/746-8383

The Green Thumb
37784 State Highway 10
607/746-2248

LONG EDDY
Andersen's Maple Farm
534 Andersen Rd
845/887-4238

ROXBURY
Quarltere's Garden and Marketplace
48850 State Highway 30
607/326-4282

WALTON
Misty Mountain Farmers Market
Bridge and Water Streets
607/865-6656

Octagon Farm Market
34055 County Route 10
607/865-7416

system that prevented them from owning the land they farmed.

Holstein and Jersey cows still graze the hillsides here, and you'll find a sampling of barns in every shape, style, and condition—from those that are barely still standing, to others that have been restored as inviting markets, homes, and bookstores.

ALONG ROUTE 28
Fleischmanns

A 40-mile drive from Kingston along Route 28 leads to Fleischmanns, at the eastern edge of Delaware County. Initially known as Griffin Corners in the early 19th century, the town is named for Charles F. Fleischmann (think yeast and whiskey). Fleishmann had emigrated from Austria-Hungary to Cincinnati in the 1860s and started the Vienna Bakery that would make him world famous. Already a successful businessman, he bought property in Delaware County in 1883 and began spending summers in the mountain air.

Soon an entire community of summer residents, mostly well-to-do families, were building lavish Victorian homes along Wagner Avenue, many of which are standing today. Dozens of resorts opened in the surrounding area, but only a handful remain in business: the old Fleischmanns Hotel, for example, is now home to **Roberts' Auction** (820 Main St., Fleischmanns (845/254-4490, www.roberts-auction.com; weekly in-house auctions) (see *Shopping*).

At the center of Main Street stands the handsome **Skene Memorial Library** (1017 Main St., Fleischmanns, 845/254-4581, www.skenelib .org; 10 A.M.–4 P.M. Mon–Fri., 10 A.M.–1 P.M. Sat.), founded with a $5,000 grant from Andrew Carnegie and completed in 1901. An old carriage barn behind the library houses the **Fleischmanns Museum of Memories** (Main St, Fleischmanns, 845/254-5514), with exhibits that document the town's history as a thriving summer resort.

Arkville

One of the most scenic railroad lines in the

as a separate county in 1797. Lumbering and stone cutting sustained the local economy at first, followed by agriculture. In the 1840s, Delaware County became a focal point of the Anti-Rent Wars, during which poor farmers across the country began to protest the feudal

THE WESTERN CATSKILLS

east connected Kingston on the Hudson to Oneonta at the western boundary of Delaware County. Over the course of its hundred-year history, the Delaware & Ulster Railroad transported lumber, bluestone, livestock, produce, coal, and tourists across 107 miles of mountains and valleys. To date, three stretches of the original route have been restored for visitor enjoyment: the New York State Trolley Museum Kingston, the Catskill Mountain Railroad in Phoenicia, and the **Delaware & Ulster Railride** (43510 Rte. 28, 845/586-3877, www .durr.org; call for schedule; adults $12, children $7) in Arkville.

The depot is the most visible attraction around as you enter Arkville on Route 28 (south side of the street). Tours leave twice daily on weekends, May–October, and also Wednesday–Friday in the months of July and August. A round-trip tour to Roxbury takes less than two hours (one hour round-trip to Halcottsville). Dogs are welcome aboard the D&U.

Next to the Arkville Fire House, on the north side of Route 28, is the **Erpf House Gallery** (Rte. 28, 845/586-2611; 9 A.M.–5 P.M. Mon.– Fri., noon–4 P.M. Sat.), featuring artwork that explores themes of nature and captures the history of the Catskill region. Rotating exhibits include paintings, photography, sculpture, installation art, and crafts. The gallery also hosts periodic lectures, workshops, and an artist-in-residence program.

Margaretville and the Pepacton Reservoir

Delaware County sustained $20 million in flood damage when the "Blizzard of 1996" was followed by unseasonably warm temperatures and heavy rains. Margaretville's Bridge Street, along the banks of the East Branch of the Delaware, suffered some of the most severe damage from the disaster, and nine buildings were ultimately condemned.

In the years since, town officials have succeeded in turning the natural disaster into an economic opportunity. With a sizable disaster-relief grant from New York State, Margaretville has constructed a new waterfront park

Pepacton Reservoir in early fall

and river walk, along with new sidewalks and landscaping along Main Street. The result is a charming downtown, with several restaurants, shops, and inns—all of which are conveniently close to endless open space for fishing, hiking, and cycling.

A scenic detour from Route 28 leads to the Pepacton Reservoir, formed by a dam at the beginning of the East Branch of the Delaware River. The reservoir is named for one of the four towns it flooded when construction was completed in 1955, and one gets the feeling that more than a few locals are still bitter over the loss.

With a capacity of 140.2 billion gallons of water, the Pepacton is the largest reservoir in the New York City Watershed and provides about 25 percent of the total supply. The man-made lake covers 15 miles and 7,500 acres, supporting a healthy population of brown trout. Fish taken from these waters average about five pounds, with record-setters exceeding 20 pounds. Fishing and rowboats are allowed with a free permit. Several outfitters supply gear and lead trips on the reservoir. No swimming or motorboats are allowed.

At the western end of the reservoir on Route 30 is the village of Downsville and the Downsville Covered Bridge, at the intersection of Route 206. This 174-foot bridge still carries one lane of traffic at a time (maximum height six feet) across the East Branch of the Delaware River.

Andes

Northeast of the Peptacon Reservoir lies the upland village of Andes (www.andesny.org), where in 1845 Moses Earle and a group of local farmers refused to pay overdue rents to protest the feudal system of land ownership. Sheriff Osman Steele intervened in the dispute and was killed by the protesters, drawing national attention to the issue. President Abraham Lincoln signed the National Homestead Act into law 15 years later, in 1862, distributing hundreds of millions of acres of land into private hands.

One of the oldest buildings in town is the 1800 **Hunting Tavern Museum** (Rte. 28, 845/676-3775; call before visiting), named for

its first proprietor, Ephraim Hunting. Sheriff Steele reportedly downed his last drink here and uttered the now-famous words, "Lead cannot penetrate Steele," shortly before he was shot. Today, the tavern hosts local art exhibits, dance performances, and period dinners.

Proximity to the reservoir and a handful of hotels and restaurants make Andes a popular stop in Delaware County. Galleries and antique shops invite visitors to explore its Main Street. In winter, snowmobilers gather at Hogans General Store on Main Street to refuel.

Andes got a face-lift in 2005, with new sidewalks, store entrances, and a visitors center and museum. Renovations were just wrapping up in late 2007. The Trailways Bus Line passes through town.

Bovina and Roxbury

Scenic Route 6 connects Margaretville to Bovina, where actors Brad Pitt and Jennifer Aniston were residents until their split in 2005. An alternative drive from Margaretville follows Route 30 north to Halcottsville and then Roxbury. In an unlikely pairing, financier Jay Gould and naturalist John Burroughs share the town of Roxbury as their birthplace and family homestead. When Gould left home to invest in railroads, Burroughs remained in the Catskills writing volumes about the natural wonders around him.

A line from "In the Southern Catskills" captures Burroughs' worldview: "Only the sea and the mountain forest brook are pure; all between is contaminated more or less by the work of man." **Woodchuck Lodge** (www.roxburyny .com), the Burroughs family farmhouse, is now a National Historic Landmark. It's located on Burroughs Memorial Road, off Hardscrabble Road, three miles north of Roxbury.

The Gould family left behind a legacy of architectural splendor. St. Lawrence marble and Tiffany stained-glass windows adorn the **Jay Gould Reformed Church** (53873 Rte. 30, Roxbury, 607/326-7101). Helen Gould Shephard, daughter of Jay Gould, built the 1911 classic Greek Revival building that has housed the **Roxbury Arts & Cultural Center** (Vega

THE WESTERN CATSKILLS

© NIKKI GOTH ITOI

Delaware County Courthouse Square, Delhi

Mountain Rd., Roxbury, 607/326-7908) since 1988. Recently restored **Kirkside Park** (Rte. 30, Main St., Roxbury, 607/326-3722, www .roxburyny.com) and the **Shephard Hills Golf Course** (Golf Course Rd. off Bridge St., Roxbury, 607/326-7121, www.shephardhills.com; greens fees $10–20, golf cart rental $8–15) were also part of her original estate. Today, Roxbury is an attractive town of 2,500 residents, many of them retirees and second-home owners who enjoy the variety of outdoor activities within reach.

Delhi

In the center of Delaware County, where Route 10 meets Route 28, is Delhi (DEL-high), the largest and most commercially developed municipality in the region. As the county seat, this town of 50,000 centers around the historic **Delaware County Courthouse Square** (3 Court St., 607/746-3959), now an open green space bounded by 2nd, Church, Main, and Court Streets, the striking 19th-century brick façade now home to county offices.

The State University of New York (SUNY) College of Technology at Delhi opened in 1913 as the State School of Agriculture and Domestic Science and currently enrolls about 2,000 students per year.

Also in town are headquarters for several regional newspapers and radio stations, a few restaurants, and a couple of banks.

The **Delaware County Historical Association** (46549 Rte. 10, Delhi, 607/746-3849, www.dchany.org; 11 A.M.–4 P.M. Tues.–Sun. Memorial Day–Oct. 15; adults $5) maintains seven historic buildings on a property located 2.5 miles north of Delhi on Route 10. Among the restored buildings are a tollgate house from the Catskill Turnpike and the 1797 Frisbee House and barn. The museum displays rotating exhibits in its two galleries, from war memorabilia to quilt shows.

Hamden Covered Bridge

The Hamden Covered Bridge spans the West Branch of the Delaware River, along Route 10 between Delhi and Walton. Built in 1859 in the long truss style, the 125-foot bridge was refurnished in 2000. Look for a dirt pullout with a visitor sign just north of the bridge, on the

© NIKKI GOTH ITOI

Hamden Covered Bridge near Walton

west side of Route 10. On a sunny day, bring lunch to the picnic table on the west side of the bridge and watch the tractors roll by.

Route 10 heads south from Delhi along the West Branch of the Delaware River, passing through the quiet towns of Hamden, Walton, and Deposit along the way.

ALONG ROUTE 23
◖ Catskill Scenic Trail

If you follow Route 23 west from Greene County, you'll reach the town of Grand Gorge just over the Delaware County line. The East Branch of the Delaware River begins here, and you can pick up the Catskill Scenic Trail (Rte. 23, Grande Gorge, 607/652-2821), which sits on top of the old railroad tracks of the Ulster & Delaware Railroad and runs 19 miles to Bloomville. The hard-packed trail is well suited for biking, jogging, horseback riding, and cross-country skiing, and it offers access to several fishing spots along the river. The railroad track foundation keeps the trail at a gentle grade, so visitors of all ages and physical conditioning can enjoy the hike. The trail may be accessed from many towns along

the way; parking lots are available in Bloomville at Route 10 and Route 33. No overnight camping is available.

At the intersection of Routes 23 and 10 lies Stamford and Mount Utsayantha (Beautiful Spring). The West Branch of the Delaware originates at this 3,214-foot peak, and it's one of the few Catskill summits that you can reach by car. A one-mile gravel road leads to the top and a view of four states on clear days. On the way to the summit is the recognized gravesite of a Mohawk princess who drowned herself in a nearby lake in grief over the loss of her son.

Stamford evolved from a distribution center for butter to a thriving resort town at the turn of the 20th century, and its 20-acre mountaintop park lured visitors from across the country. Today, the walking paths are overgrown and the abandoned observation tower shows signs of neglect. But in 2004, town officials secured a grant to restore the park to its former glory. In the meantime, the Utsayantha Flyers Organization has built several launch ramps for hang gliders and keeps a watchful eye on the property.

Turn off Route 23 onto Route 12 to reach East Meredith and the working saw and gristmill at

SKI PLATTEKILL STATISTICS

- Base: 2,150 feet
- Summit: 3,500 feet
- Vertical: 1,100 feet
- Trails: 35
- Lifts: 4
- Skiable acres: 75
- Snowmaking: 75 percent
- Snow report: 607/326-3500

the **Hanford Mills Museum** (County Rtes. 10 & 12, East Meredith, 800/295-4992, www.hanfordmills.org; 10 A.M.–5 P.M. Tues.–Sun. and holiday Mondays May 15–Oct. 15; adults $7, children $3.50).

SPORTS AND RECREATION
Winter Sports
You have to be one of the first 2,000 skiers to get fresh tracks at **Ski Plattekill** (Plattekill Mountain Rd., Roxbury, 607/326-3500, www.plattekill.com; 8:45 A.M.–4:15 P.M. Fri.–Sun.; adults $46, children $36, under 5 free) on a powder day. Normally open three days a week, the mom-and-pop mountain sells $25 tickets and runs the T-bar to expert terrain on days of 12 inches or more. But the owners stop selling tickets when they reach the 2,000 mark. Plattekill gets upwards of 200 inches of snow a year—more natural snow than even the Catskill High Peaks typically get.

The considerably smaller **Bobcat Ski Center** (Rte. 28, Andes, 845/676-3143, www.bobcatskicenter.com; 9 A.M.–4 P.M. Fri.–Sun. and holidays Dec.–Mar.; adults $25, students $12) has added snowboard rentals to its list of services.

The **Delhi College Golf Course** (Rte. 28, Delhi, 607/746-4653) is open to the public all winter long for cross-country skiing and snowshoeing. Snowmobilers congregate in the town of Andes, often to refuel at Hogans General Store (Main St., Andes, 8 A.M.–8 P.M. daily) and lunch at the Andes Hotel (Main St., Andes, 845/676-4408, lunch and dinner daily, Sun. brunch).

Hiking
The Catskill Preserve and **Utsayantha Trail System** (Stamford, 607/652-7581) offer miles of wilderness for day hikes or overnight trips. A stretch of the 552-mile Finger Lakes Trail System crosses Delaware County with several good places to camp overnight, including Beale Pond at Oquaga Creek State Park (Rte. 20, Masonville, 607/467-4160). Contact the Delaware County Chamber of Commerce or write to the Finger Lakes Trail Conference Service Center (P.O. Box 18048, Rochester, NY 14618), for a current trail map. Visit www.delaware county.org/hiking for information about access points and routes.

Cycling
Whether you want to log 15 miles or a century, Delaware County has some of the best terrain around for cycling. Plan a route to tour the county's covered bridges. In summer, Plattekill opens its lifts for mountain biking.

Golf
Hanah Country Inn & Resort (576 West Hubbell Hill Rd., Margaretville, 845/586-4849 or 800/752-6494, www.hanahcountryclub.com; greens fees $55–75) has a U.S.G.A.-rated course that's known as the Terminator. Inquire about combined room and greens fee packages. **French Woods Golf & Country Club** (17440 Rte. 97/East Newman Rd., Hancock, 607/637-1800, greens fees $28–34) is an 18-hole, 6,000-yard, par 72 course with woods and pond views.

Swimming and Boating
Paddlers head for the Delaware and Susquehanna Rivers for adventure.

Located near the Pepacton Reservoir, **Al's Sport Store** (Rtes. 30 & 206, Downsville, 607/363-7740, www.alssportstore.com;

> # BOBCAT SKI CENTER STATISTICS
>
> · Base: 1,050 feet
>
> · Summit: 3,345 feet
>
> · Vertical: 1,050 feet
>
> · Trails: 18
>
> · Lifts: 2
>
> · Skiable acres: 80
>
> · Snowmaking: 20 percent
>
> · Snow report: 845/676-3143

5:30 A.M.–6 P.M. Mon.–Fri., 5 A.M.–6 P.M. Sat., 5 A.M.–6 P.M. Sun.) offers day or overnight camping trips on the Delaware River. Shuttle service is available. **Smith's Canoe & Drift Boat Rental** (Rte. 97, Hancock, 607/637-2989) has driftboats and canoes for rent with access directly on the Delaware River.

Fishing and Hunting

Delaware County offers hundreds of miles of some of the top fishing streams, rivers, and reservoirs in the country. The season begins each April with the hatching of the blue-winged olive fly. For freestone stream fishing, the Willowemoc and Beaverkill are legendary. The Pepacton reservoir offers stillwater anglers plentiful opportunities for catching bass and occasionally huge browns.

ACCOMMODATIONS

Accommodations are hit or miss in rural Delaware County. Small country inns range from musty and neglected to positively charming. The good news is that even the best are relatively affordable.

Under $100

Located between Downsville and Delhi, **Octagon Farm Bed & Breakfast** (34055 State Highway 10, Walton, 607/865-7416;

$80–120) offers comfortable accommodations in a unique 1850s building. The main house has five guest rooms with one shared bath. A cottage has two additional bedrooms, plus a full kitchen. And the Creekside House has three bedrooms and a private outdoor space, available for $350–375 per couple. The surrounding property was once a dairy farm, and today the owners grow produce for sale at the Octagon Farm Market on-site.

Down comforters are a bonus in three guest rooms at the ◖ **Country House Bed and Breakfast** (257 East Bramley Mountain Rd., Bovina Center, 607/832-4371, www.country housebandb.com; $85–90). In addition, the 1840 farmhouse features pine floors, private baths, and tasteful, old-world furnishings, making it a solid deal all-around. Best of all, the inn is set on a 300-acre cattle farm, which means all-natural beef on your breakfast table.

For a motel with a twist, try **The Roxbury** (2258 County Hwy. 41, Roxbury, 607/ 326-7200, www.theroxburymotel.com; $100–155). Its simple rooms combine contemporary decor with the convenience of in-room kitchenettes.

One of the best-known places in Margaretville is the **Margaretville Mountain Inn** (1478 Margaretville Mountain Rd., Margaretville, 845/586-3933, www.margaretvilleinn.com; $95–150). Set in an aging Victorian on a hill above the town, the B&B has several floral rooms with brass bed frames. Some rooms share a bath. For more modern accommodations and a more convenient location, request a room in the newer building in town.

Just outside of Hancock, **Smith's Colonial Motel** (23085 State Hwy 97, Hancock, 607/637-2989, www.smithscolonialmotel.com; $65–125) is a well-kept property with an impressive list of amenities for the price, including cable TV with HBO and high-speed Internet. Guestroom walls are paneled in knotty pine, and minimal furnishings accent scenic views of the Delaware River below.

$100-150

Near Belleayre Ski Resort, **The Highlands Inn**

(923 Main St., Fleischmanns, 845/254-5650, www.thehighlandsinn.com; $115–135) surprises with wireless Internet access in a large Victorian. The downside: only three of the seven rooms have private baths, and there is a two-night minimum.

$150-200

Hanah Country Inn & Resort (576 West Hubbell Hill Rd., Margaretville, 800/752-6494, www.hanahcountryclub.com; $60–250) provides standard chain hotel-style accommodations, but the resort offers enough activities to keep you out and about the entire day. Take the free shuttle to Plattekill Mountain for some downhill mountain biking, or head out to face the Terminator golf course. A golf school on-site will help tune up your game. The resort offers numerous golf, ski, and mountain biking packages.

Campgrounds

Peaceful Valley Campground (485 Banker Rd,,Downsville, 607/363-2211, www.ny peacefulvalley.com; $10) is the place to pitch your tent. You can also rent a room in a cottage or cabin ($45–120). Canoe rentals are available by the day or by the week. An alternative is the **Little Pond Campground** (549 Little Pond State Campground Rd., Andes, 845/439-5480; $18). From Route 30 in Margaretville, go south about six miles to New York City Road and then to Barkaboom Road, and the campground will be on the right.

FOOD
Along Route 28

Margaretville has a handful of decent eateries, including **Café on Main** (Margaretville Commons, 785 Main St., Margaretville, 845/586-2343; www.domenicoscafeonmain .com; 11 A.M.–9 P.M. Mon.–Thurs., 10 A.M.–10 P.M. Fri.–Sun.; breakfast served only Sat.–Sun.; mains $5–15), serving Italian classics such as chicken cacciatore, several pasta dishes, and flank steak. Stop in for lunch while you browse the shops.

For a taste of the gourmet, head to **That**

Certain Something (496 Main St., Fleischmanns, 845/254-5155), a popular spot among weekenders that's run by Toni Perretta, a former cosmetics executive.

The unfortunately named town of Downsville hosts the upscale **Old Schoolhouse Inn** (Upper Main St., Downsville, 607/363-7814; www.oldschoolhouseinn.com; 5–9 P.M. Tues.–Thurs.; 5–10 P.M. Fri.–Sat.; 10 A.M.–9 P.M. Sun.; mains $14–23). The menu includes lobster, prime rib, and trout dishes, and you'll dine under a large collection of stuffed hunting trophies.

Get your blueberry pancakes at **Cassies Kitchen** (85 Main St., Andes, 845/676-4500; 7 A.M.–3 P.M. Thurs.–Tues.). **The Andes Hotel** (110 Main St., Andes, 845/676-3980, www .andeshotel.com; lunch and dinner daily, brunch Sun.) serves hearty fare, especially in winter when the snowmobilers ski into town. Smoky guacamole and outstanding margaritas are to be found at **Cantina** (Rte. 28 corner of Main St. and Delaware Ave., Andes, 845/676-4444, www.cantina-andes.com; 11:30 A.M.–10 P.M. Wed.–Mon.; mains $7–17).

Along Route 23

Roxbury's **Taste Buds Country Store and Restaurant** (Main St., Roxbury, 607/326-3663) is a classic: an old-fashioned soda fountain located conveniently close to Plattekill. In South Kortright, **The Hidden Inn** (Main St., South Kortright, 607/538-9259; 5–9 P.M. Tues.–Sat., noon–7 P.M. Sun.; mains $12–18) offers a long menu of surf-and-turf standards alongside more exotic offerings such as frogs' legs and escargot. The prime rib is a popular order, and the restaurant is well known for its duck à l'orange.

ENTERTAINMENT AND EVENTS
Performing Arts

The **West Kortright Centre** (49 West Kortright Church Rd., West Kortright, 607/278-5454, www.westkc.org) is one of the premier performance venues in Delaware County. Housed in a restored church on Turnpike Road in West

COMEDIANS WHO PERFORMED IN THE CATSKILLS

- Joey Adams
- Woody Allen
- Morey Amsterdam
- Milton Berle
- Shelley Berman
- Al Bernie
- Mel Brooks
- Lenny Bruce
- George Burns
- Pesach Burstein
- Red Buttons
- Sid Caesar
- Jack Carter
- Myron Cohen
- Bill Dana
- Rodney Dangerfield
- Phyllis Diller
- Betty Garrett
- George Gobel
- Shecky Green
- Buddy Hackett
- Mickey Katz
- Danny Kaye
- Alan King
- Robert Klein
- Jack E. Leonard
- Jerry Lewis
- Jackie Mason
- Jan Murray
- Carl Reiner
- Don Rickles
- Joan Rivers
- Freddie Roman
- Jackie Vernon
- Jackie Wakefield
- Jonathan Winters
- Henny Youngman

Kortright, it offers an array of musical performances throughout the summer season, as well as gallery exhibits.

Set in a historic building in downtown Franklin, the **Franklin Stage Company at Chapel Hall** (Franklin, 607/829-3700, www.franklinstagecompany.org) produces a mix of modern and classical theater. The company's free admission policy sets a fun and irreverent tone. The **Open Eye Theatre Company** (960 Main St., Margaretville, 845/586-1660, www.theopeneye.org) has moved into a permanent theater on Main Street.

Bars and Nightlife
The Red Barn (18 Kelsey Rd., Deposit, 877/560-2276, www.nyredbarn.com) is a bar, restaurant, and dance hall with live music and dinner theater in a restored barn. Catch the Folk Music Festival in late July.

Festivals
Set on a 500-acre farm and year-round campground, the **Peaceful Valley Bluegrass Festival** (Downsville, 800/467-3109) takes place in July. RV hookups and a swimming pool help beat the heat during the day, but nights can be chilly.

Listen to classical music performances at the **Honest Brook Music Festival** (off Rte. 28 between Downsville and Meridale, 607/746-3770, www.hbmf.org) or try your hand at the two-man saw during the annual **Lumberjack Festival** (Riverside Park, Deposit, 607/278-5744, www.hanfordmills.org).

SHOPPING
If you love to buy and sell goods on eBay, try the offline equivalent at one of Delaware County's professional auction houses. At **McIntosh Auction Service** (Bovina Center,

607/832-4829 or 607/832-4241 www.mcintosh auction.com), Chuck McIntosh has been in the business for 30 years. You can bid on antiques, machinery, or even a farm estate. Another reputable operation is **Roberts' Auction** (820 Main St., Fleischmanns, 845/254-4490, www.robert sauction.com). After you've won the farm, you can sample the local bounty at the **Pakatakan Farmers Market** (Kelly Round Barn, Rte. 30, Halcottsville, 845/586-4177; 9 A.M.–2 P.M. Sat.) or the Octagon Farm Market (34055 State Highway 10, Walton, 607/865-7416).

Alpacas and llamas graze the pastures at **Eastbrook Farms** (2410 Dunk Hill Rd., Walton, 607/746-3849), where you can buy woven and knitted scarves, shawls, and baby blankets. A restored carriage house holds a collection of rare and used books at **Bibliobarn** (Roses Brook Rd., South Kortright, 607/538-1555; 9 A.M.–6 P.M. daily).

Blink Gallery (454 Lower Main St., Andes, 845/676-3900, www.blinkgallery.net; 11 A.M.–6 P.M. Sat., 11 A.M.–3 P.M. Sun. and holiday Mondays) features contemporary art-ists in a wide variety of media including ceramics, glass, and paintings. At the other end of Main, **Paisley's Country Gallery** (75 Main St., Andes, 845/676-3533; 10 A.M.–5 P.M. Thurs.–Sun. Apr.–Feb.) is also worth a look for antiques and gifts.

INFORMATION AND SERVICES

The **Delaware County Chamber of Commerce** (114 Main St., Delhi, 607/746-2281, info@ delawarecounty.org, www.delawarecounty.org) is located in Delhi and maintains an informative website.

GETTING THERE AND AROUND

It's easier to rent a canoe than a car in outdoor-oriented Delaware, but you'll need wheels to get around this rural county, as public transportation is virtually nonexistent. Albany International Airport is your best bet for a rental. **Adirondack Trailways** (800/225-6815) offers bus service to Delhi.

THE UPPER HUDSON

The Catskill and Berkshire Mountains frame the upper—and most rugged—section of the Hudson River Valley. In between, small lakes and dense hardwood forests alternate with rolling hills and cultivated fields. Rural communities dot the landscape, welcoming visitors with historic sites, heirloom vegetables, antique shops, and the promise of outdoor adventure.

Striking in any season, the Upper Hudson Valley makes an exceptionally enjoyable winter getaway, when every inn has a wood fire burning and hearty meals warm you from the inside out. Greene and Columbia counties succeed in creating that cozy feeling the Austrians call *gemütlichkeit*. Cross-country skiers can explore varied terrain on private and public lands, while downhill skiers and riders can find steeps and parks for all levels at the Windham, Hunter, Bellyeare, and Catamount resorts. And for those who don't measure fun in vertical feet, snowmobiles, snowshoes, and ice skates provide a few more alternatives.

If you're the kind of person who travels to eat, the Upper Hudson Valley also holds a few hidden gems. French-inspired cuisine at Aubergine in Hillsdale, the restored art deco Ruby's Hotel in Freehold, New American at Swoon Kitchenbar in Hudson, and the multicourse tasting menu at the Basement Bistro should top any gourmet's must-try list.

And there's another way to sample the fruits of the land: by rolling up your sleeves and picking what's in season. There is at least one farmers market, roadside stand, or pick-your-own orchard in just about every town in Columbia and Greene counties.

© NIKKI GOTH ITOI

HIGHLIGHTS

◖ Kaaterskill Falls: An hour-long walk on a well-marked but strenuous trail leads to the base of the 180-foot falls that inspired many a Hudson River School painter. With the old tanneries and hotels long gone, the falls are actually more pristine today than they were 100 years ago (page 183).

◖ The Escarpment Trail: Near the town of Haines Falls, a 1,500-foot plateau marks the site of the old Catskill Mountain House, one of America's first resort hotels. The five-state view from the edge of the escarpment makes the park one of the most popular in the Catskill region today (page 184).

◖ Tannersville: This mountaintop town bustles with activity year-round. A row of colorful Victorians on Main Street holds restaurants, cafés, bars, and shops, while the Mountaintop Arboretum grows native and exotic trees and shrubs on seven acres of land (page 184).

◖ Clermont State Historic Site: The classical Clermont estate on the Hudson River north of Germantown belonged to the high-society Livingston family (page 200).

◖ Olana State Historic Site: The Persian-style Olana mansion, near the Rip Van Winkle Bridge, was the brainchild of Hudson River School painter Frederic Church (page 201).

◖ Shaker Museum and Library: This remarkable collection of artifacts offers an informative introduction to the Shaker way of life (page 205).

◖ Taconic State Park: This expansive green space encompasses 5,000 acres at the base of the Taconic Range, near the Massachusetts and Connecticut state lines (page 205).

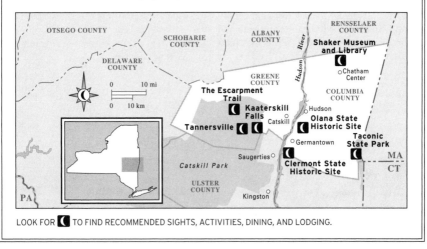

LOOK FOR ◖ TO FIND RECOMMENDED SIGHTS, ACTIVITIES, DINING, AND LODGING.

THE UPPER HUDSON

Canaan

CT

Great Barrington

5 mi

5 km

MA

New Lebanon

22

TACONIC STATE PARK

90

East Chatham

Austerlitz

NEW YORK

Hillsdale

22

Millerton

Nassau

20

RENSSELAER
COLUMBIA

Chatham Center

Ghent

66

9H

STATE PKWY

Ancram

82

Pine Plains

82

Lafayetteville

Castleton-on-Hudson

SHAKER MUSEUM AND LIBRARY

9

Kinderhook

9J

Claverack

TACONIC

COLUMBIA
DUTCHESS

199

Hudson River

144

New Baltimore

Ravena

87

9W

Hudson

OLANA STATE HISTORIC SITE

96

Germantown

CLERMONT STATE HISTORIC SITE

96

Annandale-on-Hudson

9

9G

Alcove Reservoir

ALBANY
GREENE

Greenville

Freehold

Cairo

23

Catskill

Blackhead

KAATERSKILL FALLS

Saugerties

87

9W

Kingston

209

Dormansville

19A

Greenville

THE ESCARPMENT TRAIL

Thomas Cole Mtn

Black Dome

Haines Falls

Woodstock

28

Ashokan Reservoir

Livingstonville

145

Preston Hollow

WINDAM MOUNTAIN SKI AREA

TANNERSVILLE

212

28A

19

Schoharie Reservoir

SCHOHARIE

Windham

23

Lexington

23A

HUNTER MOUNTAIN SKI AREA

Hunter Mountain 4,025ft

214

GREENE
ULSTER

Boiceville

West Shokan

42

17

Prattsville

42

Mt Tremper

Catskill Mountains

Grand Gorge

23

DELAWARE
GREENE

28

Oliverea

Winnisook

47

Catskill Park

© AVALON TRAVEL

PLANNING YOUR TIME

With a selective itinerary, you can easily tour Greene or Columbia in a day of scenic driving. (It takes less than an hour to drive the length of either one.) But you'll need a long weekend to sample the range of historic sites and outdoor activities these counties offer. Allow an hour for the round-trip hike to Kaaterskill Falls or a day to summit one of the High Peaks. Tours of the Clermont and Olana historic homes last about an hour, plus time walk the grounds and contemplate the views. Serious antique shoppers can spend a full day or more in downtown Hudson.

Many visitors to the upper Hudson plan weekend getaways around an outdoor activity or a charming inn. Others choose to take in a quick sight or memorable meal en route between New York City and New England or western New York State. Historic homes and local festivals can make good day trips, depending on your starting point.

In Greene County, the loop along Routes 23 and 23A covers about 40 miles and takes less than an hour to complete by car with no stops. An out-and-back excursion to Coxsackie along Route 385 and the Hudson River adds another hour round-trip. Columbia County has three parallel routes running north to south: Route 9G follows the river's edge, the Taconic State Parkway is the fastest, and Route 22 runs along the foot of the Taconic Hills.

Starting at the southern border with Dutchess County, a good loop is to follow Route 9G about a half hour north to the city of Hudson, then meander on local roads up to Kinderhook and Chatham. From there, you can zip back to your starting point along the Taconic, or continue east and take Route 22 south through Hillsdale and Copake. The entire loop should take about two to three hours with no stops.

Greene County

In the days before New York City residents could hop a flight to Bermuda for the weekend, they vacationed in the Catskills. If you had the means to vacation in remote Greene County during the early to mid-19th century, you might have stayed at the world-famous Catskill Mountain House—along with Alexander Graham Bell, Henry James, Oscar Wilde, Ulysses S. Grant, Mark Twain, and their contemporaries. A one-day journey from New York City began with a steamboat ride to Catskill Landing and concluded with a harrowing 12-mile, four-hour stagecoach ride to the eastern edge of the High Peaks region.

Between the Kaaterskill Creek and Sleepy Hollow, a steep and narrow road climbed to the top of a rocky plateau called Pine Orchard. Here, the classical Mountain House stood with its 13 Corinthian columns, painted stark white against a backdrop of hemlock and white pines and surrounded by hundreds of square miles of untamed forest. In the words of author Roland

Van Zandt, the hotel offered the "ideal combination of wilderness and luxury" and symbolized "a nation's young wealth, leisure, and cultural attainments."

Modern rail and jet travel changed Greene County forever, sending would-be visitors to more exotic destinations. In 1963, the New York State Department of Conservation declared the long-abandoned hotel a danger to hikers and burned what remained of the building to the ground one winter morning. Visitors today can only imagine the imposing white structure and the famous people who stayed in it, but the setting remains as enchanting as two centuries ago.

Located on the west side of the Hudson, with Albany County to the north and Ulster County to the south, Greene County features 20 miles of riverfront, several charming valley and mountain towns, and Kaaterskill Falls—at 260 feet, the highest waterfall in the east. The magical surroundings inspired American literary master Washington Irving to write the tale of Rip Van Winkle, the hen-pecked husband who wandered into the mountains and fell into a 20-year sleep.

Named after Revolutionary War General Nathanael Greene of Rhode Island, the original Greene County consisted of four towns: Catskill and Coxsackie on the river, Freehold in the valley, and Windham on the mountaintop. Agriculture, forestry, and a few dozen tanneries drove the local economy in the early days. But the opening of the Erie Canal in 1825 diverted ships and manufactured goods from Catskill to Troy, sending the once-prosperous county into a tailspin—until a group of Romantic Era writers and painters, including Thomas Cole, popularized the region for its scenic beauty.

Dairy farms and orchards came next, along with German and Irish immigrants and summer residents. From the polka dancers at the Mountain Brauhaus to the International Celtic Festival at Hunter Mountain, the county retains much of its immigrant influence today.

After a steady decline during the mid-20th century, Greene County is quietly capturing the imagination of travelers, writers, and outdoor enthusiasts again. Author Allegra Goodman chose the valley as the setting for her first novel, *Kaaterskill Falls* (Delta, 1999), which intertwines the stories of three Orthodox Jewish families from New York City who spend summers in the area. On the mountaintop, an effort is under way to revive Hunter Village with a focus on art and cultural events.

Members of the Catskill 3500 Club visit Greene County to climb many of the highest peaks in the range, including Blackhead, Black Dome, and Thomas Cole Mountain. The county also supports three winter ski resorts—Hunter Mountain, Cortina Mountain, and Windham Mountain—which offer city dwellers a convenient alternative to driving four hours to New England resorts or traveling by plane to the Rockies.

Note that the weather is often cooler, windier, and wetter on the mountaintop than at the river's edge. Bring layers in any season.

ALONG THE RIVER—ROUTE 385
Rip Van Winkle Bridge

The Rip Van Winkle Bridge spans the Hudson at mile 112, counting from the south. If you approach the crossing from Routes 9G or 82, both in Columbia County, the first sight of the Catskills' purple-gray peaks will catch you off guard. For generations, the bridge has stood as a divider between civilization and wilderness, or what many locals call "up country." The range's cluster of High Peaks rises to 4,000 feet, just 12 miles west of the sea-level river.

Begin your tour of Greene County with a walk across the mile-long span of the bridge. Built during the Great Depression at a cost of $2.4 million and opened in 1935, the bridge connects the small cities of Catskill and Hudson, ushering visitors into the forever-wild lands of the Catskill Preserve. (Car toll $1, eastbound only.) The New York State Bridge Authority has preserved the look of the original Dutch colonial toll plaza so as not to alter

THE NEW YORK CITY WATERSHED

New York City consumes 1.3 billion gallons of water a day, and most of it comes from reservoirs in the Catskill Region. The massive watershed is the largest unfiltered surface water supply anywhere in the world.

Reservoir Capacity *(billion gallons)*

Reservoir	Capacity
Ashokan Reservoir (1915)	22.9
Cannonsville Reservoir (1964)	95.7
Croton System (1842)	86.6
Neversink Reservoir (1954)	34.9
Pepacton Reservoir (1955)	140.2
Rondout Reservoir (1950)	9.6
Schoharie Reservoir (1928)	17.6

Reservoir permits are free but required in order to fish. Rowboats are allowed, but motorboats are not. Camping is also not allowed.

the view from the Olana State Historic Site directly across the river.

Park in a lot near the toll plaza on the Catskill side of the bridge. (Pedestrians only on the sidewalk. Bikes must use the narrow traffic lanes.) Pause at the middle of the span to take in the 360-degree views. The river below is tidal freshwater. To the north, Stockport Middle Ground Island is one of four sites belonging to the National Estuarine Research Reserve. The Hudson Athens Lighthouse, on a smaller island to the Northwest, was established in 1874 and had a live-in keeper until 1949. The gentle hills of Columbia County rise in the east behind the waterfront city of Hudson. And the clay-tiled rooftop of Olana, the Persian-style castle of painter Frederic Church, stands above the trees to the southeast. Turn back west, and the Catskill Mountains beckon.

Catskill

Historian Henry Brace wrote in 1876 that early Dutch settlers purchased the village of Catskill in 1684 for "a gun, two shirts, a kettle, two kegs of beer, and, as usual, a little rum." For more than two centuries, the village thrived as an agricultural crossroads and a gateway to the mountains. But the building of the Rip Van Winkle Bridge marked the beginning of a long decline. These days, the town is dreadfully quiet in winter, but come summer, the waterfront awakens with boating, outdoor dining, and an open-air market.

Recently too, the flurry of development taking place across the river in Hudson has spread to Main Street in Catskill as well. The crowds are yet to come, but optimistic entrepreneurs have opened new restaurants, cafés, and gift shops, giving the village a more upscale look and feel.

Catskill's Main Street runs parallel to Catskill Creek, which widens and empties into the Hudson just past the center of town. (There

© AVALON TRAVEL

© NIKKI GOTH ITOI

Dutchman's Landing near the village of Catskill

is a municipal parking lot off Main.) Two-story row houses line both sides of the street, many of them housing attorneys' offices, as Catskill is the county seat. The **Greene County Courthouse,** at the intersection of Main and Bridge (also Rte. 385), is a white, neoclassical structure that towers over its neighbors. Behind it is the **Catskill Public Library** (1 Franklin St., 518/943-4230, catskill@francomm.com, http://catskill.lib.ny.us; noon–8 P.M. Mon.and Wed., 10 A.M.–8 P.M. Tues., 10 A.M.–5 P.M. Thurs.–Fri., 10 A.M.–2 P.M. Sat.), in another neoclassical building. The library has a local history collection with many books about the steamboats of the Hudson.

Main Street takes a sharp turn to the left as you approach the mouth of the Catskill Creek. Follow West Main to its end to reach Catskill Point, Dutchman's Landing, and Mariner's Point Restaurant. Many community activities take place here during the summer months.

Ramshorn-Livingston Sanctuary (Grandview Ave., 845/473-4440, ext. 270, www.scenic hudson.org; dawn–dusk) is the largest tidal swamp forest along the Hudson. Paddlers can rent boats and explore some 480 acres via 3.5 miles of waterways that lead out to the river itself. Heron, waterfowl, and other birds feed here, and American shad and bass come in spring to spawn. Open dawn to dusk year-round, the sanctuary is jointly owned and operated by the Scenic Hudson Land Trust and the National Audubon Society (P.O. Box 1, Craryville, 518/325-5203, http://ny.audubon .org/ramshorn.htm).

Cedar Grove

Around the time that the Romantic Era began to take hold in America, a young artist named Thomas Cole ventured up the river from New York City in search of inspiration for a series of sketches. The canvases and exhibition that followed put him in the national spotlight and helped to make the Catskills world-famous.

Cole spent most of his adult years at Cedar Grove in the town of Catskill, now the **Thomas Cole National Historic Site** (218 Spring St., Catskill, 518/943-7465, www.thomascole.org;

10 A.M.–4 P.M. Thurs.–Sun. May–Oct.; adults
$7, seniors and students $5). He painted landscapes and taught students like Frederic E.
Church, who later established his own residence
on a hillside across the river. With a shared interest in painting mountain peaks and waterfalls
instead of portraits, Cole and his students became known collectively as the Hudson River
School of Art.

Today, the pale yellow house sits on the outskirts of town, tragically close to a busy traffic light and a Mobil gas station. Despite the
encroaching surroundings, the views continue
to inspire awe. On display inside the house and
studios are a few of Cole's paintings, as well as
furniture and family memorabilia. A $1 mil-
lion restoration of the main house was completed in 2003. A restoration of Cole's studio
was unveiled in 2004.

Athens

Head north on County Route 385 (Spring
Street) from Catskill about four miles, and
you'll come to the much smaller village of
Athens. The Dutch arrived here in 1686, and
the town was a landing point for the Athens-
Hudson ferry service, which dates back to the
late 1770s. Built into a hillside, with a splash
of color on some of its old Victorian homes, the
town hints of San Francisco, except for the two
industrial plants that frame its borders.

Several blocks of river views and a few
restaurants greet travelers right at the water's edge—though you have to look hard
to find them. Second Street, off Route 385,
leads you to the striking **Stewart House
Restaurant and Bed and Breakfast** (Second St., 518/945-1357, www.stewarthouse
.com; 5–9 P.M. Mon.–Sat., 4–9 P.M. Sun.), a
historic inn that catered to visitors who arrived
by ferry in the 1880s but fell out of favor when
trains and bridges replaced steamboat travel.
In 2000, New York City–based editor Owen
Lipstein breathed new life into the Victorian-
era venue. It's worth a peek inside to the see
the original tin ceiling and inlaid marble fireplace in the formal dining room, even if you
don't plan to stay for dinner.

riverside flower display, Athens

© NIKKI GOTH ITOI

It's rare to find many cars in the **Cohotate
Preserve** (Rte. 385, www.troop45.com/
cohotate/cohotate.htm), south of town, but the
site is worth a visit for its river views and environmental information. The parking lot is
well marked with a large sign on Route 385. A
gravel road leads to the river, and from there,
an interpretive trail describes the habitats of
local plants, animals, and fish, leading to spectacular river views. The Greene County Environmental Education Center recently added
a pond to attract and support a greater variety of wildlife for nature walkers. Students of
Columbia-Greene County College take environmental classes in a new lab on the premises.
For those who want to get on the water, there
is a well-maintained boat ramp with parking
for 25 cars just north of town.

Coxsackie

Continuing north along Route 385 brings you
to Coxsackie (cook-SAK-ee), borrowed from
an Algonquin Indian expression meaning "owl
hoot" or "place of wild geese." Reed's Landing

was once a busy center for shipbuilding and transportation, and today the town retains an industrial feel. The remains of a Hudson River freighter called the *Storm King* rest in shallow water near the town's River Park.

When the icehouses of the Hudson became irrelevant, creative entrepreneurs discovered they were ideal for growing mushrooms. The Greene County Historical Society has estimated that by the late 1930s, Coxsackie-based Knaust Brothers controlled about 85 percent of the country's mushroom business as a supplier to companies like Heinz and Campbell's.

One mile south of the Coxsackie boat launch is the **Hudson River Islands State Park** (1 Hailes Cave Rd., Rte. 157, Voorheesville, 518/872-1237), on the islands of Gay's Point and Stockton Middle Ground. Accessible only by boat, the park protects many rare and endangered species and allows picnics, fishing, and camping Memorial Day–Columbus Day.

Moving away from the river, the main attraction in Coxsackie is the oldest surviving dwelling in upstate New York, a 1663 stone house now known as the **Bronck Museum** (90 County Rte. 42, 518/731-6490, www.gc history.org/barns.phpl; 10 A.M.–4 P.M. Tues.–Sat. and holiday Mondays, 1–5 P.M. Sun., Memorial Day weekend–Oct. 15; adults $5, youth 12–15 $3, children 5–11 $ 2, under 5 free). In 1662, Pieter Bronck, a Dutchman who lived in Albany, received a land patent from the British government to settle in modern-day Coxsackie. He built a one-room structure in 1663 and expanded it 20 years later to include a loft with an Indian lookout. In 1738, Bronck's grandson added a new brick house to the property.

The museum consists of these two homes—furnished with period art, linens, ceramics, and silver—and several Dutch colonial barns. The Victorian Horse Barn contains a model of the famous Catskill Mountain House and other Greene County memorabilia. A single, center pole supports the roof of the Thirteen-Sided Barn. And the Dutch Barn has its original wood floor, made of pegged oak planks three-inches thick. The Greene County Historical Association runs the museum and holds special events

throughout the year. Check www.gchistory .org/calendar.html for a current calendar.

Unless you are continuing on to Albany via Route 9W or the New York State Thruway, now is a good time to retrace your steps to Catskill and head west on Routes 23 or 23A toward the mountaintop.

ALONG ROUTE 23A
◖ Kaaterskill Falls

Asher B. Durand, another of the Hudson River painters, spent many summers in Palenville and established one of America's first artist colonies here in the 1840s. This quiet town sits at the base of the High Peaks and the edge of Catskill Park. Washington Irving's Rip Van Winkle fell into his 20-year slumber above Palenville in the Kaaterskill Clove.

Leaving town, you enter Catskill Park, and the road becomes narrow and steep with retaining walls and hairpin turns. Ice-climbers scale the frozen waterfalls in winter, while hikers take to the trails in spring, summer, and fall. Look for the trailhead to Kaaterskill Falls about a mile into the ascent. Thomas Cole wrote of the falls:

> There is a deep gorge at the midst of the loftiest Catskills, which, at its upper end, is terminated by a mighty wall of rock; as the spectator approaches from below, he sees its craggy and impending front rising to the height of three hundred feet. This huge rampart is semi-circular. From the centre of the more distant or central part of the semi-circle, like a gush of living light from Heaven, the cataract leaps, and foaming into feathery spray, descends into a rocky basin one hundred and eight feet below.

> – "The Falls of Kaaterskill in Winter," from the *New York Evening Post*, March 29, 1843

With the old tanneries and hotels long gone, the falls are actually more pristine today than they were a hundred years ago. An hour-long walk (2.7 miles) on a well-marked but strenuous trail brings you to the base of the falls and back. (It is also possible to reach the top from the North Lake Public Campground; however, the descent along the waterfall is extremely dangerous and not advised.)

◖ The Escarpment Trail

The first town you reach on the mountaintop, driving west on Route 23A, is Haines Falls, at 2,200 feet elevation. A small green hut before the turn-off to North Lake has visitor information. Gas, groceries, and banking services are all located along Main Street (Route 23A), and several places in town rent snowmobiles and mountain bikes. Turn right on County Route 18 (North Lake Road) to reach North Lake Public Campground and trails leading to the Escarpment, a 1,500-foot plateau upon which the sprawling Catskill Mountain House once rested. Poet and journalist William Cullen Bryant described the site like this:

On that point, scarce visible on the breast of the mountain, the beautiful and the gay are met, and the sounds of mirth and music arise, while for leagues around the mountain torrents are dashing, and the eagle is uttering his shriek, unheard by human ear.

– As quoted in *The Catskill Mountain House,* by Roland Van Zandt

By virtue of its remote setting within a day's journey from thriving New York City, the antebellum Catskill Mountain House became one of America's first luxury resorts. Under the direction of Charles L. Beach, son of a stagecoach operator, the inn drew influential artists, designers, businessmen, and politicians from the entire Atlantic corridor for a period of more than 50 years. Some guests stayed a week, while others spent the full summer in the cool mountain air. Beach expanded the original Greek-style building rapidly to keep up with demand, growing from 10 rooms in 1824 to more than 300 by the 1880s.

The Catskill Mountain House remained a focal point of the American Romantic Movement until the advent of modern rail and auto transportation diverted visitors away from the region. By 1950, the building stood in ruins. Today, it is lost to history. The view, however, continues to astound first-time visitors. On a clear day, you can see five states from the edge of the escarpment, making the park one of the most popular in the Catskills.

◖ Tannersville

Tannersville bears the responsibility of reminding locals and visitors of an unfortunate episode in Catskill history. Around the turn of the 19th century, the business of manufacturing leather became lucrative for those who were willing to endure the labor-intensive process. When mountaintop tanners discovered that hemlock bark served as an effective tanning agent, they began to strip the virgin forest of its trees, peeling the bark away and leaving the trunks to rot on the forest floor. By 1855, the forest had been stripped of almost every hemlock tree, and the mountaintop had to reinvent itself.

Tannersville didn't actually incorporate until after the tannery boom had passed, but the centrally located **Mountain Top Arboretum** (Rte. 23C, 518/589-3903, www.mtarbor.org; open year-round) seems to make amends for the past. Stop by for a lesson in native and exotic trees and shrubs. You can wander across seven acres in a guided or self-led tour, or join one of many horticultural education programs.

Extending in both directions from the arboretum, Main Street is sporting a new look: charming Victorians freshly painted in purples, reds, and yellows give the place an updated yet old western feel.

Hunter Mountain

As soon as temperatures dip below freezing, the 1,100 snow guns at Hunter Mountain (Rte. 23A, 800/367-7669, www.huntermtn .com; 8:30 A.M.–4 P.M. daily) begin to paint the mountain white. A winter destination since 1960, Hunter still attracts diehard skiers from the Tri-State Area.

You can walk to the sleepy town of Hunter

from the parking lot, as long as you aren't wearing ski boots. Many of the buildings on Main Street have experienced a recent makeover; however, many more could use still some extra attention. The most inviting building in town is an enormous red barn that serves as headquarters for the Catskill Mountain Foundation (CMF), a nonprofit organization dedicated to revitalizing the mountaintop with cultural events and programs. It publishes the free *Catskill Mountain Guide* with a detailed calendar of events. Across Main Street from the red barn are two renovated buildings that house the **CMF Theater, Bookstore, and Gallery** (Rte. 23A, 518/263-5157, www.catskillmtn.org/retail; 11 A.M.–5 P.M. Mon.–Thurs., 10 A.M.–8 P.M. Fri., 10 A.M.–10 P.M. Sat., 11 A.M.–5 P.M. Sun.).

Leaving Hunter on Route 23A, you pass Route 296, a shortcut to Windham. An alternative and more scenic route, however, is to continue west until County Route 17, the turn-off to Jewett, which winds its way though orchards and historic homes up to Maplecrest, just outside of Windham.

If you skip the scenic drive and head toward Lexington, you'll soon pass the Baroque-style lanterns of the **St. John the Baptist Ukrainian Catholic Church** (518/263-3862, www.brama.com/stjohn/shop.html; 9 A.M. mass daily, additional service 10 A.M. Sun.; store hours noon–4 P.M. Tues.–Fri., 10 A.M.–2 P.M. and 6–8 P.M. Sat., 11:30 A.M.–2 P.M. Sun.) Built of cedar logs imported from British Columbia, the church serves as a spiritual and cultural center for Ukrainians living in the U.S. and represents the traditional architecture and wood-carvings of the Carpathian highland people. The church hosts art exhibits and a folk art store in a separate community center.

Prattsville

Route 23A meets up with Route 23 out of Windham in an open field at the Batavia Kill crossing. From there, it is a mile into Prattsville, another mountaintop village. You can't drive through Prattsville without learning a thing or two about its founder, the eccentric Colonel Zadock Pratt. For some 13 years in the

© NIKKI GOTH ITOI

shore of the Batavia Kill near Prattsville

early 19th century, Pratt ran one of the world's largest and most successful tanneries, and he used the profits to build present-day Prattsville. According to local lore, he completed the building of a new tannery dam in November 1824, as the first layer of ice was forming on the Schoharie Creek, and then celebrated by swimming the length of the dam.

Despite his role in destroying a large chunk of the Catskill forest, Zadock was well liked by his community, as his generosity far outweighed his shameless self-promotion. His life's achievements are depicted in a bas-relief sculpture on a large, flat rock at the outskirts of town. Called Pratt Rock, the stone carving includes the tannery, a hemlock tree, and many of Pratt's family members.

In the center of town, Pratt's former residence is now the **Zadock Pratt Museum** (Main St., Prattsville, 518/299-3395, www .prattmuseum.com; 1–4:30 P.M. Thurs.–Sun.) It contains period furnishings, a Steinway piano, photographs of Pratt, and a model of his tannery.

ALONG ROUTE 23
Windham Mountain
From the intersection of Routes 23 and 23A, it is a nine-mile drive along the Batavia Kill to Greene County's other downhill ski resort, Windham Mountain (Rte. 23, Windham, 800/754-9463, www.skiwindham.com), a smaller but more upscale version of nearby Hunter. With a base elevation of 1,500 feet and a summit of 3,100 feet, Windham attracts New York City day-trippers by the busload. Mogul experts head for the bumps on Wheelchair and Wedel, while speed demons let loose on Wolverine. Intermediate skiers enjoy the two-mile-long Wrap Around trail, and a run through the terrain park ends with an enormous gap jump at the bottom.

Windham Village is about a mile from the ski resort parking lot, too far to walk in winter weather. Along Main Street, contemporary art galleries alternate with skier-friendly eateries. A few of the ski shops rent mountain bikes in summer. **Windham Fine Arts** (5380 Main St.,

518/734-6850, www.windhamfinearts.com; 11 A.M.–5 P.M. Fri.–Mon.) rotates shows every four to six weeks and has information about other galleries and cultural events in the area.

From Windham, the Mohican Trail (Route 23) begins to descend back down to the valley floor, and the peaks of Blackhead and Black Dome come into view. A local artist runs a creative firewood stand by sculpting split wood into a new design each winter—for example, a barn or a railroad train. The western trailhead for the Escarpment Trail begins here as well. On the clearest of days, the Point Lookout Inn offers a spectacular five-state view to the northeast, with the peak of New Hampshire's Mount Washington visible in the distance.

East Durham
Irish immigrants were among the first settlers on the north side of Route 23. Stone walls mark old boundaries along County Route 31, and every sign in Durham and East Durham has a shamrock, or at least green lettering. A visit to **Guaranteed Irish** (2220 Rte. 145, East Durham, 518/634-2392, www.guaranteed irishshop.com; 9 A.M.–9 P.M.daily July–Aug., 9 A.M.–6 P.M. Sept.–June), at the corner of County Routes 31 and 145, will put you in the proper frame of mind to enjoy this town. An enormous retail space has an overwhelming selection of Irish-made goods.

Next door is Darby's Irish Pub and Restaurant, the local watering hole. (Route 145 between them goes to Freehold.) The **Zoom Flume Water Park** (Shady Glen Rd. off Rte. 145, 800/888-3586, www.zoomflume.com; 10 A.M.–6 P.M. June–Sept., some weekends until 7 P.M.; admission $18.95 adult, $15.95 kids) is a popular summertime attraction for kids. On the same road, **Hull-O-Farms** (10 Cochrane Rd., Durham, 518/239-6950, www.hull-o.com), founded in 1779, is a working dairy farm that allows overnight guests to participate in everyday farm activities.

Freehold and Greenville
There are two reasons to divert to Freehold when traveling along Route 23: to take an aerial

tour in a classic J-3 Cub or to savor the French-inspired menu at the recently opened Ruby's Hotel. The **Freehold Airport** (4000 Rte. 67, Freehold, 518/634-7626; 9 A.M.–6:30 P.M. daily Apr.–Dec.) offers daily scenic rides (weather permitting), a ground and flight school, and general aviation services. It is privately owned and operated by Clements J. Hoovler Jr. of the Catskill Valley Flying Service. The restaurant is about a 10-minute walk from the runway.

A few miles up the road from Freehold on Route 32, William Vanderbilt constructed a Queen Anne–style home in 1889. Today, the white, two-story building is a county inn set on six acres of manicured lawns and decorated in Victorian and country accents. In summer, the **Greenville Arms 1889 Inn** (Routes 32 and 81, Greenville, 518/966-5219 or 888/665-0044, www.greenvillearms.com, $115–235) hosts a series of Hudson River Valley Art Workshops in its Carriage House Studio.

Cairo

Once the center of a booming Greene County poultry business and a major producer of fresh fruits, Cairo (CARE-o) is a good place to stop for services. You'll find groceries at the Great American, gas at Cumberland Farm, and a True Value hardware store. A new set of decorative streetlights and real concrete sidewalks line Main Street, but the town is still lacking in restaurants.

The primary colors of the **Mahayana Buddhist Temple** (700 Ira Vail Rd., 518/622-3619; 7 A.M.–7 P.M. daily; donations accepted) look oddly out of place in South Cairo, 2.5 miles from Route 23B. Members of the New York City–based Eastern States Buddhist Temple of America retreat to the woods here for quiet contemplation. A red-and-yellow arch leads the way down a steep driveway to the temple, set on two small ponds. Visitors are welcome to explore the site.

Don't leave Cairo without wandering through the hamlets of Purling and Round Top. Newly built log cabins alternate here with 150-year-old farmhouses, and fields have grown up around abandoned farm equipment. Leaving Cairo on Mountain Avenue

© NIKKI GOTH ITOI

modern Catskill mountain house

MOUNTAIN STATISTICS

Location	Base	Summit	Vertical	Trails
Cortina Mountain	1,925 feet	2,650 feet	725 feet	10
Hunter Mountain	1,600 feet	3,200 feet	1,600 feet	53
Windham Mountain	1,500 feet	3,100 feet	1,600 feet	39

(County Rte. 24), you'll pass the Purling post office, Shinglekill Falls, and a roller rink that has been open more or less continuously since the 1950s. Gino Altimari at the **Round Top Raptor Center** (733 Bald Hill Rd. N., 518/622-0118, www.roundtopraptorcenter .com; 1–4 P.M. Fri.–Sun. Memorial Day weekend–Labor Day weekend; adults $7, children $2) teaches visitors about falcons, hawks, and other local birds of prey.

SPORTS AND RECREATION
Downhill Skiing and Snowboarding

You haven't skied the northeast until you've endured subzero temperatures, frostbite warnings, and the wet blast of artificial snow in your face. The après-ski whirlpool tub (there are many options) becomes an all-important finish to the day. **Hunter Mountain** (Rte. 23A, Hunter, 800/367-7669, www.huntermtn.com; $57 weekend/holiday $59 midweek) has three mountains that can handle 15,000 skiers per hour, but lift lines can still run up to an hour on busy weekends.

Windham Mountain (Rte. 23, Windham, 800/754-9463, www.skiwindham.com; $59 weekend/holiday, $46 midweek) is open 8 A.M.–4 P.M. weekends and 9 A.M.–4 P.M. midweek mid-November through mid-April, as long as the weather cooperates. You can also ski at night Thursday through Saturday and some holidays 4–10 P.M. from December until March. Adult lift tickets cost $40 nonholiday, with discounts for students and multi-day day tickets. For an additional $15, you can sign up for First Tracks to get on the slopes an hour before the lifts open

to the masses. Pick up Route 23 West at New York State Thruway Exit 21. Windham maintains a useful website through which you can book lift tickets and rental equipment, or listen to the snow report updated daily by Darrell, the mountain's head snow-maker.

A left turn off Route 23A before Selena's Diner in Tannersville leads to a hemlock-lined road and the entrance to **Cortina Mountain** (Clum Hill Rd., 866/926-7846, www.cortina mountain.com; adults Sat. $18, Sun. $16). Under new management since 2002, Cortina maintains a tubing run, terrain park, and paint ball facility. The owners are remodeling the resort with the upscale Hotel Scribner Hollow as a model. When the lifts start running, the tiny hill may once again become a fine place for kids to learn to ski or snowboard. With a base elevation of 2,200 feet, Cortina has the highest base of any ski area in Catskills; however, lifts have not been running for several years.

Bob Hostetter, a ski patroller at Hunter Mountain and licensed rock-climbing guide, shares his knowledge and experience of the Catskills' backcountry ski secrets through **Catskill Backcountry Ski Tours** (P.O. Box 712, Hunter, 518/589-6989, www.catskill-bc ski.com; half day $150, full day $200).

Nordic Skiing

Several areas on the mountaintop offer varied terrain for Nordic skiers: **White Birches Ski Area** (Nauvoo Rd., Windham, 518/734-3266) maintains 35 kilometers of groomed trails for novice to expert skiers. A cozy lodge on-site has a fireplace and snack bar. **Villaggio Resort Cross Country Skiing Area** (Haines Falls,

Lifts	Skiable acres	Snowmaking	Snow report
4	87	100 percent of terrain	866/926-7846
11	240	100 percent of terrain	800/486-8376
7	242	97 percent of terrain	800/729-4766

518/589-5000) has 300 acres and 14 kilometers of marked, groomed trails suitable for beginner and intermediate skiers. And the **Mountain Trails Cross Country Ski Center** (Rte. 23A, Tannersville, 518/589-5316, www.mtntrails .com; adult full-day $15, $12 after 2 P.M., teens $13, junior $8; full-day rental $15) has another 35 kilometers of groomed, patrolled trails with rentals, sales, a lodge, lessons, and a snack bar on-site. Daily hours vary according to snow conditions. Note: the summer Escarpment Trail is not safe for cross-country skiing.

In the valley, the **Winter Clove Inn Nordic Skiing Area** (Winter Clove Rd., Round Top, 518/622-3267, www.winterclove.com) opens 400 acres to public, with rentals available. Expert trails climb into the hills, while the easier trails follow a streambed.

Snowshoeing, Tubing, and Snowmobiles

Snowshoeing is one of the fastest-growing sports in America, and Greene County offers plenty of great trails. **Mountain Trails Cross Country Ski Center** (Rte. 23A, Tannersville, 518/589-5316, info@mtntrails.com, www .mtntrails.com) offers trails of varying grades that traverse bridges and wind through conifers. Ski patrol monitors the trails for safety. **North Lake Public Campground** (County Rte. 18, Haines Falls, 518/589-5058) has trails along wooded areas and up to the site of the Catskill Mountain House with stunning views of the Hudson River Valley. Rent equipment in nearby Hunter. The trails at **Colgate Lake** (off Rte. 78, East Jewett) run through an open meadow with great views of the Blackhead

Mountain Range. Take Route 23A to Tannersville, and turn onto Route 23C, and then right onto Route 78 by the post office.

Cortina, Hunter, and Windham all have 8- to 12-lane snow tubing runs with lift access. Tickets range from $18 all day at Cortina to $25 at Windham and Hunter. Hunter also has the **Bear Creek Landing** (Rtes. 214 & 23A, Hunter, 518/263-3839, www.bearcreek restaurant.com; 4 P.M.–10 P.M. Mon.–Thurs., noon–10 P.M. Fri.–Sun.) ice rink.

Several outfitters run guided snowmobile trips: **Rip Van Winkle Ranch** (Rte. 23A, Haines Falls, 800/804-5799) has snowmobile and ATV rentals for use on mountain trails.

Hiking

Hikers can't get enough of the northern Catskills in summer and fall. They hit the trails in search of tasty wild blueberries, wild ginseng, geological wonders, or a simply a view and a breath of fresh air. Trailhead parking lots fill early on sunny weekends, but with a little determination, it's still possible to escape the crowds. Although the most popular trails are well maintained, it's not uncommon to encounter some bushwhacking on many hikes. It's a good idea to carry water, topographical maps, and a compass or GPS, no matter how far you plan to go. *Catskill Trails: A Ranger's Guide to the High Peaks, Book One,* by Edward G. Henry (Black Dome Press, 2000), covers more than 20 hikes in the area, including the trails to Kaaterskill Falls and the Escarpment.

Major trailheads are clustered around the towns of Hunter, Jewett, and Prattsville. From

Route 23A in Hunter, you can access the Escarpment and the vista from the site of the old Catskill Mountain House, as well as Roundtop and Twin Mountains. The Big Hollow Road in Jewett leads to trails that summit the High Peaks of Blackhead, Black Dome, and Thomas Cole. Farther west, near Prattsville, you can reach trails to Westkill, Huntersfield, and Bearpen Mountains.

To see what inspired the romantic landscapes of the Hudson River School painters, hike a portion of the 23-mile-long Escarpment Trail, which connects Route 23 in East Windham with the North Lake Public Campground to the south. A three-day out-and-back hike with loops at each end traverses 30 miles of thick hardwood forests and hemlock groves, allowing time for diversions to the summits of Windham High Peak, Acra Point, and Blackhead Mountain along the way.

Dramatic elevation changes make for challenging terrain, so plan to take it slow. Camping is not restricted below 3,500 feet, but conservationists encourage hikers to set up camp in designated areas to minimize the impact on the forest. You can fill water bottles at numerous natural springs along the trail.

For a guided hike, the **Mountaintop Historical Society** (Haines Falls, www.mths .org) leads summer and fall trips. There is no charge to join, but the organization asks participants to complete a registration form in advance. The site links to online versions of area topographical maps on maptech.com.

Back at the river's edge, the Scenic Hudson Land Trust has rescued a seven-acre stretch of shoreline from development and created **Four-Mile Point Preserve** (Four-Mile Point Rd., Coxsackie, 845/473-4440; dawn–dusk daily), a nature trail that leads to an overlook 60 feet above the river. From the Rip Van Winkle Bridge, follow Route 385 almost eight miles north to Four-Mile Point Road.

For an unusual adventure, mushroom expert John Boyle of **Home and Forest** (South St., Durham, 518/239-8039) leads identification workshops and foraging trips. He also sells growing kits.

Cycling

Cyclists in Greene County can find miles of traffic-free roads to pedal, but be prepared to climb. Many old logging roads offer scenic and challenging mountain biking terrain. And when the snow melts away, Hunter opens part of its trail system to mountain bikers who want to start at the top. Hikers may try to tell you otherwise, but bikes are allowed on most of the trails in the area; take caution, however, when considering a loop on the ridge trail. The terrain is steep and rocky, making much of it unsuitable for riding.

Several shops on the mountaintop offer rentals and trail maps: **Hunter Mountain Biking** (Rte. 23A, Hunter, 888/486-8376, www.hunter mtn.com; weekends July–Oct.) has trails at the base and summit of the mountain, with lift access. **The Bike Shop at Windham Mountain Outfitters** (Rte. 296 & South St., Windham, 518/734-4700, www.windhamoutfitters.com) rents bikes and leads trips for all levels. And **White Birches Mountain Biking** (Navoo Rd., Windham, 518/734-3266) has 15 miles of trails with single and double track, but no rentals.

Golf

Green County has 10 golf courses with scenic views of the surrounding countryside. Most are open April through November. The **Blackhead Mountain Lodge & Country Club** (Blackhead Mountain Rd., 888/382-7474, www.blackhead mountaingolf.com; weekend 18 holes with cart $50, midweek $36) maintains a challenging 18-hole par 72 course with stunning views of the High Peaks. **Christman's Windham House Country Inn and Golf Resort** (5742 Rte. 23, Windham, 518/734-4230 or 888/294-4053, www.windhamhouse.com) operates two courses—an 18-hole and a 9-hole—with four sets of tees. Tannersville has two nine-hole par 35 courses that are open to the public: **Colonial Golf Club** (Main St., Tannersville, 518/589-9807) and the **Rip Van Winkle Country Club** (3200 Rte. 23A, Tannersville, 518/678-9779, www.rvwcc .com, weekdays 9 holes $14, 18 holes $17, weekends and holidays 9 holes $17, 18 holes $22, after 4 p.m. $12, cart extra).

© NIKKI GOTH ITOI

Catskill Creek at the base of Blackhead Mountain

Swimming and Boating

A dip in a mountain lake or a paddle along the river are the water sports of choice in Greene County. North Lake offers swimming and nonmotorized boating, and lifeguards are on duty Memorial Day through Labor Day. Farther west, **Dolan's Lake** (Ski Bowl Rd., Hunter, 518/263-4020) has a picnic area and lifeguard on duty in summer months.

Several marinas offer boaters convenient access to the Hudson. Part of the New York State Park System, the **Athens Boat Launch** (Rte. 385, Athens, 518/945-1551) has a hard surface ramp and parking for 25 cars. The **Coxsackie Boat Launch** (Reed St., Coxsackie, 518/731-2718), also a state facility, has a hard surface ramp and parking for 36 cars and trailers.

In Catskill, turn right at the bend in Main Street onto Greene Street to get to the full-service **Catskill Marina** (Greene St., 518/943-4170 or 800/747-2720), which has gasoline, 20 boat slips (150 feet maximum), showers, restrooms, laundry, and even a heated pool. Two other marinas, Hop-O-Nose and Riverview Marine Services, are located farther out on West Main. Riverview rents kayaks, rowboats, and canoes. **Dutchman's Landing** (Lower Main St., 518/943-3830) has four boat ramps, picnic tables, and barbecues.

The **Hudson River Water Trail Association** (www.hrwa.org) sponsors numerous outings and operates facilities for river-goers. The group is lobbying to develop a water trail from the mouth of the Hudson to the Great Lakes.

Fishing and Hunting

Whether you want to catch shad, bass, or trout, **River Basin Sport Shop** (66 W. Bridge St., Catskill, 518/943-2111) will provide all the tackle and advice you need for fishing in the area. When the ice melts, **Bear Creek Landing** (Rtes. 214 & 23A, Hunter, 518/263-3839, www.bearcreekrestaurant.com; 4 P.M.–10 P.M. Mon., Tues., Thurs., noon–10 P.M. Fri.–Sun.) opens a trout-fishing preserve on 80 mountaintop acres. Around the same time, the Batavia Kill near Prattsville becomes a mecca for fly-fishers. Bass season begins on the third Saturday in June and runs through October.

Licensed hunters may take grouse, pheasant, turkey, deer, black bear, and small game from public wilderness areas or private clubs during specified seasons. See the *Essentials* chapter for New York State Department of Environmental Conservation regulations. Upland bird hunters should head to the pheasant preserve at the **Friar Tuck Resort** (4858 Rte. 32, Catskill, 800/832-7600 www.friartuck.com).

Aviation

The **Freehold Airport** (4000 Rte. 67, Freehold, 518/634-7626; 9 A.M.–6:30 P.M. daily Apr.–Dec.) offers daily scenic rides (weather permitting), a ground and flight school, and general aviation services.

ACCOMMODATIONS

Country inns with a colonial ambience are the theme for places to stay in Greene County. You can find a few modern hotels near the ski resorts and budget motels along the highways, but the most charming accommodations include a country breakfast and a friendly chat with the innkeeper.

$100-150

The beautifully restored **Stewart House Restaurant and Bed and Breakfast** (Second St., Athens, 518/945-1357, www.stewarthouse .com; $110 with continental breakfast) attracts Shakespeare enthusiasts and city dwellers in search of a romantic weekend getaway. Five immaculate guest rooms on the second floor are decorated with cheerful colors and antique furnishings. Every room has a private bath, a couple of rooms have river views, and No. 7 has a fireplace. Hollywood trivia gurus should request No. 8, which not only overlooks the river but is the place where actress Meryl Streep dies in the 1987 film *Ironweed.*

One place in Catskill Village is worth an overnight visit: **Caleb Street's Inn** (251 Main St., Catskill, 518/943-0246, www.mhonline .net/~calebinn; $100–160), at the corner of Greene and Main, just above the Catskill Marina.

© NIKKI GOTH ITOI

Stewart House in Athens

A white 1790 house with black shutters, the inn has a veranda that overlooks Catskill Creek. Its bright guest rooms feature hardwood floors, large windows, and antique beds and dressers.

Linda and Hugh are your friendly hosts at the creekside **Tumblin' Falls House** (Rte. 24., Purling, 800/969-6895, www.tumblinfalls .com; $85–165). The inn accommodates 8–10 guests in a pale yellow Victorian that's set back from the road. All four rooms have mountain views, and a large, terraced deck and hot tub overlook the 30-foot falls. The Falls View Suite has the best view.

The Eggery Inn (288 Platt Clove Rd., Tannersville, 800/785-5364, www.eggeryinn.com; $119–159), on the mountaintop, is popular with international guests. Its 15 cozy rooms have comfortable beds, as well as cable TV, air-conditioning, and in-room phones. Owners Julie and Abe will make you feel right at home. The inn has a view of Hunter Mountain from the bar and dining room. And with a pair of binoculars, you can tell how long the lift lines are.

A mile from the slopes, on the road that connects Windham to Hunter, is the modern **(** **Hotel Vienna** (107 Rte. 296, Windham, 518/734-5300, www.thehotelvienna.com; $125–180). Straight out of the Austrian alps, rooms have beamed ceilings, cherry furniture, lace curtains, and tiled balconies. Amenities include cable TV, phones, and air-conditioning, as well as an indoor pool and Jacuzzi. For those returning from the slopes, the innkeeper serves afternoon cookies and tea by the breakfast room fireplace. Midweek specials and ski packages are available.

Sunny Hill Resort & Golf Course (352 Sunny Hill Rd., Greenville, 518/634-7642, www.sunnyhill.com; $700–850 pp per week, including all meals) is popular with golfers and families. The resort has 100 basic motel-style rooms in seven different buildings gathered around the 18-hole golf course. Some rooms have balconies and mountain views.

$150-200

The **(** **Winter Clove Inn** (Winter Clove Rd.,

Round Top, 518/622-3267, www.winterclove .com; $85–115 per person per night, including all meals) rests on 400 acres at the base of North Mountain, bordering "forever wild" state land. A creek meanders through the property, and when the winter storms roll in, guests can ski on 15 kilometers of marked cross-country trails. Inside, guest rooms feature a colonial decor, with hardwood floors, four-poster beds, and lacy white linens. The hotel attracts more suburban families than city folk. Its amenities include heated indoor and outdoor swimming pools and a nine-hole golf course. The old carriage house was converted into a bowling alley and soda fountain in the 1950s. Repeat visitors to the bowling alley quickly learn to use the warp in the floor to their advantage.

Winwood Mountain Inn (Main St., Windham, 518/734-3000, www.winwoodinn.com; $99–259), previously the Windham Arms, offers free transportation to Windham from the train station in Hudson, 40 minutes away. Its 55 modern rooms are painted in earthy tones and are minimally furnished. Ask for a mountain view, or you may end up facing the courtyard instead. Amenities include an indoor fitness center and movie theater.

Many repeat visitors at the **Greene Mountain View Inn** (132 S. Main St., Tannersville, 518/589-9886 or 877/489-9963, www .greenemountainviewinn.com; $125–175 weekends) come to attend services at the 100-year-old synagogue located four doors down the street. A 1981 Ms. Pac-Man machine and big screen TV in the lounge area complement the antique jukebox and mirror in the breakfast room. Rooms are small but clean, with natural wood accents and sloping roofs on the top floor; some have more recently updated bathrooms than others. No. 19, the newest guest room, is a mini-loft with four steps leading from the bed area up to a small sink and shower. The room has mountain views on two sides, and many guests request it in advance, despite its small size.

The expansive **Scribner Hollow Lodge** (Rte. 23A, Hunter, 518/263-4211 or 800/395-4683, www.scribnerhollow.com; $220–280) is a rustic mountain chalet with modern amenities, including an underground pool and spa called the Grotto. Deluxe rooms are decorated in a southwest, hunting lodge, or country motif. The Prospect Restaurant on the premises stocks an impressive wine cellar to accompany entrées like locally smoked Catskill rainbow trout, Hudson Valley lamb sausage, and cider-glazed breast of Long Island duckling. Mains are $21–28.

Half of the guest rooms at the **Point Lookout Inn** (Rte. 23, East Windham, 518/734-3381, www.pointlookoutinn.com; $80–175) feature the property's stunning five-state view of the Hudson River Valley and beyond. (Be sure to request the valley view.) Located a short distance from Windham, the recently renovated inn maintains a country feel. Guests are invited to help themselves to anything in the inn's refrigerator for breakfast.

The combination of antique furnishings and original, contemporary art at the **Greeneville Arms 1889 Inn** (South St., Greeneville, 518/966-5219, www.greenevillearms.com; $115–195) gives the place a unique feel. Some rooms in the main house of this country inn feature canopied or four-poster beds and private porches or balconies. Owners Eliot and Letitia Dalton recently added two rooms in a new Victorian cottage on the grounds.

Campgrounds

Greene County has two state campgrounds and more than a dozen private campgrounds to choose from. **North Lake Public Campground** (North Lake Rd., Haines Falls; early May–Oct.) has 200 tent and RV sites, plus picnic areas, hot showers, flush toilets, and a boat launch. **Devil's Tombstone State Campground** (Rte. 214, Hunter, 845/688-7160 or 800/688-2267; May 16–Sept. 1) has 24 sites, picnic tables, and a playground.

Next door to the Catskill Game Farm, **Catskill Campground** (79 Castle Rd., Catskill, 518/678-5873, catskillcamptv@cisbec.net, May 15-Columbus Day) has 50 sites for tents and RVs. You can also pop your tent at **Whip-O-Will** (County Rte. 31, Round Top, 518/622-3277 or 800/969-2267; Apr.–Oct. 15).

FOOD
Along the River–Route 385

For seafood in summer, head to **Catskill Point** (7 Main St., Catskill, 518/943-5352; mains $20–30), which features a large outdoor patio with a white picket fence and a tempting raw bar. And the **Garden Gate Café** (424 Main St., Catskill, 518/943-1994; average main dish $5) serves breakfast and lunch with a menu covering everything from omelettes to burgers.

La Conca D'Oro (440 Main St., Catskill, 518/943-3549) serves reliable Italian fare to a local clientele. Another local favorite for hearty French fare is **La Rive Restaurant Francais** (141 Dedrick Rd. off Old Kings Rd., Catskill, 518/943-4888), which opens at 6 P.M. Monday through Saturday May–October, and at 2:30 P.M. on Sundays.

Retriever Roasters (394 Main St., Catskill, 518/943-5858; mains $4–8) is the new spot for coffee drinks and café fare. Across the street, **Mod Gourmet Café** (395 Main St., Catskill, 518/943-0420; 8 A.M.–3 P.M. Mon.–Fri.; mains $4–10) is a slightly more upscale affair catering to the business lunch crowd.

Stewart House Restaurant and Bed and Breakfast (2nd St., Athens, 518/945-1357, www.stewarthouse.com; 5–9 P.M. Mon.–Sat., 4–9 P.M. Sun.; average main dish $15) has a formal dining room and a casual bistro and serves standard pub fare, as well as local specialties like Black Angus beef, grilled rainbow trout, and littleneck steamers.

Turn right at the end of 2nd Street in Athens to find **Ursula's Riverside Diner** (6 S. Water St., Athens, 518/945-2107; 6 A.M.–10 P.M. daily), located across the street from a riverfront park. With a nautical theme and inviting home-cooked food, Ursula's fills up for Sunday brunch, even in the dead of winter. The service is friendly and attentive. On the menu are omelettes and pancakes for breakfast; hot and cold sandwiches for lunch; Italian, seafood, and hearty meat dishes for dinner. Breakfast mains average $5, lunch $7, and dinner $12.

One of the Hudson Valley's culinary gems is found on a country road a few miles west of

THE MOST INTERESTING RIVER IN AMERICA

At the conclusion of an 1859 journey from the river's source to its end, Poughkeepsie resident Benson John Lossing wrote of the Hudson:

It is by far the most interesting river in America, considering the beauty and magnificence of its scenery, its natural, political, and social history, the agricultural and mineral treasures of its vicinage, the commercial wealth hourly floating upon its bosom, and the relations of its geography and topography to some of the most important events in the history of the Western hemisphere.

– *The Hudson: From the Wilderness to the Sea*, originally published by H.B. Nims & Co., 1866

12–15 courses ($50–55 per person)—many of which arrive at the table unannounced. Both options are not always available, and prices vary, depending on the ingredients. Call up to four weeks in advance for reservations (required), and follow the instructions on the machine to be sure you are confirmed. Turn your cell phone off at the door to get off to a good start with the chef. Baehrel also offers occasional cooking classes focusing on seafood, bread, and the vegetables of the season ($85 pp).

Along Route 23A

(Maggie's Krooked Café (Main St., Tannersville, 518/589-6101; opens 7 A.M.; mains $8–12) is known for a reliable cup of coffee, delicious homemade muffins, and hearty breakfast fare. Locals say the prices are high, but where else are you going to get an icy fruit smoothie?

Pancho Villa's Mexican Restaurant (3087 Main St., Tannersville,518/589-5134; 4–10 P.M. Mon.–Thurs., noon–11 P.M. Fri.–Sat., noon–9 P.M. Sun.; average main dish $13) will satisfy a craving for south-of-the-border cuisine.

Along Route 23

After an eight-year run with the popular Freehold Country Inn, the Buel and Suhner families sold the business and moved to the next town over. Their newly renovated **(Mountain View Brasserie** (10697 Route 32, Greenville, 518/966-5522, www.mountain viewbrasserie.com; Mon., Wed., Sat. noon–3 P.M. AND 4–9 P.M., Sun. noon–9 P.M.) opened in 2007 to widespread applause. Its large, U-shaped dining room maintains a cozy feel. Menu highlights include a classic French onion soup, outstanding cut of prime rib, traditional seafood bouillabaisse, and some unusual wines, including a pinot noir from Switzerland.

A 10-minute walk from the Freehold airstrip is **Ruby's Hotel** (3689 Rte. 67, Freehold, 518/634-7790; www.rubyshotel.com; 5–9 P.M. Thurs., 5–10 P.M. Fri., noon–3 P.M. and 5–10 P.M. Sat.; $18–25), in a restored art deco building that dates back to the 1800s. New York City chef Ana Sporer serves French-influenced

Coxsackie. Owner and chef Damon Baehrel established **(The Basement Bistro** (776 Rte. 45, Earlton, 518/634-2338, reservations line 518/269-1009, www.sagecrestcatering.com/ bistro.asp; from 6 P.M. Mon.–Thurs., from 5 P.M. Fri.–Sat., from 4 P.M. Sun.) in 1990 as a showcase for his catering business, Sagecrest Catering. He built and landscaped the property by hand to create a warm and elegant restaurant setting. A 2002 renovation added more elbow room and a wine cellar. Baehrel has mastered the element of surprise in fine dining. His initial à la carte menu has evolved into two prix fixe menus featuring locally grown ingredients. For example, a December menu might feature first-of-the-season winter truffles. The bistro offers two seatings per night at 5 P.M. Thursday–Saturday (at 4 P.M. Sunday) and 8:15 P.M. A Chef's Tasting includes 5–7 courses ($45–50 per person), and the Grand Tasting includes cuisine, including duck confit and coq au vin, as well as steaks and seafood. The restaurant has a bar and soda fountain in the front and a formal dining room in the back. Outdoor seating is available in the summer.

The stately **◖ Bavarian Manor** (Mountain Ave., Purling 518/622-3261, www.bavarian manor.com; 5–9 P.M. Thurs., 5–10 P.M. Fri.–Sat., 1–9 P.M. Sun.; mains $12–18) sits on 100 acres of prime Catskill forest in Purling. The business has hosted German Americans (and those who wish they were) since 1865. A decidedly old-world German restaurant serves all the requisite dishes—schnitzel, sauerbraten, spaetzle, rouladen, and bratwurst—as well as seafood and wild game. Upstairs, 19 rooms have private bath, TV, fireplace, Jacuzzi, and air-conditioning.

Maassmann's Restaurant (Blackhead Mountain Rd., Round Top, 888/382-7474, www.blackheadmountaingolf.com; 5:30–9 P.M. Wed.–Sun. May–Oct., 5:30–8:30 P.M. Fri.–Sun. Nov.–Apr.; mains $12–25), at the Blackhead Mountain Golf Course, is popular with locals for special occasions like Easter dinner. On the menu are American and German dishes. Call ahead to reserve the Stammtisch Corner, which seats five to seven people.

The Alpine Pork Store (Rte. 23B, South Cairo, 518/622-3056, www.alpineporkstore .com; 9 A.M.–5 P.M. Thurs.–Fri., 9 A.M.–3 P.M. Sat.), in South Cairo, sells German-style sausages or wursts, as well as a full menu of fresh meats cut to order. This is a good place to stop on the way to a ski condo at Windham Mountain.

Lunch is the time to dine at **The Victorian Rose at Point Lookout Inn** (Rte. 23, East Windham, 518/734-3381, www.pointlook-outinn.com; lunch and dinner Thurs.–Mon.; mains $15–32), preferably on a clear day, when the view stretches all the way to New Hampshire, 180 miles to the north. Reserve early for a fireside table.

Zerega's (5351 State Rte 23, Windham, 518/734-4655, summer hours dinner 5–10 P.M. Thurs., lunch and dinner Fri.–Sun.; mains $10–15) makes New York–style pizza by the slice or the pie. Order at the takeout window

on the right side for slices; the dining room is for people ordering whole pies.

The popular **La Griglia Restaurante** (Rte. 23, Ashland, 518/734-4499; from 4 P.M. Wed.–Mon.) has moved west of Windham to the neighboring town of Ashland. The menu consists of tempting northern Italian dishes like osso bucco, roast duck, and of course, pasta. The chef also runs a bakery and café in town, just off Main Street (La Griglia Café, Church St., Windham, 518/734-6100).

ENTERTAINMENT AND EVENTS
Performing Arts

Stewart House owner Owen Lipstein founded the **Shakespeare on the Hudson Theatre Company** (2 N. Water St., 518/731-8030, info@shakespeareonthehudson.com, www .shakespeareonthehudson.com) a few years before buying the old hotel. Summer performances begin at 8 P.M. Thursday–Saturday.

Bars and Nightlife

The German theme continues all year long in Round Top, where the **Mountain Brauhaus** (430 Winter Clove Rd., Round Top, 800/999-7376, www.mountainbrauhaus.com) pours Dinkelacker beer by the stein. Polka dancers take the floor on weekend nights. A much younger crowd gathers at **Slopes Bar** (6002 Main St., Tannersville, 518/589-5006, www.slopesniteclub.com) in Tannersville for après ski refreshments and late-night entertainment. The **Friar Tuck Resort** (4858 Rte. 32, Catskill, 800/832-7600) hosts occasional country-and-western music concerts.

Festivals

Bass tournaments draw large crowds to Catskill in Spring, when the striped bass are running. Anglers should head to **River Basin Sports** (66 W. Bridge St., Catskill, 518/943-2111; 8:30 A.M.–5 P.M. Tues.–Sat.) for dates and details. For longtime Catskill residents, the run of the American shad heralds the arrival of summer. **The Hudson River Shad Festival** (Main St., Catskill) takes place in May or June with shad tasting, music, theater programs, and even a lecture on harvesting ice from the Hudson. Contact Andy Turner for information, 518/622-9820.

At the annual **Catskill Ginseng Festival** (Catskill Point, Lower Main St., Catskill, 518/943-0989; 10 A.M.–5 P.M.; admission $5), you can taste freshly harvested ginseng, sample ginseng foods and beverages, view wild ginseng roots that are more than 100 years old, and purchase some of the highest-quality wild ginseng roots available in the United States.

For 27 years, the Michael J. Quill Irish Cultural & Sports Centre (2119 Rte. 145, 518/634-2286, www.eastdurham.org) has hosted the **East Durham Irish Festival,** drawing participants from across the Hudson Valley with Irish music performances and a one-acre "map" of Ireland, bordered with flags of the country's provinces and counties.

The Catskill Mountain Foundation theater shows a mix of independent and Hollywood films. In summer, a series of Hunter Mountain Festivals draws large crowds, with the **International Celtic Festival** and **Oktoberfest** (Belleayre Ski Center, Lower Lodge, State Rte. 28 Highmount, 845/586-3175 or 845/586-2246, www.gacnc .org/oktoberfest.htm; $8 per person, children under 12 free) among the most popular events. A calendar is available at www.huntermtn .com/calendar.htm.

In summer, beginner and experienced artists can enroll in a series of **Hudson River Valley Art Workshops** (South St., Greenville, 518/966-5219, info@artworkshops .com, www.artworkshops.com) at the Greenville Arms 1889 Inn. Weekend and weeklong programs cover watercolor, oil, acrylic, pastel, drawing, or collage. Tuition costs $300 for a weekend course and $475 for a weeklong course. A package with accommodations and dinners is $600 for three nights and $960 for six nights.

SHOPPING

Antiques, crafts, and locally made foods are among the best finds in Greene County.

Farm Stands

Local farmers bring produce to the **Riverside Market** (Dutchman's Landing, Catskill, 518/622-9820) on Saturday mornings June through October. Pop into **Traphagen's Honey and Gourmet Shop** (Rte. 23A, Hunter, 518/263-4150; 9 A.M.–5 P.M. Thurs.–Mon.) on the way out of Hunter to satisfy a craving for sugar. **Maple Hill Farm** (Route 23A, Lexington, 518/299-3195), just up the road, sells locally made maple syrup and deerskin products.

The Catskill Mountain Foundation shares its space with the **CMF Farm Market** (Rte. 23A, Main St., 518/263-2040, www.catskillmtn.org; 10 A.M.–6 P.M. Sun.–Thurs., 10 A.M.–7 P.M. Fri.–Sat.), which stocks organic produce and locally made goods. Check the fridge for outstanding Camembert and ricotta cheeses made by the Old Chatham Sheepherding Company across the river in Columbia County. The CMF bookstore across the street carries a wide range of local interest titles.

Green Acres Farm (226 Route 82, Hudson, 518/851-7460; Fri.–Mon.) opens with the summer's first harvest of tomatoes, peaches, and corn. Stop in for a weekend's worth of fresh produce and irresistible pastries baked right on the premises. The stand closes precisely at noon on Thanksgiving Day, after the holiday's homemade pies are delivered to its loyal customers.

In summer, stop by **Black Horse Farms** (Rte. 9W, Coxsackie, 518/943-9324, www .blackhorsefarms.com; 9 A.M.–6 P.M. daily) for fresh-picked corn on the cob and other seasonal produce. The family-run store also sells baked goods, plants, maple syrup, and honey.

Galleries

The hand-painted chandeliers of contemporary artist Ulla Darni are on display at **The Blue Pearl** (7551 Rte. 23, East Windham, 518/734-6525, bluepearl@mhonline.net; 11 A.M.–4 P.M. Mon.–Fri., 11 A.M.–6 P.M. Sat.–Sun.), located on Route 23, just below the Point Lookout Inn. Gallery owner Paula Cirnigliaro also maintains three floors of antiques, including Mexican and Spanish pottery,

Green Acres Farm stand on Route 82 near Hudson

Indian and Tibetan tapestries, silver tea sets, and decorative ironwork. The store has its own café on the ground floor.

Although it's not exactly a gallery, **Guaranteed Irish** (2220 Rte. 145, East Durham, 518/634-2392, www.guaranteedirishshop.com; 9 A.M.–9 P.M. daily July–Aug., 9 A.M.–6 P.M. Sept.–June), at the corner of County Routes 31 and 145, contains a wide variety of Irish-made goods, including handcrafted jewelry, tweed jackets, and Celtic music. With 5,000-square-feet of space, Guaranteed Irish bills itself as America's largest Irish import store.

Antiques
American Gothic Antiques (Rte. 23A, Hunter; 11 A.M.–5 P.M. Thurs.–Sun.) specializes in lamps from the 19th and 20th centuries. A few miles down the mountain at the eclectic **Last Chance Antiques and Cheese Café** (602 Main St., Tannersville, 518/589-6424, www.lastchanceonline.com; 11 A.M.–9 P.M. daily), a way of luring antique shoppers in the door has evolved into a full-fledged gourmet

food store and restaurant. The store is covered floor to ceiling in antique instruments and Victorian-era accessories. Enjoy an unusual brew (there are 300 beers to choose from), a cheese platter, or a rich chocolate fondue.

Opera House Antiques Center (21 2nd St., Athens; 11 A.M.–6 P.M. Tues.–Sun.) represents multiple dealers selling furniture and other collectibles.

Books
If the mountain air catches you by surprise, **Rip Van Winkle Outfitters** (Main St., Tannersville, 518/589-5541; 10 A.M.–5 P.M. Sun.–Thurs., 10 A.M.–6 P.M. Fri.–Sat.) is the place to go for an extra layer of clothes. The store carries a wide selection of local interest books, in addition to fishing, hunting, and general outdoor gear.

INFORMATION AND SERVICES
Visitor information is available at Exit 21 of the New York State Thruway/I-87. The

Greene County Tourism Office (P.O. Box 527, Catskill, 800/355-2287, tourism@discover greene.com; 9 A.M.–4 P.M. daily year-round, longer hours in summer) will answer questions through its website; by email, phone, and fax; or in person. After hours, an outdoor kiosk provides information on local sights and accommodations.

The **Greene County Council on the Arts** (398 Main St., Catskill, 518/943-3400, www .greenearts.org; 10 A.M.–5 P.M. Mon.–Sat.) keeps a calendar of countywide gallery exhibits, performances, lectures, and related events.

GETTING THERE AND AROUND
By Bus
Adirondack Trailways (800/858-8555, www .escapemaker.com/adirondacktrailways) offers daily service year-round from the Port Authority Terminal in New York City. Stops include Catskill, Palenville, Hunter, and Windham, and you can walk to town from the bus stops, or inquire about hotel and resort shuttles.

By Train
Greene County does not have its own rail service, but **Amtrak** (518/355-2287 or 800/872-7245, www.amtrak.com) stops in Hudson across the river, about eight miles from Catskill Village. You can get a taxi from the station, and some area hotels also run free shuttles.

By Car
The New York State Thruway (I-87) and Route 9W are the primary north-south arteries through Greene County. Exit the Thruway at Exit 21 for the most direct approach to the mountaintop. Routes 23 and 23A traverse the county from the Rip Van Winkle Bridge to the border with Delaware County.

Enterprise Rent-a-Car (518/943-0028) has a location in Hudson.

Columbia County

Framed by the Hudson River to the west and the Berkshire Mountains to the east, the landscape of Columbia County features rolling hills, green pastures, and extensive woodlands. Many longtime farmers in Columbia County have converted their struggling dairy operations into niche organic businesses that cater to local restaurants and residents who join community-supported agriculture programs. The transition has allowed many local growers to keep their connection to the land while earning an almost satisfactory living.

The historic city of Hudson got its start as a center for whaling and shipping in the early 19th century and later became a center for iron-ore production. An industrial past continues to haunt the city. Unfortunately for weekenders and conservationists, the St. Lawrence Cement Company wants to move its plant from south of Catskill in Greene County to just outside of Hudson. At stake are 150 jobs—enough to make a real difference to a rural community. The controversy has enraged residents on both sides of the fence, and red Stop the Plant signs have appeared on every other lawn throughout Columbia County.

Named after Christopher Columbus, Columbia County's history is closely tied to that of the powerful Livingston family. In the late 17th century, Scottish entrepreneur Robert Livingston began buying land along both sides of the Hudson from Native American tribes. In the early 1700s, King George I deeded him a large tract of land covering most of present-day Columbia County. He became the first lord of Livingston Manor, which served as the county seat with its own representation in the New York State legislature. Six more generations of Livingstons held prominent political and economic positions in the area until the mid-20th century, when the family's riverside property, Clermont, was handed over to the state.

historic Hudson row houses

© NIKKI GOTHITOI

ALONG THE HUDSON– ROUTE 9G
€ Clermont State Historic Site

Wild turkeys roam the grounds at Clermont (Clear Mountain, in French), the former riverside estate of Robert Livingston Jr., who is also known as Robert of Clermont, or simply as the Chancellor. Robert Jr. served as New York State chancellor, signed the Declaration of Independence, and later became ambassador to France. In 1728, he inherited 13,000 acres of present-day Columbia County from his father, the first lord of Livingston Manor, and built a Georgian-style riverside home between 1730 and 1750. The house was designed to catch stunning views of the Catskill Mountains across the river.

The British burned this first home to the ground during the Revolutionary War, as punishment for Livingston's support of colonial independence. Margaret Beekman Livingston, who managed the estate during the war, escaped with a grandfather clock that remains in the foyer today. She promptly rebuilt the home

in time to host George and Martha Washington in 1782.

When he wasn't involved in national affairs, Robert of Clermont turned his attention to entrepreneurial projects. For example, he introduced merino sheep from France and partnered with Robert Fulton to build the first steamship to cruise the Hudson.

Frozen in time since the start of the Great Depression, the manor reflects the tastes of the seven generations that lived in it. A crystal chandelier in the drawing room came from 19th-century France, and the library contains books from the 17th century. The dining room, newly restored in January 2004, has a marble fireplace mantel. And the original house telephone sits on a table outside the dining room. (The telephone number was 3.) A frieze over the fireplace in the study depicts Alice Livingston and her two daughters, the last residents of the estate. Oddly, an entire room upstairs is dedicated to pets of the family.

Today, the beautifully landscaped grounds of the 500-acre Clermont State Historic Site

(1 Clermont Ave., Germantown, 518/537-4240, fofc@valstar.net, www.friendsofclermont.org; 11 A.M.–5 P.M. Tues.–Sun. and Monday holidays Apr. 1–Oct. 31, 11 A.M.–4 P.M. Sat.–Sun. Nov. 1–Mar. 31; $5 adults, $4 seniors/students, $1 children 5–12, children under 5 free) are open to the public year-round. A popular time to visit is mid-May, when the lilacs are in bloom.

The visitors center, located in the old carriage house, stocks a good selection of local interest books. And a reference library in the house is open by appointment. Nearby Germantown has gas stations, ATMs, and the obligatory Stewarts Shop.

Olana State Historic Site

Ten miles north of Germantown stands another historic residence, in every way quite the opposite of Clermont. Landscape painter Frederic Edwin Church began his career in 1846 under the tutelage of Thomas Cole and went on to earn worldwide recognition. At age 24, he became the youngest artist ever elected to the National Academy of Design. As a painter who also grasped the power of marketing, Church learned how to generate hype and income for his paintings. He often showed a single painting at a time and charged admission for anyone who wished to view it.

Though he traveled extensively during his lifetime, Church held a strong connection to the Hudson River Valley and chose to settle on 126 acres just south of the present-day Rip Van Winkle Bridge. Following a trip to the Middle East, he designed a sprawling Persian-style residence on top of a hill overlooking the Hudson and landscaped the grounds as if he were composing one of his romantic paintings. New York State rescued the home in 1966 from the nephew of Church's daughter-in-law, who intended to sell all of its furnishings in a Sotheby's auction. On display are a few of Church's own works, as well as many of the paintings, sculptures, and furnishings he collected from his travels to South America and the Middle East.

Olana (5720 Rte. 9G, Hudson, 518/828-0135, www.olana.org; 10 A.M.–5 P.M.

Tues.–Sun. Apr.–Nov., 11 A.M.–4 P.M. Sat.–Sun. Dec.–Apr.) is open with guided tours on the hour. Tours cost $7 for adults, $5 for students, $2 for kids; and there is a grounds fee of $5 10 A.M.–7 P.M. on weekends and holidays. Visitors are welcome to walk the trails in summer or cross-country ski in winter.

Hudson

If you looked down Hudson's Warren Street for the first time and thought you had landed in an Atlantic seaboard beach town, you wouldn't be far from the truth. The city still reflects its heritage as a whaling port in the early 19th century.

Fearing a British retaliation after the American Revolution, a group of Nantucket whalers moved inland to the Hudson River shoreline and incorporated a city in 1785. With a strategic location and carefully planned grid of streets, Claverack Landing, later renamed Hudson, became a center for shipbuilding and sperm-oil production. By the mid-19th century, the city was firmly established as the economic and political center of Columbia County.

As the city declined in the early 20th century, it earned a reputation for its active red light district. Author Bruce Hall revisits this aspect of Hudson's history in a book called *Diamond Street: The Story of the Little Town with the Big Red Light District* (Black Dome Press, 1994). Today, antique shops have replaced the brothels, but little else has changed. Rows of restored Greek Revival and Federal townhouses line both sides of historic Warren Street for several blocks, extending from the town square to the river. New York City designers flock to more than 70 antique shops, which carry everything from Tibetan tapestries to Russian furniture.

In the 100 block is the **Robert Jenkins House & Museum** (113 Warren St., 518/828-9764; 1–3 P.M. Sun.–Mon. July–Aug., or by appointment), an 1811 Federal-style building with whaling and military exhibits that document the city's colorful past. A deserted promenade at the end of Warren Street offers river views, and the city is developing a new park south of the train station.

© AVALON TRAVEL

The Firemen's Association of the State of New York (FASNY) operates the **Museum of Firefighting** (117 Harry Howard Ave., Hudson, 877/347-3687, www.fasnyfiremuseum .com; 10 A.M.–4:30 P.M. daily, closed holidays) in downtown Hudson. Two exhibit halls include paintings, photographs, and related memorabilia. The fire engines, pumps, and clothing on display date back to the 18th and 19th centuries. Residents of New York's Volunteer Fireman's Home, next door, staff the museum and happily answer questions about the history and current state of their profession.

Kinderhook

Kinderhook received its name, which is Dutch for "children's point," from Henry Hudson himself. The story goes that when he arrived in 1609, Hudson saw a group of Mohican children staring at the *Half Moon* and named the place Kinderhook Landing, now the town of Stuyvesant. Present-day Kinderhook lies several miles inland, on Kinderhook Creek. Numerous restored homes and historical sites make this

town one of the most interesting destinations in northern Columbia County. The village hosted several notable guests during the Revolutionary War: Colonel Henry Knox passed though on his way to deliver a shipment of artillery from Fort Ticonderoga to Boston. And Colonel Benedict Arnold spent the night to recover after the victory of Bemis Heights.

Washington Irving reportedly wrote "Rip Van Winkle" during a stay in Kinderhook, and he based "The Legend of Sleepy Hollow" on local residents, though the story took place in Tarrytown. The town of Kinderhook has published a detailed guide to its many private and public historic homes at www.kinderhook connection.com/history2.htm. The walking tour begins at the Village Green, formed by the intersection of several streets that date back to the early 19th century: Albany Avenue, Broad Street, Hudson Street, and Chatham Street.

The **Columbia County Museum** (5 Albany Ave., 518/758-9265, www.cchsny.org; 10 A.M.–4 P.M. Mon.–Fri. Memorial Day–Labor Day, call for occasional Sat. hours,

10 A.M.–4 P.M. Mon., Wed., Fri., 1–4 P.M. Sat. Sept–May), run by the Columbia County Historical Society, has extensive collections of paintings and artifacts from around the county.

Take a tour of a Federal-style mansion at the **James Vanderpoel House** (Board St., 518/758-9265; 11 A.M.–5 P.M. Thurs.–Sat., 1–4 P.M. Sun. Memorial Day–Labor Day; adults $3, students $2, members and children under 12 free, discounted combination tickets with the Lukyas Van Alen House available). This restored brick building is the former home of James Vanderpoel, a prominent lawyer and politician. Inside, an elegant, curved staircase rises from a grand entryway. The home is decorated throughout with furnishings from the 1820s.

The **Luykas Van Alen House** (Rte. 9H, 518/758-9625; 11 A.M.–5 P.M. Thurs.–Sat., 1–5 P.M. Sun. Memorial Day–Labor Day weekend; adults $3, students $2, members and children under 12 free, discounted combination tickets with the James Vanderpoel House available) is a 1737 Dutch farmhouse with mid-18th century furnishings. The site appeared in Mar-

tin Scorsese's 1993 film *The Age of Innocence*. On the property is the white 1920 Ichabod Crane Schoolhouse, named after the teacher in Washington Irving's famous story "The Legend of Sleepy Hollow."

Located two miles outside of Kinderhook, the former home of Martin Van Buren, the eighth President of the United States, is now a historic site. The surrounding land was a working farm of over 200 acres. Built in 1797, the **Martin Van Buren National Historic Site** (1013 Old Post Rd., 518/758-9689, www.nps.gov/mava; 9 A.M.–4:30 P.M. daily mid-May–Oct. 31; admission $5, children under 16 free) is a Federal-style home that was remodeled in 1849, and Van Buren spared no expense: Brussels carpets and 51 elaborate wallpaper panels that form a hunting mural are on display inside.

The **Parker O'Malley Air Museum** (435 County Rte. 20, off Rte. 9H & Rte. 66, Ghent, 518/392-7200, www.parkeromalley .org; 10 A.M.–4 P.M. first Sat. of the month, or by appointment; adults $5, children $3, under 5 free) features civilian and military aircraft

© NIKKI GOTH ITOI

James Vanderpoel House, Kinderhook

from the 1920s, '30s, and '40s. Most are maintained in flying condition, and there is a wind tunnel on-site. Open cockpit airplane rides are available by appointment, starting at $75.

ALONG THE TACONIC STATE PARKWAY
Lake Taghkanic State Park

During sticky summer heat waves, Lake Taghkanic State Park (1528 Rte. 82, Taghkanic, 518/851-3631) is a popular day trip for Mid-Hudson Valley residents. The clean and refreshing lake has two beaches with lifeguard supervision and a boat launch. Overnight accommodations include tent and RV campsites, as well as cabins and cottages (May–October only, reserve online through www.reserveamerica.com). The park service maintains trails for hiking and biking. In winter, it allows cross-country skiing, snowmobiles, ice-skating, and ice fishing when the lake freezes. Hunters can take deer and turkey in season.

West Taghkanic

A large population of second-home owners have settled among the 19th-century schoolhouses in the hamlet of West Taghkanic. The name Taghkanic meant "water enough" or "full of timber" to the Algonquin Indians who once lived here. Today, the most notable building in town is the retro West Taghkanic Diner, at the intersection of Route 82 and the Taconic State Parkway.

Claverack

Continuing north on the Taconic State Parkway, you arrive at the intersection of Route 23, an old canon route from the Revolutionary War that connects Hillsdale to Hudson. Equidistant between Hudson and the Taconic is the hamlet of Claverack, best known for its 1786 stone courthouse, where Alexander Hamilton tried a famous libel case involving a Hudson newspaper publisher and President Thomas Jefferson. Today, Claverack is the center of an ongoing controversy over a proposed cement plant.

The name Claverack derives from the Dutch

for clover field. Historians believe Henry Hudson chose the name for the fields of white clover he saw when he first arrived. The 1727 Reformed Protestant Dutch Church stands as a testament to the town's first settlers, and Dutch architecture populates this stretch of Route 23.

Several pick-your-own berry farms are nearby, including **Hotalings** (518/851-9864) for cherries, apples, and strawberries, and **Philip Orchards** (Claverack, 518/851-6351) for apples and pears. Contemporary writer Leila Philip wrote a memoir of her family's longstanding connection to Claverack entitled *A Family Place: A Hudson Valley Farm, Three Centuries, Five Wars, One Family* (Viking, 2001).

Chatham

Though it is technically part of Columbia County, Chatham marks the unofficial gateway to southern New England and the Berkshires. There are actually several Chathams: At the commercial center is the town of Chatham, Route 203 off the Taconic State Parkway. The Village of Chatham, founded in 1795, has dozens of historical markers and claims one of the country's last operational one-room schoolhouses, now home to the **Riders Mills Historical Association** (at the intersection of Riders Mills Road and Drowne Road, 518/794-7156). Quiet North Chatham lies on the Valatie Kill and the Rensselaer County line, while East Chatham offers a treasure trove for book lovers: Librarium Second Hand Books.

The **Old Chatham Sheepherding Company** (155 Shaker Museum Rd., 888/743-3760, www.blacksheepcheese.com) operates one of the largest sheep farms in the U.S. and makes a Camembert that aficionados claim rivals the best that France can produce. Many of the nation's top restaurants serve the award-winning cheese, including the French Laundry, in California's Napa Valley. Stop in to observe the morning or afternoon sheep-milking (especially popular with young kids), watch the cheese-making operation, or see the newborn lambs in early spring.

◖ Shaker Museum and Library

In 1772, an Englishwoman named Ann Lee rose to the forefront of a radical dissident movement and led a small group of Shaking Quakers—so named for their tendency to break out in violent shakes during their worship services—to the New World to escape religious persecution. The United Society of Believers eventually established a leadership center in New Lebanon, New York, and grew to include some 6,000 members in 19 communities by the mid-19th century. The Shaker community evolved considerably over the years, but two ideals underpinned the religion: simplicity and celibacy. Above all, members strove to live a selfless and communal existence. Industrialization during the 19th century gradually eroded the once-thriving Shaker community (along with other utopian social experiments like it), and the few remaining followers withdrew from society, leaving only traces of the culture.

You can spend several hours exploring the Shaker Museum and Library (88 Shaker Museum Rd., Malden Bridge, 518/794-9100, www.shakermuseumandlibrary.org; 10 A.M.–5 P.M. Wed.–Mon. late May–mid Oct.; $8 adults, $6 seniors, $4 children), on the outskirts of Old Chatham. Founded in 1950, this remarkable museum contains one of the largest collections of Shaker artifacts and offers an informative introduction to the Shaker way of life. Among other values, the culture emphasizes high quality, precision, hospitality, invention, and systematic thinking. As a result, the industrious Shakers made fine furniture, tools, farm produce, and clothes. On display inside the museum are Shaker stoves, a washing machine, chairs, and textiles.

ALONG ROUTE 22
◖ Taconic State Park

Just east of Route 22, at the intersection of the New York, Massachusetts, and Connecticut state lines, lies a hidden outdoor gem: the 5,000-acre Taconic State Park (Rte. 344 off Rte. 22, Copake Falls, 518/329-3993; open year-round). The park encompasses an 11-mile stretch of the Taconic Range—the vestiges of

© NIKKI GOTH ITOI

Shaker Museum and Library near Chatham

a mountain range that geologists believe stood taller than the Himalayas during the Ordovician time period, 450 million years ago.

The state has developed two areas for year-round use—Copake Falls and Rudd Pond—with extensive hiking, biking, and nature trails, as well as fishing, swimming, and camping. In winter, the trails belong to cross-country skiers and snowmobiles. The **Copake Falls Area** (518/329-3993) is located on State Route 344 or Valley View Road. To find the **Rudd Pond Area** (59 Rudd Pond Dr., Millerton, 518/789-3059; open year-round), turn off Route 22 at Route 62 in Millerton, and head two miles north.

The highlight of this wilderness area is **Bash Bish Falls,** at 80 feet, the tallest single-drop waterfall in Massachusetts. (The falls are located just over the state line.) Beginning about a mile upstream from the town of Copake Falls, a moderate one-mile hike through a hemlock and hardwood forest takes you to the base of the falls. The water cascades over a sheer granite cliff, landing in a pristine mountain pool. Cold temperature and strong currents discourage most hikers from taking a dip. The ecosystem supports a diverse population, including coyote, red fox, and brook trout. After the falls, the Bash Bish Brook winds its way through the Mid-Hudson Valley and empties into the Hudson River. Plan to get there before 10 A.M. to enjoy the view before the crowds.

South of the state park, Columbia and Dutchess counties have teamed up to convert a 43-mile stretch of the old New York and Harlem Railroad into a pathway for walking, running, and cycling. A four-mile piece of the **Harlem Valley Rail Trail** (51 South Center St., Millerton, 518/789-9591, www.hvrt.org) now connects Ancram to the Taconic State Park entrance in Copake Falls. Lined in spots with weathered split rail fencing, the paved trail traverses the base of the Taconic Mountains. In several clearings, you can see the Catskill Mountains to the west.

According to local residents, Mohican Indian arrowheads, spears, and axes can still occasionally be found in the vicinity of Copake.

A tall clock and a Vietnam Veterans War Memorial at the intersection of Routes 22 and 7A marks the center of town, but there's not much reason to stop.

Hillsdale and Catamount

When Hillsdale residents speak of "the mountains," they mean the Berkshires, not the Catskills. Located at the Massachusetts state line, the town is part sleepy Hudson Valley, part upscale New England. The first building you see rolling into Hillsdale from Route 22 North is a 1780s brick Dutch colonial named **Aubergine** (Rtes. 22 & 23, Hillsdale, 518/325-3412, www.aubergine.com), now the restaurant of chef and owner David Lawson and his wife Stacy. Lawson—a political scientist turned restaurateur—prepares French-inspired country fare in a cozy setting that takes his guests back 150 years in time. His blend of traditional and inventive dishes attracts both weekenders from New York City and local residents for special occasions.

Catamount Ski & Snowboarding Area (3200 State Highway 23, Hillsdale, 518/325-3200, www.catamountski.com), at the Massachusetts state line, is a great mountain to hit on a midweek snow day. With seven lifts and a new terrain park, the area draws families from

CATAMOUNT STATISTICS

- Base: 1,000 feet
- Summit: 2,000 feet
- Vertical drop: 1,000 feet
- Trails: 29
- Lifts: 7
- Skiable acres: 110
- Snowmaking: 100 percent of terrain
- Snow report: 800/342-1840

across the Hudson Valley. The minimal lodge has stacks of blue lockers and cafeteria-style lunch fare. A heated tent next to the lodge houses a small gift shop with winter wear.

Austerlitz

The sale of abundant fresh blueberries helped early settlers pay their taxes in rural Austerlitz. Today, an annual Blueberry Festival commemorates the town's heritage. The Austerlitz Historical Society (518/392-0062, oldausterlitz@taconic.net, www.oldausterlitz.org) is in the process of creating Old Austerlitz, a museum site at the intersection of Route 22 and Harvey Mountain Road that collects and restores buildings, artifacts, and related town memorabilia. To date, the site includes a one-room schoolhouse from 1818 and an 1850s church. Next on the restoration list is the 1794 Morey-Devereaux house, which will serve as a research library and lecture hall. The society sponsors events and workshops year-round.

Mount Lebanon Shaker Village

The Shakers established their second community in the northeast corner of Columbia County in 1785, and the site is now a National Historic Landmark. Eight families once farmed and lived here on 6,000 acres of rolling hills, forests, and fields. More than two dozen of the original buildings have been preserved as Mount Lebanon Shaker Village (at the intersection of Rtes. 20 and 22 in New Lebanon, 518/794-9500, www.shakerworkshops.com/mt_leb.htm; 10 A.M.–5 P.M. Fri.–Sun. mid-June–mid-Oct.; adult $5, children $2, seniors $4.50, discounts for families, members, and groups). Visitors can view the original beams and chutes of the granary and the drying racks in the washhouse, as well as cemeteries, aqueducts, and the remains of several old mills. The site is a short drive from the Shaker Museum and Library, in Chatham, and the Hancock Shaker Village across the Massachusetts state line, in the Berkshires.

SPORTS AND RECREATION
Winter Sports
Catamount (3200 State Highway 23, Hillsdale,

518/325-3200, www.catamountski.com) is open 8:30 A.M.–4 P.M. weekends and holidays, 9 A.M.–4 P.M. midweek, 5–9 P.M. Wednesday–Thursday nights, and 3–10 P.M. Friday–Saturday nights. Weekend adult lift tickets cost $50 during the 2007–2008 season, with $15 days Monday through Thursday.

Nordic skiers will find more than 15 wilderness areas with groomed and ungroomed trails across Columbia County. **Clermont** (Rte. 6 just off Rte. 9G, Germantown, 518/537-4240, www.friendsofclermont.org) opens its trails and grounds free to cross-country skiers. Or explore the carriage roads and six miles of trails on the grounds of **Olana State Historic Site** (5720 Rte. 9G, Hudson, 518/828-0135). **Lake Taghkanic State Park** (1528 Rte. 82, Taghkanic, 518/851-3631) has trails around the lake. **Taconic State Park** (Rte. 344, off Rte. 22, Copake Falls, 518/329-3993) has extensive trails in both developed areas, Copake Falls and Rudd Pond. Two cottages for rent year-round each have a refrigerator, stove, microwave, dishes and utensils, a bathroom with shower, and oil heat.

Hiking

Hikers can explore state forests, historic sites, and wildlife preserves in Columbia County. Olana, Clermont, and Martin Van Buren Park have well-maintained trails for nature walks and scenic views. To get farther away from civilization, head to Beebe Hill State Forest (County Rte. 5, Austerlitz), Harvey Mountain State Forest (E. Hill Rd. off Rte. 22, Austerlitz), or the 5,000-acre Taconic State Park.

Swimming and Boating

Lake Taghkanic State Park (access from the Taconic State Parkway or Rte. 82, 518/851-3631) offers swimming and boating in a natural lake, while Taconic State Park allows swimming in the Rudd Pond area (Rte. 62 in Millerton, off Rte. 22, 518/789-3059). Queechy Lake in Canaan is another popular venue for swimming and canoeing. For Hudson River access, head to the boat launches on Front Street in Hudson or on County Route 35A (Northern Blvd.) in Germantown.

Fishing and Hunting

The New York State Department of Conservation stocks Kinderhook Creek, Claverack Creek, Roeliff Jansen Creek, and the unfortunately named Ore Pit Pond in Taconic State Park with trout. Fly-fishers head to the Taghkanic Creek or Bash Bish Falls. Queechy Lake and Kinderhook Lake allow fishing from car top boats only. A New York State fishing license is required at all locations.

Several state forests allow hunting in season: New Forge on New Forge Road off Route 82 in Taghkanic, Beebe Hill on County Route 5 in Austerlitz, and Harvey Mountain on East Hill Road off Route 22. Call the local state ranger for information: 518/828-0236. Taconic State Park permits bow and rifle hunting for deer only. Lido's Game Preserve is a private club in the town of Taghkanic (Berkshire Rd. off County Rte. 11, 518/329-1551).

Golf

A dozen golf courses are scattered among Columbia County's rolling hills. **Undermountain Golf Course** (274 Undermountain Rd., Copake, 518/329-4444, www.undermountain golf.com; 7 A.M.–7:30 P.M. Mon.–Fri., 7 A.M.–6:30 P.M. Sat.–Sun.; $17.75 midweek, $19.50 weekend and holiday, $14.75 senior/junior) operates a public, 18-hole course with views of the Taconic Range, Berkshire Mountains, and Catskills.

Copake Country Club's (44 Golf Course Rd., off County Rte. 11, Copake, 518/325-4338, www.copakecountryclub.com; 7 A.M.–7 P.M. daily, Mar.–Nov.; weekday 9 holes $25, 18 holes $35, weekend 9 holes $35, 18 holes $50) 18-hole par 72 course overlooks Copake Lake with distant views of the Catskills across the Hudson. The club offers cart rentals, a pro-shop, lessons, and a restaurant.

Cycling

Cyclists have many options for touring country roads and trails in this part of the Hudson Valley. An aggressive 83-mile road ride with a 60-mile option traverses nearly every major town in the county on back roads that meander

by old homes, farms, rolling hills, and waterfalls (www.roberts1.com/bikehudson/r/east/gt_columbia/map/index.htm). For an easier ride, the paved **Harlem Valley Rail Trail** (51 South Center St., Millerton, 518/789-9591, www.hvrt.org) follows a set of old railroad tracks along the base of the Taconic Range. Access the path at Undermountain Road, off Route 22 in Ancram or at the Taconic State Park entrance in Copake Falls. Mountain bikers will find challenging terrain in both Taconic State Park and Lake Taghkanic State Park.

Steiner Sports (301 Warren St., Hudson, 518/828-5063, www.steinersports.com; 9:30 A.M.–5:30 P.M. Mon.–Fri., 9:30 A.M.–5 P.M. Sat.) carries high-end ski, bike, and kayak equipment in three locations: Hudson, Valatie, and Glenmont. Stop in for maps, supplies, and route advice.

Aviation

Private pilots and aviation enthusiasts should head to **Richmor Aviation** (Rte. 9H, Hudson, 518/828-9461, www.richmor.com), at the Columbia County Airport, for training and scenic flights.

ACCOMMODATIONS

Aside from a couple of modern hotels that cater to business travelers, places to stay in Columbia County tend toward the upscale. A number of unique bed-and-breakfast inns are scattered about the countryside.

Under $100

Wireless Internet in every room is a plus at the **St. Charles Hotel** (16-18 Park Place, Hudson, 518/822-9900, www.stcharleshotel.com; $79–119). Rooms are basic but adequate, and the location is within walking distance of the antique shops on Warren Street.

$100-150

The **Hudson City B&B** (326 Allen St., Hudson, 518/822-8044, info@hudsoncitybnb.com, www.hudsoncitybnb.com; $125–175) occupies the former residence of Joshua T. Waterman, four-term mayor of Hudson beginning in 1853.

The house is painted green with cream trim and sits within walking distance of the Warren Street antique shops. Its comfortable rooms are decorated in 19th-century furnishings.

The **Inn at the Shaker Mill Farm** (40 Cherry Lane, New Lebanon, 518/794-9345, www.shakermillfarminn.com; $100–120, dinner $25) puts you a short drive from Berkshire attractions, including summer performances at Tanglewood, 10 miles away. As the name implies, guest rooms occupy a converted 1834 mill, and owner Ingram Paperny has embraced the Shaker philosophy with zeal. Be prepared for bare-bones decor and a communal experience, including family-style meals.

$150-200

In a region dominated by Dutch colonial and Federal structures, the clay tile roof and stucco exterior of the **The Inn at Blue Stores** (2323 Rte. 9, Hudson, 518/537-4277, www.innatbluestores.com; $125–225) offer a welcome change of scenery. The Spanish colonial building, set on a farm, dates to 1908. Guests can enjoy afternoon tea in the garden or by the fire, depending on the season. Downtown Hudson lies 10 miles to the north. Each elegant room is accented differently with period furnishings to accommodate honeymooners and business travelers alike. A gourmet breakfast is included.

Farther north at the edge of the Berkshires, pine floors, antique trunks, and down comforters lend a cozy feel to guest rooms at ❨ **The Inn at Silver Maple Farm** (Rte. 295, Canaan, 518/781-3600, www.silvermaplefarm.com; $110–295). Breakfast includes homemade breads and muffins.

Over $200

Next door to the restaurant of the same name, ❨ **Swiss Hütte** (Rte. 23, Hillsdale, 518/325-3333, www.swisshutte.com; $100–190 per person per night, including breakfast and dinner) offers immaculate, recently renovated rooms with tiled baths and mountain views.

Close to Olana, the Rip Van Winkle Bridge, and the city of Hudson, ❨ **Mount Merino**

Manor (4317 Rte. 23, Hudson, 518/828-5583, www.mountmerinomanor.com; $175–375) opened recently to rave reviews. Seven guest rooms and suites all have king- or queen-size beds, air-conditioning, and high-quality bed linens. Some have fireplaces and soaking tubs and spa showers. Hosts Patrick and Rita reportedly make a mouthwatering breakfast, too.

Campgrounds

Woodland Hills Campground (386 Fog Hill Rd., Austerlitz, 518/392-3557, www.whcg.net; May–Oct.; $23 for tents, $30 for full hookups), near the intersection of the Taconic State Parkway and the Massachusetts Turnpike (I-90), has 200 sites for tents and RVs. Amenities include hot showers, laundry, and family activities.

Taconic State Park (Rte. 344, off Rte. 22, Copake Falls, 518/329-3993; year-round) offers two recreational areas—Copake Falls and Rudd Pond—with campsites, trailer sites, and cabins available from mid-May until November. (Deer hunting is allowed in season, and camping is extended for hunters.) Reserve online through www.reserveamerica.com. Tent sites cost $13, and cabins cost $78–140. The Rudd Pond area is located off Route 22 on Route 62, two miles north of Millerton.

Camp Waubeeka Family Campground (133 Farm Rd., Copake, 518/329-4681, www.campwaubeeka.com $32–42 per day) has four rustic cabins, as well as campsites and trailer hookups. Cabins cost $60–65 per night; a basic tent site is $18.

FOOD
Along the Hudson—Route 9G

Several new and trendy eateries have opened in the city of Hudson: **Swoon Kitchenbar** (340 Warren St., Hudson, 518/822-8938, www.swoonkitchenbar.com; Thurs. –Tues. lunch 11:30 A.M.–5 P.M., dinner 5–10 P.M., Fri. –Sat. 5–11 P.M.; dinner mains $20–25) has quickly cornered the market for New American cuisine. You might start with a rhubarb sidecar cocktail and oysters on the half shell, then dive into the duck confit or pan-seared Maine scallops.

Meanwhile, **Wasabi** (807 Warren St., Hudson, 518/822-1888; mains $15–20) has filled the void for Japanese. At the more casual end of the scale, **Earth Foods** (523 Warren St., Hudson, 518/822-1396; breakfast and lunch daily; mains $5–10) treats vegetarians right, with veggie burritos, soups, salads, and other lunch fare. Cash only.

Locals fill the ◖ **Red Dot** (321 Warren St., Hudson, 518/828-3657; 5–10 P.M. and bar till 1 A.M. Wed.–Sat., 11 A.M.–3 P.M., 5–9 P.M., and bar till 1 A.M. Sun.; mains $10–20) on weekend evenings, even in the dead of winter. Entrées range from basic steak frites to the more exotic Thai beef salad. **Mexican Radio** (537 Warren St., Hudson, 518/828-7770, www.mexrad.com; 11:30 A.M.–11 P.M. daily; mains $10–17) serves upscale Mexican cuisine and has a sister restaurant in New York City. **Hudson Bakery and Grill,** at Warren and North 5th Street, is the place to go for breakfast.

Wunderbar & Bistro (744 Warren St., Hudson, 518/828-0555, http://wunderbarandbistro.com; lunch mains $6–14, dinners $12–16) up the street serves dependable Austrian and Hungarian cuisine at reasonable prices. The restaurant is open for lunch 11:30 A.M.–2 P.M. Monday–Friday and for dinner 5–10 P.M. Monday–Saturday, with live music on Saturdays.

For ribs and southern fare, head to **Carolina House** (59 Broad St./Rte. 9, Kinderhook, 518/758-1669; 5–9:30 P.M. Mon., Wed., Thurs., 5–10 P.M. Fri.–Sat., 4–9:30 P.M. Sun.; mains $14–21).

Along the Taconic State Parkway

An Indian head sign in neon pink and blue lights marks the site of the **West Taghkanic Diner** (Route 82, Ancram, 518/851-7117, www.taghkanicdiner.com; 7 A.M.–9 P.M. Mon.–Thurs., 7 A.M.–11 P.M. Fri., 7 A.M.–10 P.M. Sat.–Sun.; mains $4–13). Conveniently located at the intersection of the Taconic State Parkway and Route 82, this retro establishment has been serving breakfast and dinner all day long since 1953. Eggs, omelettes, and pancakes average $4, and dinner mains include steak, seafood, pasta, and burgers.

The **Happy Clown Ice Cream Shop** (Rtes 9 and 82, Hudson, 518/851-2177, 10:30 A.M.–9 P.M. Wed.–Mon.) is a favorite summer stop at the intersection of Routes 9 and 82. There is only outdoor seating.

Jackson's Old Chatham House (Village Square, Old Chatham, 518/794-7373; 10 A.M.–10 P.M. daily; mains $10–20) serves reliable tavern-style food, including burgers, steaks, pork chops, and reportedly the best prime rib around. The wood-burning fireplace is a plus in winter months.

Nearby, the **Old Chatham Country Store** has homemade soups and sandwiches in a casual setting (Village Square, Old Chatham, 518/794-7151).

Blue Plate (1 Kinderhook St., Chatham, 518/392-7711, www.chathamblueplate.net; dinner Tues. –Sun.; mains $12–21) is an American bistro where you can begin the meal with Maryland crabcakes, move on to "The Famous Blue Plate Meatloaf," and finish with a hot fudge sundae. At **Lipperas' at the Chatham House** (29 Hudson Ave., Chatham, 518/392-6600, www.thechathamhouse.com; Mon. –Thurs. 11:30 A.M.–9:30 P.M., Fri. –Sat. till 10:30 P.M., Sun. 11 A.M.–3 P.M. and 4–9 P.M.), inside a restored 19th-century hotel, a family that has run local eateries for several generations offers a menu of locally inspired cuisine. The famous camembert from the Old Chatham Sheepherding Company, country-style pâté, and summer strawberry salad all make appearances at various times during the year. Choose the main dining room, the tavern with fireplace in winter, or the porch in summer.

Along Route 22

Show up at ◖ **Aubergine** (Rtes. 22 & 23, Hillsdale, 518/325-3412, www.aubergine.com; opens at 5:30 P.M. Wed.–Sun.; mains $24–32) in early May, and you may be treated to fresh tomatoes or herbs from Chef David Lawson's own garden before local farms have even planted their seeds. Lawson starts the seedlings in cold frames in late February or early March and heats the soil in his garden to lengthen the season for serving fresh-picked ingredients. When the leaves begin to turn in autumn, it's worth a visit just to see the view of Mount Alander from the dining rooms. Entrées range from a straightforward sirloin steak to the more adventurous crispy veal sweetbreads. The inn has several guest rooms upstairs.

A chalet straight out of the Swiss Alps, **Swiss Hütte** (Rte. 23, Hillsdale, 518/325-3333, www .swisshutte.com; noon–2 P.M. and 5:30–9 P.M. Tues.–Sat., noon–3 P.M. and 5–9 P.M. Sun.; mains $23–28) is a restaurant and inn directly across the parking lot from the lifts at Catamount. A friendly golden retriever named Beano will likely greet you at the door. Owned since 1986 by Swiss-born Gert Alper (who is also the chef) and his wife, Cindy, the restaurant serves cheese fondue, homemade European-style hard rolls, and a full menu of hearty entrées in a cozy, mountainside setting.

The popular **Four Brothers Pizza** chain (2828 Rte. 23, Hillsdale, 518/325-7300, www .fourbrotherspizza.net; 10:30 A.M.–10 P.M. daily; mains $10–15) is open late, serving Italian, Greek, and American dishes. The restaurant is one of nine pizzerias in the Hudson Valley, which, as the name implies, were established by four Greek brothers, who immigrated to the United States.

ENTERTAINMENT AND EVENTS
Performing Arts
With support from the Catskill Mountain Foundation, the **Pleshakov Music Center** (Main St., Hunter) has moved from Hudson to the new Doctorow Performing Arts Center in Hunter; Vladimir Pleshakov and his wife Elena Winther, both accomplished pianists, have realized a lifelong dream in the Pleshakov Piano Museum, which houses 16 antique but playable pianos collectively worth $2.5 million. The idea is for the space to function as a living museum in which Pleshakov and Winther will perform from time to time. The museum opened in August 2007.

After three decades of neglect, Hudson's 150-year-old city hall building reopened in 1998 as a local performing arts center, **Hudson Opera House** (327 Warren St., Hudson, 518/822-1438, www.hudsonoperahouse .org; noon–5 P.M. daily; tickets $3–15). Artist exhibitions and concerts are hosted throughout the year.

Set in an 1847 schoolhouse, **The Spencertown Academy** (Rte. 203, Spencertown, 518/392-3693, www.spencertown .org; 1–5 P.M. Thurs.–Sun. Feb.–Dec.) has a 140-seat auditorium and four exhibiting spaces. Events range from jazz and classical concerts to yoga classes.

The quaint **Mac-Haydn Theatre** (1925 Rte. 203, Chatham, 518/392-9292, www .machaydntheatre.org; tickets about $20), on a hilltop overlooking the town of Chatham, specializes in musicals and runs a summer children's theater. The theater runs seven or eight shows per season.

Bars and Nightlife
Hudson residents congregate at the **Red Dot** (321 Warren St., Hudson, 518/828-3657; 5–10 P.M. Wed.–Sat., 11 A.M.–3 P.M. and 5–9 P.M. Sun.) after work to drink Morland Old Speckled Hen by the pint.

For maritime entertainment, **Hudson Cruises** (518/822-1014, www.hudsoncruises .com) offers afternoon or evening cruises with dinner, dancing, and scenic river views. Boats depart from Waterfont Park on Front Street in Hudson at 7:30 P.M. Wednesday, 6 P.M. Friday, 2 P.M. Saturday, and 11 A.M. Sunday.

Festivals
Folk dancers and bluegrass music lovers attend the popular **Falcon Ridge Folk Festival** (Long Hill Farm, Rte. 23, Hillsdale, 860/364-0366, www.falconridgefolk.com) each July to watch up to 40 bands perform on three stages, with plenty of flat areas for camping.

Lebanon Valley Speedway (1746 Rte. 20, West Lebanon, 518/794-9606, www.lebanon valley.com; Sat. mid-Apr.–Sept.; admission $11) holds stock car races, monster truck rallies, and hot rod events.

The **Columbia County Fair** (Columbia

County Fairgrounds, Rtes. 66 & 203, Chatham Village, 518/392-2121 or 518/758-1811, www .columbiafair.com) is an old-fashioned fair with live music, a rodeo, tractor pulls, and amusement rides. It takes place on Labor Day weekend. And the Clermont hosts various festivals and educational events throughout the year, including a sheep festival in April.

SHOPPING
Antiques

As if the 70 independent antique shops on Warren Street in downtown Hudson weren't enough to choose from, the **Hudson Antiques Center** (536 Warren St, Hudson, 518/828-9920; 11 A.M.–5 P.M. Thurs.–Tues., 10 A.M.–5 P.M. Wed.) has another 20 vendors, conveniently located under one roof. They sell an incredible range of rare goods, from Dutch antique furniture and art deco accessories to clocks, garden decorations, and custom upholstery. Most of the stores are closed on Wednesdays.

Start your tour of Hudson's antique shops at **Hudson Supermarket** (310/312 Warren St., Hudson, 518/822-0028, www.hudsonsuper market.com; Thurs.–Mon. noon–6 P.M.), a collective of six dealers that occupies a former grocery store. One of its member shops, **Colette** (310 Warren St., Hudson, 518/822-0021, www .colettedecor.com; Thurs. –Mon. noon–6 P.M.), features a wide variety of fine art, textiles, ceramics, lighting, and mirrors.

More a gallery than a store, **East Market Street Antiques** (www.eastmarketstreet antiques.com) shows its Americana, folk, primitive, industrial, decorative, and fine arts in museum-quality displays. You might find anything from barbed wire to train signs. For serious collectors, everything is for sale, and some items are also available for rent as professional props.

Away from the Warren Street bustle, **Copake Auction** (266 Rte. 7A, Copake, 518/329-1142, www.copakeauction.com; 11 A.M.–4 P.M. Mon.–Fri.) has specialized in the sale of Americana items for the past 50 years. Its annual antique bicycle auction draws cycling enthusiasts from across the nation and overseas.

Books

Bookworms will want to spend an hour or two browsing the shelves at **Librarium Second Hand Books** (126 Black Bridge Rd., East Chatham, 518/392-5209) or **Rodgers Book Barn** (467 Rodman Rd., Hillsdale, 518/325-3610; 10 A.M.–5 P.M. Sat., 11 A.M.–5 P.M. Sun., noon–5 P.M. Mon., Fri. Nov.–Mar., 10 A.M.–5 P.M. Sat., 11 A.M.–5 P.M. Sun., noon–5 P.M. Mon., Thurs., Fri. Apr.–Oct.). Better yet, save time for both. Each shop houses tens of thousands of titles in a converted barn that sets the mood for reading.

Farm Stands

There is at least one farm stand, or pick-your-own orchard in every town in Columbia County. Two farmers markets take place in Hudson during the growing season:

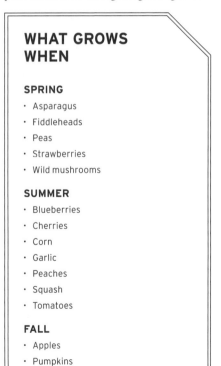

WHAT GROWS WHEN

SPRING

- Asparagus
- Fiddleheads
- Peas
- Strawberries
- Wild mushrooms

SUMMER

- Blueberries
- Cherries
- Corn
- Garlic
- Peaches
- Squash
- Tomatoes

FALL

- Apples
- Pumpkins

Hudson's Farmers Market (8432 Rte. 22, 518/828-7217; 10 A.M.–6 P.M. Sun.–Thurs., 9 A.M.–7 P.M. Fri.–Sat.), at North 6th Street and Columbia Street, and **Hudson River Farm Market** (518/828-0935; 10 A.M.–6 P.M. Sun.–Thurs., 9 A.M.–7 P.M. Fri.–Sat.), at 17 North 4th Street. To the east, near Claverack, you can pick cherries, apples, and strawberries at **Hotalings** (518/851-9864), or apples and pears at **Philip Orchards** (518/851-6351).

Just north of Hudson on Route 9, **Van Wie Natural Foods** (6798 Rte. 9, Hudson, 518/828-0533, www.vanwienaturalmeats .com; 10 A.M.–5 P.M. Tues.–Sat.) offers organic-standard meat, including pork, beef, free range chicken and turkey, lamb, seafood, pheasant, duck, rabbit, goat, and buffalo. All animals are raised without the use of chemicals, hormones, or antibiotics.

Several organic farms set up shop near Germantown in summer. **V. R. Saulpaugh and Sons** (1960 Rte. 9, Germantown, 518/537-6494) grows unusual varieties of eggplant, peppers, and squash.

Deer, buffalo, elk, antelope, and llama are just some of the animals that share the pastures at **Highland Farm** (283 County Rte. 6, Germantown, 518/537-6397). The farm sells venison and smoked venison products, breeds animals for zoos, and shelters endangered species, all under one roof.

INFORMATION AND SERVICES

The **Columbia County Office of Tourism** (401 State St., Hudson, 800/724-1846, www .columbiacountyny.org) has maps and brochures covering the county, as well as the greater Hudson River Valley region. The Columbia County Chamber of Commerce (507 Warren St., Hudson, 518/828-4417, www.columbiachamberny .com) can also provide visitor information.

GETTING THERE AND AROUND
By Bus

Adirondack Trailways (800/858-8555, www .escapemaker.com/adirondacktrailways) stops across the river in the village of Catskill, eight miles from downtown Hudson. Taxis are available, and some hotels offer free shuttle service.

By Train

Hudson is a two-hour train ride away from New York City's Penn Station. The **Amtrak Rail Station** (69 S. Front St., Hudson, 518/355-2287 or 800/872-7245, www.amtrak.com) is located at the water's edge. A one-way ticket from Penn Station to Hudson costs $31–47. You can hop a cab from the train station or rent a car from Enterprise Rent-a-Car.

By Car

From New England, turn off I-90 at Exit B2 to reach the northern end of the Taconic State Parkway, the speediest north–south route through Columbia County. Route 23 crosses northern Columbia County, connecting Hillsdale to Hudson. Route 9 and its many spinoffs form a major commercial corridor along the river, while the more rural Route 22 runs along the base of the Taconic Range at the eastern edge of the county.

THE CAPITAL-SARATOGA REGION

The Capital-Saratoga Region of Albany, Rensselaer County, and Saratoga Springs marks the end of the tidal Hudson River and offers a symbolic bookend to a journey through the Hudson River Valley. After Albany and industrial Troy, the river becomes part of the Champlain Canal before veering west to its origin, high in the Adirondack Mountains.

Henry Hudson reached Albany in September of 1609 and had to turn the 122-ton *Half Moon* around when the river became too shallow. Word spread after that maiden voyage, and Fort Orange became one of the earliest and largest Dutch settlements along the river. Today's state capital is a destination in its own right, but with an international airport and modern train station, the city also serves as a gateway to surrounding towns and wilderness areas.

Across the Hudson River from Albany lies sleepy Rensselaer County, home of the nation's first engineering school, Rensselaer Polytechnic Institute (RPI), two attractive state parks, and a large concentration of Tiffany glass.

Although it's best known for its summer horse racing scene, Saratoga Springs offers a much wider appeal. A charming Victorian-era village is packed with boutique shops selling treasures old and new. Wellness spas, historic homes, a world-class outdoor performing arts theater, and several chefs of Food Network television fame make for a rich and varied travel experience. Apple orchards and art shows also have their place. Ideally situated at the edge of the Adirondack State Park, the largest publicly protected area in the contiguous United States, this small city of 26,000 residents offers hikers

HIGHLIGHTS

◖ **Empire State Plaza:** The centerpiece of downtown Albany is a 98-acre plaza with an impressive collection of art displayed indoors and out (page 218).

◖ **The Capitol Building:** Elaborate stone carvings line the imposing outdoor stairway that leads from the Empire State Plaza to the entrance of New York's state capitol building. Built by hand over a period of 30 years, the building defines the Albany skyline and serves as headquarters for the New York State Assembly (page 219).

◖ **Lark Street and Washington Park:** Downtown Albany has a bohemian enclave at the east end of Washington Park, with several blocks of eclectic boutiques and trendy restaurants (page 219).

◖ **Grafton Lakes State Park:** A pleasant sandy beach and rare peace pagoda draw visitors from near and far to this corner of Rensselaer County (page 232).

◖ **Saratoga Spa State Park:** Natural hot springs, towering pine trees, and an outdoor concert venue are highlights in Saratoga's 2,300-acre park (page 236).

◖ **Saratoga Race Course:** The Saratoga racetrack is the oldest continuously operating thoroughbred track in the U.S., and the town's population triples during the summer racing season (page 237).

◖ **Tang Teaching Museum and Art Gallery:** Skidmore College has opened a state-of-the-art museum dedicated to presenting and teaching contemporary works (page 238).

LOOK FOR ◖ TO FIND RECOMMENDED SIGHTS, ACTIVITIES, DINING, AND LODGING.

and backpackers convenient access to supplies and outfitters. Lake George is just 30 minutes farther up the Northway (I-87) for summer swimming and boating.

PLANNING YOUR TIME

One day allows plenty of time to explore most of downtown Albany, but you'll need extra time to schedule a tour of the Capitol Building or Executive Mansion. Popular Albany itineraries include dinner downtown followed by an evening event at the Times Union Center (Pepsi Arena), a weekend of historic colonial sights, or a day of holiday shopping at the malls.

Rensselaer County is easily explored in a day or two of driving scenic back roads. The drive from Albany to Saratoga Springs should take about half an hour with light traffic; however, a large number of government workers commute into Albany each day, so be sure to time your drive to avoid the rush. Ideal as a weekend getaway, Saratoga Springs can also work well as a side trip from Lake George, or as a day of civilization before or after a multi-day hike through the Adirondack backcountry.

THE CAPITAL-SARATOGA REGION

CAPITAL-SARATOGA REGION

Adirondack

WARREN
SARATOGA
Park

Lake
George

Lake
George

Fort Ann

Conklingville

Lake
Luzerne

Glens
Falls

Hudson Falls

Northville

Corinth

Fort Edward

FULTON
MONTGOMERY
Sacandaga

Batchellerville

Mayfield

Great
Sacandaga
Lake

Salem

East
Galway

TANG TEACHING MUSEUM
AND ART GALLERY

Saratoga
Springs

Schuylerville

Greenwich

SARATOGA
RACE COURSE

Broadalbin

SARATOGA SPA
STATE PARK

Ballston
Spa

Saratoga
Lake

Amsterdam

SARATOGA

Malta

Bemis
Heights

Buskirk

WASHINGTON
RENSSELAER

Minaville

MONTGOMERY

East
Glenville

Mechanicville

Hoosick
Falls

Schaghticoke

Schoharie Creek

Rotterdam

Mohawk River

Tomhannock
Reservoir

Pittstown

Delanson

SCHENECTADY
ALBANY

Gifford

Cohoes

GRAFTON LAKES
STATE PARK

Berne

Loudonville

Cropseyville

LARK STREET

Troy

Berlin

ALBANY

WASHINGTON PARK

Delmar

EMPIRE
STATE PLAZA

Averill
Park

Cherry Plain
State Park

THE CAPITOL
BUILDING

MA

Clarksville

SCOHARIE

Stephentown

0   5 mi
0   5 km

Nassau

RENSSELAER
COLUMBIA

Pittsfield
State Forest

Preston
Hollow

Alcove Reservoir

Ravena

ALBANY
GREENE

East
Chatham

© AVALON TRAVEL

Albany

From names like Ten Broeck to its annual tulip festival, New York's capital city retains much of its early Dutch roots. As the New York State capital since 1797, the city has also preserved much of its 19th- and 20th-century architecture. Walk a few of the city's historic blocks and you'll find many examples of the Italianate, Federal, and Greek Revival styles, in conditions ranging from perfectly restored to borderline run-down.

Albany today contains an appealing mix of architectural masterpieces, art collections, and historic sights. Meanwhile, students from several area colleges support a vibrant sports and nightlife scene. With a population of 100,000, the city is large enough to offer a rich urban experience, but compact enough that you can tour the downtown in a day. Unfortunately however, many parts of Albany have yet to recover from the economic turmoil of the mid-20th century. As a result, showy state government buildings alternate with equally powerful signs of urban decay.

DOWNTOWN ALBANY

The modern Empire State Plaza and giant Times Union Center (Pepsi Arena) have done much to revitalize downtown Albany since most of its factories shut down in the 1950s; however, the new and restored buildings contrast sharply with the low-income neighborhoods that surround them. City leaders are targeting the dynamic technology industry— from nanotechnology to fuel cells—as a key source of future economic growth.

The majority of visitors find themselves in Albany for one of three reasons: a business convention, a school field trip, or a concert or sporting event. Whatever the draw, it's well worth the time to absorb a slice of New York state history while you're in town.

◖ Empire State Plaza

The centerpiece of downtown Albany is the 98-acre Empire State Plaza (State St.), where most of the government's 11,000 employees show up for work each day. Ten dazzling skyscrapers surround an open plaza and fountain, including the Corning Tower, which at 42 stories is the state's highest building outside New York City.

In the 1960s, then-governor Nelson A. Rockefeller envisioned an architectural wonder and cultural center that would bring jobs and visitors to downtown Albany again. He commissioned Wallace Harrison, the same architect who built Rockefeller Center, and construction began in 1965. Thirteen years later, the city had a gorgeous new public space. The best view in town is found atop the **Corning Tower Observation Deck** (42nd floor of the Corning Tower, off the Empire Plaza exit in Albany, 518/474-2418; 10 A.M.–2:30 P.M. daily).

One of the most unusual sights on the plaza is a sculpture-like building called **The Egg** (Empire State Plaza, 518/473-1061, www.theegg .org), a custom-built performing arts center with two theaters and state-of-the-art acoustics.

Key to Rockefeller's vision was the incorporation of art into public spaces. (His mother, Abby Aldrich Rockefeller, had been instrumental in the founding of the Museum of Modern Art in New York City.) Accordingly, scattered throughout the plaza, inside and out, are pieces of the impressive **New York State Art Collection** (2978 Corning Tower, 1 Empire State Plaza, 518/473-7521; 6 A.M.–6 P.M. Mon.–Fri.), featuring the work of New York State artists from the 1960s and 1970s. It is considered one of the most important collections of modern art in the country.

Currently, there are 92 paintings, sculptures, and tapestries displayed on the concourse, in building lobbies, and in outdoor spaces. The collection is especially strong in abstract art. Alexander Caldwell and Mark Rothko are among the best-known artists in the collection. Visitors may view the works anytime government offices are open.

The **Plaza Information Office** (518/ 474-2418), located off the main concourse, near The Egg, has information on maps and tours. Additional information booths are located at the north and south ends of the concourse. Take the Empire Plaza exit from I-787. There are several visitor parking lots around the plaza on Madison and Grand Streets. Rates range from $5–7 per day up to $1/hr. (max. $10/day).

New York State Museum

At the south end of the plaza, the New York State Museum (Madison Ave., 518/474-5877, www.nysm.nysed.gov; 9:30 A.M.–5 P.M. daily; suggested donation $2) began in 1836 as a center for geological and natural history exhibits. Over the years, it has maintained a core focus on geology, biology, anthropology, and history as they relate to the state. A photography exhibit in 2004 commemorated the 35th anniversary of the 1969 Woodstock Music Festival (see *The Western Catskills* for more information on Woodstock).

The Executive Mansion

Governor Pataki lives in the New York Executive Mansion (138 Eagle St., 518/473-7521), one block south of the Empire State Plaza. The home was built in the 1850s and has housed governors and their families since 1875, including Theodore and Franklin Delano Roosevelt. Public rooms contain exquisite artwork and furnishings from the 18th, 19th, and 20th centuries. Guided tours are offered at noon, 1 P.M., and 2 P.M. on Thursdays, except during the month of July (reservations required).

❰ The Capitol Building

The capitol building (Washington Ave., 518/474-2418) that towers over State Street hill, adjacent to the north end of the Empire State Plaza, looks more like a European castle than a U.S. state capitol. A stunning set of stairs climbs up to three grand archways, featuring elaborate stone carvings. Construction began by hand in 1867 and took 30 years to complete, by which time Theodore Roosevelt had become governor. The final price tag was an astronomical $25 million.

The New York State Assembly conducts its business inside. You can take a guided tour of the building at 10 A.M., noon, 2 P.M. and 3 P.M. Monday–Friday, and at 11 A.M., 1 P.M., and 3 P.M. on weekends. It's closed holidays. A number of lively inns and restaurants are clustered along State Street, within a short walk for business travelers and midweek lunch-goers.

From the Empire State Plaza, it is a short walk down State Street to Broadway and one of Albany's newest outdoor spaces: the **Hudson River Way** is a pedestrian bridge that crosses over I-787 to **Albany Riverfront Park,** in the Corning Preserve (518/434-2032), where residents come to walk their dogs or read a book on warm afternoons. Along the path are a series of murals depicting Albany's long and colorful history.

Follow Broadway a few blocks farther north to reach the **Albany Heritage Area Visitors Center** (Clinton Ave. and Broadway, 800/258-3582; 9 A.M.–4 P.M. Mon.–Fri., 10 A.M.–4 P.M. Sat.–Sun.), a good place to get an overview of the history and culture of the Capital Region.

From there, it's a short drive to the handsome **Ten Broeck Mansion** (9 Ten Broeck Pl., 518/436-9826, www.tenbroeck.org; 10 A.M.–4 P.M. Thurs.–Fri., 1–4 P.M. Sat.–Sun. May–Dec.; adults $5) where the Albany County Historical Association has set up shop. The Federal-style home was originally built by Abraham Ten Broeck, a distinguished general and statesman who fought at the Battle of Saratoga and later served as mayor of Albany. More than two decades after the wealthy Olcott family had donated the renovated building to the city, museum staff discovered a fully stocked wine cellar in the basement. Many of the surrounding buildings in the once-exclusive Arbor Hill district have been converted into urban apartments.

❰ Lark Street and Washington Park

Many of Albany's events, including the popular spring tulip festival, take place in Washington Park (www.washingtonparkconservancy.com), a 90-acre green space in the center of the city that has been public property since the 17th century. Jogging trails circle a small lake and a handful of statues and monuments across the park. A bronze statue of Scottish poet Robert Burns was created by a local sculptor in 1888. The King Fountain was made of rocks from Storm King Mountain in Orange County. Though the park is well loved, it's rarely crowded, and students can always find a quiet place to read. Playgrounds are a draw for kids.

At the east end of the park, bohemian Lark Street is Albany's answer to Manhattan's East Village and San Francisco's Haight-Ashbury. This is the neighborhood of choice for Friday drinks or Sunday brunch. Several blocks of shops and restaurants between State and Madison streets got a fresh new look in 2003. You'll find everything from cozy cafés to chic new establishments serving Kobe beef.

The historic Center Square neighborhood, bound by Lark, State, Swan, and Jay streets, connects the Lark Street district to the Empire State Plaza. Stroll through its quiet streets to see rows of brick, brownstone, and clapboard houses more than 100 years old.

Albany Institute of History and Art

For a lasting impression of Hudson Valley history and culture, head to one of the oldest museums in the United States. Older than the Smithsonian, the Metropolitan Museum of Art, and the Louvre, the Albany Institute of History and Art (125 Washington Ave., 518/463-4478, www.albanyinstitute.org; 10 A.M.–5 P.M. Wed.–Sat., noon–5 P.M. Sun.; adults $8, seniors and students $6, children (6–12) $4, under 5 free) dates back to 1791. The museum has increasingly broadened its focus over the years to include Hudson River School paintings, artifacts from colonial times, and 19th-century American sculpture.

Schuyler Mansion

Major General Philip Schuyler's home (32 Catherine St., 518/434-0834, http://nysparks.state .ny.us/sites/info.asp?siteID=27; 11 A.M.–5 P.M. Wed.–Sun. mid-Apr.–Oct., 11 A.M.–5 P.M. Tues.–Sun. June–Aug., 10 A.M.–4 P.M. Mon.– Fri. Nov.–Mar. by appointment only) was an important base of operations during the Revolutionary War and is now a New York state historic site. Tours begin on the hour and the last tour begins at 4 P.M.

USS Slater

After a 10-year restoration, the last remaining World War II *Destroyer Escort,* once part of a fleet of more than 500 ships, now rests on the Hudson River at the Port of Albany. In summer, the *USS Slater* is open for guided tours (141 Broadway, Albany, 518/431-1943, www.ussslater.org; Apr.–Nov. Wed. –Sun. 10 A.M.–4 P.M.; adults $7, seniors $6, children 6–14 $5, under 6 free). In winter, it moves one mile south to Rensselaer.

ALBANY COUNTY
Historic Cherry Hill

South of downtown Albany, Historic Cherry Hill (523 1/2 South Pearl St., 518/434-4791, www.historiccherryhill.org; Tues.–Sun. Apr.– Dec. by guided tour; adults $4, seniors $3, students $2, children $1) was once the center of a

USS Slater **destroyer on the Hudson**

working farm that belonged to the Van Rensselaer family. A hodgepodge of collections inside the 1787 Colonial-style home document the lives of four generations of the family, ending with Catherine Bogart Putnam Rankin, the great-granddaughter of Philip and Maria Van Rensselaer. On display are ceramics, silver, textiles, books, and photographs.

The home is also known as the site of a famous murder in 1827. Author Louis C. Jones chronicled the story in a book called *Murder at Cherry Hill* and also referred to the murder in a better-known book of ghost stories, *Things That Go Bump in the Night.* From I-787, take Exit 2.

Watervliet Shaker Historic District

In the shadow of the Albany airport stands an intriguing slice of history, the Watervliet Shaker Historic District and the site of the first American Shaker settlement (875 Watervliet Shaker Rd., 518/456-7890; 9:30 A.M.–4 P.M. Tues.–Sat. Feb.–Oct., 10 A.M.–4 P.M. Mon.–Sat. Nov.–Dec.). The first group of Shakers arrived here in 1776 with the founder of the movement, Ann Lee, and built a log cabin as the first communal dwelling. Over the years, the community grew to 350 people, and the last members left the site in 1938.

Visitors can explore several buildings, beginning with a museum in the 1848 Shaker Meeting House. Outside are an herb garden, barnyard, and network of trails around a nature preserve. Lee and other early members are buried in the Shaker Cemetery on the property. Guided tours are offered at 11:30 A.M. and 1:30 P.M. Saturdays June–October.

John Boyd Thacher State Park

A short drive farther west, John Boyd Thacher State Park (1 Hailes Cave Rd., Voorheesville, 518/872-1237; 8 A.M.–dusk daily; admission $6) encompasses the Helderberg Escarpment, a six-mile-long limestone cliff that contains billion-year-old fossils and rock formations. Even amateur geologists will be able to spot the distinct change in rock formations as they

© NIKKI GOTH ITOI

Shaker family barn and church

climb and descend the staircases of the Indian Ladder, an 80-foot cliff on top of the escarpment. This geological wonder leads one back to the time when the area surrounding Albany was covered by a warm tropical sea. For an informative geology lesson, call to sign up for a guided tour with the park interpreter (518/872-0800).

Besides the geological wonders, the park offers panoramic views of the Adirondack and Berkshire Mountains and of Vermont's Green Mountains. Twelve miles of trails accommodate hiking, mountain biking, cross-country skiing, snowshoeing, and snowmobiling. Also on the premises are an Olympic-sized swimming pool, basketball and volleyball courts, playgrounds, ball fields, and picnic areas.

Rensselaerville

In the southwest corner of Albany County lies the 200-year-old hamlet of Rensselaerville (not to be confused with the Rensselaer County city of Rensselaer), named for the Dutch patron who ran the local manor. Due to its remote location, the site was settled relatively late by colonial standards—in the 1780s—by Revolutionary War veterans from Long Island and New England. A number of handsome 19th-century buildings have been preserved along Main Street. Today, they house a mix of antique shops and restaurants. To get to Rensselaerville, take I-90 to Exit/Route 85 West and follow Route 85 for 12 miles.

SPORTS AND RECREATION
Winter Sports

Hockey and figure skating are popular winter activities in the Albany area. Empire State Plaza and Albany County Hockey Training Facility have rinks with public skate sessions. Nordic skiers will find trails at John Boyd Thacher State Park and at the 400-acre Five Rivers Environmental Education Center (56 Game Farm Rd., Delmar, 518/475-0291, www.dec.state.ny.us/website/education/5river.html). And for downhill skiers, Windham and Hunter Mountains are a half hour away (see the *Upper Hudson* chapter).

Albany yachts

Hiking

Four short hiking trails loop through John Boyd Thacher State Park, ranging 0.9–2.5 miles in length. The park also marks the northern terminus for the 326-mile Long Path, named for a line in a famous Walt Whitman poem, *Song of the Open Road:*

> Afoot and light-hearted I take to the open road, Healthy, free, the world before me, The long brown path before me leading wherever I choose.

The Long Path begins at the George Washington Bridge and meanders across the Hudson River Valley, eventually entering the park from the west.

Cycling

The 41-mile-long Hudson-Mohawk Bikeway connects Albany, Schenectady, and Troy along the Hudson and Mohawk Rivers. Call 518/372-5656 or 800/962-8007 for a free map. The **Mohawk Hudson Cycling Club** organizes road and mountain biking trips within an 80-mile radius of the Albany-Schenectady-Troy area, including a September Century Weekend that begins in Saratoga Spa State Park and Mountain Bike Festival at **Grafton Lakes State Park** (61 North Long Pond Rd., Grafton, 518/279-1155) outside of Troy.

In addition, several hundred cyclists participate each summer in the **Cycling the Erie Canal Tour** (518/434-1583, www.ptny.org/canaltour; $520), an eight-day ride from Buffalo to Albany covering roughly 50 miles a day. The fee includes camping, meals, entertainment, and riding support. In its 10th year in 2008, the event is sponsored by Parks & Trails New York, a local nonprofit.

Stop by the **Down Tube Cycle Shop** (466 Madison Ave., Albany, 518/434-1711) in a convenient downtown location, for gear and information.

Golf

Capital Hills at Albany (65 O'Neil Rd., 518/438-2208; $24), designed in 1929, maintains a challenging public course (18 holes) with tough closing holes and considerable elevation change. Rent a cart unless you're looking for a cardio workout. Ten miles north of Albany, **Mill Road Acres Golf Course** (30 Mill Rd., Latham, 518/785-4653, www.millroadacres.com; weekdays 9 holes $13.50, 18 holes $18.50; weekends 9 holes $17, 18 holes $23) has a well-maintained nine-hole course.

You can mix and match the four nine-hole courses at the **Town of Colonie Golf Course** (418 Consaul Rd., Schenectady, 518/374-4181; www.colonie.org/parks/golf; weekdays 9 holes $15, 18 holes $20; weekends 9 holes $17, 18 holes $22). The Red/White course combination has water hazards on six holes.

Swimming and Boating

Dutch Apple Cruises (Madison and Broadway, Albany, 518/463-0220, www.dutchapplecruises.com) operates several cruises per week from Snow Dock in the Port of Albany.

ACCOMMODATIONS

Albany's many business hotels are clustered downtown and near the airport. Unique properties are more difficult but not impossible to come by. Look near Washington Park and the Empire State Plaza.

Under $100

In 1997, Rensselaerville residents Steve and Marlene Omlor restored an 1806 home to create the **Catalpa House B&B** (Main St., Rensselaerville, 518/797-3484, www.catalpahouse.com; $65–90), named for a giant Catalpa tree that stands on the front lawn. The inn has six country-style rooms, two of which have private baths. The reasonable rates include breakfast and afternoon tea.

$100-150

In the shadow of the state capitol buildings, the **State Street Mansion Bed & Breakfast** (281 State St., Albany, 518/462-6780 or 800/673-5750, www.statestreetmansion.com; $125–150) is a three-story brownstone B&B with 12 amply furnished rooms and off-street parking. Smaller doubles with private bath run $125/night, while larger rooms with two queens go for $150/night. Cable TV, wireless Internet, and continental breakfast included.

Two heated pools and a day spa are among the modern amenities at ☿ **The Desmond** (660 Albany Shaker Rd., 518/869-8100 or 800/448-3500, www.desmondhotelsalbany .com; $120–185), primarily a business hotel and conference center with well-appointed rooms in a complex of brick colonial buildings. There are two restaurants on-site: Scrimshaw serves steak au poivre, veal Oscar, and cedar-plank salmon in an 80-seat dining room, while Simpson's is a casual venue for all-American fare. Weekend packages include rooms and meals at discounted rates. Take Exit I-87 to Exit 4.

$150-200

One block from the state capitol and the Pepsi Arena, the **Crowne Plaza Albany City Center** (corner of State St. & Lodge St., 518/462-6611 or 800/227-6963, www.cpalbany.com; $190–260) is one of the largest business hotels in downtown Albany. The facility includes 384 modern rooms on 15 floors, plus a health club and business center. High-speed Internet is a plus at the eight-story **Albany Marriott** (189 Wolf Rd., 518/458-8444 or 800/443-8952 www.marriott.com; $299), a 350-room establishment located four miles from downtown.

Among the most posh in Albany accommodations is the four-room ☿ **Morgan State House** (393 State St., www.statehouse.com; $135–260), where feather beds, robes, and down comforters make for a cozy night's stay. A 12-foot ceiling with skylights makes room No. 4B one of the best in the house.

74 State (74 State St.,518/434-7410, www.74state.com; $155–265) is a boutique hotel with 74 rooms—some with city views.

FOOD

There are hundreds of restaurants to choose from in the Albany metropolitan area. A steady stream of politicians and financial executives support a diverse and upscale restaurant scene downtown.

Surf and Turf

One of the oldest establishments is ☿ **Jack's Oyster House** (42 State St., 518/465-8854; www.jacksoysterhouse.com; 11:30 A.M.–10 P.M. daily; mains $19–27), a turn-of-the-20th-century tavern with a dark wood interior that creates a formal but not stuffy air. At the busy lunch hour, waiters dressed in snappy uniforms whisk about the dining room carrying trays of fresh oysters from the raw bar. Steaks pair well with the restaurant's private-label red wine from Silverado Vineyards in California.

For French cuisine in a romantic setting, make reservations at **Nicole's Bistro** (25 Quackenbush Sq. at Broadway, 518/465-1111; lunch Mon.–Fri., dinner Mon.–Sat.; mains $19–28 or $28 prix fixe), at the Quackenbush House. In summer, courtyard dining next to a colonial herb garden is a plus. The restaurant also hosts occasional cigar nights.

Inside the Hampton Inn & Suites, the award-winning **Yono's Restaurant** (25 Chapel St., 518/436-7747, www.yonosrestaurant .com; dinner Mon.–Sat.; mains $18–36) serves a blend of Indonesian and Continental cuisine. Chef Yono also oversees the more casual **dp An American Brasserie** (www.dpbrasserie.com; lunch and dinner Mon.–Sat.; mains $10–20), with a menu of small plates, steak *frites,* main plate salads, and burgers.

Angelo's 677 Prime (677 Broadway at Clinton Ave., 518/427-7463, www.677prime .com; lunch 11:30 A.M.–2 P.M. Mon.–Fri., dinner 5:30–10 P.M. Mon.–Sat., bar menu available 2–10 P.M.) is an upscale steakhouse and wine bar centrally located in Albany's theater district. Chopped or wedge salads, caviar, and a full raw bar complement a menu of Kobe beef, steak *au poivre,* and a 40-ounce Porterhouse for two. You can also start with French onion soup or lobster bisque, and order the potato of your choice. Live music plays Wednesday–Saturday 6:30–10 P.M.

Southern cuisine defines the menu at **Magnolias On the Park** (462 Madison Ave., 518/449-2492, www.magnoliasonthepark .com; mains $16–22), which ranked second only to Hattie's Chicken Shack in Saratoga for best southern/soul food in the Capital Region. Choose among baby back ribs, pan-fried Georgia catfish, and of course, the classic buttermilk fried chicken.

Taverns and Pubs

Three-story **DeJohn's Restaurant and Pub** (288 Lark St., 518/465-5275, www.dejohns .com; lunch 11:30 A.M.–4 P.M. Sat.–Sun., dinner 4–11 P.M. Sun.–Thurs., 4 P.M.–midnight Fri.–Sat.; mains $17–20) has a basement sports bar and rear patio. The middle level is a casual restaurant serving trout and several vegetarian options. The top floor has a banquet room. Owner John DeJohn also runs **Justin's** (301 Lark St., Albany, 518/436-7008; www .justinsonlark.com; 11:30–1 A.M. Mon.–Fri., 11–1 A.M. Sat.–Sun., mains $17–23), an eclectic basement restaurant with a small street-side patio that is packed at almost any time of day on the weekend. The bar stays open till 4 A.M. daily. The corned-beef hash is deserving of its reputation. Wicker furniture, dim lighting, and dark paint won't detract from the experience of eating the *ropa vieja* sandwich made of braised Cuban brisket.

There are only two river-based restaurants in the Capital Region: The 11-year-old **RiverFront Bar & Grill** (Corning Preserve, 518/426-4738; open seasonally, call for hours; mains $12–18) in Albany and the **Rusty Anchor** (1 Selke Drive, Watervliet, 518/273-2920; 11:30–2 A.M. Mon.–Fri., noon–2 A.M. Sat.–Sun.; mains $8–12) in Watervliet, both run on floating barges and modeled on the successful Gully's restaurant at the Newburgh Landing.

Italian

More than 100 Italian restaurants are scattered across the Albany area, and a few of them manage to rise above the crowd: Locals choose (**Lombardo's** (121 Madison Ave., 518/462-9180; 11 A.M.–2 P.M. and 4–11 P.M. Mon.–Fri., 3–11 P.M. Sat.) for delicious and reasonably priced Italian fare. For northern Italian convenient to downtown, grab a table at **Café Capriccio** (49 Grand St., 518/465-0439;

OUTDOOR DINING IN ALBANY AND SARATOGA SPRINGS

ALBANY
- Ballinger's
- Bayou Cafe
- DeJohn's
- Elda's
- Envy Lounge
- Franklin's Tower
- Jillian's
- Justin's
- McGeary's
- Provence
- Real Seafood Co.
- Scratch Bakery Café
- Tess' Lark Tavern
- Totem Sushi
- Victory Cafe
- Yono's/DP

SARATOGA SPRINGS
- Chianti
- Forno Toscana
- Stadium Café
- Uncommon Grounds
- Wheatfields

5:30–10 P.M. Mon.–Thurs., 5:30–11 P.M. Fri.–Sat., 5:30–9 P.M. Sun.).

After a day of shopping, super-sized plates of pasta and giant bottles of chianti define the southern Italian experience at **Buca di Beppo** (44

Wolff Rd., Colonie, 518/459-2822 www.buca dibeppo.com; 11 A.M.–10 P.M. Mon.–Thurs., 11 A.M.–11 P.M. Fri.–Sat., 11 A.M.–9 P.M. Sun.; mains $15–25), outside of Albany.

International

Albany also has its share of exotic cuisine, including **Shalimar Restaurant** (31 Central Ave., 518/434-0890) for Indian or **Mr. Pio Pio** (160 Quail St., 866/501-1675, www.mrpiopio. com; mains $10) for Ecuadorian.

El Mariachi (locations at 289 Hamilton St., 518/432-7580, and 52 Central Ave., 518/465-2568; 11 A.M.–10 P.M. Mon.–Fri., 1–10 P.M. Sat.–Sun.) serves authentic Mexican fare in two downtown Albany locations. The full tequila bar and homemade sangria are a plus. Locals prefer the cheap eats and Ms. Pac-Man game at ◖ **Bombers Burrito Bar** (258 Lark St., 518/463-9636; www.bombersburrito bar.com; 11–2 A.M. Sun.–Wed., 11–3 A.M. Thurs.–Sat.; mains $6–8).

Nightclub Restaurants

Restaurants that turn into nightclubs are a growing trend in Albany. Some patrons like the high-energy atmosphere; others feel rushed and overwhelmed when the DJ starts to spin.

Crab and lobster frangelico, filet mignon, and lobster-stuffed shrimp are among newer entrées on the dinner menu at **Pearl Restaurant & Lounge** (1 Steuben Pl. on South Pearl St., 518/433-0011, www.pearlalbany.com; lunch 11 A.M.–4 P.M. Mon.–Fri., dinner 5–9 P.M. Mon.–Wed., 5–10 P.M. Thurs.–Sat.; lunch mains $8–12, dinner mains $16–26). Prices are moderate for the high quality of the food, and the restaurant offers free valet parking.

Newcomer Envy Lounge (99 Pine St., Albany, 518/694-3689, www.envyalbany.com) offers a full menu of martinis and other cocktails for $8–12. But among the local set, the club gets higher marks for its food than its music. For example, "new school macaroni and cheese" consists of butter-poached lobster with manchego and mascarpone cheese, while pan-seared scallops are accompanied by basil whipped potatoes, slivered black truffles, con-

fetti sweet potatoes, white truffle oil, and lavender honey.

Cafés and Quick Bites

With 50 years of experience, **Bob and Ron's Fish Fry** (1007 Central Ave., 518/482-9747) does seafood right. Impatient locals will stand in line forever for a basket of fish and chips. Meanwhile, **Paesan's** (289 Ontario St., 518/435-0312, www.paesanspizza.com; 11–12:30 A.M. daily; mains $7–11) has mastered the art of the thin-crust pizza. Most weekdays, a host of vendors congregate on the lawn behind the Capitol Building serving lunch to go. A slice of pizza or a couple of tacos are among the best deals around.

In business since 1976, **The Daily Grind** (204 Lark St., 888/876-3222, www.dailygrind .com; 7 A.M.–10 P.M. Mon.–Sat., till 8 P.M. Sun.) is a European-style coffee bar and café that roasts its own beans.

Culinary Events

Twice a year since 2004, the Downtown Albany Business Improvement District has organized Restaurant Week, inviting thousands of restaurant-goers to enjoy a three-course meal at participating eateries across the city for $16.09 per person. The price reflects the year that Henry Hudson first set foot in Albany. Some of the city's most upscale establishments participate, including Marché, Nicole's Bistro, Jack's Oyster House, the Mansion Hill Inn, and Pearl Restaurant & Lounge. Search the dining section of www.downtownalbany.org for information.

If you're visiting in August, check the calendar for the **Empire State Plaza Food Festival,** a one-day event including more than 70 food vendors and live music (www .www.ogs.state.ny.us/visiting/cultural/events/ Summer2007Food.html). Another new food-themed event is the **Wine & Dine** series, which focuses on award-winning or hard-to-find wines paired with a special menu for the evening. The event rotates to various upscale restaurants around town, including Marché, Envy Lounge, and Angelo's 677 Prime to date. Contact sponsor SMB Selections (518/452-6049, www.smdselections.com).

Learn techniques for grilling and how to cook with farm fresh ingredients at **Mezzo Marketplace & Eatery** (340 Hamilton St., 518/463-6240, www.mezzomarket.com; $60). Mezzo Cooks classes are held on Tuesday evenings beginning at 6:30 P.M. Book ahead, as classes have become popular and fill up quickly.

ENTERTAINMENT AND EVENTS
Performing Arts
The twin theaters inside **The Egg** (Empire State Plaza, 518/473-1061, www.theegg.org) show theater, dance, music, and comedy. **Spectrum 8 Theatres** (290 Delaware Ave., 518/449-8995, www.spectrum8.com; adults $8.50, seniors $6.75, children 13 and under $5.50) is the place to catch an indie film along with some of the best movie snacks around.

Founded in 1931, the **Albany Symphony Orchestra** (19 Clinton Ave., 518/465-4755, www.albanysymphony.com) plays at the Palace Theatre near Quackenbush Square. Its programs often emphasize contemporary or overlooked American works.

Bars and Nightlife
Albany boasts a colorful nightlife scene, with many bars and clubs along Pearl Street and Lark Street. The free alternative weekly *Metroland* (www.metroland.net) covers Capital Region happenings in exhaustive detail. Copies are available at many bars, restaurants, and convenience stores, and on many street corners.

Steps away from the Pepsi Arena, the martini bar at **Pearl Restaurant & Lounge** (1 Steuben Pl. on South Pearl St., 518/433-0011, www.pearlalbany.com) is open till midnight on school nights, 1 A.M. on Thursdays, and 4 A.M. on most weekend nights.

Jillian's (59 N. Pearl St., 518/432-1997; 11–1 A.M. Mon.–Wed., 11–3 A.M. Thurs.–Sat., 11:30–1 A.M. Sun.; mains $8–14) is a three-story complex with a bar on each floor, plus a video café, dance floor, and numerous large-

screen TVs. You'll find a wider-than-average selection of standard pub fare on the menu. A block away is the **The Skyline,** also three floors, with pool tables and a third-floor dance club that often has an additional cover charge.

It's standing room only most nights at **Mahar's Public Bar** (1110 Madison Ave., 518/459-9416; 4 P.M.–midnight Mon.–Sat.), near Washington Park. Beer aficionados are crazy about this tiny pub with a bar, limited seating, and old taps on the wall. There are 25 beers on tap and 300 bottles to choose from at any given time. Regulars keep their own mug on a shelf by the bar, and a free T-shirt goes to anyone who tries 50 different brews. Computerized menus keep track of which ones you've already sampled. Five hundred tastings get you a plaque on the wall. The food menu is intentionally limited.

Choose from among 30 wines by the glass and 160 bottles at **The Ginger Man** (234 Western Ave., 518/427-5963, www.albany gingerman.com; lunch 11:30 A.M.–4 P.M. Mon.–Fri., dinner 4–11:30 P.M. Mon.–Thurs., 4 P.M.–12:30 A.M. Fri., 4:30 P.M.–12:30 A.M. Sat.), a wine bar near Washington Park. Justin's Café (301 Lark St., 518/436-7008) draws a steady late-night crowd as well.

Live bands often play at the **Lark Street Tavern** (453 Madison Ave., 518/463-9779,

FOUR HUNDRED YEARS AND COUNTING

In 2009, communities up and down the Hudson River will celebrate the 400th anniversary of Henry Hudson's trip up the river from Manhattan to present-day Albany, as well as the 200th anniversary of Robert Fulton's steamship voyage on the Hudson.

Festivities are in the works for New York and Amsterdam, plus a celebratory transatlantic voyage to commemorate the event. Visit www.henryhudson.com for details.

www.larktavern.com). A more refined alternative for live music is **The Larkin Lounge** (199 Lark St., 518/463-5225), which hosts local and national performances, including a Wednesday-night piano bar.

Festivals

For almost 60 years, Albany residents have celebrated their Dutch heritage with the annual **Albany Tulip Festival** (Washington Park, 518/434-2032 www.albanyevents.org/tulip_festival), which coincides each year with Mother's Day in May. Sample an array of foods and live music while you admire the massive display of flowers. For one Saturday each September, trendy Lark Street closes to traffic to host a wildly popular street fair, called **Larkfest,** with music, food, and entertainment.

Spectator Sports

Before visiting Albany, check the **Times Union Center** (formerly the Pepsi Arena, 51 South Pearl St., Albany, 518/487-2000, www.pepsi arena.com) website for upcoming events. You might be able to catch a monster truck show, the latest mega-concert, or an NBA game.

The arena is the home to the AHL (American Hockey League) River Rats, Albany Conquest (arena football), and the Siena Saints college basketball team.

Performing Arts

The Rolling Stones once played at the **Palace Performing Arts Center** (19 Clinton Ave., 518/465-3334, www.palacealbany.com; $5), a restored 1933 theater.

Recent performances at **The Egg** (Empire State Plaza, 518/473-1061, www.theegg.org), have included Golden Dragon Chinese Acrobats, Hot Tuna, and Steven Wright.

SHOPPING

Albany-area shopping malls draw consumers from hours away for a healthy dose of retail therapy. With anchor stores including Macy's, Lord & Taylor, Filene's, and JC Penney, the **Crossgates Mall** (1 Crossgates Mall Rd., Guilderland, 518/869-9565, www.shop crossgates.com; 10 A.M.–9:30 P.M. Mon.–Sat., 11 A.M.–6 P.M. Sun.), in Guilderland, a suburb of Albany, bills itself as the largest mall in New York State. For a funkier selection of clothing and

pumpkins for sale

locally made crafts, head to the shops on Lark Street in Albany. Among the many boutiques and antique shops is **Elissa Halloran Designs** (229 Lark St., 518/432-7090, www.ehdesigns.com; 11 A.M.–6 P.M. Tues.–Wed. and Sat., 11 A.M.–7 P.M. Thurs.–Fri., noon–5 P.M. Sun.), which carries women's apparel and handmade jewelry.

Bookstores

The Book House of Stuyvesant Plaza (Western Ave. and Fuller Rd., 518/489-4761, www.bhny.com; 10 A.M.–9 P.M. Mon.–Fri., 10 A.M.–6 P.M. Sat., noon–5 P.M. Sun.) is a reliable independent bookstore featuring local authors in Albany's Stuyvesant Plaza strip mall.

Farm Stands

After checking out the Helderberg Escarpment, pay a visit to **Indian Ladder Farms** (342 Altamont Rd., Altamont, 518/765-2956, www.indianladderfarms.com; 9 A.M.–6 P.M. daily) to pick your own apples, raspberries, and blueberries. You can also pick your own strawberries at **Altamont Orchards** (6654 Dunnsville Rd., Altamont, 518/861-6515, www.altamontorchards.com). **W.F. Ryan Produce** (114 Railroad Ave. Extension, between the Northway Mall and Filler Rd., Colonie, 518/459-5776, www.ryansproduce.com; 8 A.M.–6 P.M. Mon.–Fri., 7 A.M.–6 P.M. Sat., 11 A.M.–5 P.M. Sun.) is an indoor farmers market that stays open year-round.

INFORMATION AND SERVICES

The **Albany Visitor Center** (25 Quackenbush Sq., 518/434-1217 or 800/258-3582, www.albany.org; 9 A.M.–4 P.M. Mon.–Fri., 10 A.M.–4 P.M. Sat.–Sun.) has a wealth of information on local attractions.

GETTING THERE AND AROUND

As a major transportation hub for the Catskill and Capital Regions, Albany is easily reached by air, train, car, or bus. Many residents as far south as Dutchess County prefer to fly in and out of Albany International Airport than fight traffic around the New York City airports.

By Bus

Dozens of local bus lines serve the Albany metro area. Check the **Capital District Transportation Authority** website (www.cdta.org) for current routes and schedules.

By Train

One of the most pleasant ways to get from New York City to the Capital Region is to board an **Amtrak** (800/USA-RAIL, www.amtrak.com) train at Penn Station and follow the Hudson River for two hours north. Be sure to get a seat on the left side to catch the views the whole way north. Cabs are readily available from the Rensselaer Station (East St., Rensselaer).

By Car

Albany is a major metropolitan area with heavy traffic during commuting hours. I-87 and I-787 are the main north-south highways. The Albany Airport is Exit 13N on I-87. You can rent a car from all the major chains at the Albany Airport.

Rensselaer County

Look at a Grandma Moses painting and you will have a good idea of the atmosphere of much of eastern Rensselaer County, which contrasts greatly with the formerly industrial towns along the Hudson on the western border of the county. The Taconics, Berkshires, and Green Mountains provide the backdrop for the pastoral setting of the east while the cities of Troy and Rensselaer hug the Hudson.

The Van Rensselaer family were the original patroons of the area around Albany and their name graces not only the county but the town and the original engineering school in this country—Rensselaer Polytechnic Institute (RPI). This premier institution was founded in a city that once made detachable men's shirt collars—there was an Arrow Factory in town, and by 1925, 9 out of 10 people in the country were wearing collars made in Troy—and invented the Ferris wheel. Indeed, Troy did its part to churn along the Industrial Revolution. That history is best explored at the RiverSpark Visitor Center in downtown Troy.

The meat packing industry produced Troy's arguably best known resident, Uncle Sam, whose statue pays tribute to him near **Riverfront Park** downtown. He is buried in the nearby historic Oakwood Cemetery in the northern part of Troy. Industry brought great wealth to the area, as witnessed by the elegant homes and the plethora of Tiffany glass found in this community.

The city quickly gives way to quieter small-town settings that dot the rest of the county. Opportunity for outdoor recreation abounds in two state parks, Grafton Lakes and Cherry Plain. Sinuous roads lead to oft-surprising small treasures of communities tucked away in the country. Farm markets sell honey, maple sugar, and produce and range from small roadside stands to larger, well-developed markets. Troy has a weekly farmers market down on the Hudson.

TROY AND RENSSELAER
Troy

Known as the Collar City, Troy was at the heart of the Industrial Revolution. Stroll along its streets to see some of the finest examples of urban architecture in a concentrated area. The streetscapes appeared in the 1993 movie *The Age of Innocence.* Stop in at the **RiverSpark Visitor Center** (251 River St., 518/270-8667; 10 A.M.–5 P.M. Tues.–Sat.) to start your tour of Troy and view a short film about its past.

Known for its superb acoustic properties, the **Troy Music Hall** (30 Second St., 518/273-0038, www.troymusichall.org) reflects beaux arts and French Renaissance influences. George B. Post, who also designed Chickering Hall in New York City, was the architect. The building was completed in 1875.

Just a few steps away, the **Rensselaer County Historical Society** is located in the Joseph B. Carr Building (57 Second St., 518/272-7232,

old brick building, Troy

© NIKKI GOTH ITOI

www.rchsonline.org; noon–5 P.M. Tues.–Sat. Feb.–Dec. 23, closed major holidays; adults $5, seniors $4, youth 12–18 $3, under 12 free). Admission includes tours of the neighboring Federal-style **Hart-Cluett House,** which opens at 2 P.M. on the same days at the historical society. Guided walking tours of Troy are also offered on Saturdays at 11 A.M., or you can pick up a map from RiverSpark and opt for a self-guided tour.

Antique shops, restaurants, and other stores line the streets of the downtown area. The

Troy Waterfront Farmers Market (www .troymarket.org) is held in the summer at Hedley Park Place (433 River St., 9 A.M.–1 P.M. Sat.) and moves indoors for the winter at the Uncle Sam Atrium (Third St. and Broadway, 10 A.M.–2 P.M. Sat.).

South of downtown is the **Burden Iron Works Museum,** which used to cast bells, including the Centennial Bell that hangs in Independence Hall in Philadelphia, but now offers tours of Troy with themes including Tiffany Glass and the Iron Works (1 E. Industrial

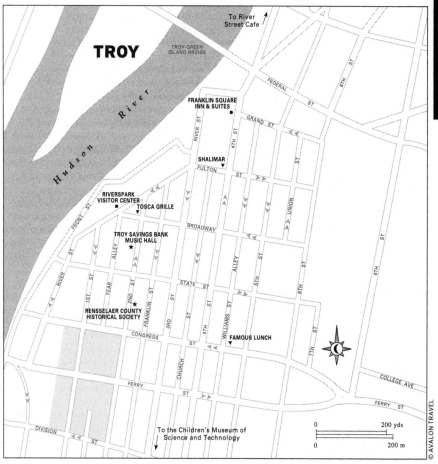

Parkway, 518/274-5267; open when staffed by volunteers, call ahead).

The **Children's Museum of Science and Technology** (250 Jordan Rd., 518/235-2120, www.childrensmuseumonline.org; 10 A.M.– 5 P.M. Thurs.–Sat., noon–5 P.M. Sun., extended days and hours in summer, but closed Sundays; $5) offers a variety of daily programs including the Lally Digital Dome Planetarium, which features the Molecularium as one of its four daily shows. The Molecularium is the first of its kind in the United States and teaches kids about science at the molecular level. Other shows include an animal show and a Hudson River show.

Rensselaer

Eight miles south of Troy, smaller Rensselaer (pop. 8,000) has the **Crailo State Historic Site** (9 1/2 Riverside Ave., 518/463-8738, http://ny sparks.state.ny.us/sites/info.asp?siteID=7). Part of the Van Rensselaer patroonship, this farm bears the name of the Van Rensselaer estate in the Netherlands. Now used as a museum, its exhibits focus on the colonial history of New Netherland in the area.

BEYOND TROY

The urban landscape of Troy quickly gives way to small towns and open vistas as you travel toward the eastern parts of the county. The Taconics, Berkshires, and Green Mountains come into view as you pass through towns like Averill Park, Petersburgh, Grafton, and Hoosick Falls.

◀ Grafton Lakes State Park

Local residents recently voted the beach at this pretty state park the best in the Capital Region, beating out even Lake George in the Adirondacks. The park is located at 61 North Long Pond Road, off Route 2, Grafton, 518/279-1155, http://nysparks.state.ny.us/ parks/info.asp?parkID=116.

Watch for the tiny sign on Route 2, near Grafton Lakes, for the entrance to the **Grafton Peace Pagoda** (87 Crandall Rd., 518/ 658-9301, www.geocities.com/dharmadoors/ grafton_peace_pagoda.html; open year round,

call 7–9 P.M.). Peace Pagodas date back 2000 years and are a symbol of nonviolence. This is one of only a few peace pagodas located in the United States.

Cherry Plain State Park

Cherry Plain State Park (6 State Park Rd., Cherry Plain, 518/733-5400, http://nysparks .state.ny.us/parks/info.asp?parkID=115) offers swimming beaches, hiking, biking, and winter sports.

Hoosick Falls

Celebrated American folk artist Anna Mary Moses, who became known as Grandma Moses, was first discovered in this present-day town of a few thousand residents near the Vermont border. The town boasts a Grandma Moses–inspired mural on the wall of a building on Main Street, and the artist was buried here in 1961, at the age of 101.

Hoosick Falls is also the gateway to the **Bennington Battlefield** (north side of Rte. 67 between Walloomsac, NY, and VT state line), site of a Revolutionary War encounter. Contact Grafton Lakes State Park for info: http://nys parks.state.ny.us/sites/info.asp?siteID=3.

SPORTS AND RECREATION

Grafton Lakes State Park is known for its network of mountain biking trails. Visit http:// capitalmtb.org/Resources/Grafton_Lakes_ State_Park_Trails for a trail map. Both Grafton Lakes and Cherry Plain State Parks offer swimming holes in the shadows of the mountains to the east, as well as cross-country ski trails in winter.

ACCOMMODATIONS

The options in Rensselaer County are limited, and you will need to book in advance if your trip coincides with a graduation or other important weekend. There are a few bed-and-breakfast inns scattered throughout the region and some interesting motels from which to choose. (See *Accommodations* under *Albany* and *Columbia County* in *The Upper Hudson* chapter for other options nearby.)

© NIKKI GOTH ITOI

marina on the Hudson, near Troy

Under $100

In the eastern part of the county, the **Sedgwick Inn** (17971 Rte. 22, Berlin, 518/658-2334, www.sedgwickinn.com; $85–115) offers a small pet-friendly motel on the property with simple rooms decorated in a variety of pleasant, if generic, styles.

Franklin Square Inn & Suites (1 Fourth St., Troy, 518/274-8800 or 866/708-2233, www.franklinsquareinn.com; rooms $89–134, suites $229–260) is a slightly more upscale reincarnation of a former chain motel, with 63 "elegantly casual" rooms. Centrally located in downtown Troy, the inn is walking distance to the Hudson River and downtown attractions. Rooms include continental breakfast; complimentary coffee, tea, and juice are available round the clock.

$100-150

Twelve uniquely themed rooms, including a Nautical Room, Adirondack Room, and Rose Garden, welcome guests to the 🌜 **Gregory House Country Inn** (Rte. 43, Averill Park, 518/274-3774, www.gregoryhouse.com; $110–150). All rooms have private baths, and there is a pool for guests. The on-site La Perla Restaurant offers authentic Italian cuisine.

Hidden off the road, the hilltop setting of the contemporary-style **Berkshire Mountain House** (150 Berkshire Way, Stephentown, 800/497-0176,www.berkshirebb.com;$109–209) allows panoramic views of the nearby mountains. The main house consists of nine individually decorated rooms and one apartment. A separate house can accommodate up to 12 people or be rented as two separate two-bedroom apartments. Guest may walk the trail or take a dip in the pond. The inn is pet-friendly.

FOOD

Ask the innkeepers in the eastern part of the county what they recommend for dining, and they suggest eating in Troy. Restaurants are few and far between in the east, but you will find a few local establishments in some of the larger villages.

Known for hot dogs that it ships worldwide, **Famous Lunch** (111 Congress St., Troy, 518/272-9481; 5 A.M.–10 P.M. Mon.–Sat., mains under $10) is a Troy institution serving breakfast, lunch, and dinner.

For an ethnic food fix, **Shalimar** (407 Fulton St., Troy, 518/273-8744; 11 A.M.–10 P.M. Mon.–Thurs., 11 A.M.–11 P.M. Fri.–Sat.; mains under $10) offers a great lunch buffet of Indian and Pakistani dishes. The buffet is served 11 A.M.–2:30 P.M. Monday–Friday ($5.99) and 11 A.M.–3 P.M. Saturday ($6.99).

Check out the small **C River Street Café** (429 River St., Troy, 518/273-2740; 5:30 P.M.–close Tues.–Sat.; mains $18–24) for tempting Continental fare at reasonable prices. The café is known as well for its extensive wine list. Reservations recommended.

Tosca Grille (200 Broadway, Troy, 518/272-3013, www.toscagrille.com; 5–10 P.M. Mon.–Sat., brunch 10 A.M.–3 P.M. Sun.; mains $18–46) serves up a summer menu of light Italian fare, including wild mushroom risotto and a grilled beef tenderloin insalata.

At the Gregory House Inn, La Perla serves pizza, pasta, veal, beef, chicken, and seafood (Rte. 43, Averill Park, 518/274-3774, www.gregoryhouse.com; 4–10 P.M. Mon. and Wed.–Thurs., 4–11 P.M. Fri., 3–11 P.M. Sat., 2–11 P.M. Sun.; mains $8–30).

ENTERTAINMENT AND EVENTS

Nationally known artists perform at the **Troy Music Hall** (30 Second St., 518/273-0038, www.troymusichall.org) throughout the year. **Music at Noon** is a free concert series usually held the second Tuesday of the month from October to May. Check the music hall website for information.

INFORMATION AND SERVICES

The **RiverSpark Visitor Center** serves as a tourism office for the county (251 River St., Troy, 518/270-8667; 10 A.M.–5 P.M. Tues.–Sat.).

GETTING THERE AND AROUND
By Bus

The **Capital District Transportation Authority** (110 Watervliet Ave., Albany, 518/482-8822, www.cdta.org) provides public bus service within Troy and to surrounding cities. The base fare is $1; an unlimited day pass is $3. The nearest Greyhound station is in downtown Albany.

By Train

The closest rail connection is the Albany/Rensselaer Amtrak station, located approximately eight miles south of Troy and across the river from Albany. Taxis are available at the station.

By Car

Rental cars are available at the Albany Airport; it takes approximately 20 minutes to reach Troy from the airport, depending on traffic.

Saratoga County

For the 40-mile stretch from Troy to Fort Edward, the Hudson River becomes an industrial conduit for the Champlain Canal, a shipping channel built in the early 19th century that extends all the way to the Canadian border. A series of locks and dams enables ships to navigate the changing elevation. The most impressive feat of aquatic engineering takes place at Waterford, where the Hudson merges with its largest tributary, the Mohawk River. Managing an elevation difference of 165 feet, the **Waterford Flight of Locks** are the highest in the world.

Route 4 follows the Hudson shoreline northward, passing by a handful of historic sites: On October 17, 1777, British General Burgoyne surrendered to American General Gates in a decisive victory that convinced the French to join the American cause and marked the turning point of the Revolutionary War. **Saratoga National Historic Park** (648 Rte. 32, Stillwater, 518/664-9821; seven-day pass $3), in the town of Stillwater, commemorates the battles of Saratoga. A nine-mile toll road ($5) open to motorists and cyclists reenacts the battles that took place on surrounding farmlands and woods. Park facilities include a visitors center, museum, and bookstore. The Battlefield Visitors Center is open 9 A.M. to 5 P.M. daily, and the Tour Road is open April 1 to mid-November.

George Washington, Alexander Hamilton, and the Marquis de Lafayette all stayed at the summer residence of General Philip Schuyler, a few miles north in Schuylerville. Visitors can tour the **General Schuyler House** (Rte. 4, Schuylerville, 518/664-9821; adults $3, children $1). The Schuyler House has guided tours 9:30 A.M. to 4:30 P.M. Thursday–Sunday, May 28 through Labor Day. Just off Route 4 is the 155-foot tall **Saratoga Monument** (Rtes. 4 & 32, Victory, 518/664-9821), built in 1877 to honor the historic victory.

Recently, local organizations have renamed Route 4 the **Lakes to Locks Passage** (www .lakestolocks.com) in an attempt to draw more visitors to the area. But other than these scattered historic sites, the prevailing mood along the Hudson here is one of neglect. One abandoned factory after another serves as a poignant reminder that this region was once a busy port of commerce.

SARATOGA SPRINGS

History lessons aside, the main reason to visit Saratoga County is to explore the charming Victorian town of Saratoga Springs. Natural hot springs, world-class horse racing, autumn apple picking, and a vibrant artistic community that revolves around Skidmore College draw an enthusiastic crowd of students, weekenders, and permanent residents.

◖ Saratoga Spa State Park

The Iroquois were first to discover the healing powers of Saratoga's natural hot springs, created by a layer of limestone in the ground that produces carbonated mineral water. Like the spa town of Baden-Baden in Germany's Black Forest, Saratoga's legacy as a spa resort dates back to the turn of the 19th century. Envisioning a well-developed destination for rest and relaxation, Gideon Putnam built the first tavern and boarding house and drew the first plans for a town around the hot springs.

In 1930, the state of New York got in on the action and built a Georgian Revival hotel in Putnam's name. In its day, the Gideon Putnam Hotel hosted the likes of entertainers Bob Hope and Fred Astaire, as well as Chief Justice of the U.S. Supreme Court Charles Evans Hughes.

Today, Saratoga Spa State Park (19 Roosevelt Dr., 518/584-2535, www.saratogaspastatepark .org) covers 2,300 acres of tall pines, steaming mineral baths, and tranquil walking paths. Visitors can access the mineral baths through the Gideon Putnam Hotel or the Lincoln Mineral Baths. At a price tag of $1.7 million, the family-oriented Peerless Pool Complex has a zero-depth entry and a waterslide. A second swimming area, the Victoria Pool, is surrounded by brick buildings and arched walkways.

© NIKKI GOTH ITOI

Roosevelt Baths, Saratoga Spa State Park

In addition to the great outdoors, the park holds several cultural attractions: There is no better way to spend a summer afternoon than listening to live music at the **Saratoga Performing Arts Center** (SPAC; 108 Avenue of the Pines, 518/584-9330, www.spac .org). From opera and ballet to pop and rock'n' roll, this custom-designed amphitheater offers something everyone. Initially conceived to give the New York Philharmonic a proper summer home, SPAC opened in 1966 and celebrated its 40th season in 2005. Today, the New York City Ballet and Philadelphia Orchestra both move to Saratoga for summer performances May–September. The theater holds 5,000 people under an open shelter and has room for 7,000 more on the lawn.

SPAC also operates the **National Museum of Dance & Hall of Fame** (99 S. Broadway, 518/584-2225, www.dancemuseum.org; 10 A.M.–5 P.M. Tues.–Sun.; adults $6.50, seniors $5, children 12 and under $3), in the old Washington Bath House (1918). The Greek Revival building contains five galleries full of photographs, videos, books, and costumes that document all forms of dance, from ballet to tap.

After a multiyear renovation that cost $5 million, the original Roosevelt Bathhouse (1930) is back in business as part of the **Gideon Putnam Hotel** (24 Gideon Putnam Rd., 800/732-1560, www.gideonputnam.com; $170–360). Inside are a 13,000-square-foot spa with 42 private spa rooms. From Route 9, turn left onto Avenue of the Pines to reach the park entrance.

◖ Saratoga Race Course

At the next exit on I-87 is Saratoga's other main attraction, the Saratoga Race Course (267 Union Ave., www.nyra.com/saratoga; free parking). Featured in the contemporary book and movie *Seabiscuit,* the racetrack dates back to 1863, making it the oldest continuously operating thoroughbred track in the country. Horse racing became wildly popular in the 1940s and '50s, and the Saratoga Race Course has been a local institution ever since.

Saratoga's population of 27,000 literally tri-ples during the month-long summer racing season, from the end of July through Labor Day weekend. Tickets are affordable, and the scene is at once traditional and exciting. Women still don their Sunday finest to watch from the grandstand. At the other end of the spectrum, diehard fans barbecue at their cars and watch from the parking lot without buying tickets at all. The hoopla concludes each year with the famous **Travers Stakes,** named for racetrack co-founder William Travers.

Grandstand tickets go on sale at 8 A.M. each morning for that day's races. Purchase them at the Union Avenue Gate, or at the Holiday Inn in downtown Saratoga Springs (cash only, limit four per person). You can also rent binoculars at the track for up-close viewing. Take Exit 14/ Union Avenue from I-87.

For information before or after the meeting dates, call 718/641-4700 or 516/488-6000. For information during the meeting (late July through Labor Day), call 518/584-6200.

National Museum of Racing

Across from the racetrack, an informative museum demonstrates what traits make the best thoroughbreds and re-creates famous scenes on the track. Recent additions to the National Museum of Racing (191 Union Ave., www.racing museum.org; 518/584-0400; 10 A.M.–4 P.M. Mon.–Sat., noon–4 P.M. Sun.; adults $7, students $5) archives include newspaper articles from the mid-19th century. Florida-bred Skip Away and Kentucky-bred Flawlessly became the newest inductees into the museum's Hall of Fame in 2004.

Beyond the racetrack and museum on Union Avenue is the 400-acre Yaddo estate, an artist community established in 1900 and housed in an imposing Tudor mansion. Its terraced **Yaddo Rose Garden** (Union Ave., Saratoga Springs, 518/584-0746, www.yaddo.org), modeled after classical Italian designs, has been gradually restored over the last 15 years.

Downtown Saratoga Springs

Broadway and Union Avenue both lead to the open lawns of **Congress Park** and the heart

© NIKKI GOTH ITOI

Caroline Street, Saratoga Springs

of Saratoga Springs. Kids will want to head straight to the park's working merry-go-round or to feed the ducks in the pond. The **Canfield Casino** (Congress Park, 518/584-6920, www .saratogahistory.org; 10 A.M.–4 P.M. daily Memorial Day–Labor Day, 10 A.M.–4 P.M. Wed.–Sun. the rest of the year; adults $5, seniors and students $4, under 12 free), a major attraction during the spa town's heyday, is now a local history museum.

Along Broadway, between Congress Street and Van Dam Street are a host of tempting options for shopping, entertainment, and dining out. To get oriented, stop by the information booth at the corner of Broadway and Congress. Then continue up Broadway to one of Saratoga Springs's most famous landmarks, the **Adelphi Hotel** (365 Broadway, 518/587-4688, www .adelphihotel.com; $140–320), a four-story Victorian that has stayed in business since the turn of the 20th century. Note the hand-painted stencils in the lobby before settling in for a drink in the garden out back. These days, the hotel is unfortunately surrounded by a sea

of chain stores, including Gap, Banana Republic, Eddie Bauer, and Starbucks.

◖ Tang Teaching Museum and Art Gallery

North Broadway leads to the Skidmore College campus and an innovative museum that hosts programs with titles like "Why is Contemporary Art So Weird?" The Tang Teaching Museum and Art Gallery (815 N. Broadway, 518/580-8080, www.tang.skidmore.edu; 10 A.M.–5 P.M. Tues.–Thurs., 10 A.M.–7 P.M. Fri., noon–5 P.M. Sat.–Sun.) combines an outstanding permanent collection with provocative lecture topics to engage an audience of students, as well as adults and children in the local community. Exhibits are designed to involve other college departments, from dance to history. Rooftop concerts are a favorite local pastime in summer.

Petrified Sea Gardens

West of downtown on Route 29 is a 30-acre outdoor museum called the Petrified Sea

Gardens (off Rte. 29, Saratoga Springs, 518/691-0150, www.petrifiedseagardens.org; adults $3.25, students and seniors $2.25; hours vary), where you can view stromatolite fossils that formed 500 million years ago, when the Hudson River Valley marked the edge of a tropical sea. Beyond the half-acre fossil area, walking trails lead to other glacial formations, a sundial park, and a Native American medicine wheel.

SPORTS AND RECREATION
Winter Sports
When a good nor'easter buries the North Country in snow, Saratoga Spa State Park becomes a winter playland, and the cross-country skiing is sublime. You can rent equipment at a ski shop at the golf course and ski 20 kilometers of trails. **Lapland Lake** (139 Lapland Lake Rd., Northville, 518/863-4974, www.laplandlake.com; 9 A.M.–4:30 P.M. Sun.–Fri., 9 A.M.–9 P.M. Sat.; adults $12–15, juniors $7) has another 38 kilometers of groomed trails for classic and skating-style cross-country. A four-kilometer portion of the trail is lighted for night skiing. Rentals and lessons are available. For off-piste skiing and snowshoeing, try one of the local apple orchards.

Downhill skiers continue farther north to resorts in the Adirondack Park, including Gore Mountain (Peaceful Valley Rd., North Creek, 800/342-1234 or 518/251-2411, www.goremountain.com). Adult lift tickets cost $64 per day on weekends. Teens are $52, juniors $34, and under 6 ski free.

Hiking
As the gateway to the Adirondack Mountains (beyond the scope of this handbook), the Capital Region affords convenient access to some of the best—and most challenging—hiking and backpacking in the northeast. The highest peaks in New York State, including 5,344-foot Mount Marcy, are within a 100-mile drive. The Mount Marcy trailhead is located at Adirondack Loj on Heart Lake. Bugs and black bears can be minor or major annoyances, depending on your tolerance. The steep and rocky ter-

---

ADIRONDACK STATS

- The original forest preserve was established in 1885.

- The park encompasses approximately 6 million acres.

- It is larger than Yellowstone, Everglades, Glacier, and Grand Canyon National Parks combined.

- About half of the park is constitutionally protected to remain a "forever wild" forest preserve.

- The remaining half of the park is designated private land which includes settlements, farms, timber lands, businesses, homes, and camps.

- There are more than 3,000 lakes and 30,000 miles (48,000 km) of streams and rivers inside the park.

- 7-10 million tourists visit the park annually.

- It is the largest area without a city in New York state.

---

rain will challenge even the strongest of hikers: Routes are often longer than they look at first glance, and it's not unusual to encounter thunderstorms, mosquitoes, bears, and flat-out fatigue all in one overnight hike.

Cycling
The **Saratoga Mountain Biking Association** (518/587-0455, www.saratogamtb.org) maintains trails on 538 acres north of Skidmore College. Trails suit riders of all abilities, with single track, steep climbs, and fast descents. **The Bike Shop** (35 Maple Ave., Saratoga Springs, 518/587-7857; 10 A.M.–6 P.M. Mon.–Fri., 9 A.M.–5 P.M. Sat.) has rentals, maps, and gear. **All Outdoors** (35 Van Dam St., Saratoga Springs, 518/587-0455) is another popular shop for cycling supplies. **Blue Sky Bicycles** (71

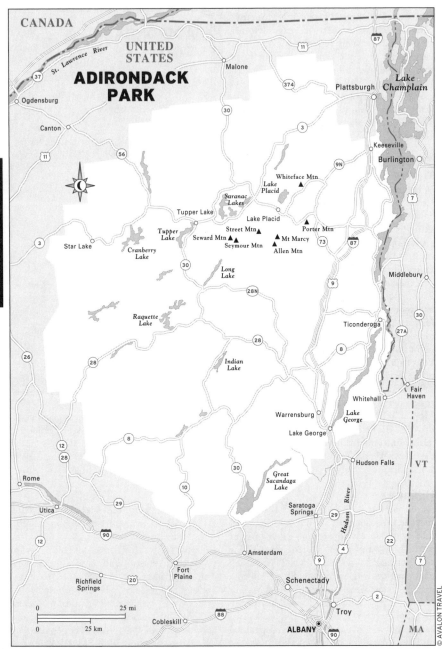

CANADA

UNITED STATES

ADIRONDACK PARK

St. Lawrence River

Ogdensburg

Canton

Star Lake

Cranberry Lake

Tupper Lake

Malone

Saranac Lakes

Tupper Lake

Seward Mtn ▲ ▲
Seymour Mtn ▲

Street Mtn ▲

Lake Placid

Whiteface Mtn ▲

Plattsburgh

Keeseville

Burlington

Lake Champlain

Porter Mtn ▲

▲ Mt Marcy
Allen Mtn ▲

Long Lake

Raquette Lake

Indian Lake

Middlebury

Ticonderoga

Fair Haven

Whitehall

Warrensburg

Lake George

Lake George

Hudson Falls

Great Sacandaga Lake

Rome

Utica

Saratoga Springs

Hudson River

Richfield Springs

Fort Plaine

Amsterdam

Schenectady

Troy

ALBANY

Cobleskill

VT

MA

0   25 mi

0   25 km

© AVALON TRAVEL

Church St., Saratoga Springs, 518/583-0600, www.blueskybicycles.com; 10 A.M.–7 P.M. Mon.–Fri., 9 A.M.–5 P.M. Sat.) sells cycling gear, maps, and high-end bikes. Visit the shop to stock up on supplies and ask for ride directions. Better yet, download a cue sheet online before you go. Blue Sky doesn't offer rentals.

Golf

There are at least a dozen golf courses in the immediate Saratoga area. One of the best is **Saratoga Spa Golf Course** (60 Roosevelt Dr., Saratoga Springs, 518/584-3137, www .saratogaspagolf.com; Mar.–Dec.; weekends $34, weekdays $29), a 27-hole complex with a 7,098-yard championship course. Before your round, you can hit a bucket of balls from the grass tees at the driving range. Private pilots should reserve a tee time at the **Airway Meadows Golf Course** (262 Brownville Rd., Gansevoort, 518/792-4144, www .airwaymeadowsgolf.com; weekends $30, weekdays $26), adjacent to an airstrip and skydiving school.

Slide into a GPS-equipped cart at the **Saratoga National Golf Club** (458 Union Ave., Saratoga Springs, 518/583-4653, www .golfsaratoga.com; summer weekends $150, summer weekdays $130), and you'll forget about the $150 you paid to get away from the crowds. After the round, you can enjoy a meal at Sargo's, which is now managed by one of Albany's top restaurant management companies.

Elevation changes are a challenge at the relatively new **Saratoga Lake Golf Club** (35 Grace Moore Rd., Saratoga Springs, 518/581-6616; www.saratogalakegolf.com; weekends $32, weekdays $26). Greens are in good condition.

Swimming and Boating

The busiest lake in the Capital Region is **Lake George,** 30 minutes from downtown Saratoga Springs along I-87. Known for its clear water and summer resort scene, the lake measures 32 miles long and three miles across. Several towns have public beaches. Scuba divers can explore underwater shipwrecks with remark-

ably good freshwater visibility. **Million Dollar Beach** has public parking. An **Antique Classic Boat Show** takes place in August.

In addition to Lake George, several smaller lakes offer ample space for aquatic adventures. You can rent a kayak, canoe, or rowboat from **The Kayak Shak** (Saratoga Outdoor Center, 251 Staffords Bridge Rd., 518/587-9788, www.saratogaoutdoorcenter .com/kayak.htm; $15 half day, $20 full day for single kayaks) to paddle around **Saratoga Lake.** The larger **Great Sacandaga Lake** is a man-made lake that allows powerboats, personal watercraft, and fishing. Swimming and windsurfing are also popular summer activities. **Moreau Lake State Park** (605 Old Saratoga Rd., Gansevoort, 518/793-0511, http://nysparks.state .ny.us/parks/info.asp?parkID=119) has a sandy beach and wooded campsites, though it tends to be crowded in the summertime. Boating and fishing are allowed.

Fishing and Hunting

Anglers cast for largemouth bass, northern pike, and panfish in Saratoga Lake. You can rent a boat and stock up on tackle at **Lake Lonely Boat Livery** (378 Crescent Ave., Saratoga Springs, 518/587-1721). For more serious sport fishing and charter operations, head to Lake George, where the catch includes lake trout and landlocked salmon, as well as bass.

ACCOMMODATIONS

Overnight visitors to Saratoga Springs have more than 100 establishments to choose from, including business hotels, smaller inns, motels, and bed-and-breakfasts. The Marriott Courtyard opened in spring 2004, and the historic Gideon Putnam completed its overhaul in summer 2004. Expect higher rates during the month-long horse racing season.

$150-200

Enjoy high-speed wireless Internet access as you sit among the genuine antique furnishings in an elaborately decorated suite at the **Adelphi Hotel** (365 Broadway, Saratoga

© NIKKI GOTH ITOI

CAPITAL-SARATOGA REGION

the Adelphi Hotel, Saratoga Springs

Springs, 518/587-4688, www.adelphihotel
.com; $155). The property features 39 indi-
vidually decorated guest rooms and a piazza
that overlooks Broadway.

Six miles south of Saratoga Springs in
the town of Ballston Spa, the newly opened
Medberry Inn and Spa (48 Front St., Ballston Spa, 518/885-7727 or 800/508-1804;
www.medberyinnandspa.com; $125–175) has
11 rooms decorated in pastel colors and floral
linens. Data ports and whirlpool tubs lend a
modern touch to the 200-year-old property.
There is a day spa on-site.

Bob and Stephanie Melvin are your
hosts at the **Westchester House Bed and
Breakfast Inn** (102 Lincoln Ave., Saratoga
Springs, 518/587-7613 or 888/302-1717, www
.westchesterhousebandb.com; $125–245, dur-
ing the horse racing season $270–450), inside a
colorful Victorian on a quiet residential street.
Rooms are decorated in country-print wallpa-
per and lacy window coverings. Wireless Internet is an unexpected perk.

East of Saratoga Springs and just north

of Hoosick Falls on Route 22, the historic
Cambridge Hotel (4 West Main St., Cambridge, 518/677-5626, www.cambridgehotel
.com; $135–185) recently reopened to great
fanfare. In the 1880s, the 40-room hotel was
modern for its time; today, it has been converted into a 17-room bed-and-breakfast,
complete with private baths, air-conditioning,
and wireless Internet access throughout. Each
room is individually decorated in a Victorian
or country theme.

Over $200

Spacious and well-appointed guest rooms and
suites cost up to $550 a night at the recently
restored **Gideon Putnam Hotel** (Rte. 50,
Saratoga Springs, 800/732-1560, www.gideon
putnam.com; $195). You'll be walking dis-
tance to SPAC, but beware that rates go
sky-high during the month-long horse racing season.

Campgrounds

You can pitch a tent or park an RV under the

pine trees at the **Whispering Pines Campsites & RV Park** (550 Sand Hill Rd., Greenfield Center, 518/893-0416 www.saratogacamping.com; tent sites $24/day). Services include hot showers, swimming pool, a trout brook, and two ponds.

FOOD

The food scene in Saratoga Springs has blossomed in recent years, as a result of both visitor demand and exposure on The Food Network cable channel. Today, you can find everything from classic French and traditional Italian to international cuisine—and everywhere its chefs who make the most of the farm-fresh ingredients at their fingertips.

Surf and Turf

The well-heeled leave the racetrack behind and retreat to **43 Phila** (43 Phila, Saratoga Springs, 518/584-2720, www.43philabistro.com; 11:30 A.M.–3 P.M. and 5–10 P.M. Mon.–Sat.; mains $28–46) to savor a tender milk-fed veal rib chop for $46. *Steak frites* and swordfish round out the menu, and even the requisite chicken dish is prepared with a twist: hoisin sauce and kimchi.

The Olde Bryan Inn (123 Maple Ave., Saratoga Springs, 518/587-2990, www.oldebryaninn.com, 11 A.M.–10:30 P.M. Sun.–Thurs., 11 A.M.–11 P.M. Fri.–Sat.; mains $12–26) is a historic affair serving a Continental menu of prime rib, chicken Français, and crab-stuffed shrimp.

When other restaurants have filled their tables for the evening, you can sometimes still get in at **Springwater Bistro** (139 Union Ave., Saratoga Springs, 518/584-6440, www.springwaterbistro.com; 5:30–10 P.M. Wed.–Mon.; mains $12–26). The menu ranges from paella to coq au vin, and Monday is Tapas Night.

Known up and down the Hudson Valley for its classic French cuisine, **⟨ Chez Sophie Bistro** (The Saratoga, 534 Broadway, Saratoga Springs, 518/583-3538, www.chezsophie.com; breakfast 7–10 A.M. Mon.–Sat.; brunch 7 A.M.–2 P.M. Sun.; lunch 11:30 A.M.–2 P.M. Mon.–Fri., dinner 5–10 P.M. daily, bar menu available 2–10 P.M.

daily; dinner mains $26–40) relocated to The Saratoga hotel on Broadway a few years back.

Fried Chicken

Chef Jasper Alexander, a graduate of the Culinary Institute of America, became a local legend when he triumphed over Food Network host Bobby Flay in a surprise fried chicken cooking contest. The celebrated "Throwdown with Bobby Flay" took place in 2007, and **⟨ Hattie's Chicken Shack** (45 Phila St., Albany, 518/584-4790, www.hattiesrestaurant.com; 5–10 P.M. daily; mains $14–18) has continued serving its legendary fare ever since.

Taverns and Pubs

A block away on Phila is **The Original Saratoga Springs Brewpub** (14 Phila St., Saratoga Springs, 518/583-3209, www.saratogabrewpub.com; mains $7–25), where you can wash your burger down with a microbrew. Outdoor seating is a plus in summer.

Italian

Chianti Il Ristorante (371 Broadway, Saratoga Springs, 518/580-0312, www.chiantiristorante.com; mains $16 and up) serves a full menu of Italian specialties, from pasta to risotto to filet mignon and rack of lamb. The restaurant is open daily for lunch and dinner.

Cafés and Quick Bites

Don't leave Saratoga without sampling a pastry at **⟨ Mrs. London's** (464 Broadway, Saratoga Springs, 518/581-1652 www.mrslondons.com; 7 A.M.–6 P.M. Tues.–Thurs. and Sun., 7 A.M.–10 P.M. Fri.–Sat.; mains $4–9). Tempting first courses include grilled panini on ciabatta, pizzas, soups, and sandwiches.

Vegetarians and visitors with a case of late-night munchies won't go hungry at **Esperanto** (6 1/2 Caroline St., Saratoga Springs, 518/587-4236, 11:30–2 A.M. Sun.–Wed., 11:30–3 A.M. Thurs., 11:30–4 A.M. Fri.–Sat.). It has a tempting selection of quick eats, including burritos, pizza, and soups, as well as a number of international cuisines, such as Thai, Mexican, and Middle Eastern.

Locals flock to **Beverly's** (47 Phila St., Saratoga Springs, 518/583-2755; 8 A.M.–3 P.M. daily; mains $5–10) for diner-style fare served with a twist. Curried chicken salad and grilled cheese made wth havarti are some of the more creative items on the menu.

ENTERTAINMENT AND EVENTS
Performing Arts

The story goes that the **Saratoga Performing Arts Center** (108 Avenue of the Pines., Saratoga Springs, 518/584-9330, www.spac.org) was originally built to keep the New York Philharmonic from moving to Vermont as its summer home. While the Philharmonic never came to Saratoga Springs, the new venue did become one of the largest producers of first-rate music, dance, and opera performances in the state. Recent concerts have included everything from Bon Jovi to the Grateful Dead. A night of ballet or opera will be simply unforgettable. For opera aficionados, **Lake George Opera** (480 Broadway, Ste. 336, Saratoga Springs, 518/584-6018, www.lakegeorgeopera.org) stages performances at the Spa Little Theater in Saratoga Spa State Park.

Bars and Nightlife

Between its racetrack spectators and student population, Saratoga Springs has earned a reputation as a party town: Jazz bars, dance clubs, and Irish pubs, as well as coffeehouses and wine bars, offer venues for spirited entertainment. Several of the late-night establishments are on Caroline Street.

Located in a 19th-century brick building on Broadway, **The Wine Bar** (417 Broadway, Saratoga Springs, 518/584-8777; 4 P.M. till close Tues.–Sat.; small plates $3–9, wine flights $12–20) has earned recognition from *Wine Spectator* for its list and praise from patrons for a menu of small plates that pair nicely with the wines.

At cocktail hour, head to the bar and outdoor garden at the Adelphi (365 Broadway, Saratoga Springs, 518/587-4688, www.adelphihotel .com). One block off Broadway, jazz aficionados settle in at the beautiful wooden bar of **9 Maple Avenue** (9 Maple Ave., Saratoga Springs, 518/583-2582, www.9mapleavenue.com; opens at 4 P.M. daily) for a night of live music, well-made cocktails, and a large selection of single malts. The **Parting Glass** (40-42 Lake Ave., Saratoga Springs, 518/583-1916, www.partingglasspub. com) plays live Irish music. **Saratoga Gaming & Harness Raceway** (Crescent Ave., Saratoga Springs, 518/584-2110, www.virtualflow.com/ gaming) has 1,300 video gaming machines.

Festivals

Each September since 2001, SPAC has hosted the popular **Saratoga Wine & Food Festival** (Saratoga Performing Arts Center, 108 Avenue of the Pines, Saratoga Springs, 518/584-9330 ext. 3021, www.spac.org/spac-festivals/spac-festivals.asp?varID=16), drawing food and wine enthusiasts from across New England and the mid- Atlantic states. A selection of tapas and a premium sherry tasting were among the highlights of one past event.

SHOPPING

Storefronts crowd both sides of Broadway in Saratoga Springs, offering a mix of boutique jewelry and apparel, high-end retail chains, and straight-up kitsch. **Silverado Jewelry Gallery** (446 Broadway, Saratoga Springs, 518/584-1044; Mon.–Sat. 10 A.M.–6 P.M., Sun. 11 A.M.–5 P.M.) sells unique silver and semiprecious jewelry from a number of New York City artists. At the corner of Broadway and Phila, you can browse the selection of sundresses, hats, and handbags at **Lifestyles** (436 Broadway, Saratoga Springs, 518/584-4665; Sat.–Wed. 10 A.M.–6 P.M., Thurs.–Fri. till 8 P.M.). **Symmetry Gallery** (348 Broadway, Saratoga Springs, 518/584-5090, www.symmetrygallery.com; 10 A.M.–6 P.M. Mon.–Sat., till 8 P.M. Thurs., noon–4 P.M. Sun.), also on Broadway, features art glass works by local artists. And, as the name implies, the **Pink Paddock** (380 Broadway, Saratoga Springs, 518/587-4344, www.pinkpaddock.com; Mon. –Thurs. 10 A.M.–8 P.M., Sat. 10 A.M.–6 P.M., Sun. 11 A.M.–5 P.M.) sells a unique collection of pink apparel, as well as other shades. You'll find everything from seersucker pants and argyle sweaters to ribbon headbands, flip-flops, and flirty summer dresses.

Farm Stands

The **Saratoga Farmers Market** (High Rock Ave., Saratoga Springs, 800/806-3276, www .saratogafarmersmarket.org; 9 A.M.–1 P.M. Sat. and 3–6 P.M. Wed. May–Oct.) is a summer tradition, with 50 local vendors set up under a permanent pavilion. If you're planning a whole meal, pick up some fresh-baked bread, organic beef, and smoked salmon while you're there.

Putnam Market (435 Broadway, Saratoga Springs, 518/587-3663, www.putnammarket .com; 9 A.M.–6 P.M. Mon.–Sat., 11 A.M.–6 P.M. Sun.) supplies the gourmands in town with an impressive display of cheeses and pâtés. Order sandwiches, desserts, and chocolates or pick up fresh fish to cook yourself. The adjoining wine store (Putnam Wines) offers free tastings every day and stays open on Sundays.

Visit **Bowman Orchards** (141 Sugar Hill Rd. Rexford, 518/371-2042, www.bowman orchards.com), **Charlton Road Apple Orchard** (140 Charlton Rd., Ballston Lake, 518/381-3601), or **Stetkar Orchards** (Fitch Rd., Saratoga Springs, 518/584-6839) for an afternoon of apple-picking and cider-sipping.

Bookstores

Browse through a wide selection of used books from every genre at **Twice Told Used Books** (19 Phila St., Saratoga Springs, 518/587-2427, www.ttubbs.com; summer 10 A.M.–9 P.M. daily), and then hang out with a cup of coffee while you watch others pass through. Also on Phila, **Lyrical Ballad Bookstore** (7-9

Phila St., Saratoga Springs, 518/584-8779; 10 A.M.–6 P.M. Mon.–Sat., 11 A.M.–6 P.M. Sun.) displays some of its fine old books and prints in a former bank vault.

INFORMATION AND SERVICES

In Saratoga Springs the **Saratoga County Chamber of Commerce** (297 Broadway, Saratoga Springs, 518/587-3241; 9 A.M.–5 P.M. daily) operates an information center near Congress Park late June–Labor Day.

GETTING THERE AND AROUND
By Bus

The **Saratoga Summer Visitors Shuttle** stops at Congress Park, Skidmore College, and SPAC. It does not operate on Mondays ($1 round trip). The **Capital District Transportation Authority** (110 Watervliet Ave., Albany, 518/482-8822, www.cdta.org) provides public bus service within Saratoga Springs and to surrounding cities. The base fare is $1; an unlimited day pass is $3.

By Train

Saratoga Springs opened a new rail station a few years ago (West Ave., Saratoga Springs) with Enterprise and Thrifty car rentals onsite.

By Car

The Capital Region is a major metropolitan area with heavy traffic during commuting hours. I-87 and I-787 are the main north–south highways. The Albany Airport is Exit 13N on I-87; Saratoga Springs is Exit 14. You can rent a car from the Albany Airport or from several independent companies in the Saratoga area.

BACKGROUND

The Land

Abundant natural resources in the Hudson River Valley played a critical role in the development of trade and commerce in colonial America. The lush display of trees, bushes, and wildflowers astounded Henry Hudson when he first sailed up the river. Native American and European settlers found ample water, arable land, and lumber, fish, and game to support their growing communities.

Nearly half the land in the Hudson Valley has been developed for urban, residential, and agricultural use, and the rest remains second- and third-growth forest. Elevation in the region ranges from 150 feet in the lowlands to 4,000 feet in the mountains. Lowlands consist of fertile farmland, rolling hills, marshes, and swamps. Mountainous areas feature sheer cliffs, escarpments, and rocky lookout points. In addition, the Catskill region is known for its red clay soil.

GEOLOGY

Dramatic rock formations in the Hudson River Valley tell a story of mountain-building, erosion, and glacial movement that began a billion years ago. The oldest exposed bedrock in the region is found in the Hudson Highlands of Orange and Putnam Counties. Limestone and shale marine sediments remind us that the valley was once the edge of a shallow, tropical sea, much like the Red Sea, complete with pink sand and delicate coral formations.

The Taconic Mountains were formed next in an event known as an orogeny, followed by the Acadian Mountains, which stretched as high as the Himalayas. Runoffs from the mountain range deposited sandstone and shale to create the Devonian Catskill Delta, which forms the Catskill and Shawangunk Mountains of today. Farther south, molten rock carved the sheer cliffs of the Palisades.

In recent geologic history, 40,000 years ago, glaciers carved the fjord we now call the Hudson River. When the ice melted, it formed glacial Lake Albany and a submarine canyon that extends 500 miles offshore from Manhattan.

GEOGRAPHY

The Hudson River Valley is bound by New York City and New Jersey to the south, New England to the east, the Adirondack Mountains to the north, and the Appalachian Plateau and Mohawk Valley to the west. At the center of the valley is the river itself, 315 miles long, 3.5 miles across at its widest point, and 216 feet at its deepest. The river originates from Lake Tear of the Clouds in the Adirondack Mountains and becomes navigable at Troy, above Albany. Dozens of tributaries feed the Hudson, draining the Catskill Mountains to the west and the Taconic Range to the east. The largest rivers and creeks include the Croton, Wallkill, Rondout, Esopus, and Catskill.

A second major river, the Delaware, traverses the western part of the region and empties into the Atlantic to the south.

CLIMATE

The Hudson River Valley enjoys a temperate, continental climate. Four distinct seasons range from the muggy days of summer to the crisp, clear-blue days of fall and below-freezing temperatures in winter. The first frost comes in late September, ending a growing season that lasts 160–180 days. According to U.S. Department of Agriculture Forest Service data, average rainfall is about 40 inches, while snowfall measures 165 inches at the mountaintops and

AVERAGE TEMPERATURE BY MONTH		
Month	High	Low
January	34	15
February	38	16
March	47	26
April	59	36
May	70	46
June	78	55
July	84	60
August	82	59
September	74	50
October	62	38
November	51	30
December	39	21

40–60 inches on the valley floor. Extreme weather events include ice storms and blizzards in winter and thunderstorms and the occasional hurricane in summer and fall. The fall foliage season lasts mid-September through late October, with the peak typically around Columbus Day weekend.

ENVIRONMENTAL ISSUES

The Hudson River absorbed a barrage of industrial waste, raw sewage, and agricultural runoff during the late 19th and early 20th centuries. The river was on the verge of recovery by the 1970s, when scientists tested striped bass for polychlorinated biphenyls (PCBs) and found alarming levels of contamination. The discovery shut down all commercial fisheries along the river, and in 1977, General Electric (GE) was ordered to stop dumping PCBs into the river. But the Hudson was unable to heal itself. The Environmental Protection Agency finally agreed in 2002 to conduct a massive dredging effort to clean up the river, but GE continued to fight the decision for years. As of August 2007, GE had begun construction of processing and transportation facilities that will store sediment dredged from the river.

By many accounts, the Hudson River is cleaner than its has been in a generation. American shad are considered safe to eat again, people are swimming in its waters again, and the river continues to support an astonishing diversity of life. However, PCBs and the efforts to rid the river of them continue to pose a challenge to the community.

Flora and Fauna

The constant mixing of saltwater and freshwater as far north as Albany creates a rich supply of nutrients that in turn support a remarkably diverse set of interdependent plants and animals.

TREES
Sixty percent of the entire Hudson River Valley is covered in second- or third-growth forest. Towering red and white oaks and a variety of northern hardwoods—white and yellow birch, sugar maple, hickory, basswood, and ash—make up the majority of the deciduous forest.

Riverside red maple

Acorns and beechnuts provide a key source of food for wildlife populations. Common conifers include blue spruce, hemlock, white pine, and yellow pine. The sand plains around Albany support the growth of pitch pine-scrub oak forests.

FLOWERS
Across the Hudson Valley, bright yellow forsythia mark the arrival of spring, adding the first splash of color to the barren winter landscape each May. Cultivated daffodils and tulips are close behind, and more than 100 different kinds of wildflowers bloom by midsummer, including goldenrod, buttercups, and daisies, as well as jack-in-the-pulpit, sarsaparilla, and winterberry.

MAMMALS
A variety of critters big and small make their home in wooded valleys, fields, and mountainous areas. Among them are the black bear, gray squirrel, coyote, raccoon, river otter, and bobcat. In addition, many of the Hudson Valley's suburbs are overrun with white-tailed deer that munch on everything in sight, from geraniums to apple blossoms.

SEALIFE
The Hudson River once held a large number of saltwater creatures, including oysters, mussels, crabs, and turtles. Most of the shellfish are gone today—blue crabs are an exception—but the river still supports more than 150 types of fish, such as bass, shad, and sturgeon, many of which

are prized catches for determined anglers. At the water's edge, muskrats, snapping turtles, and ospreys feed on cattails and other marsh plants.

BIRDS

Ornithologists flock to the Hudson Valley's wilderness areas to view more than 100 types of nesting birds, migrating raptors, and waterfowl. Among the more unusual species are the Red-Eyed Vireo, found in woodland areas; American Redstart, which arrives to nest in late spring to early summer; gray and yellow Canada Warbler, found at lower levels of the forest; and Western Wood-Pewee, which prefers the dense upper canopy. Wild turkeys, grouse, and pheasant are abundant in wooded areas as well. The noisy pileated woodpecker likes a moist habitat

wild turkey in the Catskills

where it can feed on carpenter ants. Observing one in action is a treat. Mallard ducks paddle calm, sheltered waters across the valley, while Canada geese enjoy spending the winter near local golf courses. And the American bald eagle has made a comeback along the Delaware River, with sightings as far east as Greenwood Lake.

REPTILES AND AMPHIBIANS

The Hudson Valley has its share of snakes, frogs, salamanders, and turtles. The friendly garter snake, water snake, and white striped milk snake are common. The only two poisonous snakes are the copperhead, found south of Kingston, and the timber rattlesnake, which lives in parts of the Catskills and along the river valley.

Come March, spring peepers fill the evening air with a familiar song. One of the most common amphibians in the region, peepers live anywhere that standing water is found. Other types of frogs and toads live at the water's edge, including wood frogs, bullfrogs, green frogs, and two dark-spotted frogs, the northern leopard and pickerel.

Motorists often encounter feisty snapping turtles crossing back roads to lay their eggs. Painted turtles are another common species. Less common are the box turtle, wood turtle, the yellow-spotted Blanding's turtle in the lower Hudson Valley, and the map turtle in the Hudson River. A dozen kinds of salamander also inhabit area rivers and ponds. The mudpuppy is found in the Hudson, while the hellbender lives in the southern part of the region.

INSECTS

Mosquitoes and mayflies are a nuisance in wet and wooded areas May through July, while fireflies light up the forest on hot summer nights. Deer ticks, found in fields and woods, can spread Lyme disease.

History

EARLY INHABITANTS

Anthropologists believe the earliest inhabitants settled the Hudson River Valley as many as 10,000 years ago. By the 17th century, three main Native American nations lived along the river: the Mahicans (Algonquin) claimed the east bank of the river, from Long Island Sound to Albany, as well as the west bank from Albany to Catskill; the Mohawks (Iroquois) lived in the Catskill area; and the Lenni Lenapes (Delaware) occupied the west, from the Catskills south to the Potomac. Modern town names like Wappingers, Tappan, Hackinsack, and Minnisink all refer to Native American tribes.

EUROPEAN EXPLORATION AND SETTLEMENT

Technically speaking, Giovanni Verrazano was the first European explorer to enter the Hudson River at New York Harbor in 1524. But it was Henry Hudson, commissioned by the Dutch, who made it famous. Hudson sailed the *Half Moon* as far north as Troy in 1609, in search of a northwest passage to the Indies. Hudson did not succeed and turned around when the river became too shallow near Troy, but Dutch settlers returned soon after to settle Fort Orange at present day Albany.

Despite ongoing conflicts, the Native American and European populations began to trade fur, tobacco, wheat, oysters, beans, corn, pumpkins, and other goods. Dutch settlements grew at Albany, Manhattan, and Kingston.

The Dutch introduced the patroon system of land management, in which an individual was granted proprietary rights to a tract of land in return for bringing 50 new settlers to the colony. When the English took over in the mid-17th century, they introduced a similar approach, the manor system. Robert Livingston, Frederick Philipse, and other historic figures were all benefactors of these preferential land-management practices.

REVOLUTIONARY WAR TIMELINE

1774	New York "Tea Party"
1775	Americans capture Fort Ticonderoga and Crown Point
1776	British invade New York City
1777	Saratoga Campaign – the turning point
1778	Fortress West Point begun
1779	Battle of Stony Point
1780	Benedict Arnold and John André treason
1781	Siege of New York City and Battle of Yorktown
1783	British evacuate New York City

REVOLUTIONARY WAR

Nearly two centuries after the first Europeans arrived, the Hudson Valley's communities found themselves in the crossfire of the war for independence. Major battles took place at Stony Point, Kingston, White Plains, and Saratoga. Soldiers wheeled canons along Route 23 between the Hudson and the Berkshires. George Washington established headquarters in Newburgh and other towns along the river, and West Point was fortified to keep the British out.

EARLY INDUSTRY

After the revolution, abundant natural resources created the foundation for industry in the newly independent country: tanneries, bluestone quarries, sawmills, and gristmills opened to support a growing population. Dairy farms and orchards flourished, and the first icehouses appeared along the Hudson.

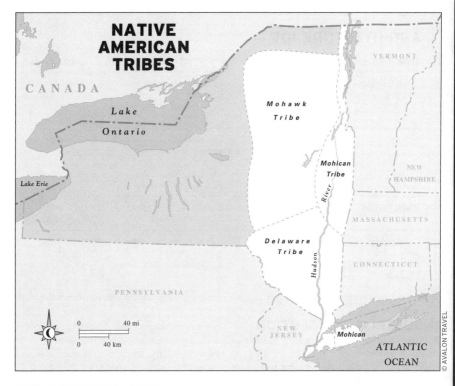

NATIVE AMERICAN TRIBES

CANADA

Lake Ontario

Lake Erie

Mohawk Tribe

Mohican Tribe

Delaware Tribe

Mohican

VERMONT

NEW HAMPSHIRE

MASSACHUSETTS

CONNECTICUT

PENNSYLVANIA

NEW JERSEY

Hudson River

ATLANTIC OCEAN

0   40 mi
0   40 km

© AVALON TRAVEL

STEAMBOAT TRAVEL

Inventor Robert Fulton shattered previous Hudson River records on August 14, 1807, when he made the first successful steamboat journey from New York to Albany in 32 hours. Backing the venture was Chancellor Robert R. Livingston, who had met Fulton in France a decade earlier.

Engines powered by steam would eventually revolutionize the transport of goods and passengers on the Hudson, spurring a new wave of economic development. Change might have proceeded at a faster clip, had New York State not granted Livingston a 20-year monopoly on steamboat travel between New York City and Albany. Livingston and Fulton were free to seize and impose fines on any competitors. But the sovereign state of New Jersey understandably objected to the arrangement, and the Supreme Court intervened to settle the dispute. In the landmark decision of 1824, *Ogden vs. Gibbons,* the court ruled to end the mo-

nopoly, setting a precedent for federal control over interstate commerce. In the wake of the decision, between 1819 and 1840, the number of steamboats on the river rose from 8 to more than 100.

RAIL TRAVEL AND RIVERSIDE ESTATES

The advent of the railroad brought a new wave of prosperity to the Hudson River Valley and Catskill Mountain towns. Summer resorts flourished in Greene, Sullivan, and Delaware Counties. Westchester County became a commuter base as early as the 1800s, when rail travel made it possible to reach New York City in just a few hours. In this era of prosperity, families including the Rockefellers, Vanderbilts, Philipses, and Van Cortlandts built or expanded their sprawling country estates along the banks of the Hudson.

ARCHITECTURE 101

Style	Time Period	Characteristics	Example
Dutch Colonial	late 19th century until the 1930s	Symmetrical two-sided roof with two slanted sides (gambrel) and curved roof edges	Val-Kil
Federal	1780-1830	Low-pitched roof, semicircle over the front door, and large windows with usually six panes per window	Clermont
Greek Revival	late 18th and early 19th centuries	Greek detailing applied to American homes	Roxbury Arts & Cultural Center
Neoclassical (also called Classical Revival/ beaux arts)	late 1800s to the early 1900s	Symmetry and differences in hierarchy; grand entrances and staircases	Mills Mansion (Staatsburg)

INDUSTRIAL REVOLUTION

Factories grew like weeds along the banks of the Hudson during the early 20th century, manufacturing everything from cars to paper to poultry. General Electric began to make appliances in Troy, and IBM settled near Poughkeepsie. As the industrial economy transformed into the information economy and jobs moved overseas, most of these factories shut down. Today's many abandoned plants in Beacon, Newburgh, Poughkeepsie, and other river cities testify to the volume of industry that once thrived across the valley. By the 1960s, the Hudson had earned designation as an industrial river—a body of water polluted beyond repair.

RECESSION AND REVIVAL

Modern auto, rail, and jet travel changed the region forever, sending would-be visitors to ever more exotic destinations in the same amount of time it once took to reach the Catskills from New York City. Farmers, manufacturers, and vacation resorts alike struggled to compete on the international stage, and most towns along the Hudson River fell into a deep and prolonged recession.

The economic boom of the late 1990s triggered a long overdue recovery for many area towns. Weekenders bought second homes, supporting riverfront restaurants and festivals from Newburgh to Kingston. To meet the needs of increasingly sophisticated palates, local farmers began to experiment with boutique crops, such as heirloom vegetables, shiitake mushrooms, organic meat, and microgreens. Winemakers planted French hybrid grapes to produce award-winning labels. Together, these factors set the stage for the intriguing region visitors can experience today.

Government and Economy

ORGANIZATION AND POLITICAL PARTIES

New York State consists of 64 counties, 12 of which are covered in this handbook. Four of the group were established when the first New York General Assembly convened in 1683, with the rest to follow by the early 19th century. Several Hudson Valley cities, including Fishkill, Poughkeepsie, and Kingston, hosted the early state government, before it eventually settled in Albany.

Hudson Valley communities have representation in 10 of the state senate's 62 districts, and the majority of today's senators are members of the Republican party. Three districts, covering Westchester County and the city of Albany, currently have Democratic representatives.

The New York State Assembly is made up of 150 districts, with one representative from each. Ron Canestrari, a Democrat representing the 106th District, which covers parts of Albany, Rensselaer, and Saratoga Counties, plays a leadership role in the current Assembly. He was first elected to the Assembly in 1988 and appointed majority leader in 2007 by the Speaker of the Assembly.

AGRICULTURE

Some 4,000 farms cover nearly 20 percent of all land in the Hudson Valley, producing everything from beef, poultry, milk, and cheese to apples, sweet corn, organic produce, wine, hay, and flowers. Most of the area's longtime farmers are struggling to make ends meet in the globalized economy. They face a host of challenges, from achieving profitability and resisting development pressure on land to updating infrastructure and raising public awareness and support for an endangered way of life.

The current Buy Local movement, which is gaining momentum across the nation, stands to benefit Hudson Valley growers. Community-supported agriculture and "agri-

NEW YORK'S NOTABLE GOVERNORS

- George Clinton (1st: 1777-1798) is remembered as the Father of New York.

- DeWitt Clinton (6th) served two nonconsecutive terms in 1817-1822 and 1825-1828, during which he led the construction of the Erie Canal.

- Martin Van Buren (9th: January-March 1829) was known as Old Kinderhook. His tenure as governor is the second shortest on record for the state.

- Theodore Roosevelt (33rd: 1899-1901) was elected in 1899 after returning from the Spanish American War. He served for two years before becoming vice president to William McKinley.

- Franklin Delano Roosevelt (44th: 1928-1932) mobilized New York state's government to aid the economy during the Great Depression.

- W. Averell Harriman (48th: 1955-1959) was famous for his diplomacy skills. Prior to becoming New York's 48th governor, he served as ambassador to Moscow and England.

- Nelson A. Rockefeller (49th: 1959-1973) was elected governor of New York four times. He grew the State University of New York into the largest provider of public higher education in the country and also improved and expanded the New York State Parks system.

Source: www.ny.gov/governor/nygovs

FORTY TO ONE

While McDonalds is trying to win your breakfast dollars with the McGriddle – featuring maple-flavored sugar crystals baked into your pancakes – a handful of Hudson Valley farmers continue to produce real maple syrup the old-fashioned way. They drill holes in hard maple trees, collect the sap that drips out, and boil excess water away in a wood-fired evaporator. The end result is Grade A maple syrup that turns a quick breakfast into a gourmet feast.

Once an off-season income supplement for dairy farms, maple sugarhouses today draw late-season skiers and other visitors for a lesson in culinary science. The process begins in late February or early March, when temperatures climb into the 40s during the day and return to the low 20s at night. For about four to six weeks, the fluctuating temperatures move tree sap from roots to leaves and back again, allowing the farmer to catch some of the flow without harming the tree. The most authentic sugarhouses hang aluminum buckets on each trunk to collect the sap, although larger operations have upgraded to plastic pipes in order to speed up the process.

Straight out of the tree, sap runs clear, with just a hint of sweetness. Back in the sugarhouse, the farmer boils the frothy liquid in the long flutes of a steel evaporator, staying up all night long when necessary to finish the day's harvest. An instrument called a hydrometer measures the specific gravity of the liquid and tells the boiler when the sap has officially reached the distinctive amber color and thickness we associate with the real stuff. It's a precise and labor-intensive operation – for every 40 gallons of raw sap, a sugarhouse will produce approximately 1 gallon of syrup.

SUGARHOUSES IN THE HUDSON VALLEY

Delaware County
- Catskill Mountain Maple
  65 Charlie Wood Rd., De Lancey
  607/746-6215

- Shaver-Hill Farm
  Shaver Rd., Harpersfield
  607/652-6792

Greene County
- Maple Glen Farm
  Scribner Hollow Rd., East Jewett
  518/589-5319

- Maple Hill Farms
  107 C. Crapser Rd., Cobleskill
  518/234-4858 or 866/291-8100
  www.maplehillfarms.biz

Sullivan County
- Andersen's Maple Farm
  534 Andersen Rd., Long Eddy
  845/887-4238

- Muthig Farm
  1036 Muthig Rd., Parksville
  845/292-7838

Ulster County
- Lyonsville Sugarhouse & Farm
  591 County Road 2/Krumville Rd.,
  Kripplebush
  845/687-2518

- Mountain Dew Maple Products
  351 Samsonville Rd., Kerhonkson
  845/626-3466

tourism" activities such as farm tours, tasting rooms, and educational programs, promise a sustainable future for farmer and community alike. The Hudson Valley Agricultural Partnership is a network of farmers, consumers, business, and other organizations working together to strengthen agriculture and protect farmland in the region. Visit www.hvap.org for more information.

INDUSTRY

The larger cities and towns along the Hudson River reached their peak at the height of the Industrial Revolution, when area factories made everything from automotive parts to ball bearings to men's shirt collars. In the 1980s and 1990s, globalization sent most of those jobs overseas, shutting the old factories down.

Today, employment in the manufacturing sector continues to decline. (It has dropped 15.3 percent since 2002, affecting 10,700 workers.) In the meantime, employment in a variety of service industries is on the rise. And new jobs are appearing in real estate; educational services; arts, entertainment, and recreation; and healthcare and social assistance industries. The largest employers (excluding agriculture) in the area are in the government, healthcare, retail, and food and accommodations sectors.

Despite the cutbacks of the early 1990s, IBM remains the largest private employer in the region, with offices and plants from Somers to Hawthorne and Poughkeepsie to East Fishkill. AT&T, Altria/Kraft, Fuji Photo Film, GAP/Old Navy, the Indian Point Nuclear Energy plant, MasterCard, PepsiCo, and Verizon Wireless are some of the other top employers. Tourism (leisure and hospitality) accounts for about 9 percent of employment in the region.

Unemployment in the Hudson Valley measured 3.89 percent in 2006, down from 4.10 in 2005 and lower than the national rate.

DISTRIBUTION OF WEALTH

Per capita income varies widely across the valley. In Westchester ($64,045), Rockland ($46,505), and Putnam ($43,992) counties, it is well above the state ($39,967) and national averages ($34,471). But Dutchess County, at $36,467, measures just slightly above the national level, and well below the state level. The rest of counties in the region fall below the national and state averages.

Accordingly, more than half the businesses in the region are based in Westchester County; the vast majority (90 percent) are small businesses with fewer than 20 employees. Only 32 companies in the region had more than 1,000 employees as of a 2005 study.

Inflation is strong in the Hudson Valley region. Prices are rising faster than national average. And property values rose by more than two-thirds from 2000 to 2004. Home prices are still rising, but at a much slower rate than earlier in the decade. In 2005, the average selling price of a single-family home was $568,486 (well above the national average of $268,200 and the state average of $336,060). More than 80 percent of residents in the region drive or carpool to work. As the Hudson Valley becomes its own economic center, distinct from New York City, it is encountering the associated challenges of providing affordable housing and managing traffic congestion.

TOURISM

Tourism is a growing part of the overall Hudson Valley economy (7.3 percent at last check), as new historic sites, museums, and cultural attractions draw visitors from New York City, the greater Tri-State area, and beyond. West Point alone draws more than 3 million visitors a year and is one of the top three tourist destinations in New York State.

The People

DEMOGRAPHICS

Historically, Hudson Valley immigrants were German, Dutch, or Irish. Today, more than 2 million area residents are a mix of commuters to New York City, farmers, small business owners, artists, students, second-home owners, and blue-collar workers. The majority of counties in the region exceed the national average in percentage of high school and college graduates that make up their population.

From 2000 to 2004, nearly 24,000 people moved into the Hudson Valley from New York City, but overall migration was negative, with about 20,000 more people leaving the valley than moved in.

ETHNIC GROUPS

All major socioeconomic groups are represented in the Hudson Valley, and the ethnic makeup has become increasingly diverse as new immigrants arrive in New York City and gradually make their way north in search of jobs and homes. Black, Hispanic, and Asian minorities live throughout the region, representing the highest percentages of total population in Westchester and Rockland counties.

Although they played a pivotal historical role in the development of the Hudson Valley, Native American tribes unfortunately have little presence in modern-day communities. In Ulster and Sullivan counties, several tribes have been in negotiations with government officials to open casinos that some argue could revive struggling local economies, as well as benefit the tribes; however, a strong contingent opposes this kind of development on the grounds that it would encourage the spread of gambling without generating the kind of economic momentum that's promised.

As immigrant communities take hold and expand in more remote areas, they are introducing international foods and traditions that were once limited to urban areas like New York City. The result for residents and visitors alike is an increasingly diverse mix of options for dining and entertainment throughout the region.

ESSENTIALS

Getting There and Around

BY AIR

The Hudson River Valley is easily accessible from several international airports, including John F. Kennedy (JFK; Van Wyck Expressway, 718/244-4444), LaGuardia (LGA; Grand Central Pkwy., 718/533-3400), and Newark (EWR; I-95 and I-78, 973/961-6000) in the New York City area, as well as Albany (ALB; 737 Albany-Shaker Rd., Albany, 518/242-2200, www.albany airport.com), Stewart (SWF; 1180 First St., New Windsor, 845/564 2100, www.stewart intlairport.com), and Westchester (HPN; 240 Airport Rd., White Plains, 914/995-4850) airports upstate. Numerous county and private airstrips provide local shuttle service.

Stewart and Albany offer convenient access to many Hudson River Valley attractions; however busier JFK and Newark airports often have better rates and more choice in flight times for travelers coming from afar.

Stewart Airport has just one terminal with four rental car agencies and one limousine service inside. Taxis are also available. The only food option outside the terminal is a Quizno's sandwich chain. Hudson's has books and snacks. There is an ATM near baggage claim.

Newark is closest to destinations in Orange and Rockland Counties, while JFK and LaGuardia serve Westchester and Putnam counties best. Newark also has the best public

© JASON EGLIT

transportation to and from New York City. Its AirTrain service connects to NJ Transit and Amtrak, which offer frequent express trains out of Penn Station. Rail service to JFK is a trickier proposition that requires a long subway ride to Queens and then an AirTrain connection to the terminals. Information about all three New York City airports, as well as AirTrain services at Newark and JFK, is available at the Port Authority of NY & NJ website: www.panynj.gov.

Car services are often the best option for getting to and from Stewart and Albany airports, and listings are available on the airport websites; cabs, rental cars, and shuttle services are also readily available to most destinations.

BY TRAIN

Metro-North (800/638-7646, www.mta .nyc.ny.us/mnr/index.html) and **New Jersey Transit** (800/772-2222, www.njtransit.com) run commuter lines out of New York City's Grand Central and Penn Stations, reaching Poughkeepsie and Wassaic in the north, Port Jervis in the west, and Connecticut in the east. Metro-North offers discount rail fare and admission to popular destinations, including Boscobel, Clearwater, Dia:Beacon, Nyack, and Kykuit.

Amtrak (800/872-7245, www.amtrak.com) offers service beyond the commuter zone, following the eastern bank of the Hudson all the way to Albany and Saratoga Springs. Taxis are readily available at most major stations.

BY BUS

Greyhound (800/229-9424, www.greyhound .com) buses stop in major cities and towns throughout the valley, including Albany, New Paltz, Newburgh, Poughkeepsie, Saratoga Springs, and White Plains. **Shortline Bus** (800/631-8405, www.shortlinebus.com) and **Adirondack Trailways** (800/858-8555, www .escapemaker.com/adirondacktrailways.com) offer regional connections and package trips.

Public transportation gets less reliable the farther you travel into the countryside, but most counties run some sort of local bus sys-

© NIKKI GOTH ITOI

tem to connect major town centers and some rural areas.

BY BOAT

Several companies run daytime and evening cruises along the river. Major ports include Newburgh, Kingston, and Hudson. The Hudson River Sloop *Clearwater,* based out of Poughkeepsie, produces environmental education programs and riverfront festivals. **NY Waterway** (800/53-FERRY or 800/533-3779, www.nywaterway.com) runs commuter ferries as well as sightseeing tours to and from Manhattan. Some packages include admission to popular destinations.

BY CAR

Traveling by car affords the opportunity to meander along scenic back roads, across one-lane bridges, and down bumpy dirt roads; however, drivers should be aware that along with the rural scenery comes some inevitable runins with traffic congestion. And once you leave the highway, few roads are straight and flat; hills and curves are part of any Hudson Valley road trip.

Two major interstates traverse the Hudson River Valley: I-84 connects Pennsylvania to Connecticut through southern Dutchess County. And I-87, the New York State Thruway, runs from New York City to Albany and then on to Buffalo.

Toll Roads

The New York State Thruway (I-87) holds the record as the longest toll highway in the United States. It costs $5.10 to drive the length of the Hudson Valley northbound, from the New York City line to the downtown Albany exit (141 miles). The return trip costs $9.10, due to one-way bridge fees. Exits are often 15 miles or more apart, so watch carefully for signs to avoid missing your turn. Occasional rest areas have gas, restrooms, and an array of fast food, including Starbucks.

The following five Hudson River crossings have a $1 toll in the eastbound direction:

- Bear Mountain Bridge (Westchester and Orange)

- Newburgh-Beacon Bridge (I-84)

- Mid-Hudson Bridge (southern Dutchess and Ulster)

- Kingston-Rhinecliff Bridge (northern Dutchess and Ulster)

- Rip Van Winkle Bridge (Columbia and Greene)

There is a $4 toll to cross the Tappan Zee Bridge between Westchester and Rockland counties, and a $6 toll for the George Washington Bridge. All bridges and toll roads in New York State are equipped with the EZ-Pass (www.ez-pass.com) automatic transponder system, which is compatible with most systems in the northeast. If you want to use an EZ-Pass in a rental car, you must first call EZ-Pass to have the license plate registered on your account. Some agencies, including Avis, are beginning to rent cars with EZ-Pass installed. Cash-only lanes are clearly marked at most toll plazas.

Highway Information

The best sources of real-time traffic updates for the Lower Hudson Valley and New York metropolitan area are AM radio 880 "on the eights" (1:08, 1:18, 1:28, etc.) and AM 1010 "on the ones" (1:01, 1:11, 1:21, etc.). **Radio Catskill** is a hydropowered community radio station serving the Catskills, the Upper Delaware, and Mid-Hudson regions (FM 90.5 and FM 94.5, www.wjffradio.org). In Albany, tune to **WAMC Northeast Public Radio** (FM 90.3 in Albany and FM 90.9 in Kingston, www.wamc.org).

Consult www.nycroads.com/crossings/hudson-river for bridge conditions. Also online is the New York State Travel Information Gateway at www.nysdot.gov/portal/page/portal/tig, with information by region.

The Taconic State Parkway

The scenic Taconic State Parkway runs north-south from the Sprainbrook Parkway, which comes out of New York City, to I-90 near the Massachusetts state line and offers convenient access to many of the Hudson Valley's inland towns. Unlike the six-lane interstates that run parallel to it, the Taconic has just two lanes in each direction with a wide, green median in between. It crosses some of the prettiest woodlands, marshes, and fields of Westchester, Dutchess, and Columbia Counties, making it a popular route for motorists.

Several risks make the route one of the more dangerous in the state. When driving the Taconic for the first time, take these factors into consideration:

Narrow lanes: The Taconic's narrow lanes are unforgiving, particularly on icy or wet roads. There are drains every few hundred feet on both sides and no emergency breakdown lanes. If you must stop for any reason, pull all the way onto the grass, as far as possible away from traffic.

Cross traffic: Except for a few of the busiest intersections, the Taconic does not have on- and off-ramps. After one too many accidents, the state closed most of the hazardous crossroads in Dutchess County, but many in Columbia County remain open. Watch for cars braking suddenly in the left lane to turn, or for cars accelerating slowly in the right lane.

Deer: The Hudson Valley supports a healthy population of white-tailed deer, and many of them feed on the shrubs and bushes that line both sides of the Taconic. Watch for eyes at night, and remember that a deer caught in the glare of oncoming headlights will often freeze in its tracks. When you see one, others are likely feeding nearby.

Speed traps: The speed limit on the Taconic is 55 miles per hour, and New York State troopers are serious about enforcing it. Although traffic moves much faster during rush hour, troopers frequently lurk in the median to catch drivers who exceed the limit by as little as five miles per hour. Bulls Head Road near Rhinebeck and the town of Fishkill are known hot spots.

U.S. Route 9 and Route 9W on the east and west sides of the Hudson River are slower north–south routes through the valley.

Driving Guidelines

The maximum speed limit on New York State highways is 65 miles per hour, and limits are often lower through congested areas or on older highways. Seatbelts are required at all times, and it is illegal to talk on a cell phone while driving, unless you have a hands-free connection. Right turns on red are permissible outside of New York City, unless otherwise marked.

Rental Cars

Rental agencies are easy to come by in the Lower Hudson Valley, but more difficult as you venture north, until you reach Albany. Major brands cluster around the airports, and most sizable towns have at least one independent rental service.

Car rentals are generally much less expensive in the Hudson River Valley than they are at the New York City airports. If you are traveling from these airports to the Mid-Hudson region or farther and plan to stay more than a couple of days, try this cost-saving strategy: arrange a one-way rental at the higher airport rate, then return the car the next day and reserve a new vehicle at the lower upstate rate for the remainder of your trip.

BY BICYCLE

Mountain bikes are easier to find as rentals than road bikes, but a number of shops in the area cater to the cycling community. For example, The Bicycle Depot on Main Street in New Paltz rents aluminum road bikes in good condition. Cycling enthusiasts Ken Roberts and Sharon Marsh Roberts have posted a wealth of useful information, including maps, online at www.roberts-1.com/bikehudson. You can travel with bikes on Shortline Bus and Metro-North.

Washington, D.C.–based **Escapades Bike Tours** (202/232-1531, www.bikeescapades.com/hudson) organizes an eight-day fall-foliage tour in October for cyclists of all levels ($1,895). Average daily mileage is 25–45, depending on individual preferences and abilities. A shorter six-day version costs $1,595.

The fourth annual **Great Hudson Valley Pedal** (www.ptny.org/hudsontour), sponsored by Parks & Trails New York, was to take place in August 2008. Participants ride from Albany to New York City in a fully supported six-day, 200-mile tour.

Sports and Recreation

Excellent outdoor recreation is one of the top reasons people come to the Hudson River Valley. You can escape the crowds in summer or winter on the expansive network of trails in the Catskills or in one of the region's many state parks. Approximately 100,000 acres of wilderness are preserved in more than a dozen state parks, including Bear Mountain, Harriman, Minnewaska, and Saratoga Spa. Catskill State Park encompasses another 900 square miles of "forever wild" state land. And the expansive Taconic State Park encompasses 5,000 acres at the base of the Taconic Range, near the Massachusetts and Connecticut state lines. Hiking, boating, and fishing rank among the most popular activities.

State Parks

All told, the Hudson Valley, Catskills, and Capital-Saratoga regions encompass more than 40 state parks and 20 designated state historic sites. The state plays an active role in preserving the Catskill Park: It runs the Belleayre ski resort, maintains a network of 33 trails, stocks rivers and creeks with fish, and operates a number of campgrounds. See individual chapters for specific park profiles. Or contact the New York State Office of Parks, Recreation and Historic Preservation at Empire State Plaza in downtown Albany (518/474-0456). The New York State Historic Preservation Office is located at the Peebles Island Resource Center in Waterford (518/237-8643). For camping reservation, call Reserve America (800/456-CAMP).

Hiking

Most state parks maintain their own trail systems and camping facilities, and some 200 miles of trails traverse the Catskill Forest Preserve. High above the Hudson River Valley are **Kaaterskill Falls** and the **Escarpment Trail,** a magical wilderness setting where the Hudson River School of painters found inspiration and the Catskill Mountain House entertained prominent guests. **Slide Mountain** in Ulster

---

THE BEST GREENS FOR THE FEES

Golf is ubiquitous throughout the Hudson Valley region, and you can spend as little or as much as you like. Here are some of the best deals around:

- Apple Greens Course, Highland, Ulster County

- Beekman Country Club, Hopewell Junction, Dutchess County

- Carvel Country Club, Pine Plains, Dutchess County

- Casperkill Golf Club, Poughkeepsie, Dutchess County

- Centennial Golf Club, Carmel, Putnam County

- Grossingers Country Club, Liberty, Sullivan County

- Hudson Hills Golf Course, Ossining, Westchester County

- Links at Union Vale, LaGrangeville, Dutchess County

- Rondout Golf Club, Accord, Ulster County

- Silo Ridge Golf Course, Amenia, Dutchess County

County is the highest peak in the Catskills and offers a challenging day hike.

In Minnewaska State Park, part of the Shawangunk Ridge, hikers may see two rare species: the dwarf pitch pine and peregrine falcon. Taconic State Park has Bash Bish Falls, as well as miles of trails that invite exploration.

Camping in all of these areas is unrestricted below 3,500 feet, although backpackers are encouraged to camp in designated areas to lessen the impact on the forest.

Cycling

Cyclists enjoy endless miles of rolling hills on quiet country roads, and several counties have converted long stretches of abandoned train tracks into paths for walking, jogging, or biking. **Piermont** and **New Paltz** are popular cycling towns, and many local clubs plan group rides on summer weekends. You might tour one county at a time, or attempt the 180-mile multiday ride from New York City to Albany. Include as many bridge crossings as possible, and allow time to take in some of the sights along the way. Several companies offer guided bike tours of the area; an amateur bike race is another way to discover many of the back roads.

Swimming and Boating

The Hudson and its tributaries support all manner of water sports. Boats are available for rent at marinas on both shores—the **Village of Catskill** is a good place to launch. Tubing on the **Esopus** in Ulster County is especially popular in summer. Sailing school is an option out of Kingston. **Greenwood Lake** in Orange County, **Lake Taghkanic** in Columbia County, and several lakes near Saratoga Springs have beaches for swimming and facilities for boats.

Kayakers can paddle lakes, ponds, creeks, and of course the Hudson River in Dutchess County. **Hudson Valley Pack & Paddle** (45 Beekman St., Beacon, 845/831-1300, www .hvpackandpaddle.com; 10 A.M.–5 P.M. Mon.–Sat., noon–5 P.M. Sun.) rents kayaks and canoes April through November. Rates are $45/day for a single kayak and $60/day for a double kayak or two-person canoe. Look for the shop on the west side of Route 9D, just before the turn for the train station. For a Hudson River tour, you can launch nearby at Dennings Point in Beacon.

Another reputable shop, **The River Connection** (9 West Market St., Hyde Park, 845/229-0595 or 845/242-4731, www.the-river-connection.com), offers water sports instruction, as well as equipment sales and rentals. Certified instructors lead trips from various launch points along the river, including Norrie

fishing the Wallkill River near High Falls

© NIKKI GOTH ITOI

Point (Staatsburg), Tivoli, Croton Point, and Poughkeepsie ($100 pp). Experienced paddlers may join the guided day trips from Athens to Saugerties, Saugerties to Norrie Point, and Cold Spring to Annsville Creek, which make up the annual Great Hudson River Paddle (ages 16 and up only, $100 pp).

Fishing

Anglers can fish the tidal Hudson River, freshwater creeks and streams, or reservoirs. Guided tours are available in many locations, including the Willowemoc and Beaverkill Rivers near **Roscoe (Trout Town U.S.A.)** and the **Pepacton Reservoir.** Popular catches include American shad, striped bass, perch, herring, and sturgeon in the Hudson; and wild trout and bass in lakes, streams, creeks, and ponds throughout the region. The **Catskill Fly Fishing Museum** in Sullivan County pays tribute to the fathers of the sport in a series of informative exhibits. Bass tournaments draw large crowds to the river near the town of Catskill in summer.

Winter Sports

New Yorkers flock to **Windham, Hunter,** and **Belleayre mountains** for downhill skiing and snowboarding. Runs are relatively short at all three resorts; Belleayre caters to beginners, while Windham and Hunter have more terrain for experienced skiers and boarders. Resorts with snow-making equipment open in late November or early December, as soon as temperatures dip below freezing. Spring conditions typically last through the end of March.

For more of a wilderness experience, many state parks—especially **Harriman, Minnewaska,** and **Saratoga Spa**—maintain trails for Nordic skiing, snowshoeing, tubing, and tobogganing.

ACCOMMODATIONS

Hudson Valley accommodations range from budget motels to modest inns to luxury resorts. In most counties, there is an appealing option for just about every type of trip and budget.

Resorts

Scattered throughout the region—mostly in the Catskill Mountains—are a handful of full-service resorts that offer golf, spa treatments, and other activities on-site. Prices are often given per person per week and include meals. The Mohonk Mountain House near New Paltz, and the Emerson Resort and Spa near Woodstock are a couple of examples. Most of the area's ski resorts have a variety of slopeside and nearby rooms and condos for rent.

Hotels and Motels

You can find everything from major chains to boutique hotels along the Hudson River. Some of the most charming properties are housed in historic homes that have been restored and converted for guest use. Many of the top establishments also run award-winning restaurants, staffed by graduates of the prestigious Culinary Institute of America in Hyde Park. Belvedere Mansion and the Beekman Arms, both located in Rhinebeck (Dutchess County), and the Inn at Lake Joseph in Forestburgh (Sullivan County) are a few examples.

Pig Hill Inn B&B, Cold Spring

© NIKKI GOTH ITOI

Bed-and-Breakfast Inns

By far the most popular places to stay in the Hudson Valley are bed-and-breakfast inns, which range from a few rooms in someone's house to rooms with private entries in a converted barn or carriage house. With this type of accommodations, you may have the opportunity (or obligation, depending on how you see it) to socialize with the owners over breakfast. Another bonus: Innkeepers often hire CIA-graduates to prepare gourmet country-style breakfasts. Some B&Bs are centrally located in the valley's most popular towns; others are more remote. Quality varies widely too, so it pays to do your homework before you book. Sparrow Hawk Bed and Breakfast (Ulster County) and Octagon Farm Bed & Breakfast (Sullivan County) are a couple of top picks.

Efficiency Cabins

Many motels and campgrounds also provide rustic one-room cabins with kitchenettes. These are often heated by wood-burning stoves or fireplaces. Expect a cozy atmosphere but very basic amenities in this type of accommodations.

Camping

From dozens of state parks to the Catskills and Shawangunks, outdoors enthusiasts can choose from hundreds of appealing places to pitch a tent. For car camping, Yogi Bear's Jellystone Camp-Resort has several locations in the Mid-Hudson region. Some parks, such as Taconic State Park, also rent cabins for year-round activities. Backpackers can camp anywhere below 3,500 feet elevation in the Catskills, but rangers ask that you choose designated camping areas to lessen the impact on the forest.

Other Options

Simple guesthouses—a room or two in someone's home—are another possibility, as are vacation rental homes. Yoga institutes and alternative lifestyle centers like the Omega Institute in Rhinebeck offer yet more choices in accommodations. Another interesting option is the rustic two-room Saugerties Lighthouse.

FOOD

Whether you intend to build a trip around the valley's good eats or simply want to know where to get sustenance while you're on the go, it will be extremely difficult to go hungry in this part of New York State. Gourmet restaurants are scattered all over the area, while numerous taverns, pubs, delis, and diners reflect their individual locations and communities. Many of the best places to eat are not centrally located in the valley's towns and villages, but either a few miles away on a scenic country back road or hidden in a commercial plaza. Either way, it's often worth the drive to seek out a memorable culinary experience.

In summer, you can get your fill roaming from one roadside farm stand to the next, with an occasional pause to pick your own fruit and vegetables. Ice cream stands pop up in every town, and the hardest decision will be whether to choose home made or soft-serve. If all of this fails to please, fast-food chains are everywhere, too.

Tips for Travelers

STUDENTS

Students will find a range of programs at the Hudson Valley's many colleges and universities. The State University of New York has campuses in Albany, New Paltz, and Purchase. Private institutions include Vassar College, Marist College, Bard College, Skidmore College, and the Culinary Institute of America. Jobseekers should consult local newspapers and county websites for current listings.

FEMALE TRAVELERS

Women traveling alone should feel safe throughout the Hudson Valley, but be aware of surroundings when exploring urban areas like Albany, Newburgh, and Poughkeepsie.

Get detailed directions for places you want to visit in these areas so you don't wander too far off-course, and leave valuables behind. In general, take the same precautions you would in any mid-sized U.S. city.

GAY AND LESBIAN TRAVELERS

In 2004, the town of New Paltz brought same-sex marriage to the national spotlight. A year later, the New Paltz Pride March and Festival brought together a group of volunteers who soon after formed the **Hudson Valley LGBTQ Community Center** (300 Wall St., Kingston, 845/331-5300, www.lgbtqcenter.org). Some 800 members have joined the organization since it was founded. Among other awareness- and community-building initiatives, the center sponsors an annual Come Out & Find Out conference, covering hot-button topics facing the lesbian, gay, bisexual, transgender, and queer/questioning community of the Mid-Hudson Valley.

While many of the Hudson Valley's towns are diverse in their makeup and progressive in their way of thinking, gay and lesbian travelers are still likely to encounter a quietly conservative attitude in rural areas. For accommodations, New Paltz, Woodstock, Rhinebeck, and Hyde Park all have a number of inns that are especially welcoming to gay couples—specifically, Cromwell Manor Inn (Cornwall), Ecce B&B (Barryville), Journey Inn B&B (Hyde Park), Morgan State House (Albany), Old Drovers Inn (Dover Plains), and Sparrow Hawk B&B (Stone Ridge).

The Day to Be Gay in the Catskills Festival draws a crowd of residents and visitors with music and entertainment (www.daytobegay.org). Check Out in the Catskills (www.outinthecatskills.com) for a list of gay-friendly establishments in Sullivan County.

The annual **Winter Explosion** (www.winterexplosion.com) music festival has been held at the Hudson Valley Resort and Spa on President's Day weekend in February every year since 2000 (except for 2003–2004 when it moved temporarily to King of Prussia, Pennsylvania). In 2007, the festival was sponsored entirely by black, gay-owned businesses; this incredibly popular event stages the likes of Chaka Khan and Patti LaBelle in sold-out concerts. The producers organize bus transportation from major cities and airports, and the price of $520–575 per person includes accommodations for the weekend.

New York City–based *Go Magazine* (www.gomag.com) occasionally features lesbian-friendly destinations in the Hudson Valley.

TRAVELERS WITH DISABILITIES

With a few exceptions, travelers with disabilities will find most major attractions in the region easily accessible. The exceptions are some of the outdoor garden tours, which may not be wheelchair-friendly. Travel plazas along the New York State Thruway are fully accessible, and people with disabilities can purchase full-service fuel at self-serve rates.

FAMLIES TRAVELING WITH CHILDREN

Families will find many kid-friendly establishments across the Hudson River Valley, including historic museums, interpretive nature trails, and water parks. (See the *Where to Take the Kids* callout in the *Hudson Highlands* chapter.) Restaurants often have special menus for children, and many historic sites and attractions offer reduced admission fees for families. Students also often receive preferential rates. A few of the region's luxury inns do not allow young children. Check before making reservations.

SENIORS

Senior citizens enjoy reduced admission fees at most attractions throughout the region; however, some walking tours of historic homes and gardens, such as the Rockefeller Estate, may be dangerous for travelers with limited balance or mobility. If you're concerned, call ahead for details.

PETS

Pets are welcome at many, but not all, outdoor spaces throughout the Hudson Valley. Inquire at inns and hotels before bringing your dog along. Restaurants do not allow pets inside, but many don't mind if your pooch curls up at your feet outside.

ANGLERS AND HUNTERS

Trout fishing on lakes and streams is open April 1–October 15. You can fish for crappie, whitefish, shad, and perch year-round. Certain rivers and counties have additional restrictions. Trout fishing on New York City reservoirs is open year-round with size limitations. A free New York City Public Access permit is required to fish on the reservoirs. The application can be downloaded and printed from the Department of Environmental Protection at http://nyc.gov/html/dep/watershed/html/wsrecreation.html.

A wide variety of game is available for hunting in designated seasons within the Hudson Valley region. Deer, turkey, bear, ducks, and upland game are popular species. You'll know you're in a hunting town when you see signs advertising Hunter Breakfasts.

New York State is divided into four hunting zones: Northern, Southern, Westchester, and Suffolk. Seasons are divided into regular (for rifles), archery, and special firearms. Hunting season dates and regulations vary from year to year.

Before hunting or fishing, make sure you have the correct license, tag, and federal stamps. Licenses are available in many sporting goods stores. Contact the New York State Department of Environmental Conservation (518/357-2450, www.dec.state.ny.us) for the latest information.

HEALTH AND SAFETY

The Hudson Valley has a severe problem with ticks and Lyme disease. Wear long sleeves and pants when hiking in grassy or wooded areas, and always check for ticks when you return. Poison ivy is another nuisance that can cause minor skin irritation and itching.

Hypothermia is a concern for hikers, paddlers, and cyclists who may be subject to rapid temperature changes. Bring layers and plenty of fluids for any outdoor adventure.

Campers need to take precautions against black bears, who often visit campsites in search of food. Don't cook near your tent, and bring rope or a bear canister to store your food out of reach.

Deer are a perennial hazard when driving roads at night; take it slow and watch for their eyes.

Dial 911 for emergencies, or 0 for the operator. Area hospitals are open around the clock to treat injuries and illnesses. Bring proof of medical coverage.

Crime in New York State has dropped steadily over the past few years, and Hudson River Valley communities are known to be among the safest in the United States. Crime rates in the largest towns and cities measure average or better across the valley. Albany and Newburgh are the exceptions, with the highest crime rates in the region. Take the same precautions you would at home.

Information and Services

Businesses in New York are generally open 9 A.M.–5 P.M. Monday–Friday. Banks close earlier, around 3 P.M., although some are open on Saturday mornings as well, and ATMs are accessible 24/7. Shops in tourist destinations stay open on Saturday and part or all of Sunday, and some grocery stores are open 24 hours. (Price Chopper is often open 24 hours, and ShopRite stores are generally open 6–1 A.M.).

Most stores, hotels, and restaurants accept credit cards for payment, but there are excep-tions, so be sure to ask before you attempt to pay with plastic. The state sales tax is 4 percent as of January 2007, but when you add local county taxes, the markup usually exceeds 8 percent.

MAPS AND TOURIST INFORMATION

Jimapco publishes one of the best atlases to the region. The spiralbound *Hudson Valley Street Atlas* covers Greene, Columbia, Ulster, Dutchess,

Sullivan, Orange, and Putnam counties, with detailed maps of the largest cities (Kingston, Poughkeepsie, Newburgh, Middletown, Monticello, Catskill) and the tiniest hamlets (Maplecrest, Freehold, Ancram). The fourth edition is available at www.jimapco.com for $24.95. Hagstrom (www.hagstrommap.com) publishes a laminated foldout map to the Hudson Valley and Catskills for $8.95. Individual county maps from both companies are available in convenience stores throughout the region. Cyclists can print detailed route maps for scenic road rides on the website of cycling enthusiasts Ken Roberts and Sharon Marsh Roberts (www.roberts-1.com/bikehudson).

COMMUNICATIONS AND MEDIA

Post offices, found in even the most rural towns, are generally open 8:30 A.M.–5 P.M. Monday–Friday and 8:30 A.M.–noon Saturday.

Public libraries across the region offer Internet access free or for a nominal charge. In addition, Internet cafés and wireless hotspots have been making their way up the valley to Barnes & Noble, Starbucks, and a growing number of independent locations.

Telephone Area Codes

There are four main area codes in the Hudson River Valley.

- 518: Albany, Saratoga, Greene, Columbia

- 607: Parts of Delaware

- 845: Rockland, Putnam, Orange, Sullivan, Dutchess, Ulster, and parts of Delaware

- 914: Westchester

Local Media

The *New York Times* is a daily national newspaper with regular coverage of upstate towns and issues. The *Poughkeepsie Journal* is a respected regional paper owned by a national publisher. Many other towns have small circulation newspapers, and several regional magazines contain useful information for travelers: *Hudson Valley Magazine* (Suburban Publishing, www.hvmag.com), *Dutchess Magazine* (Taconic Press), *Westchester Magazine* (Spotlight Publications, www.westchestermagazine.com), and *Kaatskill Life* (The Delaware County Times, www.kaatslife.com). *Chronogram* is a free, large-format print magazine focused on art and culture in the valley. Look for copies in tourism offices, hotel lobbies, and visitors centers. **The Hudson River Valley Review,** published by the Hudson River Valley Institute at Marist College (3399 North Rd., Poughkeepsie, 845/575-3052, www.hudsonrivervalley.net/hrvr.php), prints scholarly research and literature connected with the region.

Most local television networks are based out of New York City or Albany. Albany radio station WAMC 90.3 is an NPR-member station, as is WNYC 93.9 out of New York City.

RESOURCES

Suggested Reading

FICTION

Adams, Arthur G., ed. *The Hudson River in Literature: An Anthology.* New York: Fordham University Press, 1980. This anthology, which includes the writings of James Fenimore Cooper and William Cullen Bryant, provides a good overview of writers who wrote about and were influenced by the Hudson River Valley.

Cooper, James Fenimore. *The Last of the Mohicans.* New York: Bantam Classics, 1982. The second Leatherstocking Tale and the most popular of Cooper's novels, this adventure of the French and Indian Wars in the Lake George county takes place in 1757.

Cooper, James Fenimore. *The Leatherstocking Tales.* New York: Library of America, 1985. The five books that make up Cooper's Tales are set in the Hudson River Valley.

George, Jean Craighead. *My Side of the Mountain.* New York: Puffin Books, 1988. Many young readers have fallen in love with this story about a boy who runs away from home to the Catskills.

Goodman, Allegra. *Kaaterskill Falls.* New York: Delta, 1999. This book, about three Jewish families who spend summers in the Catskills, is contemporary novelist Allegra Goodman's first.

Irving, Washington. "The Legend of Sleepy Hollow." Rockville, MD: Wildside Press, 2004. Washington Irving lived in Sleepy Hollow and found inspiration for his writing in local residents and villages.

Irving, Washington. "Rip Van Winkle." Hensonville, NY: Black Dome Press Corp, 2003. Irving's classic tale of a very sleepy man takes place in the Catskills.

HISTORY

Chernov, Ron. *Titan: The Life of John D. Rockefeller, Sr.* New York: Vintage Books, 1999. This biography has sections on Kykuit and the Pocantico Hills and gives a good overview of the economy and culture that defined the Hudson River Valley in the 19th century.

Diamant, Lincoln. *Chaining the Hudson: The Fight for the River in the American Revolution.* New York: Fordham University Press, 2004. This book tells the story of defending the river at West Point.

Evers, Alf. *The Catskills: From Wilderness to Woodstock.* Woodstock, NY: Overlook Press, 1982. This book is the definitive history of the Catskills.

Hall, Bruce Edward. *Diamond Street: The Story of the Little Town with the Big Red Light District.* Hensonville, NY: Black Dome Press, 1994. This book tells the story of Hudson's red light district.

Ruttenber, E. M. *Indian Tribes of Hudson's River to 1700* and *Indian Tribes of Hudson's*

River 1700–1850. Saugerties, NY: Hope Farm Press, 1992. These present a thorough history of the Native Americans who first inhabited the valley.

Van Zandt, Roland. *The Catskill Mountain House: America's Grandest Hotel.* Hensonville, NY: Black Dome Press, 1991. Roland Van Zandt offers in in-depth look at one of the most famous hotels in U.S. history.

CULINARY

Greenberg, Jan. *Hudson Valley Harvest: A Food Lover's Guide to Farms, Restaurants and Open-Air Markets.* Woodstock, VT: Countryman Press, 2003. This fascinating overview of the region's microterroirs covers everything from heirloom beans to shiitake mushrooms. Chapters are organized by type of food.

Manikowski, John. *Wild Fish & Game Cookbook.* New York: Artisan, 1997. Not only is Manikowski an accomplished outdoorsman, he wrote and illustrated his own book.

New York State Farm Fresh Guide Metro Region. New York State Department of Agriculture and Markets. This free guide on what to expect when and where is available through the New York State Department of Agriculture and Markets (718/722-2830).

The Valley Table. The Valley Table, Inc. This quarterly print publication maintains an informative website (www.valleytable.com) of local culinary news and events.

Zagat. *Zagat Westchester/Hudson Valley Restaurants 2007–2007.* New York: Zagat Survey, 2007. Comprehensive restaurant listings with extensive coverage of Westchester County and select coverage across the valley. This guide does not cover Albany or Saratoga Springs.

TRAIL GUIDES

Henry, Edward G. *Catskill Trails: A Ranger's Guide to the High Peaks.* Hensonville, NY:

Black Dome Press, 2000. This pair of trail guides are an essential resource for hikers. Book 1 covers the Northern Catskills, and Book 2 covers the Southern Catskills.

Green, Stella and H. Neil Zimmerman. *50 Hikes in the Lower Hudson Valley: Hikes and Walks from Westchester County to Albany.* Woodstock, VT: Countryman Press, 2002. Hikes on both sides of the lower Hudson, from the past vice president and president of the New York–New Jersey Trail Conference.

Kick, Peter. *Catskill Mountain Guide (Hiking Guide Series).* Boston, MA: Appalachian Mountain Club Books, 2002. A guide with more than 90 trail descriptions and a pullout map by a local outdoorsman.

Kick, Peter. *25 Mountain Bike Tours in the Hudson Valley: A Backcountry Guide (25 Bicycle Tours).* Woodstock, VT: Countryman Press, 1996. Somewhat dated information on rail trails, bikeways, and shops.

NATURE

Boyle, Robert H. *The Hudson River: A Natural and Unnatural History.* New York: W. W. Norton & Company, 1979. This is required reading for anyone who takes an environmental interest in the Hudson River.

Burroughs, John. *In the Catskills.* Charleston, SC: BiblioBazaar, 2007. One of America's first conservationists and a contemporary of Walt Whitman and John Muir, Burroughs writes about Slide Mountain and his hometown of Roxbury in a collection of eight essays.

Cole, Thomas. *Thomas Cole's Poetry: The Collected Poems of America's Foremost Painter of the Hudson River School.* York, PA: George Shumway Publisher, 1972. Cole was a poet as well as a painter. More than 100 of his poems and a chronology of his life are included in this edition.

Klinkenborg, Verlyn. *The Rural Life.* New York: Back Bay Books, 2002. This memoir of life on a farm takes place largely in Columbia County.

Titus, Robert. *The Catskills: A Geological Guide.* Fleischmanns, NY: Purple Mountain Press, 1998. This must-read for armchair geologists contains basic explanations and recommended fieldtrips.

TRAVEL ESSAYS

Carmer, Carl. *The Hudson.* NY: Farrar and Rinehart, 1939. In the early 20th century, Carl Carmer wrote a guide to the region, filled with personal anecdotes and observations.

James, Henry. *The American Scene.* Reprinted in *Henry James: Collected Travel Writings.* New York: Library of America, 1993. This book, first published at the turn of the 20th century, captures Henry James's reflections on his return to upstate New York.

Lossing, Benson J. *The Hudson: From the Wilderness to the Sea.* Hensonville, NY: Black Dome Press, 1995. Lossing presents a 19th-century perspective of the region in a travel narrative format.

Lourie, Peter. *River of Mountains: A Canoe Journey down the Hudson.* Syracuse, NY: Syracuse University Press, 1998. This contemporary travel narrative follows a paddler from the Adirondacks to New York Harbor.

Van Zandt, Roland. *Chronicles of the Hudson: Three Centuries of Travel and Adventure.* Hensonville, NY: Black Dome Press, 1992. This book captures an interesting cross-section of travel writing related to the Hudson River.

Internet Resources

Most New York State counties maintain a tourism website with information on attractions, activities, lodging, and dining out. In addition, most establishments maintain at least a basic website with general information. Here are some of the unique sites that cover broader issues and trends in the region.

Black Dome Press
www.blackdomepress.com
This publisher has a large online catalog of regional fiction and nonfiction titles.

Chronogram
www.chronogram.com
Online version of the free, monthly print publication dedicated to supporting the arts in the Hudson Valley.

Clearwater
www.clearwater.org
This organization gathers information about the ongoing clean-up of the Hudson River.

Historic Hudson Valley
www.hudsonvalley.org
This organization publishes information about visiting several National Historic Landmarks in the area, including Kykuit, Lyndhurst, and Montgomery Place.

Hudson River Bridges and Tunnels
www.nycroads.com/crossings/hudson-river
Check here for current traffic conditions before you drive the next leg of your trip.

The Hudson River Valley Institute
www.hudsonrivervalley.net
This Marist College organization is dedicated to scholarly research and writing about the Hudson River Valley National Heritage Area.

Hudson Valley Agricultural Partnership
www.hvap.org
This network of farmers, consumers, business, and other organizations works together to strengthen agriculture and protect farmland in the region.

Hudson Valley Magazine
www.hvmag.com

This regional print publication has timely information for residents and visitors and articles about local food, business, and culture.

Hudson Valley Tourism
www.travelhudsonvalley.org

A promotional agency, connected with the I Love New York state tourism office, representing the counties in the region with a detailed calendar of events.

I Love NY
www.iloveny.com

The central New York State tourism site contains trip ideas, event information, and more.

Index

Acknowledgments

Many experienced travelers, local residents, and fellow writers contributed their time and talents to the second edition of Moon Hudson River Valley. Gretchen Boehm and Jason Eglit shared photos and stories from their weeklong tour of the Mid-Hudson region. And through regular blog postings, Gretchen's parents, Dick and Char Boehm, helped me update and improve coverage of Hudson River's marinas as they cruised from New York City to the Erie Canal aboard their new boat, the Ellen Leigh.

Pawling resident Andy Busby shared notes on some of the hotspots around town, while dear friends Mavis and Charlie Wright turned me on to Millerton. Barbara and Ken Kull called attention to some of the popular eateries near Poughkeepsie. Kathy Herlihy gave me the scoop on some of the valley's nightlife venues and offered invaluable childcare while I was in town. Special thanks to Christopher Winn for insight into Hudson's antique shops.

Ever the supportive parent and travel companion, Sue Goth accompanied me through Delaware and Sullivan Counties to remote outposts that even she had never seen before. My sisters, Jenn Nisi and Kathryn Goth, sent tips on new restaurants and festivals throughout the year. Kathryn also led me on a driving tour of Putnam County. Tanya Lujbli joined me for a hot summer day around Greenwood Lake and Warwick. And Adrienne Mohadjerin sent a report of her first skydiving adventure.

Elizabeth Itoi generously offered the use of her sporty car, Jean Claude, during my extended visits. And my husband, Paul Itoi, shouldered the challenging responsibility of solo parenting while I disappeared on several research trips.

Many thanks to Theresa Russell, who scouted out Rensselaer County for me, and Sarah Anderson, who updated contact information for nearly every business covered in the book. And back at the ATP offices, Erin Raber and Tiffany Watson provided good ideas for shaping the second edition, as well as professional hands-on editing of the manuscript.

To everyone who influenced and supported me in the effort to deliver a thorough and accurate update, my sincerest gratitude.

www.moon.com

For helpful advice on planning a trip, visit www.moon.com for the **TRAVEL PLANNER** and get access to useful travel strategies and valuable information about great places to visit. When you travel with Moon, expect an experience that is uncommon and truly unique.

HANDBOOKS | METRO | OUTDOORS | LIVING ABROAD

MAP SYMBOLS

Symbol	Name	Symbol	Name	Symbol	Name	Symbol	Name
	Expressway		Highlight		Airfield		Golf Course
	Primary Road	○	City/Town		Airport		Parking Area
	Secondary Road	◉	State Capital	▲	Mountain		Archaeological Site
	Unpaved Road	⊛	National Capital	+	Unique Natural Feature		Church
	Trail	★	Point of Interest				Gas Station
	Ferry	•	Accommodation		Waterfall		Glacier
	Railroad	▼	Restaurant/Bar	▲	Park		Mangrove
	Pedestrian Walkway	■	Other Location		Trailhead		Reef
	Stairs	Λ	Campground		Skiing Area		Swamp

CONVERSION TABLES

°C = (°F - 32) / 1.8
°F = (°C x 1.8) + 32
1 inch = 2.54 centimeters (cm)
1 foot = 0.304 meters (m)
1 yard = 0.914 meters
1 mile = 1.6093 kilometers (km)
1 km = 0.6214 miles
1 fathom = 1.8288 m
1 chain = 20.1168 m
1 furlong = 201.168 m
1 acre = 0.4047 hectares
1 sq km = 100 hectares
1 sq mile = 2.59 square km
1 ounce = 28.35 grams
1 pound = 0.4536 kilograms
1 short ton = 0.90718 metric ton
1 short ton = 2,000 pounds
1 long ton = 1.016 metric tons
1 long ton = 2,240 pounds
1 metric ton = 1,000 kilograms
1 quart = 0.94635 liters
1 US gallon = 3.7854 liters
1 Imperial gallon = 4.5459 liters
1 nautical mile = 1.852 km

MOON HUDSON RIVER VALLEY

Avalon Travel
a member of the Perseus Books Group
1700 Fourth Street
Berkeley, CA 94710, USA
www.moon.com

Editors: Erin Raber, Tiffany Watson
Series Manager: Kathryn Ettinger
Copy Editor: Valerie Sellers Blanton
Graphics Coordinator: Stefano Boni
Production Coordinator: Darren Alessi
Cover Designer: Stefano Boni
Map Editor: Kevin Anglin
Cartographer: Kat Bennett
Cartography Director: Mike Morgenfeld
Indexer: Rachel Kuhn

ISBN-10: 1-59880-036-1
ISBN-13: 978-1-59880-036-4
ISSN: 1554-2327

Printing History
1st Edition – 2005
2nd Edition – March 2008
5 4 3 2 1

Front cover photo: © Hardie Truesdale
Title page photo: Kykuit, the Rockefeller Estate at Pocantico Hills, Courtesy of Historic Hudson Valley/ www.hudsonvalley.org
Interior photos: page 4, Jason Eglit; page 5, 7, 8, Nikki Goth Itoi; page 6, Courtesy of Historic Hudson Valley/ www.hudsonvalley.org

Printed in the United States by RR Donnelley

KEEPING CURRENT

If you have a favorite gem you'd like to see included in the next edition, or see anything that needs updating, clarification, or correction, please drop us a line. Send your comments via email to feedback@moon.com, or use the address above.